Immigration and Race

Immigration and Race

New Challenges for

American Democracy

Edited by Gerald D. Jaynes

Yale University Press

New Haven and London

Printed in the United States of America.

Library of Congress Cataloging-in-Publication Data

Immigration and race : new challenges for American democracy / edited by Gerald D. Jaynes.

    p.   cm.

    Includes bibliographical references and index.

    ISBN 0-300-07380-1 (cloth : alk. paper)—ISBN 0-300-08005-0 (pbk. : alk. paper)

    1. United States—Race relations—Congresses. 2. United States—Race rela-tions—Political aspects—Congresses. 3. United States—Emigration and immi-gration—Government policy—Congresses. 4. United States—Emigration and immigration—Social aspects—Congresses. 5. Afro-Americans—Social condi-tions—1975—Congresses. 6. Immigrants—United States—Social condi-tions—Congresses. 7. Afro-Americans—Politics and government—Congresses. 8. Immigrants—United States—Political activity—Congresses. I. Jaynes, Gerald David.

E184.A1 I4365 2000

305.8′00973—dc21   99-057178

A catalogue record for this book is available from the British Library.

The paper in this book meets the guidelines for permanence and durability of the Committee on Production Guidelines for Book Longevity of the Council on Library Resources.

10 9 8 7 6 5 4 3 2 1

Contents

v

Politics: Coalition and Competition

Acknowledgments

This volume is the result of a collaboration of several academic and social policy analysts who were drawn together because of their common interests in the topics of immigration and race and ethnicity in a changing America. Thanks to a generous grant from the Andrew Mellon foundation, we were able to meet several times to discuss the issues that are covered in the various chapters of this volume. At an early meeting authors agreed to write research papers covering several of the topics of interest to the group. Initial drafts of the papers contained in this volume were presented by their respective authors during a working conference in Washington, D.C. This conference produced a round of criticism and revisions. Revised drafts were then presented during a more formal symposium treating the topic of immigration and race relations. This symposium also occurred in Washington, D.C., during the summer of 1994.

Chapter 1 Introduction: Immigration and the American Dream

Gerald D. Jaynes

It was a beautiful April day. As the van pulled away from the border checkpoint and into California, my thoughts were of the hills outside Tijuana. The image of dozens of women, men, and children, bundles in their arms, milling about on hills, would not leave me. They were waiting, we had been told, for the darkness that would camouflage their run across the border into the land of the American dream that we took for granted. The van sped on its way up Interstate 895 carrying Cynthia and me in the rear seats and our friends Pat and Nick from San Diego in the front—four privileged members of the middle class ending a day in northern Mexico.

My thoughts turned to the fall of 1957 when, as a boy living in a small town in northern Illinois, a ten-year-old named Hector gave me my first lesson in relative poverty. Hector's parents were poor migrant farm workers from Mexico, in town for a few months to help harvest crops. During the time that his parents worked, Hector and his younger sister were enrolled in school. Hector's English wasn't very good, and his family's seasonal migration pattern had kept him well behind the academic level of the fourth-grade class. The tall, bronze-colored Hector

1

sort of naturally gravitated into friendships with the half-dozen African Americans at the school: soul people, bonded through our poverty and our brown skins. One day, in the middle of the term, as suddenly as he had arrived, Hector was gone. I never saw or heard from him again. Many times I have pondered what became of Hector and his sister.

I hid my face from my friends as a tear traced its way down my cheek. Abruptly, my thoughts were interrupted as Nick braked and the shadowy figure of a woman darted across the highway. Then there was a man, then another. Suddenly, we were in a traffic jam: it was a checkpoint of the U.S. Immigration and Naturalization Service (INS). Officers were more or less randomly stopping cars to check for undocumented immigrants. I knew we would be checked. Our van was sprinkled with an assortment of brown skins, and the driver was of Mexican ancestry.

After the check, we continued our journey to San Diego in silence. My thoughts remained with the desperate human beings trying to evade the INS, and I wondered if they experienced feelings similar to those my ancestors must have felt running from slave patrols under cover of night in antebellum America. I felt very close to these Mexicans who were making a desperate and daring bid for a better life. Surely there had to be a better way to manage immigration policy.

A few days later, back in suburban Washington, D.C., I drove into a housing development under construction. The carpenters, bricklayers, and assorted laborers were busily at work. All the supervisors were white men, and all the others were Latino men. I instantly thought of the hundreds of African American men and women I had just seen milling about on the streets of Washington.[1] And I thought of all the historical and social science work I had read and done concerning the vicious discrimination against African Americans by the construction industry in the United States. Why were all the supervisors white men, all the workers Latinos? Where were the African Americans and women? At that moment, I knew the meaning of ambivalence.

RACE, IMMIGRATION, AND THE DISCOURSE OF AMBIVALENCE

Few contemporary topics evoke more conflicted attitudes than does immigration. Many Americans may feel compassion for Florida-bound Cubans and Haitians braving the Atlantic in small boats, for hard-working Vietnamese immigrants whose life savings and livelihood went up in flames when their fishing boats were bombed during a dispute with Texas fishermen; but the same people may be apprehensive about the consequences of immigration for their own livelihoods and for the stability of "their" cultural and social institutions.

Such ambivalence poses dangerous risks for a democratic society. Frequently, people with conflicted attitudes either suppress the less salient, popular, or economically expedient attitude or they remain silent, leaving public debate and policy-making to the less ambivalent. Public debate diverges to extreme positions, and elected officials dismiss the search for a middle position that may exist but will be nearly impossible to discern given the complexity of voters' opinions and the simplicity of public debate and opinion poll questions. A chilling effect on free discourse may result. Individuals and organizations may remain silent because of anxiety toward their own conflicted attitudes and the possibility that raising certain issues may identify them with more extreme and personally repugnant viewpoints.

Something akin to this is now occurring in the debate over immigration. On the whole, immigration is beneficial to the United States. But it does have both positive and negative effects, often on different people and places. Our task as citizens of a democratic society is to restructure the debate on firmer, more honest grounds.

My own ambivalence toward immigration reflects my cultural position as an African American. On the subject of immigration, African Americans may be the most ambivalent group in America, reflecting a powerful tension between a widespread belief that increased immigration is detrimental to blacks' economic well-being and a moral commitment to equality and the rights of dispossessed peoples.

Polling data reveal that African American respondents are more likely than other Americans to associate immigration with detrimental labor market competition. Even so, a nationwide poll found that blacks were more supportive of both immigration and immigrants than were nonblacks. Nearly two-thirds of all Americans agreed that immigrants take jobs from the native-born, and more than three-quarters of African Americans believed that "businesses would rather hire immigrants than black Americans." Yet African Americans were evenly split between those who thought that the United States should continue accepting immigrants at current or higher rates and those favoring fewer immigrants, whereas other Americans favored lower immigration quotas by a margin of two to one. Furthermore, whereas a majority of white Americans were against bilingual education in the public schools, African Americans favored it by a margin of nearly four to one (Mandel and Farrell 1992, 118–19).[2]

Effects on economic well-being are but one consequence of immigration. Intuitively, Americans understand that the nation is undergoing a period of profound changes. And they sense that these changes will have major consequences for the nation's social fabric. Throughout America's history, immigration has had an enormous impact on the development of the nation's economic, political, and social institutions. Correspondingly, immigration has also had great effects on the character of ethnic and race relations. Today's immigration will continue this pattern. This chapter discusses how contemporary immigration's most profound effect may well be its alteration in the very manner in which Americans conceive of race and ethnicity and in race relations.

The Black-White Paradigm

Slavery and African Americans' central position during several constitutional crises that literally defined the meaning of American democracy and citizenship have made black-white relations the dominant paradigm for comprehending race in the United States for four centuries. Moreover, because they continue to be disproportionately poor, African Americans remain at the forefront of American discourse on the precise nature of pluralism and equality. But the demographic effects of immigration foreshadow the demise of this bimodal conceptualization of racial identity and race relations. I am convinced that revolutionary change for this cultural paradigm is inevitable, yet I understand why black and white Americans resist it.

A major source of resistance to the demise of the black-white paradigm is the fact that it transcends its apparently simple function as a way of understanding race and ethnicity. The paradigm, fully internalized by many generations of Americans, is built into the fabric of American social ideology and culture. Fundamental American social values are understood through reference to it. To illustrate, one function of the black-white paradigm has been its role in supporting the frequently voiced claim that class distinctions assume no structural role in maintaining inequality in the United States. Although it has been the most open society in history, the claim that there are no class barriers is false. Frequently, race, as both a primary determinant and as a shield for class, has assumed that role.

Throughout American history, the black-white paradigm (which conveniently ignored the presence of other groups) has been inextricably connected to and a fundamental support of the American dream of equality of opportunity because anyone espousing it is challenged to accept the proposition that African Americans are the exception that proves the rule. What are the core elements of the American dream and the black-white paradigm? I define the American dream in simple terms. It is that all members of the United States polity are free to define success and to strive for it under conditions of equal opportunity. It is understood that the existence of equal opportunity is consistent with both success and failure. Attainment of one's goals is dependent on individual talent, hard work, and, to some extent, luck. The black-white paradigm, no less simple, holds that African Americans' perpetual subordinate status presents no significant challenge to the validity of the American dream because blacks' status is due to their own inadequacies.

The black-white paradigm has also served the immigration ideology that is central to the American dream. Even in the colonial era the dream and the paradigm served important cultural functions. Structural barriers to upward mobility for poor white immigrants, although remarkably lower than in Europe, perpetuated a lower class of unruly whites mired in poverty. But the presence of black slaves mitigated the cultural significance of the imperfect social mobility. The historian David Brion Davis, drawing on work of Edmund S. Morgan (1972), argues that the "paradox" of slaveholders declaring the freedom and equality of all men is resolved once we understand that the enslavement of Africans reduced the need for lower-class white indentured servants. Morgan argues that increased importations of slaves allowed "a decrease in the number of dangerous new [white] freedmen who annually emerged seeking a place in society that they would be unable to achieve" (Davis 1975, 260–62).

In effect, Morgan argues that Americans "bought their independence with slave labor." The highly visible and constrained slaves at the bottom of society enabled colonists to promulgate ideas of freedom and equality for all whites in a competitive society. After their emancipation, black Americans remained consigned to the bottom rungs, serving as the exception proving the rule of American egalitarianism. Deeply ingrained in the nation's history and culture has been a profound need to have a population of lower-class blacks assuring whites that their values hold true.

Abraham Lincoln, who characterized the American dream in all its ramifications as well as anyone, stressed the freedom to compete and the freedom to fail. But he, unlike any previous president, chastised the nation for not living up to its creed and giving blacks a fair chance to succeed or fail: "As a nation, we began by declaring that 'all men are created equal,'" wrote Lincoln. "We now practically read it 'all men are created equal, except negroes'" (Schlesinger 1991, 9).

From Alexis de Tocqueville in the early nineteenth century to the present, virtually all Europeans who made a careful study of our peoples and institutions have subscribed to some form of the indomitable egalitarianism of Americans. "No novelty in the United States struck me more vividly during my stay there than the equality of conditions" are the first words to appear in de Tocqueville's (1966) analysis of American democracy. But it was the Swedish scholar Gunner Myrdal who, during the early 1940s, formulated the American ideal of equal social opportunity as a way of describing the national character. He wrote that "the essential dignity of the individual human being, of the fundamental equality of all men, and of certain inalienable rights to freedom, justice, and a fair opportunity represent to the American people the essential meaning of the nation's early struggle for independence" (1944, 4).

Yet Myrdal was also aware of what surveys undertaken throughout the 1940s would prove: majorities of white Americans believed that black Americans' second-class citizenship was justified by their intellectual and moral inferiority to whites (Schumann et al. 1985). Nevertheless, unlike many other European students of American culture, Myrdal rejected whites' beliefs as a rationalization of the disjuncture between their professed commitment to the creed of equal opportunity and the actual legal and social status of blacks. He viewed African Americans' socioeconomic status to be a fundamental challenge to the validity of the American dream.

Many Americans accepted Myrdal's critique as applying to the color-caste system of social and legal segregation in the South, but in the North, despite pervasive discrimination against blacks, the absence of an elaborate legal machinery of segregation allowed most whites to convince themselves that African Americans' failure to succeed could be attributed to their own shortcomings. Black-white relations in the North were usually subsumed under a model of ethnic group competition. Blacks were assumed to be just one of a number of ethnic groups who in different areas and times competed for political and economic resources. This competition generally resulted in winners and losers. The resulting hierarchy of group status changed over time as different immigrant groups entered the competition at the bottom rungs and managed to move up.

Often the final stage in this vertical movement into the dominant class structure of American society was postulated to be symbolized by an ethnic group's moving out of a residential enclave to a "middle-class American neighborhood." Thus, the ethnic competition model was simply a restatement of the creed of equal opportunity and the American dream. Without denying that assimilation was tougher for blacks, Asian Americans, and nonwhite Hispanics, proponents of the model argued that the difference between them and white ethnic groups was one of degree but not of kind (Moynihan and Glazer 1963; Drake 1965).

Thus, sanguine social commentators assured the nation during the 1960s that the increasing visibility of rising urban poverty was merely a temporary problem. Black rural migrants to cities were hypothesized to be facing a situation just like that faced by European immigrants to America in 1900. In time, the argument went, the southern migrants would adjust to city folkways and mores, be absorbed by industry, and join the ranks of the American middle class. Twenty years later, although a great many African Americans had secured middle-class status, a great many hadn't. African Americans, nearly a third of them officially counted as poor and as a whole registering at or near the bottom of most measures of success, remained low in most Americans' hierarchies of groups.

When blacks didn't re-create the European immigrant model of intergenerational success, many analysts ignored the different conditions that newly arrived black migrants had faced in comparison with European immigrants of earlier decades. And they ignored the fact that African Americans were not immigrants; many were not even migrants to the urban North or South. Instead, they explained blacks' inability to re-create the "ethnic miracle" on the basis of putative pathologies in black culture. The sole explanation of blacks' continuing low status became the cultural attributes of lower-class blacks. The resilient black-white paradigm was raised again.

Social and economic conditions in the United States during the past few decades have accentuated the salience of the black-white paradigm. Immigration, estimated at ten million documented and undocumented entrants during the 1980s alone, continues to orchestrate tremendous changes in U.S. social and cultural institutions. The 1980s figure exceeded the previous record for decadal immigration, set during the first decade of the twentieth century (see figure 1.1). Expectations of continuing large flows of immigrants into the nation in the near future imply that the effects of immigration during the late twentieth century will be comparable to the great immigrations of southern and eastern Europeans into the United States during the late nineteenth and early twentieth centuries.

Moreover, the countries of origin for today's immigrants form a much more diverse group than during the previous wave. In addition to immigrants from Europe, much larger proportions of entrants into the United States during the 1980s arrived from Asia, Latin America and Mexico, the Caribbean, and Africa. As a consequence, the racial and ethnic diversity of the U.S. population has been significantly changed. One in four Americans is now a member of an ethnic group of non-European heritage: Hispanic Americans reached 9 percent of the U.S. population in 1990 and Asian Americans 3 percent; African Americans compose less than half of the so-called minority population. The impact of this

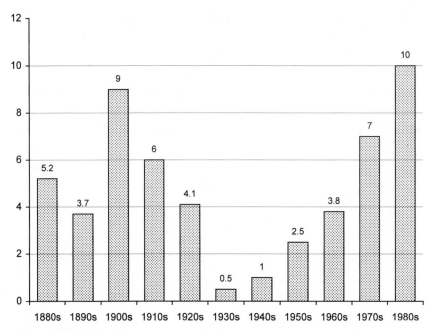

Figure 1.1 Millions of Immigrants to the United States by Decade, 1880–1990

revolution in population and cultural diversity is having and will increasingly have profound effects on intergroup relations and on the socioeconomic positions of various groups. Many analysts understand that we are in a transition period of race relations in the United States. But in the search for a new conceptualization of intergroup relations, commentators have not recognized that the old conceptualization, what I call the black-white paradigm, continues to exert a powerful influence on ideas of race and ethnicity. Contemporary race relations, although in a state of flux, are not as chaotic and incoherent as is often suggested.

The black-white paradigm continues to be the dominant ideological force in American race relations; it is still the framework within which the vast majority of Americans think about race and class. Americans interpret and anticipate intergroup relations through its jaundiced eye. Consequently, even though the paradigm must undergo drastic changes, currently and perhaps paradoxically, we can only understand such relations by first examining them through the veil of the black-white paradigm.

The survival of the paradigm will depend on both the future course of race relations and the attainment—or nonattainment—of incorporation into American society of the major minority groups whose populations are currently growing through immigration. The black-white paradigm will survive only if all new immigrant groups become successful in the United States, leaving the black poor at the bottom of the social structure. If, however, significant proportions of some immigrant groups join poor African Americans at the bottom, a new paradigm of race and class relations may well emerge. To phrase the issue differently, will a growing lower class composed of many races undermine the historic association of blacks with the lower class and lead to new socioeconomic ideologies?

Rising intergroup inequality will place enormous strains on political institutions. Class differences within racial and ethnic groups will force the economically advantaged members of these groups either to adopt an extended version of the black-white paradigm, abandoning the more disadvantaged members of their groups, or to adopt explanations of group inequality based on class and racial barriers. Most will choose the latter. White Americans' unequal treatment of minorities undermines the possibility that minorities will completely assimilate whites' belief structures concerning group inequality in the United States. As alternative minority perspectives enter the culture, many whites, no longer so dominant a majority and members of a far more complex society, will be forced to consider racialized class barriers to success.

In the remainder of this chapter I attempt to elucidate these ideas. Along the way, I also discuss the issues addressed by the authors of the other chapters of this book.

Race Through the Veil of the Black-White Paradigm

For roughly twenty years after the Immigration Act of 1965 changed the volume and geographic origin of immigration into the United States, white and black Americans viewed the growing Asian and Latino American populations solely through the veil of the black-white paradigm. Well into the 1980s, the increasing ethnic and racial diversity of the U.S. population had minimal influence on American ideals and social values. Black and white Americans have viewed Asian and Latino Americans through self-reflecting mirrors rather than as Americans with new contributions to make to the society's ever-changing culture. Blacks have hoped to accept these groups as comrades who, finding themselves discriminated against and denied opportunities, would become similar to blacks in political consciousness. Whites have tended to invoke the "model minority" theme and perceive the immigrants, especially Asians, as groups whose social status is between those of themselves and blacks but rising. As blacks are routinely ranked last in studies of group achievement—in income, earnings, occupations, education, residential distribution, and so on—this ideology has served to strengthen the exception-that-proves-the-rule argument. Proponents of the classic competition model point to these groups and say that others of color can make it, therefore African Americans fail because of their own faults.

Interpreting all intergroup relations through the lens of the black-white paradigm has encouraged invidious comparisons between groups with vastly different historical experiences. Thus the journalist Nicholas LeMann, in a widely acclaimed essay published in the *Atlantic* during 1986, buttressed his proposition that the poverty of urban African Americans was due to cultural pathologies by pointing to the fact that certain immigrant Asians to the same cities were thriving economically because, in LeMann's words, the immigrants "maintain a separate culture" (35–36). The ability of LeMann and many other writers to ignore the vast class differences between the immigrant Asian business owners in the United States and the poor African Americans whom these merchants often serve is a tribute to the cultural power of the ideology of the American dream and the black-white paradigm.

It is well known among demographers who study immigrant and migrant populations that, except in rare instances of forced movement of entire peoples, the personal characteristics of immigrants are on average quite different from those of their population of origin. Because of this selective migration, which, depending on the circumstances, can favor the poor and least prepared or the highly skilled and most prepared, immigrant groups are rarely comparable to the native-born populations they join or the ones they leave.

The many examples of selective migration are taken for granted and yet ignored in most discussions of immigration. Owing to the structural features of international migration into Great Britain, its most highly educated demographic group is Africans (T. Cross 1994). In contrast, because of differences in their legal status in Britain and the United States, English-speaking black Caribbean immigrants to these two countries occupy very different positions in the social discourse of the two nations. In Britain, where Caribbean migration has involved a more representative sample of the Caribbean population, black Caribbeans are seen as low in status. In the United States, black Caribbeans are typically held up as successful and as proof of the cultural failures of native-born blacks. Cuban refugees to the United States during the late 1950s and the 1960s represented a spectrum of the business classes and the professional elite who had the most to lose from the social disruption of the Cuban revolution. Korean and

Cuban immigrants to the United States are in many ways the cream of their respective societies. Among Korean immigrants to the United States, 47.3 percent of adult men are college graduates. Korean immigrants to the United States overwhelmingly represent members of Korea's post-1950s middle class. Highly educated and motivated for upward mobility, the immigrants to America were without essential family connections to people with power and were therefore constrained within Korea's hierarchically controlled and traditional social structure.

Calling attention to the special advantages of these immigrants should not detract from the impressive achievements they have made through hard work and great personal sacrifice. But the conditions of their immigration do mean that simple comparisons between their social and economic achievements and those of poor and disadvantaged members of native-born groups are meaningless. Those who try to make the comparison always do so in terms of the black-white paradigm. And examples of immigrants' successes serve to bolster the ideology of the American dream. These arguments ignore both the historical conditions that discriminated against blacks and the severe structural barriers to upward mobility among the poor and the lower middle classes that arose during the past three decades of economic change in the United States.

The model minority myth serves both the ideology of the American dream and the black-white paradigm. But to invoke it for these purposes requires ignoring ethnic differences among Asians: explaining the great differences in status among Asian American groups requires a class and historical analysis that weakens the model minority view and undermines the black-white paradigm. Status differences between groups of various national origins among Asian and Pacific Islander Americans and Hispanic-origin Americans are illustrated in table 1.1. It is clear from these data that for these groups there are vast differences in education and income, ranging from the highly educated and urbane Asian Indian population to the poorly educated and impoverished agricultural peoples from Laos and Cambodia. Although the American dream appears intact for the individuals and groups it has historically benefited, urbanized middle-class-oriented immigrants, it is clearly inappropriate for uneducated peasant populations.

RACE, CLASS, AND SOCIAL MOBILITY

During the past two decades, changes in the education and skill levels of arriving cohorts of Asian and Latino immigrants, combined with structural changes

Table 1.1
Selected Social Characteristics of Native-Born Asian Americans and
Latino Americans, 1990

	Income	Percentage in Poverty	Years of Education	Percentage High School Dropouts
Cambodian	$21,546	45.1	12	44.6
Chinese	45,764	8.4	16	8.8
Japanese	44,543	4.2	14	11.7
Korean	32,115	8.6	14	12.3
Laotian	20,446	40.9	11	56.4
Thai	24,681	8.5	14	17.6
Central American	31,472	20.5	14	19.3
Cuban	32,273	13.5	14	18.6
Dominican	23,840	39.2	12	34.4
Mexican	25,396	24.5	12	39.3
Puerto Rican	21,079	31.7	12	46.5

Sources: *Persons of Hispanic Origin in the United States,* 1990 CP-3-3, tables 3 and 5. Bureau
of the Census, August 1993. *Asians and Pacific Islanders in the United States,* 1990 CP-3-5,
tables 3 and 5. Bureau of the Census, August 1993.
Note: "Income" refers to median household income in 1989. "Percentage in Poverty" is the
percentage of all persons below the poverty line in 1990. "Years of Education" is an estimate
of median years of education of all persons age twenty-five or older. "Percentage of High
School Dropouts" is the percentage of all persons aged twenty-five or older with less than a
high school diploma or equivalent. Central Americans include Costa Ricans, Guatemalans,
Hondurans, Nicaraguans, Panamanians, and Salvadorans.

in the United States economy, may be slowing socioeconomic incorporation of
some of these groups. Research shows that more recent cohorts of immigrants
in general have arrived with lower levels of education than earlier cohorts originating from the same countries (Borjas 1985).

This is especially true for immigrants from Mexico and Central and South
America. Among Mexicans, there was a difference of as much as two years in the
amount of schooling of immigrants arriving during the 1960s and those arriving during the 1980s. Among Central and South Americans the differences in
schooling between these cohorts appear to be even larger. There is similar evidence that Asian immigrants who arrived during the late 1980s had mean educational attainment levels of roughly two and one-half years less than those

who arrived during the decade beginning in 1975 and three and one-half years less than those who arrived prior to 1975 (Bean et al. 1991; Lee and Edmonston 1991).

The declining educational attainments of recently arriving cohorts of immigrants coincides with declining wage and employment opportunities for workers with only high school educations or less. The deterioration in the average wages of American men and women that began during the early 1970s continued in the 1980s, while the incomes of wealthier, more educated Americans rose dramatically. Reductions in real earnings were generally greatest for men and women with the least education. Thus, the real mean weekly wages of black and white men lacking high school educations were actually less in the mid-1980s than their respective wages in 1960. The earnings of black male high school graduates, two-thirds those of black male college graduates during the entire 1939–1969 period, fell to one-half in the mid-1980s (Farley and Neidert 1985).

There were also significant reductions in labor force participation and employment of men between 1970 and 1980. And as manufacturing jobs continued to be lost at a rapid pace, they were replaced with jobs in the service sector that either required high education and skills or offered very low wages. Many of the low-paying jobs were filled by immigrants.

Overall, the late 1970s and especially the 1980s were times when Americans of every racial group were finding it ever more difficult to escape from poverty. Poverty rates rose dramatically during this period as the American economy faltered. In 1973 the poverty rate among whites was 8.4 percent; in 1992 it was 11.6 percent. For blacks the increase during this same period was from 31.5 percent to 33.3 percent. No group was safe; the rates among Latinos were 21.9 percent in 1973 and 29.3 percent in 1992. Figures for Asian Americans for the earlier year are not available, but their 12.5 percent poverty rate in 1992 was higher than for preceding years.

The largely hidden poverty of some Asian subgroups verges on a national disgrace. An astounding two of three native-born Hmong (Vietnamese) Americans lived in poverty during 1990, as did more than two of five Cambodian and Laotian Americans. Although the many children of Vietnamese immigrants who have excelled academically have received great news coverage, bolstering the myth of the American dream, the widespread poverty of native-born Vietnamese Americans is barely mentioned—one in four lived in households with incomes below the poverty line in 1990.

These conditions coincide with signs of slowing socioeconomic incorporation of some Asian and Latino groups. Among Mexican-origin Americans, members of the second generation have higher levels of educational attainment than their parents, but younger cohorts of the third generation have lower mean levels of educational achievement than their parents. Larger proportions of the younger cohort have not completed high school, and smaller proportions attend college than did their parents. Evidence consistent with intergenerational deterioration of income status among Asian American households has been reported, but it is not yet clear whether that evidence will be explained differently with better data. All Asian groups except for Chinese Americans had significantly higher household incomes than whites in 1980, but most lost this advantage during the 1980s (Bean et al. 1991; Lee and Edmonston 1991).

Declining real wages and rising unemployment were accompanied by pessimistic outlooks toward the future among many young Americans as successive cohorts of high school graduates entered an economy that appeared to promise them a standard of living that would be worse than their parents'. The effects of these conditions have been most evident in the severely deteriorating socioeconomic status of poor black youth and, to a lesser extent, poor white youth. But the stagnating educational attainments of the later generations of native-born Hispanics, combined with the deteriorating prospects of lower-skilled men and women in the job market generally, strongly suggest that social conditions among Hispanic youth from poor and lower-class backgrounds may be replicating conditions among the African American lower class. Moreover, findings of greater perceptions of discrimination against Hispanics among Hispanics of later generations provide further evidence of a change in attitudes toward opportunities in the United States among immigrant Hispanics and their children.

Much about these changes can be explained by the deteriorating economy and the end of the selective immigration of highly educated people from the origin countries. Post-1980 Chinese immigrants to the United States have poverty rates nearly three times those of pre-1980 Chinese immigrants, and the poverty rate of post-1980 immigrants from South America is twice that of their pre-1980 counterparts.

Because it is much more difficult for any American to work herself out of poverty now than it was in the past, these conditions suggest that the United States may become home to larger numbers of poor minorities who will influence the course of American race relations.

VIEWS OF OPPORTUNITY: A MINORITY-WHITE DIVIDE

Intergroup relations among African, Asian, and Latino Americans are largely propelled by competing pressures within each group. I mentioned above the ambivalence among blacks between fear of the economic and political effects of immigration and their commitment to equal opportunity and the eradication of poverty. Below I call attention to an analogous ambivalence that in its own way simultaneously attracts and repels Asian and Latino Americans to and from blacks. This love-hate relationship among Asians, blacks, and Latinos presents social analysts with a particularly difficult problem. It is easy to pursue a path of analysis that emphasizes only one side of the picture; striking a balance may be extremely difficult and, even more difficult, at any given time there may be no balance. We must confront the possibility that for some time to come the essence of relations between African, Asian, and Latino Americans may involve highly competitive relationships that are frequently interrupted by significant coalitional efforts.

Striking confirmation of the existence of this tension in the views of African Americans is provided by findings of a survey of racial attitudes among Los Angeles County residents (see note 2). The survey shows that there is virtually no difference in the opinions of whites and blacks about the economic and political effects of immigration on themselves: both groups see them as primarily negative. But whereas whites' negative evaluation of the effects of immigration on their personal well-being is matched by their support for curtailing current high levels of immigration, blacks give significantly more support for high immigration quotas than do whites. This is likely a manifestation of blacks' strong commitment to equality of opportunity. Clearly, it is also an example of the competing pressures vying for the political souls of African Americans.

For Asian Americans and Latinos, minority status creates an inherent tension in their attitudes toward American society. Their status exposes them to discrimination from the larger society, giving them an affinity with African Americans, but it also entitles them, under programs instituted under the aegis of the black-white paradigm, to special benefits and preferences as "protected groups" under conditions that often throw them into competition with blacks. Moreover, the spatial distribution of housing and business opportunities frequently places immigrant Latinos and Asians into direct contact with lower-income African Americans. Ethnographic studies and theoretical research on the formation of prejudiced attitudes suggest that such contact reinforces negative stereotypes of blacks that would tend to make Asians and Latinos assimilate white Americans' ideas of race and equal opportunity.

The results of the Los Angeles County survey confirm that persons of Asian descent appear to have the most negative images of blacks. Moreover, the survey revealed that negative attitudes toward blacks among Asians rose considerably immediately after the riots following the verdict in the Rodney King trial during the spring of 1992. And in a nationwide survey commissioned by the National Conference of Christians and Jews, Latinos were found to have images of blacks that were substantially more negative than those held by non-Hispanic whites (see note 2).

Yet both surveys found that, in stark contrast to the views of whites, substantial majorities of Asians and Latinos agreed with African Americans that their respective groups do not enjoy opportunity equal to whites'. Moreover, majorities of Asian and Latino Americans expressed approval of the principle of affirmative action. They believed, in contrast to whites, that African Americans are subject to considerable discrimination, and they were far more likely than whites to support government social spending programs. A majority of whites in these same surveys approved of affirmative action. But since a large majority of whites believe that all groups have equal opportunities, this finding suggests that whites may have a different interpretation of the meaning and purposes of affirmative action. (This question is discussed further in the next section.)

There is a clear-cut minority-white divide in views of the American social order, especially with regard to access to economic opportunity. One likely explanation for the minority agreement is the fact of discrimination. Evidence of discrimination against Asians and Latinos is accumulating rapidly. Indeed, compelling evidence of discrimination against these groups in seeking employment and housing has been demonstrated in an impressive array of statistical analyses and discrimination audits in which the treatment of matched pairs of white and Asian or Hispanic housing or job seekers is compared.

Bendick and his co-authors (1991) report the following examples of discrimination in their test of the Washington, D.C., metropolitan area:

A vacancy for a receptionist in an optometrist's office in suburban Virginia was advertised in a suburban newspaper. When a Latino tester called the next day to apply, she was put on hold and then called by the wrong name (Carmen, when she had given her name as Juanita) and told that they were not taking any further applications. When the Anglo tester called thirteen minutes later, she was given an appointment for an interview the following morning.

Another test involved a vacancy advertised in the *Washington Post* for an assistant manager of a suburban health club. When a Latino tester called, the call lasted one minute, and he was instructed to mail in his résumé. When the Anglo tester called four minutes later, the call lasted two minutes. He was told that an open house would be held the following day, that he should bring in his résumé at that time, and that he would then be interviewed.

But the case for a shared minority experience can be overargued. The great ethnic and class diversity among Asian and Latino Americans places strong limits on the strength of this supposedly shared perspective. Douglas S. Massey, in *The Residential Segregation of Blacks, Hispanics, and Asians, 1970–1990*, Chapter 2 of this book, stressing the empirical connection between a group's socioeconomic well-being and its spatial position within a society, reports findings that provide insights on these questions. African Americans stand apart from the other two groups in displaying much higher levels of segregation and isolation. The largest and most segregated Asian American communities are much less isolated from whites than are the most integrated African American communities. Despite high rates of population increase through recent immigration, a condition that would be expected to increase ethnic residential concentration, the degree of Asian-white and Latino-white segregation proved to be moderate, with the Latino-white index actually falling during the study period while Asian-white levels of segregation were approximately constant. Asian-Latino segregation is moderate and has remained stable over two decades.

Although Asian and Latino Americans do encounter prejudice and discrimination in seeking housing, measures of Asian and Latino segregation from whites decrease as their socioeconomic attainments increase. But increased socioeconomic attainment for blacks has little affect on black-white segregation indices. African Americans are also highly segregated from Asian and Latino Americans, although less so than from whites. Massey also reports evidence indicating that among Latinos levels of discrimination and segregation from whites are highly correlated with Latino skin colors.

Caribbean immigrants with African ancestry appear to have much greater difficulty achieving socioeconomic incorporation into American society than do their white counterparts. Furthermore, the influence of customs and racial attitudes in the United States may be sharpening divisions among Hispanics of color and those who are white. Cuban Americans, who are disproportionately white in comparison with the population of Cuba, represent a salient case. For example, a black Cuban complained of the treatment received from some of his fellow Cubans: "I was never rejected on racial grounds by Cubans until I came to Miami. . . . Cubans in Miami act more like white Americans than Latinos" (*New York Times,* 2 December 1987, D26). And, indeed, among the three largest Latino groups in the United States, Cuban Americans' attitudes and beliefs about issues of race relations and equal opportunity appear to be much closer to those of white Americans generally than do those of Mexican Americans and Puerto Ricans (*Washington Post*, 26 October 1989, A18; de la Garza et al. 1992).

In addition to differences in wealth and other indices of socioeconomic status among these groups, Cuban Americans' attitudinal differences may also flow from different social experiences in America. Among respondents to the Latino National Political Survey of 1984, 14 percent of Cuban but 33 percent and 30 percent of Mexican and Puerto Rican respondents, respectively, reported that they had personally experienced discrimination. And, consistent with this self-evaluation, each of the three groups believed that there is less discrimination against Cubans than against the others. How these perceptions correlate with skin color is not known.

Overall, there seems to be a clear division in how Americans view the structure of opportunity and rewards in this society. Whites and blacks represent two extremes. Asians and Latinos fall between but are far enough from whites to conclude that there is a fundamental divide in views of the opportunity structure between whites and all minorities.

I read this point to be a major conclusion of John A. Garcia's "Coalition Formation: the Mexican-Origin Community and Latinos and African Americans" (Chapter 10). Garcia's discussion of the great diversity within the Mexican-origin community as a subgroup of Latinos, and more generally among Latinos as a whole, provides a stark reality check of the difficulties that must be overcome if political coalitions are to be formed between Latino and African Americans. Nevertheless, he argues that sociopolitical experiences such as the act of immigration itself underlie links between all persons of Mexican origin and serve as the basis for community formation and collective action. Similarly, he argues that the basis for coalitional activities between Latinos and African Americans is centered around a "common minority experience" based on actual discrimination, social distance from the American mainstream, and perceived discrimination by non-Latino whites.

Statistical analysis of this hypothesis reveals that Latino support for programs to help blacks can be explained by four independent variables: personal experience with discrimination, views of discrimination against Latino subgroups and African Americans, empathy (social distance) from those groups, and attitudes toward social programs in general. Garcia's analysis and data support the conclusion that ultimately the issue of coalition or competition among all the minority groups will depend on how much discrimination and poverty Asian and

Latino Americans experience in the United States. If the level of discrimination remains significant, then the minority-white divide is likely to persist.

INTERPRETATIONS OF INTERGROUP CONFLICT

Viewing race relations through the veil of the black-white paradigm, the news media tend to report negative incidents involving immigrants and "jealous" African Americans disproportionately to their frequency among all intergroup conflicts. Racial and ethnic conflicts have been too numerous to report and are more complicated than blacks against various newcomers, for example, ongoing conflicts between Cambodians and Latinos in Long Beach, California, blacks and Cubans in Miami, white and Vietnamese fishermen in Texas, Florida, and California, and a violent attack against a Chinese American grocer preceded and followed by prolonged harassment by white citizens and local government officials in Castro Valley, California. One cannot attribute these conflicts to any one cause. Elements of scapegoating, competition for scarce resources, racial and ethnic prejudice, and cultural differences are clearly factors in many of these incidents. Contrary to some popular beliefs, white reactions are often similar to those of blacks. Especially in the context of the changed economy of the 1980s, the response of the native-born has become more increasingly negative. For example, violence in New Jersey targeted toward Indians became prevalent in the mid-1980s as a Jersey City gang calling themselves the Dotbusters, referring to the bindi that Indian women wear on their foreheads as a sign of marital fidelity, swore to drive the Indians out. Again in 1990, a gang calling themselves the Lost Boys began a campaign of violence against the Asian Indian community in Middlesex County. The Lost Boys' multiethnic makeup confounds all stereotypes of native-born perpetrators of hate crimes. The fifteen gang members arrested included one black, one Jew, a number of Greek and Italian heritage, three Filipinos, and several Anglos. According to a police officer involved in the case, the boys were a middle-class "yuppie gang" with several members who drove Porsches and BMWs.

This kind of conflict may reflect the changed composition of the immigrant Indian population. According to the 1980 census, of the 400,000 Asian Indians in the United States, 11 percent of the men were physicians and 17 percent were engineers, architects, or surveyors; among women, 8 percent were physicians and 7 percent were nurses. In many communities such as those in northern New Jersey where many Asian Indians settled, the small numbers of college-educated professional Indian immigrants of the 1970s and earlier were received by whites as examples of the Asian model minority success story. When Asian Indians arrived during the early 1960s they were seen as a glorified minority group. But the arrival of the initial cohort of immigrants was followed by large numbers of their relatives and friends, many of whom were less educated and followed more traditional immigrant occupations such as shopkeeping, laboring, and driving taxis. The median household incomes of pre-1980 Asian Indian immigrants was $59,976 in 1990, compared with $32,365 for those who immigrated after 1979.

Among the more law-abiding native-born population, reactions to the influx of Asian Indians paralleled to a remarkable degree those of African Americans reacting to the arrival of Cubans and other Hispanics to Miami. Residents made statements such as "look what has happened to our town"; "they [immigrants] get interest free Small Business Administration loans"; "they are clannish"; and "they drive out the whites" (U.S. Commission on Civil Rights, 1992).

But the most salient example of the continuing ascendancy of the black-white paradigm is revealed by "informed" interpretations of the Los Angeles riot of 1992. Most commentators interpret the riot as a repeat of the Watts Rebellion of 1965 or as a black vendetta against Korean merchants. But in fact there was substantial participation by all major racial groups. Various kinds of evidence indicate that the most represented group may have been immigrant Latinos from Central America, a possibility not too difficult to understand when the composition and economic conditions of central Los Angeles are considered.

The multiracial character of the 1992 riot suggests that there may have been many different motivations for taking part. That is one of the points that local Asian and Latino leaders were trying to make when they felt it necessary to tell the media, encumbered by the blinder of the black-white paradigm, "we were there too."

In "The Politics of Black-Korean Conflict: Black Power Protest and the Mobilization of Racial Communities in New York City" (Chapter 3), Claire Jean Kim challenges us to rethink contemporary race and ethnic relations by questioning the efficacy of conventional wisdom that assigns simple causal motivations to highly complex situations. She discusses the Red Apple Boycott of 1990, a thirteen-month-long boycott by African Americans and Haitian immigrants of two Korean-owned stores in the Flatbush section of Brooklyn.

Kim notes that conventional wisdom holds that the boycott is best understood as scapegoating. Black protesters, frustrated by their disempowerment, were misdirecting their anger away from either themselves or the social system and toward innocent Korean merchants. Kim suggests that the scapegoating explanation ignores how the protesters themselves understood their actions and circumstances and what purposes and meanings they attached to their own behavior. Furthermore, she argues, the conventional wisdom is based on stock racial myths involving Korean immigrants as a model minority and African Americans as an underclass; the public's susceptibility to this conventional wisdom was adeptly manipulated by a newly politically conscious Korean American merchants' association whose efforts to combat the boycott changed Korean American politics in New York. One of the more interesting features of this conflict was that it did not simply pit native blacks against immigrant Asians: the Haitians who participated in the boycott were themselves recent immigrants, an important fact that erodes the power of the scapegoating explanation.

By setting the boycott within its political-historical context, Kim shows how diverse native-born and immigrant groups appropriate American ideologies to frame definitions of a political situation in terms meant to influence public opinion and mobilize supporters. Kim argues that the Red Apple Boycott was not an isolated campaign but part of a resurgence of black nationalism in New York City. The boycott was a protest campaign organized by black nationalists and Haitian community activists to mobilize blacks by constructing a sense of racial community to serve as a power base. In other words, Kim concludes that black-Korean conflict is about black political activity and that the campaign was purposeful, not purposeless. Using the classic strategy of protest outlined by Martin Luther King in his "Letter From a Birmingham Jail," the boycotters sought to draw attention to their political agenda by using the incident with the Korean grocers as a focal point for gaining the sustained attention of the media and the political power structure in New York City. The Korean merchants were merely the means to an end.

This conclusion does not negate the existence of more mundane motives on the part of many of the participants. Kim's examination of the attitudes and behaviors of the African American and Korean American communities toward one another, along with the political and socioeconomic conditions underlying these attitudes and behaviors, suggest a myriad of individual motives that enabled the boycott leaders to sustain a long, difficult campaign. Wherever such conditions and attitudes are replicated, the close contact between lower- and working-class blacks and middle-class immigrant merchants is bound to periodically precipitate open conflicts.

COMPETITION FOR RESOURCES

Competitive conditions fostered by individuals' seeking scarce resources is an important contributor to the instability of minority group relations. In a society in which people perceive others in terms of ethnicity and race, such competition inevitably leads to questions of whether receipt of resources by members of one group implies less for the others.

Although there is now a large literature of serious research treating competition between the native-born and immigrants for jobs and between various racial and ethnic groups for political power, less attention has been paid to competition over public services. In Chapter 4, "Educating Immigrant Children: Chapter 1 in Changing Cities," Michael Fix and Wendy Zimmermann contribute to the public services debate. They address the degree to which limited-English-proficient (LEP) children receive services under Chapter 1, a multi-billion-dollar program that supports compensatory education for children who are economically disadvantaged and performing below national norms.

Fix and Zimmermann discuss a number of equity and policy issues common to the delivery of public services in general. There are a large number of recently arrived children in the public schools who do not speak English well, live in concentrated poverty, and perform poorly in school. They fit the profile of students who should receive compensatory education services under Chapter 1. Do they, and what are the implications for native-born children if they do?

Fix and Zimmermann's findings suggest that, in many cities, whether statutorily eligible immigrant children receive Chapter 1 services depends on local politics and on the organization of the educational bureaucracy. Demographics and raw political power appear to be instrumental in determining who gets served, and it is often not immigrant children. Moreover, where immigrant children are included, we should be careful not to jump to the simplistic conclusion that immigrants are displacing native-born Americans or that Americans of Latino and Asian descent are displacing those of African and European descent. The belief that immigration has had no effect on the delivery of Chapter 1 services to native-born whites and blacks is not supportable either. The authors find that during the 1980s, while the proportion of Asian and Latino American students increased at dramatic rates, in many cities the political process simply expanded the enrollment of the Chapter 1 programs to accommodate all groups. But this accommodation appears to have had a cost: the inflation-adjusted expenditures per pupil served by the program declined significantly. It is likely that services to the native-born were less than they might have been in the absence of immigration.

This process of competitive dilution, whereby racial and ethnic groups that are growing more slowly than others find their share of a resource shrinking as immigration increases the competition for the resource, appears to be far more prevalent than displacement from the competition altogether. Anecdotal reports from a variety of sources suggest that recipients of public services have experienced longer waiting periods and fewer services as the size and political savvy of Asian and Latino American populations increase.

Labor Market Effects

The labor market effects of immigration on the native-born have emerged as an important public policy issue. Both common sense and straightforward economic reasoning suggest that an influx of millions of people, many of them ready and able to work, would have a significant effect on the wage and employment opportunities of workers previously available. Common sense has been supported by the concurrence of the surge in immigration with a dramatic decline in the real wages of less-skilled American workers during the 1970s. Furthermore, compensation of less-skilled workers continued to fall relative to wages of the highly skilled during the 1980s, and unemployment rose during the late 1980s and early 1990s. What's more, numerous case studies of particular industries in specific places have reported strong evidence that low-wage immigrant workers have displaced native-born workers. And, in survey after survey, significant percentages of Americans have responded that they believe that immigrants lower wages and displace native-born workers from jobs.

But common sense and what appears to be straightforward economic reasoning can sometimes be misleading. Throughout the 1980s and into the 1990s, virtually every sophisticated study of the effects of immigration on the economic status of the native-born population has concluded that it is difficult to determine if the effects of immigration have been positive or negative. In any case, measured effects have been quite small. These results have held for native-born workers who are skilled and those who are unskilled, for women, minorities, and whites.[3]

More recently, however, Borjas, Freeman, and Katz (1992), using methods of analysis different from those in the earlier studies, estimated that two important factors in the decline in weekly wages of lower-skilled American workers (high school dropouts) relative to higher-skilled ones (college graduates) during the 1980s were increased imports of goods produced with lower-skilled labor and increased immigration of lower-skilled workers. They concluded that 30 percent to 50 percent of the estimated decline in the relative weekly wage of high school dropouts between 1980 and 1988 should be attributed to trade and immigration flows.

What might explain these authors' findings in view of the earlier studies? The standard method used in most analyses of the effects of immigration on native-born workers has been based on a straightforward idea. If immigration has neg-ative effects, then, other economic factors being equal, the wages or employ-ment conditions of native-born workers should be worse in areas with more im-migrant workers. Thus, researchers have compared the wages or unemployment rates of native-born workers in cities with few immigrants in the labor force to those in cities with relatively high numbers of immigrants: controlling for such independent factors as the state of local economies, skill levels of the local labor forces, and racial, ethnic, gender composition, they estimate the independent effect of the presence of immigrants.

It has been suggested that the preponderance of findings with small effects is due to a shortcoming of the comparative method. Put simply, some economists and demographers believe that negative effects have not been found because the native-born workers whose wages or employment would have been worsened by the presence of immigrants leave the metropolitan areas that have attracted relatively large numbers of immigrants. If so, the comparative model must un-derestimate immigration's effects on native-born workers for two reasons. First, the native-born workers who remain in areas with large numbers of immigrants would be those with relatively high wages and good employment opportunities. Second, those leaving such areas for places with few immigrants increase the la-bor supply and thus worsen the employment and wage conditions in the areas of destination, making the conditions in both kinds of areas similar. If true, then even if immigration had substantial effects on the labor market condition of na-tive-born workers nationwide, those effects could not be found by comparing different metropolitan areas.

Recent studies by demographers, notably William Frey of the University of Michigan (1995), have reported evidence that provides support for this hypothe-sis. This research has shown that, during the 1980s, the states that attracted rela-tively large numbers of immigrants were precisely the states that low- and lower-middle-income whites were most likely to leave for states with relatively few immigrants. Moreover, the states with relatively large numbers of immigrants also disproportionately attracted highly skilled native-born workers. One study esti-mates that for every seven immigrants who moved into an area during the 1980s, one blue-collar worker left. Perhaps typical of this pattern is Stan Godek, a thirty-four-year-old carpenter who, with his family, left California in the spring of 1993 for Las Vegas. "All the illegal aliens in L.A. drive the wages for construction way down, I mean way down," complained Godek, who obtained a construction job in Las Vegas at three times his last wage in Los Angeles, where in the end he could only find part-time work (*The Oregonian*, 9 August 1993, A5).

Borjas, Freeman, and Katz avoid these problems by estimating the effects of immigration and trade on the aggregate labor market. Put simply, they estimate the "implicit" increase in lower-skilled labor consonant with the increased volume of U.S. imports and add that figure to the increase in the labor supply due to immigration. They then estimate the change in the relative wages of high- and low-skilled workers that would be due to the implicit increase in the relative supply of low-skilled workers to get an estimate of the wage effect of immigration and trade on the aggregate labor market.

In "Labor Market Dynamics and the Effects of Immigration on African Americans" (Chapter 6), Frank D. Bean, Mark A. Fossett, and Kyung Tae Park reexamine the comparative approach. They seek to discover if local labor markets with higher concentrations of immigrants exhibit higher African American unemployment rates, especially in areas in which overall employment opportunities are relatively scarce. They report two findings. First, in metropolitan areas with low unemployment rates, an increase in the number of immigrants *reduces* the unemployment rate of blacks. Evidently, the immigrants' positive effect on the demand for goods and services is larger than their negative effect on the competition for jobs. Second, relatively larger numbers of mostly Latino immigrants in places with high overall unemployment rates tend to raise African American unemployment rates.

Bean et al. argue that earlier conclusions that immigration exerts a negligible effect on African American labor market outcomes may be premature for several reasons. Foremost is that previous research has tended to rely on highly aggregated measures of immigration and has overlooked variations in the structural features of local labor markets likely to influence intergroup labor market competition. One way of looking at the highly aggregate methods of combining data that Bean et al. criticize is to focus on the term *immigrant*. Although immigrants do enter labor markets, they seldom self-identify or organize themselves in social networks in those terms. Rather, immigrants such as Salvadorans, Haitians, Soviet Jews, and Laotians tend to form social networks with others of the same nationality. These networks play important roles in determining in what localities and for what jobs individuals actually seek and obtain work. As a consequence, for significant periods of time after entry to the host country, immigrant groups tend to congregate within areas and labor markets that already contain relatively large numbers of their counterparts. For example, 20 percent of the former population of a small village in El Salvador now lives in one section of the District of Columbia.

The importance of such social networks suggest that many immigrant and native-born groups may be noncompeting groups, whereas others may be quite competitive. Or to phrase the issue in the language of neoclassical economics, certain groups may serve as labor substitutes for some groups and thus compete for the latters' jobs, but as complements who actually increase the jobs available for other groups. In the U.S. labor market, highly segmented by race, ethnicity, and gender, as well as by education, it would hardly be surprising that ethnically diverse flows of immigrants might have very different effects on the labor market status of an ethnically varied native-born population. There may be enough variation, in fact, that statistical analyses of the effects of a composite category, "immigrants," on a composite category, "native-born," are, on average, null.

In this regard it is interesting that Bean and his co-authors report especially significant effects of Latino immigrants on the unemployment of African American males. In "Immigrants, Puerto Ricans, and the Earnings of Native Black Males" (Chapter 5), Thomas J. Espenshade provides a direct test of this minority competition hypothesis by examining the disparate effects of "immigrants" and Puerto Rican–born men on the labor market status of black males in New Jersey. Puerto Rican migrants are a distinctive and self-identified minority group with strong internal social networks. Although they are not immigrants to the United States, Puerto Ricans born on the island who migrate to the mainland represent additions to mainland labor markets just as do immigrants. Therefore, comparing the effects of Puerto Rican migrants on the wages of native-born blacks to the effects of immigrants, an amorphous conglomeration of distinctive groups with separate social networks, is an ideal test of the minority competition hypothesis.

New Jersey is a state well suited to Espenshade's analysis. It contains large Puerto Rican and African American populations, and it ranks sixth in the nation in the number of foreign-born residents. Espenshade's results support two major conclusions. First, there is evidence of direct labor market competition between native-born black and Puerto Rican–born males in New Jersey. A 1 percentage point increase in the share of Puerto Rican males in a local labor market is associated with a 4 percent decline in the average annual or weekly earnings of black men. Second, there is no evidence that the presence of immigrants per se affects black males earnings, positively or negatively.

Jaynes and Wilson (1996) made findings similar to these in their study of immigration and changing employment during the 1980s. For example, although the effects of immigrants per se on the labor market position of native-born workers may not necessarily be strong, preliminary analysis of changing employment of particular groups is instructive. The construction industry is especially noteworthy in this regard. During the 1980s, Latinos' share of unskilled laborer employment in the Chicago construction industry rose from 12 to 22 percent while the African American and white shares were falling. Overall the magnitude of the changes in employment among unskilled laborers in this industry is striking: in 1980 Latino unskilled labor construction employment was 58 percent of black, but by 1990 black employment was 80 percent of Latino; total black employment had fallen while Latino employment had nearly doubled. Similar transformations occurred in skilled craft positions in construction. In such metropolitan areas as Dallas–Fort Worth and Los Angeles, huge increases in Latinos' shares of employment in these jobs occurred, as they did for Asians in Los Angeles. Similarly, in New York, Latinos held far fewer of these jobs than blacks in 1980 but had surpassed them by 1990. Asian shares, although smaller than all groups, grew much faster.

The reader should be cautioned that findings of sharply changing employment shares among unskilled black and white labor do not prove that these workers have been made worse off by the increased employment shares of Latinos and Asians. It may be that black and white workers who left the Chicago construction industry or those who might have entered if there had been no immigration of Latinos and Asians found alternative employment in Chicago or elsewhere that was preferable to what they would have had in Chicago in the absence of immigration. Given the likely alternatives for unskilled construction workers, however, this outcome does not seem likely. Moreover, Jaynes and Wilson's statistical analysis of three industries and fifty-two major metropolitan areas concludes that immigration during the 1980s was especially detrimental to the employment of semiskilled blue-collar natives. Early consensus that immigration has had negligible effects on native-born workers may yet prove correct, but the issue is far from settled.

Lest we dwell only on group competition, let me note that Jaynes and Wilson also find that levels of pay for Asians, blacks, and Hispanics were all below those of whites working at similar jobs in the same metropolitan areas. Thus, in Chicago, Dallas–Fort Worth, New York City, and Los Angeles, in both 1980 and 1990, non-Hispanic whites earned considerably higher hourly wages than did Asians, blacks, or Latinos with similar qualifications and working in the same industry and occupation.

Affirmative Action

"Affirmative action" programs provide another salient example of the tensions between Asian, Latino, and African Americans. Civil rights law in the United

States, in all its manifestations, was predicated on the experience of discrimination against blacks. During the 1960s, when the corpus of equal opportunity laws and government affirmative action programs to increase minority participation in various sectors of society was being initiated, African Americans represented nearly nine of ten people of color in the United States. The term *minority* was automatically used by most people synonymously with *black* and, in theory and practice, affirmative action and equal opportunity meant African Americans vis-à-vis Americans of European descent.

During the ensuing two decades, however, the immigration of Asians and Hispanics of color and the expansion of the term *minorities* to include white Latinos changed the practice if not the theory. By 1991, African Americans, although still the largest "minority" group (48 percent), were a minority of the peoples belonging to at least one of the groups deemed by the federal government to be eligible for affirmative action programs. Latinos, Asian Americans and Pacific Islanders, and Native Americans and others were 37 percent, 12 percent, and 3 percent, respectively. These changing numbers have produced large alterations in the operation of and the receipt of benefits from these programs.

The redistribution of program benefits between African Americans and the other groups has resulted in some bitter conflicts. For example, one benefit of affirmative action policies to African Americans has been reduced discrimination in public-sector employment, where, since the 1960s, blacks have found a haven from the higher levels of discrimination in the private sector. By 1990, African Americans were disproportionately employed by government at both the federal and the municipal levels.

But changing population dynamics and pressures at all levels of government to pursue policies of equality and diversity have led to increased penetration of Asian and Latino Americans into public employment. For example, in 1988 the Los Angeles County Board of Supervisors announced a goal of achieving population parity in public-sector employment for all groups. In a metropolitan area where in 1990 Hispanics' share of public-sector jobs was less than half their 40 percent of the population, this policy would seem to have an obvious implication for African American employment. In fact, Latinos' share of employment at all levels of government within the Los Angeles metropolitan area rose from 14.4 to 19 percent between 1980 and 1990; Asians' share grew from 5.5 to 8.2 percent; blacks' share fell slightly, from 16.3 to 15.8 percent; and whites' share declined considerably, from 63.6 to 56.8 percent. Similar employment patterns occurred in many cities as Latino and Asian Americans increased their share of public-sector employment.

The response by some African Americans has been a repudiation of affirmative action. Mamie Grant, head of an organization representing African American city workers in Los Angeles, referring to Hispanics, complained, "They're trying to siphon off all our gains." She asked plaintively, "Whatever happened to merit?" and declared, "I'm not in favor of affirmative action [because] it shuts blacks out" (*The Sunday Oregonian,* 19 December 1993, A4). Similar conflicts are arising in other cities.

Hispanics searching for greater representation in government employment have turned attention to the federal postal service. In the early nineties, Postmaster General Marvin T. Runyon publicly stated that the Postal Service needed more Hispanic employees and that it was "committed to making progress in affirmative action and being a leader in work force diversity" (*Washington Post,* 3 August 1994, A5). Nationwide, Hispanics compose just 6.4 percent of the Postal Service workforce, but they are 8.1 percent of the nation's nonmilitary workforce. In contrast, African Americans compose 20.8 percent of postal workers but just 10.3 percent of the national workforce.

In a number of large cities with appreciable Hispanic populations, the relative numbers for Hispanics and African Americans are disproportionately greater than the national figures. For example, in Chicago, blacks account for 79.7 percent of postal workers but only 18.2 percent of the general labor force, whereas Hispanics comprise 3.9 percent of postal workers and 11 percent of the labor force. In Los Angeles, blacks comprise 63 percent of postal workers but 9.6 percent of the labor force, whereas Hispanics comprise 15 percent of postal workers but 34 percent of the area labor force. And in the Washington, D.C., area, blacks comprise 86.4 percent of postal workers and Hispanics just 1.1 percent.

Both Asian and Latino underrepresentation in government employment can be partly explained by large percentages of noncitizens, poor English-language skills, and lack of education among many immigrants. But there may be other reasons. Tirso del Junco, a Cuban American and the vice chair of the Postal Service Board of Governors, claimed that blacks "think it is a right to have this overrepresentation" (*Washington Post,* 3 August 1994, A1). He further charged black postal managers in many large cities with a failure to make the effort to find qualified Hispanics because they preferred to hire blacks.

African American postal officials dispute del Junco's charges. They claim that blacks are not overrepresented on the Postal Service workforce and that their large numbers reflect a long history dating to the early twentieth century, when the Post Office, because of civil service examinations and hiring rules, was practically the only federal employment available to blacks other than menial jobs.

This history, blacks argue, has resulted in a tradition of strong networks of community organizations and current workers ensuring that many highly qualified blacks apply for postal positions (*Washington Post,* 3 August 1994, A1, A5). For what is probably a combination of all of these explanations, Latino and Asian American shares of public-sector jobs remain below their proportion of the labor force in many large metropolitan areas.

Awards to minority-owned firms by public agencies operating under an assortment of minority business set-aside programs present another area of intergroup competition. A study of contract awards to minority firms in the District of Columbia during the period 1989–1991, when the district operated a minority business set-aside program, reported several interesting findings. During those three years, African American–owned firms received 50 percent of the contracts awarded to minorities, Hispanic-owned firms 28 percent, Asian American–owned firms 1.6 percent, and unidentified "other minorities" 20 percent. During an earlier period, 1984–1985, Hispanic-owned firms had been awarded contracts worth more than twice the amount awarded to black-owned firms. The high utilization of Hispanic-owned firms by the city government may have had a role in the sometimes acrimonious city council debates during the early 1980s over which groups would be considered minorities and thus eligible for program participation. Some black advocacy groups strongly opposed the inclusion of Hispanics and Asians. The council spent considerable time discussing just what constituted a minority; it decided on groups that were "economically and socially disadvantaged because of historical discrimination practiced against these groups by institutions within the United States." The city council, with the support of Mayor Marion Barry, thus included all major minority groups (A.D. Jackson 1990).

The views expressed by some black organizations that opposed inclusion of Hispanics and Asians in the District of Columbia minority business program were similar to those expressed by an African American in Miami who argued, "The question is whether the Hispanic community has been harmed the same way the black community has. . . . There is a priority, and if you have only limited resources, you have to look at the community that has the longer baseline and history [of victimization from discrimination]" (*New York Times,* 30 May 1992).

How these changes in the benefits of affirmative action, equal opportunity, or diversity are viewed depends on one's understanding of the origins of and the public policy objectives of affirmative action. One commonly held view takes a strict interpretation from within the perspective of the black-white paradigm.

Clyde Johnson, who represents black employees of Los Angeles County, presented this view well: "When you think of affirmative action you think of black and white. All the laws really were directed specifically at eliminating patterns of discrimination against blacks. . . . All the others are latecomers and bandwagon jumpers" (*The Sunday Oregonian,* 19 December 1993, A4). Or, according to James C. Burke, an African American politician from Miami, referring to the redistricting of the Florida state legislature during the early 1990s: "If the basis of an extra minority seat is the Voting Rights Act, then we ought to look and see who it was standing on the Edmund Pettus Bridge in Selma getting trampled" (*New York Times,* 30 May 1992).

But commitment to the black-white paradigm is not limited to people with obvious personal interests to protect. The lens of the black-white paradigm obscured even the business of the highest judicial courts. In the famous 1979 Supreme Court case *Regents of the University of California v. Bakke,* Bakke, an unsuccessful white applicant to the University of California medical school, had sued the state for admission on the ground that he had been discriminated against because sixteen minority students with allegedly weaker admissions credentials than his had been admitted under a special process for "disadvantaged students." Justice Powell, who cast the decisive vote in a 5 to 4 ruling in favor of Bakke, recognized the multiethnic scope of the case and found it disturbing that the university seemed to only consider "Negroes, Mexican-Americans, American Indians, and Asians" as disadvantaged (LaNoue 1993, 425; see also Schwartz 1990).

Yet, despite Justice Powell's comments and the fact that African Americans were actually a minority of the students who had been admitted through the special admissions process during its existence (the proportions were 48 percent Hispanic, 33 percent black, and 19 percent Asian), the news media, the four dissenting judges, and the general public discussed this inflammatory case only in terms of the black-white paradigm.

Justice Brennan, writing a dissenting opinion for three of the justices, and Justice Marshall, dissenting for himself, both argued in favor of the program on the basis of the historical discrimination against African Americans. The opinions virtually ignored the other three groups benefiting from the admissions policy. Similarly, the highly inflamed debates that followed this opinion were nearly always couched in terms that referred to affirmative action for blacks and reverse discrimination against whites. The ensuing black-white debate, framed in language that disparaged the academic abilities of blacks, encouraged negative critiques of all affirmative action programs without the broader discourse that would have been required if the roles and social conditions of participating Asians and Latinos had been included.

Ironically, despite the fact that the rhetoric surrounding affirmative action programs and equal opportunity laws has always been strongly based on the black-white paradigm, both real-world politics and constitutional requirements ensured that statutes and presidential executive orders were worded in general terms covering race, color, and creed. Thus, while the rhetoric of civil rights law and public policy seemed to refer to reparations for African Americans, the actual political and legal institutions that developed were founded on the principle of antidiscrimination and pursuit of equal opportunity for all minority Americans. This fact provides an alternative to the black reparations perspective.

The juxtaposition of the two interpretations has been stated ably by Latino activist and Los Angeles radio personality Xavier Hermosillo: "Nobody can really compete with 400 years of slavery. [Blacks have] got the lock on worst history of oppression by an ethnic minority. But, it depends on how you view affirmative action. If you view it as a never-ending wheel of fortune in which blacks come up a winner on every spin, then I've got a problem with that. If you view affirmative action as a tool for allowing everybody the opportunity to participate, than I find that very acceptable" (*The Sunday Oregonian,* 19 December 1993, A4). Hermosillo's position has gained considerable support from the changing politics fueled by increases in Asian and Latino voters and a legal system that appears to be moving in a direction consistent with the equal opportunity and antidiscrimination interpretation of affirmative action.

The judiciary has been moving in concert with demographically driven politics. In 1989, in *City of Richmond v. J. A. Crosen Co.,* the Supreme Court delivered one of its most important decisions on civil rights. Ruling against the minority set-aside program for city construction projects in Richmond, Virginia, the Court took issue with the city's designation of an array of minority groups as eligible for participation in the program. The majority opinion declared that it is not clear that any members of some of the covered groups, such as Aleuts, had ever lived in the city, much less been victims of discrimination there.

In the future, all similar programs of state and local governments must pass a strict two-pronged test. If a set-aside program is to satisfy the equal protection clause of the Fourteenth Amendment to the Constitution, it must be implemented to achieve a compelling government interest and be narrowly tailored. The Court ruled that the Constitution does recognize that remediation of governmental fostering of state or private discrimination is a compelling governmental interest, but narrow tailoring requires that the government unit must demonstrate, through objective evidence, that any covered group has been the victim of discrimination relevant to the activity being addressed by the program and in the government's jurisdiction. In considering the Richmond case, the Court wrote: "There is absolutely no evidence of past discrimination against Spanish-speaking, Oriental, Indian, Eskimo, or Aleut persons in any aspect of the Richmond construction industry" (*J.A. Croson v. City of Richmond* [4th Cir. 1987], 822 F.2d 1355).

Strict scrutiny places considerable constraints on affirmative action programs. The immediate effect is that there can be no demonstration of a history of discrimination for groups with no history in a given area. To the extent that other groups are unable to document relevant types of discrimination in the given jurisdictions, African Americans might benefit by being a smaller class of protected groups. But if groups newer to the jurisdiction are unable to qualify for such programs, their political support for the programs may be reduced, leaving blacks and their allies to defend programs that are increasingly under attack.

Even though various polls suggest that large pluralities or even small majorities of whites favor affirmative action, broad support for it can hardly be taken for granted. The fact that nearly two-thirds of whites agree that minorities now enjoy equal opportunity implies that they do not see affirmative action as necessary to battle discriminatory barriers to equal opportunity for minorities. One may reasonably speculate that whites who support some type of affirmative action and believe that equal opportunity for minorities has been achieved probably consider affirmative action as some kind of reparation for past injustices to blacks. They may also think that such past discrimination may have lingering contemporary effects on blacks' ability to take advantage of the equal opportunities they believe exist.

How much support people with these views would be willing to give to affirmative action that is increasingly rewarded to groups other than blacks is unknown. Recent attacks on affirmative action have been based on the participation of so-called undeserving groups, however.

There are also no simple conclusions that can be drawn about the competitive as opposed to the cooperative interests of the minority groups who currently qualify for a variety of affirmative action programs. As the rationale of affirmative action programs, if not the public rhetoric, moves from reparations for blacks to remediation of discrimination and pursuit of equal opportunity of discriminated minorities, interests that such minorities have in common may or may not provide a basis for their cooperation.

Who gets discriminated against becomes an important question. There is a good deal of evidence of significant discrimination against Asians and Latinos. As the numbers of people of Asian and Hispanic descent in the nation's population increases through immigration and birth, discrimination is unlikely to decrease soon. Nevertheless, the circumstances underlying the disadvantages faced by Asian and Latino Americans are frequently different from the most salient conditions relevant to African Americans.

Differences in social background and racial ancestry do exacerbate tensions over the role of equal opportunity and affirmative action. Many African Americans who accept the concept of equal opportunity question the eligibility of some groups for affirmative action programs. A state senator from Miami Beach put this position in the bluntest of terms: "The Cubans have ridden on the backs of Mexicans and Puerto Ricans to claim privileges which, as the only middle-class emigrés of any size that we have had in this country, they don't need" (*New York Times*, 30 May 1992). Similar criticisms have been directed at some Asian nationalities whose heavily middle-class social backgrounds enable them to compete for scarce resources with very high success rates (LaNoue 1993).

POLITICAL EMPOWERMENT AND THE
BLACK-WHITE PARADIGM

The Voting Rights Act of 1965 was a major achievement of the civil rights movement. It gave the federal government the power to enforce the rights of minorities to participate in elections, and, under certain conditions, it empowered state legislatures to create congressional districts in which a member of a protected minority group is likely to win election. This important legislation is one of the major reasons that there are more than seven thousand African American elected officials in the United States today.

In Chapter 8, "Legislative Redistricting and African American Interests: New Facts and Conventional Strategies," Bruce E. Cain examines the efficacy of the act as a means of enhancing minorities' electoral influence during the 1990s. His discussion is a compelling illustration of the inadequacies of the black-white paradigm in our multiethnic society. Cain argues that because there now exist several groups competing for electoral representation, the premises underlying the act are not applicable to the 1990s.

Cain argues that because the law interpreting the act assumes the historical model of African American vote dilution, its application to the voting rights of Latinos and Asians is often highly problematic. The barriers to electoral participation these groups face are quite different from those the legislation addressed on behalf of African Americans. He considers three implicit assumptions of the Voting Rights Act for a protected group: that it has a large core of eligible voters who have been prevented from voting by institutional barriers, that it has a history of discrimination and a pattern of electoral frustration, and that it is politically coherent.

Each of these criteria is generally satisfied by blacks but not by Asians and Latinos. For example, among Latinos there are twenty-two distinct nationalities with different cultures and histories. This fact confounds the assumption that Latinos are a politically coherent group, and it frequently makes concerted political action difficult if not impossible. A similar diversity of nationalities and ethnic backgrounds complicates the political coherence assumption for Asian Americans.

Moreover, Cain shows that even applying the voting rights act to African Americans in areas with significant numbers of Asians and Latinos is by no means straightforward. In this situation, a number of complicated zero-sum political problems can arise because various "protected" racial and ethnic groups may have competing claims to representation in a particular geographic area. Cain argues that in such multiracial cases the biracial model underlying the Voting Rights Act offers courts and legislatures little guidance for balancing complex competing interests.

Finally, Cain examines how the complications introduced by multiracialism have fueled a debate within and outside the African American community about the limits of legislative redistricting as a strategy for achieving political empowerment. He suggests that coalitional strategies, whereby minorities spread their voting strength to influence a large number of congressional districts, may now be preferable to concentrating voters in a few districts in order to elect a few officials.

As the debate over political empowerment strategies continues among African Americans, the increasing presence of Latinos and Asians in communities where they were barely discernible two decades ago increases both their need for public services and their political aspirations. This process of enhanced political consciousness leads these groups to make new demands on political institutions. Throughout the country, these pressures are changing the face of politics.

Most often, political activity begins at the local level and is expressed through an organization representing a group of specific national origin. Thus, an association of Korean merchants or Cambodian residents may pressure city governments—in such places as New York City, the District of Columbia, Camden, New Jersey, or Lowell, Massachusetts—for better police protection, or a Vietnamese civic association may demand cleaner streets. These mundane political activities may then pull persons of diverse nationalities together to pursue common interests and provide leaders with incentives to address issues in the wider public arena from a more pan-Asian or pan-Hispanic perspective. In the early 1990s, for instance, various Latino nationality groups organized to protest the state of Virginia's policy of denying drivers' licenses to applicants who could not produce a green permanent resident card. Such active political participation may be reinforced by black and white politicians who are accustomed to thinking in terms of racial and ethnic categories and are impressed by growing blocks of voters.

In the heavily populated communities of northern Virginia that border Washington, D.C., the 1990 census revealed that Asian Americans outnumber blacks in Fairfax County and Latinos outnumber blacks in Arlington. This growth in the numbers of Latino American and Asian groups has increased their political activity, and the political structures of many communities are responding to these conditions. To cite a few instances, the president of a coalition of Vietnamese self-help groups in the area traveled to the capital in Richmond to lobby area delegates and the governor's office in early 1991. Democratic Party leaders in Arlington hosted a wine and cheese reception to woo a group of people identified as leaders in the Arlington Latino communities. The Democratic chair of the Fairfax County Board named a Hispanic activist to the county's Human Rights Commission. "She beat me to it," complained the county supervisor, a Republican, referring to the appointment made by the board chair.

As Cain points out, Asians and Latinos represent much lower proportions of registered voters than of residents in many communities. This severely reduces their political power, but it does not mean they have no political leverage at all. As the preceding examples demonstrate, elected officials who are keeping their eyes on future voting potential ensure that these groups are not ignored. As Maria Isabel Hoyt, president of the Arlington, Virginia, chapter of the League of United Latin American Citizens, said: "They'll have to come to terms with the numbers" (*Washington Post,* 3 February 1991, B1, B4). Hard data suggest that northern Virginia's elected officials are not the only ones wooing Asian and Latino constituents.

Thomas E. Cavanagh, in "Political Representation and Stratified Pluralism" (Chapter 7), presents the first comparative analysis of public office holding among African, Asian, Latino, and Native Americans in the United States. He provides descriptive statistics for elected and appointed officials over time, with regional breakdowns for each group. Cavanagh's detailed research also provides separate numbers for subgroups among Latinos and Asians. His comparative discussion of each group's political history in the United States offers insights into the particular events and nuances that explain the different trajectories.

Cavanagh reports that the numbers of elected officials from these groups have risen considerably from a handful just a generation ago. Whereas elective and appointive office holding among minorities is increasing dramatically for every group, however, Asian Americans lag behind the others. Among elected officials in 1990, there were more than 7,000 African American and 4,000 Latino but only 316 Asian elected officials in the United States.

One key explanation for this underrepresentation of Asian Americans is their underparticipation in the electoral process. In "Political Activity and Preferences of African Americans, Latinos, and Asian Americans" (Chapter 9), Carole Jean Uhlaner's examination of electoral participation (campaign contributions, voter turnout, party preferences, and issue preferences) among whites, blacks, Asians, and Latinos, she concludes that relatively little ethnically specific political organizing has occurred in Asian American communities. Moreover, she finds that strong tendencies to organize within national-origin groups suggest that there is no politically relevant "Asian" community in the United States. This provides a sharp contrast to the strong political organizations of African Americans, with their high focus on racial identity. And despite the existence of great diversity along national-origin lines among Latinos, Uhlaner finds that they are developing common political structures.

Rates of voting among citizens tend to be highest among African Americans and lowest among Latinos. Although the data show that all groups contain more Democrats than Republicans, there is variation among groups, with African Americans most likely to be Democrats and Asian Americans having the largest minority of Republicans.

Both the Asian American and Latino groups contain substantial numbers of natives and immigrants from many national backgrounds. Political behavior and attitudes can differ across these dimensions. For example, native-born Asian Americans are more likely to identify with the Democratic Party than are Asian immigrants. How will cultural assimilation affect party affiliation among Asians in the future? More generally, how will it affect political activity? In her study of black-Korean relations in New York City, Claire Jean Kim found that the black boycott of Korean merchants had the unintended consequence of provoking racial or ethnic countermobilization strategies within the Korean American community.

Uhlaner concludes that in a comparison of the compatibility of these groups' political concerns, there exist important "minority" commonalities as well as points of potential friction both across groups and within them. The possibilities for coalition and competition between these groups in the future will depend heavily on the ability and desire of their political leaders to foster collective rather than competitive actions. In particular, African Americans, still the largest and most influential of minority groups, need to take the initiative in forging new coalitions to meet the needs of a dynamic and changing world.

As I read Cain, Garcia, and Uhlaner, coalitional ties among major minority groups are not to be understood as permanent utopian arrangements that end all or even most forms of intergroup competition. Rather, as I suggested earlier, intergroup coalitions are likely to be frequently formed but temporary arrangements aimed at specific issues. And they are just as likely to be recurring interruptions of more competitive intergroup relations. In order to illustrate how a shared minority perspective can be a major cohesive factor for these coalitions, I turn to a discussion of a recent major political coalition whose existence has confounded analysts who fail to take into account what I call African Americans' ambivalence toward immigration and immigrants and the competing tensions involved in relations between minority groups.

THE POLITICAL ECONOMY OF IMMIGRATION

In the long term, immigration policy is primarily driven by economic considerations. This is true despite the experience of the 1970s and early 1980s when U.S. immigration policy appeared to be driven by purely humanitarian considerations such as admittance of political refugees and reunification of family members of legal residents. The fundamental economic basis of immigration policy has prevailed since the importation of slaves and indentured servants in the seventeenth century.

The major reason is that, irrespective of what other motives may be operative, the reception of large numbers of immigrants must have significant effects on the labor market specifically and on the competition for many kinds of scarce resources generally. These effects assume great importance to employers and at least some native workers. Thus, although various immigration issues are important to many citizens and organizations, much higher priority is given to immigration by interest groups such as large farm owners dependent on cheap labor, labor unions, business organizations, ethnic group organizations, and human rights advocates. This induces these interest groups to allocate far greater amounts of their time and resources to immigration-related issues than do other groups or the general public (see Schuck 1991). As a consequence, these special interests exert influence on immigration politics that is disproportionate to their numbers. Over any reasonably long period of time, any immigration policy initiative that seeks the approval of the legislative and executive branches of government must win the support of some of these groups if it is to become law.

The Debates of the 1980s

These factors were conclusive during the policy debates concerning the passage of the Immigration Reform and Control Act of 1986 (IRCA) and the Immigration Act of 1990. These debates revealed several deep fissures separating the positions of key groups in U.S. society. First, there was a split along class lines: employer organizations were overwhelmingly in favor of relaxed immigration rules, whereas blue-collar workers in general, and labor unions in particular, desired more restrictive policies. The combined effect of IRCA and the 1990 act represented something of a compromise between the two groups.

The key provisions of IRCA were the introduction of sanctions against employers found hiring undocumented immigrants and an amnesty program that enabled thousands of undocumented aliens already in the country to become documented. The Immigration Act of 1990 liberalized immigration policy by enlarging the quotas available in many immigrant categories. It also featured diversity goals that disproportionately favor Irish immigrants, and it enlarged quotas for immigrants with scarce skills. Although labor unions largely opposed the amnesty program, they were somewhat mollified by passage of employer sanctions. Labor unions had unsuccessfully sought employer sanction legislation as early as the 1960s and again in the 1970s. And western growers were strongly proimmigration, but they were opposed to the amnesty program—a pair of positions that can only be understood when the growers' desire for docile as well as cheap labor is recognized.

The key debates over these bills hinged on several economic factors: employers' demand for cheap labor, discrimination against minority immigrants, and the impact of immigration on state and local government budgets (Schuck 1991; Fix and Passel 1991). Important in the political alignments were the positions taken by racial and ethnic groups with strong self-identified interests in the future course of immigration. Given their high level of representation among lower-skilled and semiskilled workers and the fact that polling data taken during the 1980s revealed that majorities of African American respondents associated immigration with detrimental labor market competition, it is not surprising that there was very vocal black opposition to increased immigration. Moreover, such opposition was strengthened when a number of proponents of immigration used the argument that increased immigration was necessary to the economic competitiveness of the nation. That argument was predicated on a thinly veiled negative critique of the economic worth of the African American and Latino populations in the United States.

The gist of the argument was that the native-born population, by virtue of the low birthrate of whites and the increasing proportions of Latinos and blacks in the workforce, was not capable of producing the high-quality skilled labor force required by the high-technology economy of the twenty-first century. Therefore, skilled immigrants should be encouraged to enter (Johnston and Packer 1987). Whatever else this argument implied, it carried a strong implication for future public policy. Disadvantaged native populations, disproportionately African American and Latino, would be abandoned, and immigration policy favoring skilled foreign workers would be substituted for government policies committed to improving the educational and training opportunities available to underprivileged Americans (Bach and Meissner 1990; Mishel and Teixeira 1990; Brown 1990).

Given these facts, widely covered by the news media, a number of commentators expressed surprise that a major force in the passage of both pieces of legislation was the supportive coalition of the congressional black and Hispanic caucuses. But such surprise would seem to be due to a lack of recognition of the fact that although some African Americans were highly visible members of the opposition, there was great ambivalence toward immigration reform among African Americans generally. Thus, as noted above, even though most blacks' views of the effects of immigration were highly negative, blacks were more supportive of immigration and immigrants than were nonblacks.

The alignment of African American political and civic leaders with pro-immigration forces reflected the adhesive power of a shared minority experience. These leaders balanced the widespread belief among blacks that increased immigration was detrimental to their well-being with blacks' moral commitment to the rights of the underprivileged and their civil rights ties to Latinos, who heavily favored liberalized immigration policies. Furthermore, opposition to liberal immigration reform by African American leaders would have aligned them with anti-immigration forces that, throughout the decade, had espoused policies in terms of "cultural purity." By the 1990s, an economic recession and increased media attention to the economic costs of immigration returned the debate over immigration policy back to long-term economic impact.

Benefits and Costs of Immigration

Despite the near-hysteria created by the pronouncements of some politicians and some interest groups, the most methodologically sound studies of the net costs of immigration support the conclusion that the United States, as a whole, benefits from contemporary immigration. During a period of time reasonably long enough to allow immigrants to adjust to their new situations, they produce more than they require in government services.

Some of the confusion over this issue has been caused by a failure to make appropriate distinctions between immigration's impact on local and state governments and its impact on the whole nation. Although many of the benefits of immigration, such as lower prices for consumer and producer goods and greater federal tax revenues, accrue to the nation as a whole, nearly all of the costs for public services are borne by local and state governments. As a consequence, some of the studies that find positive net benefits for the nation also find that the net cost of immigration to particular state and local governments are negative. But some of these findings have been overstated by inappropriate analyses. And frequently, although sometimes not reported, the methods used also indicate that native-born residents also impose net costs.

An easy way to understand this is to note that one of the largest costs at the state and local levels is education. These costs, often greater for immigrant pupils because of the need to supply English-language instruction, are obviously legitimate expenses and should be included in any cost-benefit calculation of immigration's impact. But a correct balancing of costs and benefits would also have to take into account the expected benefits from future tax, production, and civic contributions of the students. Cost-benefit analyses made at a given moment in time tell us something about the current net costs to the state, just as they would for any native-born household. But because immigrants bring children with them and give birth to children after arriving, the full net costs or benefits of immigration will unfold only over time.

On average, residents of the nation gain from immigration but, at least in the short run, residents of particular states may lose. But cost-benefit analyses of immigration are only concerned with a comparison of aggregate costs and benefits: who derives the benefits and who bears the costs are not considered. But in any large-scale disruption of a society there are inevitably winners and losers. The welfare principle that legitimates cost-benefit analysis as a decision-making criterion for social policy is based on what economists call the Hicks Compensation Principle. If a cost-benefit analysis produces a positive bottom line, then the summed gains of all the winners is, by definition, sufficient to compensate all the losers for their losses. In theory, such payments from winners to losers would make everyone in the society better off. In practice, such compensation is never made.

An important illustration of this phenomenon is connected to the fact that immigration into the United States during the 1980s did not have equal effects on all fifty states. California and New York received 49 percent of all legal immigrants, and the top six receiving states received 75 percent. The politics of immigration during the 1990s has been affected greatly by this differential geographic incidence of costs and benefits. Thus, one can well understand the demand of the states that have received disproportionate numbers of immigrants for some form of compensation from the federal government.

But the differential incidence of the benefits and costs of immigration among states is not the only major failure of our current immigration policy to address the inadequacies captured by the Hicks Compensation Principle. Employers and consumers gain at the expense of some workers who are already in the country. We have seen that the losers are likely to be low-skilled, poorly paid, and disproportionately minority workers.

CONCLUSIONS

Economic justice requires that the least advantaged members of the society should not be forced to pay the costs for benefits that the nation enjoys from immigration. The question we should be debating is not whether we should end immigration. The nation benefits from immigration. We should be debating how society should be compensating less-skilled workers through combinations of better training, relocation, and educational opportunities and how the federal government should address the unequal burdens of immigration among the states.

The economic effects of immigration are of immense importance. Nevertheless, they represent a mere fraction of immigration's influence on American society. As it has throughout American history, immigration continues to promise major changes in our economic, political, and social institutions. In these pages I have discussed a number of these effects as they are occurring now. Where they may ultimately lead depends on Americans' commitment to equality and pluralism.

Surely we may agree with some commentators that these changes could be detrimental to the future well-being of African Americans if their institutions and leaders do not adapt themselves to a newly emerging sociopolitical environment. But despite the natural tendency toward intergroup competition inherent in a diversifying, ethnically plural society, past successes at intergroup cooperation and a shared commitment to justice and equality suggest that such an outcome can be avoided. Indeed, if faced squarely and boldly, contemporary immigration and its effects on our conceptions of race and ethnicity could offer African, Asian, and Latino Americans an opportunity to forge new coalitions and new visions of the American dream for all Americans.

Chapter 2 The Residential Segregation of Blacks, Hispanics, and Asians, 1970–1990

Douglas S. Massey

Social scientists have long studied patterns of racial and ethnic residential segregation because of the close connection between a group's spatial position in society and its socioeconomic well-being. Opportunities and resources are unevenly distributed in space: certain neighborhoods have safer streets, higher home values, better services, more effective schools, and more advantageous peer environments than others. As people and families improve their socioeconomic standing, they move in order to gain access to these benefits. That is, they attempt to convert their achievements into improved residential circumstances, which not only yield immediate tangible benefits but also enhance the prospects for success by providing greater access to important resources such as higher education.

Racial and ethnic groups moving into urban areas historically have settled in enclaves located close to the urban core in areas of mixed land use, old housing, poor services, and low or falling socioeconomic status. As group members spend time in the city, however, and as their socioeconomic status rises, they tend to move out of these enclaves into neighborhoods that offer more amenities and improved conditions, areas in which members of the majority group are likely to predominate.

The twin processes of migrant settlement, on the one hand, and spatial assimilation, on the other, combine to yield a diversity of segregation patterns across groups and times, depending on the particular histories of inmigration and socioeconomic mobility (Massey 1985). Groups experiencing recent rapid inmigration and slow socioeconomic mobility tend to display relatively high levels of segregation; those with rapid rates of economic mobility and slow rates of inmigration tend to be more integrated.

When avenues of spatial assimilation are blocked by prejudice and discrimination, however, high levels of residential segregation result. Migrants arrive in a city and settle within enclaves, but then their mobility is blocked; ethnic concentrations rise, enclaves are filled, densities rise, and then homeseekers are forced into adjacent areas, thereby expanding the boundaries of the enclave (Duncan and Duncan 1957). In the United States, most immigrant groups faced few residential barriers, so levels of ethnic segregation historically were quite moderate. Using a standard segregation index that ranges from 0 to 100, European ethnic groups rarely have scored higher than 60 or 65 (Massey 1985; Massey and Denton 1992).

Blacks, in contrast, traditionally have experienced more severe discrimination than other groups in urban housing markets. As they became more urbanized from 1900 to 1960, their segregation levels rose to unprecedented heights. By 1960 black segregation scores exceeded 60 in virtually all urban areas, and in the largest black communities they were between 80 and 90 (Massey and Denton 1993).

Such high levels of residential segregation imply a restriction on the opportunities and resources available to African Americans in comparison with other groups. The existence of discriminatory barriers in urban housing markets means that individual blacks are unable to capitalize fully on their attainments to achieve desirable residential conditions. In comparison with whites of similar social status, blacks are more likely to live in systematically disadvantaged neighborhoods, even in suburbs (Schneider and Logan 1982; Massey et al. 1987; Massey and Fong 1990; Massey and Denton 1992).

In a very real way, therefore, barriers to spatial mobility are barriers to social mobility, and a racially segregated society is not a "race-blind" society. The way that a group is spatially incorporated in a city is as important for its socioeconomic well-being as the manner in which it is incorporated in the labor force. It is important, therefore, that levels and trends in residential segregation be documented. This chapter presents and interprets trends in the residential segregation of blacks, Hispanics, and Asians in large metropolitan areas of the United States during the period from 1970 to 1990.

TRENDS IN SEGREGATION

Blacks

Table 2.1 displays indicators of black residential segregation for the thirty U.S. metropolitan areas with the largest African American populations. These data consider racial segregation from two vantage points. The first three columns show trends in the degree of spatial separation between blacks and whites using the index of dissimilarity, the most widely accepted measure of residential segregation. This index computes the relative percentage of blacks that would have to change their neighborhood in order to achieve an even residential distribution (Massey and Denton 1988). Evenness is defined to occur when all neighborhoods replicate the racial composition of the urban area as a whole, so that if an area is 20 percent black, each neighborhood is also 20 percent black (James and Taeuber 1985; White 1986). The index of dissimilarity ranges from 0 to 100: scores above 60 are generally considered to be high; those between 30 and 60 are viewed as moderate (Kantrowitz 1973).

The next three columns of the table show trends in the extent of black residential isolation, or the degree to which blacks inhabit homogeneous, all-black neighborhoods. This facet of segregation is captured by the P* index popularized by Stanley Lieberson (1980, 1981), which gives the percentage of blacks within the neighborhood of the average black person. Like the index of dissimilarity, it varies from 0 to 100 and represents the probability that a typical black person has residential contact with other blacks.

Indices of segregation and isolation for 1970 and 1980 were obtained from Massey and Denton (1987), with metropolitan areas defined by 1970 boundaries. The 1990 figures were obtained from Harrison and Weinberg (1992), who used 1990 geographic definitions. Both sets of researchers defined whites and blacks to exclude both white and black Hispanics. Both computed indices using census tracts as units of analysis: tracts are relatively small, homogenous spatial units of three thousand to six thousand people delineated by the Census Bureau to approximate urban neighborhoods (White 1987). Although the Census Bureau endeavors to maintain constant boundaries between censuses, population shifts and physical changes invariably require reclassifications that yield small inconsistencies over time. These changes, however, are unlikely to affect the broad trends and patterns being considered in this chapter.

If segregation levels at any time reflect the offsetting effects of processes of migrant settlement and spatial assimilation, then in principle one would expect to observe widespread declines in the level of black-white segregation between 1970

Table 2.1
Trends in Black Segregation and Isolation in the Thirty Metropolitan Areas
with the Largest Black Populations, 1970–90

	Dissimilarity Index			Isolation Index		
	1970	1980	1990	1970	1980	1990
North						
Boston	81.2	77.6	68.2	56.7	55.1	51.2
Buffalo	87.0	79.4	81.8	71.2	63.5	68.1
Chicago	91.9	87.8	85.8	85.5	82.8	83.9
Cincinnati	76.8	72.3	75.8	59.1	54.3	61.0
Cleveland	90.8	87.5	85.1	81.9	90.4	80.8
Columbus	81.8	71.4	67.3	63.5	57.5	52.5
Detroit	88.4	86.7	87.6	75.9	77.3	82.3
Gary-Hammond-E. Chicago	91.4	90.6	89.9	80.4	77.3	84.2
Indianapolis	81.7	76.2	74.3	64.5	62.3	61.0
Kansas City	87.4	78.9	72.6	74.2	69.0	61.6
Los Angeles-Long Beach	91.0	81.1	73.1	70.3	60.4	69.3
Milwaukee	90.5	83.9	82.8	73.9	69.5	72.4
Newark	81.4	81.6	82.5	67.0	69.2	78.6
New York	81.0	82.0	82.2	58.8	62.7	81.9
Philadelphia	79.5	78.8	77.2	68.2	69.6	72.2
Pittsburgh	75.0	72.7	71.0	53.5	54.1	53.1
St. Louis	84.7	81.3	77.0	76.5	72.9	69.5
San Francisco-Oakland	80.1	71.7	66.8	56.0	51.1	56.1
Average	84.5	80.1	77.8	68.7	66.1	68.9
South						
Atlanta	82.1	78.5	67.8	78.0	74.8	66.5
Baltimore	81.9	74.7	71.4	77.2	72.3	70.6
Birmingham	37.8	40.8	71.7	45.1	50.2	69.6
Dallas-Ft. Worth	86.9	77.1	63.1	76.0	64.0	58.0
Greensboro-Winston Salem	65.4	56.0	60.9	56.1	50.1	55.5
Houston	78.1	69.5	66.8	66.4	59.3	63.6
Memphis	75.9	71.6	69.3	78.0	75.9	75.0
Miami	85.1	77.8	71.8	75.2	64.2	74.1
New Orleans	73.1	68.3	68.8	71.3	68.8	71.9
Norfolk-Virginia Beach	75.7	63.1	50.3	73.5	62.8	55.9
Tampa-St. Petersburg	79.9	72.6	69.7	58.0	51.5	51.0
Washington, D.C.	81.1	70.1	66.1	77.2	68.0	66.7
Average	75.3	68.3	66.5	69.3	63.5	64.9

Sources: For 1970 and 1980: Massey and Denton 1987. For 1990: Harrison and Weinberg 1992.

Note: For explanations of dissimilarity and isolation indices, see text.

and 1990. Black migration to urban areas had largely ceased by 1970 (Farley and Allen 1987), and the passage of the Fair Housing Act in 1968 theoretically opened up white neighborhoods to blacks.

Among northern metropolitan areas, however, there is little evidence of any trend toward black residential integration. As table 2.1 shows, black-white dissimilarity indices averaged about 85 in 1970, 80 in 1980 and 78 in 1990, a decline of only 8 percent in twenty years. At the rate of change observed between 1970 and 1990, the average level of black-white segregation in northern areas would not reach the lower bound of the high range (60) until the year 2043; at the slower rate of change prevailing from 1970 to 1980 it would take until 2067. As of 1990, no northern black community yet approached a moderate level of segregation (between 30 and 60).

Indeed, in most metropolitan areas racial segregation remained very high throughout the twenty-year period. Dissimilarity indices were essentially constant in six metropolitan areas—Cincinnati, Detroit, Gary, New York, Newark, and Philadelphia. In seven others—Buffalo, Chicago, Cleveland, Indianapolis, Milwaukee, Pittsburgh, and St. Louis—small declines still left blacks extremely segregated. All of the latter areas had dissimilarity scores exceeding 70 in 1990, and in four areas the value was more than 80. No other ethnic or racial group in the history of the United States has ever, even briefly, experienced such high levels of residential segregation (Massey and Denton 1992).

A few metropolitan areas experienced significant declines in the level of black-white segregation between 1970 and 1990, although the pace of change slowed considerably during the 1980s. In Columbus, Ohio, for example, black-white dissimilarity fell by more than ten points from 1970 to 1980 (from 82 to 71), but then dropped only 4 points from 1980 to 1990. Likewise, San Francisco dropped from 80 to 72 during the 1970s but then dropped only to 67 by 1990.

The only areas that experienced a sustained decline in black-white segregation across both decades were Los Angeles and Boston, but in each case the overall level of segregation remained in the high range. The drop in Los Angeles probably reflects the displacement of blacks by the arrival of large numbers of Asian and Hispanic immigrants (Massey and Denton 1987). By 1990, for example, Watts, the core of the 1960s black ghetto, had become predominantly Hispanic (Turner and Allen 1991). The arrival of more than one million new immigrants in Los Angeles County between 1970 and 1980 put substantial pressure on the housing stock and increased intergroup competition for residential units, especially at the low end of the market, leading to considerable neighborhood mixing.

When large black communities are subject to high levels of segregation, intense racial isolation is inevitably produced. In 1990, five metropolitan areas (Chicago, Cleveland, Detroit, Gary, and New York) displayed isolation indices of 80 or more, meaning that the average black person lived in a neighborhood that was at least 80 percent black. Detailed analysis of neighborhoods shows, however, that even this overall average was misleading: it represents a balance between a small number of blacks who reside in integrated neighborhoods and a large majority of blacks who live in all-black areas (Denton and Massey 1991). In four of the six metropolitan areas, the level of black isolation actually *increased* between 1970 and 1990.

In some northern areas, the prevailing pattern of change in racial isolation scores was one of stability, with shifts of fewer than five percentage points in the years 1970–1990. The average northern isolation index of 68.9 in 1990 was virtually identical to that of 68.7 two decades earlier. Twenty years after the Fair Housing Act, in other words, blacks were still unlikely to be in residential contact with members of other groups. The large ghettos of the north were largely unaffected by the civil rights legislation of the 1960s and remained intact.

Trends in black segregation and isolation are somewhat different in the South, where segregation levels traditionally have been lower because of the distinctive history and character of southern cities. With social segregation enforced by Jim Crow legislation, blacks and whites before 1960 frequently lived in close physical proximity, with black-inhabited alleys being interspersed between larger, white-occupied avenues (Demerath and Gilmore 1954). During the postwar housing boom, moreover, rural black settlements were often overtaken by expanding white suburbs, thereby creating the appearance of racial integration. For these and other reasons, black-white segregation scores in the South traditionally have averaged about 10 points lower than in the North (Massey and Denton 1993).

This regional differential shows roughly in table 2.1, but southern areas display considerably greater diversity beneath the regional averages than those in the North. In some metropolitan areas, such as Baltimore, Houston, and Tampa, significant declines in segregation occurred during the 1970s but then slowed during the 1980s. Others, such as Dallas, Miami, and Norfolk, experienced steady declines across both decades. Two southern areas—Memphis and New Orleans—experienced relatively small changes in both decades, and two others displayed *increasing* levels of black-white segregation: Birmingham, where the increase was very sharp after 1970, and Greensboro, where an initial decline during the 1970s was reversed during the 1980s.

In general, then, black-white segregation scores in the South appear to be converging on values between 60 and 70, yielding an average of 67 and maintaining the traditional differential compared with the North. Metropolitan areas with segregation levels above this 60–70 range in 1970 experienced falling segregation, those with indices below it displayed increases in segregation, and those lying within it did not change much. Only Norfolk–Virginia Beach departed from this pattern, displaying a very significant and sustained decline in segregation across both decades, producing by 1990 a level of black-white dissimilarity well within the moderate range. This singularity probably reflects the fact that many Norfolk residents are in the military, which has been more successfully integrated than other institutions in American life. Frey and Farley (1993) have demonstrated that areas dominated economically by military bases have significantly lower levels of black-white segregation than others, controlling for a variety of other factors.

Although levels of black-white dissimilarity may be lower in the South, the relative number of blacks in urban areas is greater, so the average level of racial isolation within neighborhoods is not much different than in the North. Across the two decades, there was relatively little change in the overall degree of black isolation, with the average index falling from 69 in 1970 to 65 in 1990. In four southern areas (Baltimore, Memphis, Miami, and New Orleans), black isolation was more than 70 in both decades, and in Birmingham the level of black isolation *rose* from 45 to 70 between 1970 and 1990. Only in Norfolk–Virginia Beach, which was rapidly desegregating, and in Tampa, which had relatively few blacks, did isolation levels fall much below 60. In most cities of the South, as in the North, blacks were relatively unlikely to share neighborhoods with members of other racial or ethnic groups.

Overall, despite some evidence of change in the South, African Americans living within the nation's largest urban black communities are still highly segregated and spatially isolated from the rest of American society. Of the thirty northern and southern areas we examined, nineteen still had black-white dissimilarity indices above 70 in 1990, and twelve had isolation indices over 70. Either in absolute terms or compared with the historical experience of other groups, African Americans remain a very residentially segregated and spatially isolated group.

Hispanics

From recent demographic trends for Hispanics, one would generally predict increasing levels of segregation over the past two decades. The 1970s and 1980s witnessed a remarkable resurgence in Hispanic immigration to the United States, yielding rapidly growing Latino populations in many metropolitan areas. In the Los Angeles metropolitan area alone, for example, the number of Hispanics increased by 1.3 million between 1970 and 1980, and the proportion of Hispanics jumped from 28 to 38 percent. Since migrant networks channel new arrivals to neighborhoods in which immigrants have already settled, such rapid inmigration can generally be expected to increase the concentration of Hispanics within enclaves and raise overall levels of isolation and segregation.

Although processes of spatial assimilation may function simultaneously to reduce ethnic concentration among Hispanics, socioeconomic mechanisms require considerably more time to operate, and they occur at a much slower pace than immigration and settlement. During periods of rapid immigration, such as has occurred over the past two decades, segregation levels therefore tend to rise, and the greater and more rapid the immigration, the more pronounced the anticipated increases in segregation and isolation.

Table 2.2 presents indicators of Hispanic-white dissimilarity and Hispanic residential isolation for the thirty metropolitan areas containing the largest Latino communities in the United States. As above, 1970 and 1980 figures were taken from Massey and Denton (1987) and 1990 figures were drawn from Harrison and Weinberg (1992). Because the Massey-Denton computations did not include several metropolitan areas that housed large Hispanic populations in 1990, additional indices have been taken from Lopez (1981) and Hwang and Murdock (1982). These figures, however, were computed for central cities rather than metropolitan areas and are therefore somewhat higher, thereby underestimating increases and overestimating declines in the level of Hispanic-white segregation.

In a significant subset of the metropolitan areas shown in table 2.2, Hispanics constitute an absolute majority of the total population, a condition that does not exist for any of the black communities examined in table 2.1. Because large minority populations increase the demographic potential for isolation, and because theorists have hypothesized high minority proportions to foment greater discrimination on the part of majority members (see Allport 1958; Blalock 1967), indices have been tabulated separately for areas where Hispanics comprise a majority or near-majority (48 to 49 percent) of the metropolitan population.

Despite the fact that demographic conditions in these metropolitan areas maximize the potential for segregation, the degree of Hispanic-white dissimilarity proved to be quite moderate, and it fell over the two decades, from an average of 55 in 1970 to 47 in 1990. Levels of Hispanic-white segregation were es-

Table 2.2

Trends in Hispanic Segregation and Isolation in the Thirty Metropolitan Areas with the Largest Hispanic Populations, 1970–90

	Dissimilarity Index			Isolation Index		
	1970	1980	1990	1970	1980	1990
Hispanic Majority areas						
Brownsville-Harlingen	54.0	42.0	39.8	—	—	85.2
Corpus Christi	55.9	51.6	47.5	63.5	63.6	67.8
El Paso	49.6	51.2	49.7	71.5	74.1	80.0
McAllen-Pharr	62.0	48.0	37.9	—	—	87.4
Miami	50.4	51.9	50.3	46.5	58.3	73.4
San Antonio	59.1	57.2	53.7	67.5	67.5	69.1
Average	55.2	50.3	46.5	62.3	65.9	77.2
Other Metropolitan Areas						
Albuquerque	45.7	42.5	41.9	54.4	50.6	53.4
Anaheim-Santa Ana	32.0	41.6	49.9	19.4	31.0	50.1
Bakersfield	50.8	54.5	55.4	34.9	42.1	55.7
Chicago	58.4	63.5	63.2	25.1	38.0	51.3
Dallas-Ft. Worth	42.5	47.8	49.5	18.6	24.0	41.1
Denver-Boulder	47.4	47.4	46.5	27.4	27.5	33.8
Fresno	40.8	45.4	47.8	37.6	44.6	58.7
Houston	45.3	46.4	49.3	26.9	32.8	49.3
Jersey City	54.8	48.8	42.9	34.5	46.5	56.0
Los Angeles	46.8	57.0	61.1	37.8	50.1	71.5
Nassau-Suffolk	29.1	36.2	42.3	6.0	9.6	22.1
Newark	60.4	65.6	66.7	16.7	26.3	48.5
New York	64.9	65.6	65.8	36.1	40.0	66.6
Oxnard-Simi Valley	—	—	52.3	—	—	51.2
Philadelphia	54.0	62.9	62.6	10.6	21.6	42.9
Phoenix	48.4	49.4	48.1	32.1	32.1	39.8
Riverside-San Bernadino	37.3	36.4	35.8	30.2	31.6	42.7
Sacramento	34.7	36.4	37.0	16.3	16.5	23.9
San Diego	33.1	42.1	45.3	19.8	26.9	43.6
San Francisco-Oakland	34.7	40.2	43.9	19.2	19.3	41.1
San Jose	40.2	44.5	47.8	29.6	31.7	47.1
Tampa	56.0	48.4	45.3	25.0	18.2	21.5
Tucson	52.6	51.9	49.7	46.7	43.1	48.8
Washington, D.C.	31.8	30.5	40.9	4.3	5.4	22.5
Average	45.3	48.0	49.6	26.5	30.8	45.1

Sources: For 1970 and 1980: Massey and Denton 1987. The 1970 figures for Brownsville-Harlingen and McAllen-Pharr were taken from Lopez 1981. The 1980 figures for these same areas were taken from Hwang and Murdock 1982. For 1990: Harrison and Weinberg 1992.

sentially constant in El Paso and Miami, they changed little in San Antonio and Corpus Christi, and Brownsville and McAllen experienced pronounced declines in segregation: in no case was there an increase in the level of Hispanic segregation from whites within Hispanic-majority areas.

Levels of isolation, in contrast, were very high and rose somewhat from 1970 to 1990. The increases did not stem from an increasing tendency for whites and Hispanics to live apart, however, but from the large size and rapid growth of the Hispanic population. Even if Hispanics were evenly distributed, their chances of encountering non-Hispanics would be limited in these areas. Isolation indices of 85 and 87 in Brownsville and McAllen, for example, mainly reflect the fact that Hispanics represent 82 percent and 85 percent of the metropolitan populations, respectively. High levels of Hispanic-white contact are impossible to achieve in areas that are so predominantly Hispanic.

This pattern is unlike that for blacks, for whom isolation indices in the 1980s (as in Chicago and Detroit) generally reflect the intense segregation of African Americans, not high black proportions; in both metropolitan areas blacks constitute about 22 percent of the population. The contrast between Hispanics and blacks is put into perspective by comparing San Antonio's indices with the black indices shown for northern areas in table 2.1. Although Hispanics constitute 48 percent of San Antonio's population, its Hispanic-white dissimilarity index of 54 is lower than the black-white dissimilarity score observed in any northern area, and its Hispanic isolation index of 69 is below seven of the eighteen black isolation indices.

A better indication of what happens to Hispanics in U.S. cities can be seen by examining segregation measures computed for metropolitan areas where Latinos do not constitute a large share of the population. On average, the level of Hispanic-white dissimilarity changed very little in these areas, moving upward slightly from 45 in 1970 to 50 two decades later. In about one-third of these metropolitan areas (in Chicago, Denver, Houston, New York, Phoenix, Riverside, Sacramento, and Tucson), Hispanic segregation remained nearly constant from 1970 to 1990, and in three areas (Albuquerque, Jersey City, and Tampa), the level of Hispanic-white dissimilarity decreased somewhat over the decades.

In all the other areas, levels of Hispanic segregation increased. In most cases, the increases were modest, but in several instances segregation increased substantially over the period. In Los Angeles, for example, the level of Hispanic-white segregation rose from 47 to 61, and in Anaheim-Santa Ana the increase was from 32 to 50. Large increases were also recorded in Nassau-Suffolk, San Diego, San Francisco, and Washington. All of these metropolitan areas were places that experienced rapid rates of Hispanic population growth and immigration from 1970 to 1990. Frey and Farley (1993) have shown that population growth among Hispanics was a significant factor in increasing their segregation during the 1980s.

Despite these increases, levels of Hispanic-white segregation still remained moderate in 1990. Only five of the twenty-four metropolitan areas have indices of more than 60. Three of these—New York, Newark, and Philadelphia—were areas where Puerto Ricans predominate. Since 1970 this group has stood apart from other Latino populations in displaying uniquely high levels of segregation from whites (Jackson 1981; Massey 1981), a pattern largely attributable to the fact that many Puerto Ricans are of African ancestry (Massey and Bitterman 1985; Denton and Massey 1989a). The two remaining areas are Los Angeles, which experienced more Hispanic immigration than any other metropolitan area, and Chicago, which contained a large population of Puerto Ricans in addition to a rapidly growing immigrant Mexican population.

Reflecting the increase in the proportion of Hispanics in most metropolitan areas, Hispanic isolation indices rose markedly throughout the nation. In the few areas where the rates of Hispanic population increases were relatively slow— Albuquerque, Denver, Phoenix, and Tucson—the level of Hispanic isolation hardly changed, but as the rate of Hispanic immigration rose, so did the extent of spatial isolation. As would be expected, levels of Hispanic isolation rose most in southern California, going from 19 to 50 in Anaheim-Santa Ana, from 38 to 72 in Los Angeles, and from 20 to 44 in San Diego.

By 1990, isolation indices equaled or exceeded 50 in about one-half of the metropolitan areas under consideration, but in only two cases—New York and Los Angeles, the two largest Hispanic communities—did the index exceed 60. By way of contrast, only eight of the thirty African American communities examined above had black isolation indices *below* this level. Thus, although contemporary demographic conditions favor high segregation and rising isolation among Hispanics, they still do not display the high levels that are characteristic of black Americans in large urban areas.

Asians

Although the immigration of Asians to U.S. urban areas has accelerated since 1970, Asian populations are still quite small in comparison with either blacks or Hispanics. Moreover, they are more highly concentrated regionally and are found in a relatively small number of metropolitan areas. Table 2.3 therefore presents indices of Asian segregation and isolation for only the twenty largest Asian communities, rather than the thirty largest as we did for the other groups. This table draws on the same sources as table 2.1.

Demographic conditions for Asians, as for Hispanics, favor substantial increases in segregation and isolation. In most metropolitan areas, rapid immigration has led to substantial growth from a rather small 1970 population base. In some cases, the number of post-1970 migrants exceeded the size of the original Asian community by several times. Only 25,000 Asians lived in the Anaheim-Santa Ana metropolitan area in 1970, for example, but by 1990 their number had grown tenfold to 249,000. Over the same period, the Asian community of Los Angeles quadrupled, from 243,000 to 954,000, and Chicago's Asian population grew from 62,000 to 230,000. In such cases, where a sudden massive immigration overwhelms a small established community, levels of segregation often decline initially as new arrivals distribute themselves widely and then rise as these pioneers attract subsequent settlers to the same areas.

Such a falling and rising is the most common pattern of change among the metropolitan areas shown in table 2.3. Asian-white dissimilarity averaged 44 in 1970, fell to 36 in 1980, and then rose to 41 in 1990. This basic trend occurred in twelve of the twenty metropolitan areas. In three more areas an initial decline was followed by no change from 1980 to 1990. Only one area (San Jose) experienced a sustained increase in Asian segregation, but it began from a very low level of segregation in 1970. Four areas displayed uninterrupted declines in segregation across both decades: Boston, Nassau-Suffolk, Newark, and Paterson.

Despite rapid immigration and population growth, Asian segregation levels remained quite moderate in 1990. The increases observed between 1980 and 1990 simply restored the indices to their 1970 levels, showing little net change in segregation over the period. Thus, Asian-white dissimilarity indices ranged from scores in the low 30s (in Anaheim–Santa Ana, Nassau-Suffolk, Newark, Riverside, and Washington) to 50 in San Francisco-Oakland. In no area did the level of Asian segregation approach the high levels characteristic of blacks in the nation's largest metropolitan areas.

Rapid Asian immigration into moderately segregated communities produced increases in Asian isolation, consistent with a process of enclave consolidation. Sharp increases occurred in areas where southeast Asian refugees settled in large numbers: Anaheim, where the isolation index rose from 3 in 1970 to 22 in 1990; Fresno, where the increase was from 6 to 33; and San Diego, where the increase was from 6 to 29. Despite these increases, however, Asians still are not very iso-

Table 2.3

Trends in Asian Segregation and Isolation in the Twenty Metropolitan Areas with the Largest Asian Populations, 1970–90

	Dissimilarity Index			Isolation Index		
	1970	1980	1990	1970	1980	1990
Anaheim	27.4	24.9	33.3	2.6	7.7	22.4
Boston	49.9	47.4	44.8	8.0	10.5	12.9
Chicago	55.8	43.9	43.2	7.6	8.7	15.9
Dallas	43.9	29.1	40.5	1.7	2.6	9.6
Fresno	35.1	22.9	43.4	5.7	5.3	33.1
Houston	42.7	34.6	45.7	1.5	4.5	15.7
Los Angeles	53.1	43.1	46.3	12.3	15.2	40.5
Minneapolis	45.2	36.9	41.2	3.0	6.2	15.1
Nassau-Suffolk	42.2	34.5	32.4	1.0	2.2	5.9
Newark	50.2	34.4	29.6	1.5	2.9	7.5
New York	56.1	48.1	48.4	11.6	14.3	32.8
Paterson-Clifton-Passaic	46.6	40.4	34.4	1.3	3.1	12.1
Philadelphia	49.1	43.7	43.2	2.4	4.0	11.0
Riverside-San Bernadino	31.9	21.5	32.8	2.5	4.1	10.2
Sacramento	47.6	35.5	47.7	11.8	11.6	23.6
San Diego	41.3	40.5	48.1	5.9	11.1	29.1
San Francisco-Oakland	48.6	44.4	50.1	21.0	23.2	46.0
San Jose	25.4	29.5	38.5	5.3	11.6	36.6
Seattle	46.6	33.3	36.5	11.7	12.4	20.0
Washington, D.C.	36.5	26.8	32.3	2.2	5.7	12.6
Average	43.8	35.8	40.6	6.0	8.3	20.6

Sources: For 1970 and 1980: Massey and Denton 1987. For 1990: Harrison and Weinberg 1992.
Note: For explanations of dissimilarity and isolation indices, see text.

lated anywhere, including San Francisco–Oakland, where they constitute a higher percentage of the population (21 percent) than in any other area. The isolation index of 46 means that Asians in the Bay Area are still more likely to share a neighborhood with non-Asians than with each other. In Los Angeles, which received the largest number of Asian immigrants between 1970 and 1990, the isolation index rose to just under 41. Thus, the largest and most segregated Asian communities in the United States are much less isolated than the most integrated black communities.

THE UNIQUENESS OF BLACK SEGREGATION

Intergroup Segregation

The data above underscore the distinctive nature of black residential segregation in urban America. More than two decades after the passage of the Fair Housing Act, blacks are still extremely segregated and very isolated within U.S. metropolitan areas, particularly those outside the South. Although Hispanics and Asians experienced rising segregation and increasing isolation from 1970 to 1990, these changes reflect mass immigration more than a lack of spatial assimilation, and levels of Hispanic and Asian segregation and isolation generally still remain far below those of blacks.

Table 2.4 further documents the exceptional nature of black segregation by presenting intergroup dissimilarity indices between blacks, Hispanics, and Asians in the thirty largest metropolitan areas of the United States in 1970 and 1980. These indices were calculated directly from summary tape files obtained from the U.S. Bureau of the Census (1970, 1980) and have not been previously published. Harrison and Weinberg (1992) did not calculate measures of interminority segregation, so indices for 1990 are not available.

Because many metropolitan areas do not contain significant numbers of all minority groups, indices have been tabulated separately for ten metropolitan areas where all three populations are well represented. In these areas, a common pattern clearly emerges: not only are blacks very segregated from whites, they are also highly segregated from Hispanics and Asians. The average level of black-Hispanic segregation was 73 in 1970 and 66 in 1980; the respective levels of black-Asian segregation were 74 and 70. Only San Diego (which contains a large military population) displayed a clear and consistent trend toward intergroup residential integration. Everywhere else segregation levels between blacks and other minority groups remained at 60 or above in both 1970 and 1980.

In contrast, Hispanic-Asian segregation scores were quite moderate and remarkably stable across the decade of the 1970s. The average level of Hispanic-Asian dissimilarity increased from 44 in 1970 to 47 in 1980, and only one area, Newark, displayed a substantial increase. The highest indices are generally in four areas with substantial Puerto Rican populations—Chicago, Newark, New York, and Philadelphia—all of which had 1980 Hispanic-Asian indices from 50 to 60.

In metropolitan areas where either Hispanics or blacks were not well represented, the pattern of change in their mutual segregation was more varied. In some areas (Baltimore, Boston, Cincinnati, Phoenix, and Seattle), pronounced declines left segregation levels between blacks and Hispanics in the moderate range in 1980. In other areas (Cleveland, Denver, Detroit, Kansas City, Miami), there was relatively little change, and intergroup segregation persisted at very high levels. In one metropolitan area, San Jose, segregation between blacks and Hispanics was moderate in 1970 and was even lower by 1980. On average, the level of black-Hispanic segregation fell by 12 points in these metropolitan areas, to an average of 61 in 1980.

Patterns of black-Asian segregation were also quite varied in metropolitan areas where one of the groups was not well represented. In two areas (Cincinnati and Detroit) the degree of segregation between blacks and Asians *increased* from 1970 to 1980, and in ten others (Atlanta, Baltimore, Boston, Cincinnati, Cleveland, Kansas City, Milwaukee, Nassau-Suffolk, Pittsburgh, and St. Louis) relative stability left both minority groups quite segregated from each other in 1980.

Nonetheless, there were significant declines in the level of black-Asian segregation in some areas. In four (Denver, Miami, Minneapolis, and Tampa), the declines left segregation levels still within the high range, but in four (Anaheim, Phoenix, Riverside, and Seattle), segregation moved into the moderate range. In San Jose, Hispanics and blacks actually achieved a low level of segregation (a dissimilarity index below 30). On average, black-Asian segregation fell by about 9 points over the decade in these metropolitan areas.

Whether one considers areas where all groups are present in significant numbers or those where at least one is not well represented, the pattern of Hispanic-Asian segregation is always low to moderate. The average level of Hispanic-Asian segregation in areas where all three groups are not present fell from about 46 to 40, and as of 1980 the highest level observed in any of these areas was 53, in Cleveland. Seattle had a remarkably low level of Hispanic-Asian segregation in 1980 (25), and in Atlanta the index was almost as low (29).

In summary, levels of segregation between blacks and other minority groups are generally high and relatively stable in areas where all groups are well represented, a pattern that holds in any metropolitan area with a sizable black community. The only significant declines in black-Hispanic segregation occurred in areas with relatively small black or Hispanic populations, and the only downward trends in Hispanic-Asian segregation occurred in areas with small black or Asian communities. In contrast, no matter what the relative size of the Asian or Hispanic communities, these two minority groups were never highly segregated from one another and, in a few cases, the index of intergroup dissimilarity was remarkably low.

Table 2.4
Patterns of Intergroup Residential Dissimilarity Between Blacks, Hispanics, and
Asians in the Thirty Largest Metropolitan Areas, 1970–80

	Black-Hispanic		Black-Asian		Hispanic-Asian	
	1970	1980	1970	1980	1970	1980
Areas with Significant Concentrations of All Groups						
Chicago	87.4	86.2	85.9	86.2	53.5	59.9
Dallas	76.8	66.6	85.3	75.4	43.4	44.9
Houston	74.0	63.2	74.5	67.9	39.0	48.8
Los Angeles	84.4	72.7	78.9	74.9	43.8	44.8
Newark	63.7	64.8	64.9	72.0	48.7	60.4
New York	54.7	57.7	70.4	74.6	51.2	54.9
Philadelphia	69.1	69.0	64.7	68.8	53.6	59.4
San Francisco-Oakland	72.6	62.6	69.6	63.8	44.2	39.9
San Diego	71.5	48.4	67.2	48.0	26.5	30.1
Washington	74.8	64.9	73.4	66.6	33.4	25.4
Average	72.9	65.6	73.5	69.8	43.7	46.9
Other						
Anaheim-Santa Ana	73.9	40.8	81.0	38.5	31.0	34.9
Atlanta	79.4	63.8	76.0	74.4	50.6	28.6
Baltimore	67.9	58.4	73.9	68.9	50.4	38.3
Boston	62.5	54.3	76.5	69.7	51.2	49.5
Cincinnati	72.2	56.7	58.2	62.3	44.7	33.2
Cleveland	83.3	79.2	80.0	77.7	52.8	52.9
Denver	79.3	71.2	76.7	60.6	37.5	36.5
Detroit	75.5	74.8	68.3	75.4	49.8	47.0
Kansas City	80.3	73.6	76.1	74.2	45.7	37.6
Miami	87.3	78.9	79.9	67.5	41.9	47.9
Milwaukee	83.5	75.4	82.0	75.2	52.2	47.9
Minneapolis	79.9	62.4	73.0	62.4	54.0	40.4
Nassau-Suffolk	68.3	60.5	71.8	69.1	47.1	42.2
Phoenix	62.5	40.5	72.4	49.2	36.6	36.0
Pittsburgh	74.6	64.8	75.2	74.9	62.7	51.0
Riverside-San Bernadino	59.5	44.6	63.0	43.4	35.8	31.8
St. Louis	80.0	68.7	76.3	75.7	47.0	38.4
San Jose	43.2	31.0	52.2	29.2	33.7	32.6
Seattle	73.9	58.8	57.1	46.9	43.9	25.3
Tampa	76.1	68.8	79.0	68.3	58.2	45.9
Average	73.2	61.4	72.4	63.2	46.3	39.9

Sources: For 1970: U.S. Bureau of the Census (1970). For 1980: U.S. Bureau of the Census
(1980).

Hypersegregation

The data presented above actually understate the extent of African Americans' isolation in U.S. society because they only consider two dimensions of segregation. Massey and Denton (1988, 1989b) conceptualize segregation as a multidimensional construct composed of five dimensions of spatial variation. In addition to dissimilarity (unevenness) and isolation, discussed above, they define segregation in terms of clustering, concentration, and centralization.

Clustering is the extent to which minority areas are next to one another: it is maximized when black neighborhoods form one large, contiguous ghetto; it is minimized when they are scattered widely, as on a checkerboard. Centralization is the degree to which blacks are distributed in and around the center of an urban area, usually defined as the central business district. Concentration is the relative amount of physical space occupied by African Americans: as segregation rises, blacks are increasingly confined to small, geographically compact areas.

A high level of segregation on any single dimension is problematic because it isolates a minority group from amenities, opportunities, and resources that affect socioeconomic well-being. As high levels of segregation accumulate across dimensions, however, the deleterious effects of segregation multiply. Indices of dissimilarity and isolation, by themselves, cannot capture this multidimensional layering of segregation and so they actually misrepresent the nature of black segregation and understate its severity. Blacks are not only more segregated than other groups on any single dimension of segregation, they are also more segregated across all dimensions simultaneously.

Massey and Denton (1993) identified fifteen metropolitan areas that were highly segregated (with index values of more than 60) on at least four of the five dimensions of segregation, a pattern they called hypersegregation: Atlanta, Baltimore, Buffalo, Chicago, Cleveland, Dallas, Detroit, Gary, Indianapolis, Kansas City, Los Angeles, Milwaukee, Newark, New York, and St. Louis. In these areas, the average level of black-white dissimilarity was 82, the average isolation index was 71, the mean clustering index was 58, the mean centralization index was 88, and the average concentration index was 83. In contrast, neither Hispanics nor Asians were hypersegregated in *any* metropolitan area.

These fifteen areas are among the most important in the country, containing six of the ten largest in the United States. Blacks in these areas live in large, contiguous settlements of densely inhabited neighborhoods that are packed tightly around the urban core. Typical inhabitants are unlikely to come into contact with nonblacks in the neighborhoods where they live. Moreover, if they travel to an adjacent neighborhood they are still unlikely to see a white face; and if they go to the next neighborhood beyond that, no whites would be there, either. People growing up in such an environment have little direct experience with the culture, norms, and behaviors of the dominant group of American society and have few social contacts with members of other racial groups.

Denton (1992) examined the issue of hypersegregation using data from the 1990 census. According to her analysis, not only has black hypersegregation continued, in many ways it has worsened. Of the sixteen metropolitan areas defined as hypersegregated in 1980, fourteen remained so in 1990, but the apparent improvement is illusory. In Atlanta the index of spatial concentration fell to 59, and in Dallas the isolation index fell to 58: since both of these figures are just below the threshold value of 60, Atlanta and Dallas in effect remained hypersegregated in 1990. More telling, all the areas showed an increase on at least one dimension of segregation by 1990 (Denton 1992). In ten areas the level of isolation increased, and in nine concentration grew more acute; clustering increased in eight. In Newark and Buffalo, segregation increased on all five dimensions, and in Detroit segregation increased on all dimensions but one.

In sum, areas that were hypersegregated in 1980 generally remained so in 1990, or close to it, and there was little movement away from this extreme residential pattern. Furthermore, hypersegregation spread to several new urban areas during the 1980s. Of the forty-four nonhypersegregated metropolitan areas studied by Massey and Denton in 1980, Denton (1992) found that six satisfied the criteria for black hypersegregation by 1990—Birmingham, Cincinnati, Miami, New Orleans, Oakland, and Washington—bringing the total number of defined hypersegregated areas to twenty. Together, these areas contain roughly eleven million African Americans, 36 percent of the black population.

Explanations and Evidence

In light of the foregoing analysis, the principal fact to be explained is the exceptional nature of black segregation in U.S. metropolitan areas: the high degree of residential dissimilarity from whites; the profound level of black racial isolation; the high degree of spatial separation from other minority groups; and the cumulative nature of black segregation across multiple dimensions simultaneously—hypersegregation.

CLASS AND PREFERENCES

A variety of explanations have been posited to account for the unusual depth and persistence of black segregation in American cities. One is that racial segregation reflects class differences between blacks and whites. Because African Americans have lower incomes and fewer socioeconomic resources than whites, it is argued, they cannot afford to move into white neighborhoods in significant numbers. According to this view, black-white segregation reflects little more than income segregation between poor households, which happen to be predominantly black, and affluent households, which are disproportionately white. Empirically, however, this explanation has not been sustained.

Differences in socioeconomic status in no way account for the high degree of segregation between blacks and whites. When indices of racial segregation are computed within categories of income, occupation, or education, researchers have found that levels of black-white segregation do not vary by social class (Farley 1977; Simkus 1978; Massey 1979, 1981). According to Denton and Massey (1988), black families earning at least $50,000 are just as segregated as those earning less than $2,500. Indeed, black families earning more than $50,000 are more segregated than Hispanic or Asian families earning less than $2,500. In other words, the most affluent blacks are more segregated than the poorest Hispanics or Asians. Moreover, in contrast to black segregation, Hispanic and Asian segregation levels fall steadily as income rises, reaching low or moderate levels at incomes of $50,000 or more (Denton and Massey 1988).

Another explanation that has been posited for racial segregation is that blacks prefer to live in predominantly black neighborhoods and that segregated housing simply reflects these preferences. But this position is not supported by survey evidence on black attitudes. Most African Americans express strong support for the ideal of integration, and when asked on opinion polls whether they favor "desegregation, strict segregation, or something in-between," they answer "desegregation" in large numbers (Schuman et al. 1985). Blacks are virtually unanimous in agreeing that "black people have a right to live wherever they can afford to," and 71 percent would vote for a communitywide law to enforce this right (Bobo et al. 1986).

Black respondents are not only committed to integration as an ideal; survey results also suggest they strongly prefer it in practice. When asked about specific neighborhood racial compositions, blacks consistently select racially mixed areas as most desirable (Farley et al. 1978, 1979; Clark 1991). Although the most popular choice is a neighborhood that is half black and half white, as recently as 1992 nearly 90 percent would be willing to live in virtually any racially mixed area (Farley et al. 1993).

Although blacks express a reluctance about entering all-white neighborhoods, this apprehension does not indicate a rejection of whites per se but stems from a well-founded fear of hostility and violence. Among black respondents to a 1976 Detroit survey who expressed this reluctance, 34 percent believed that white neighbors would be unfriendly and make them feel unwelcome, 37 percent said they would be made to feel uncomfortable, and 17 percent expressed a fear of violence (Farley et al. 1979). On this survey, four-fifths rejected the view that moving into a white neighborhood constituted a desertion of the black community.

The evidence thus suggests that racial segregation in urban America is not a voluntary reflection of black preferences. African Americans support the ideal of integration in large numbers, and they express a clear desire to live in racially mixed neighborhoods. But blacks' preferences interact with those of whites to produce the residential outcomes actually observed. Even though blacks may prefer neighborhoods with a 50–50 racial balance, this pattern will not occur if most whites find this level of racial mixing unacceptable.

On the surface, whites seem to share blacks' ideological commitment to open housing. On national surveys, the percentage of whites who agree that "black people have a right to live wherever they can afford to" approached 90 percent by the late 1970s, and the percentage who disagreed with the view that "white people have a right to keep blacks out of their neighborhoods" reached 67 percent in 1980. At present, very few whites express support for the strict segregation of American society (Schuman et al. 1985).

Yet whites remain uncomfortable about the implications of open housing in practice. Although most whites agree that blacks have a right to live wherever they want to, only 40 percent in 1980 said they would be willing to vote for a communitywide law stating that "a homeowner cannot refuse to sell to someone because of their race or skin color" (Schuman and Bobo 1988). In other words, 60 percent of whites were willing to vote against an open housing law that had been on the federal books for twelve years. Furthermore, white support for open housing generally declines as the number of blacks increases: in a 1978 survey, 86 percent of whites said they would not move if "a black person came to live next door," but 46 percent stated they would not move out if "black people came to live in large numbers," and only 28 percent of whites were willing to live in a neighborhood that was half-black and half-white (Schuman et al. 1985).

When questions are posed about specific neighborhood compositions, moreover, it becomes clear that white tolerance for racial mixing is quite limited. According to Farley et al. (1993), 16 percent of whites responding to a 1992 Detroit survey said they would feel uncomfortable in a neighborhood where only 7 percent of the residents were black, and 13 percent would be unwilling to move to such an area. When the black percentage reaches 20 percent, one-third of all whites say they would be unwilling to enter, 30 percent would feel uncomfortable, and 15 percent would try to leave. Once a neighborhood reaches about one-third black, the limits of racial tolerance are exceeded for most whites: 59 percent would be unwilling to enter, 44 percent would feel uncomfortable, and 29 percent would try to leave. Beyond a 50–50 balance, a neighborhood becomes unacceptable to all but a small minority of whites: 73 percent said they would not be willing to enter such a neighborhood, 65 percent would feel uncomfortable, and 53 percent would try to leave.

Thus, whereas most blacks pick a 50-50 racial mix as most desirable, the large majority of whites are unwilling to enter such a neighborhood and most would try to leave. This fundamental disparity between the races has been confirmed by surveys conducted in Milwaukee, Omaha, Cincinnati, Kansas City, and Los Angeles, all of which show that blacks strongly prefer a 50-50 mix and that whites have little tolerance for black-white mixes that are more than 20 percent black (Clark 1991).

These contrasting attitudes create a large disparity in the demand for housing in racially mixed neighborhoods. Given the violence, intimidation, and harassment that historically have followed their entry into white areas, blacks express considerable reluctance at being first across the color line. After one or two black families have entered a neighborhood, however, black demand grows rapidly given the high value placed on integrated housing. This demand escalates as the black percentage rises toward 50 percent, the most preferred neighborhood configuration; beyond this point, black demand stabilizes and then falls off as the black percentage rises toward 100 percent.

The pattern of white demand for housing in racially mixed areas follows precisely the opposite trajectory. Demand is strong for homes in all-white areas, but once one or two black families enter a neighborhood, white demand begins to falter as some white families leave and others refuse to move in. The acceleration in residential turnover coincides with the expansion of black demand, making it very likely that outgoing white households are replaced by black families. As the black percentage rises, white demand drops ever more steeply as black demand rises at an increasing rate. By the time black demand peaks at the 50 percent mark, practically no whites are willing to enter, and the large majority are trying to leave. Thus, the racial segregation widely observed appears to be created by a process of racial turnover fueled by the persistence of significant antiblack prejudice by whites.

This model of racial change was essentially proposed by Schelling (1971). According to Schelling, integration is an unstable outcome because whites prefer lower proportions of minorities in neighborhoods than do blacks—even though they might accept *some* black neighbors. Yet by itself, Schelling's explanation is incomplete. Whites can only avoid coresidence with blacks if mechanisms exist to keep blacks out of other neighborhoods to which whites can retreat. They can only flee a neighborhood where blacks have entered if there are other all-white areas to go to, and this escape will only be successful if blacks are unlikely to follow. Some method must exist, therefore, to limit black entry to a few neighborhoods and to preserve racial homogeneity in the rest. Although white prejudice is a necessary precondition for the perpetuation of segregation, it alone is insufficient to maintain the residential color line; active discrimination against blacks must also occur.

DISCRIMINATION IN THE HOUSING MARKET

Racial discrimination was institutionalized in the real estate industry during the 1920s, and it was well established in private practice by the 1940s (Massey and Denton 1993). Evidence suggests that discriminatory behavior was widespread among realtors at least until 1968, when the Fair Housing Act was passed (Helper 1969; Saltman 1979). Since then, outright refusal to rent or sell to blacks has become rare, given that overt discrimination could lead to prosecution under the law.

Black homeseekers now face a more subtle process of exclusion. Rather than encountering "white only" signs, they encounter a series of covert barriers: blacks who inquire about an advertised unit may be told that it has just been sold or rented; they may be shown only the advertised unit and told that no others are available; they may be shown houses only in black or racially mixed areas and systematically led away from white neighborhoods; they may be quoted a higher rent or selling price than whites; they may be told that the selling agents are too busy and to come back later; they may give their phone number but never receive a return call; they may be shown units but offered no assistance in arranging financing; or they simply may be treated brusquely and discourteously in hopes that they will leave. Although each individual act of discrimination is small and subtle, together they have a powerful cumulative effect in lowering the probability of black entry into white neighborhoods. Because the discrimination is not overt, however, it is unobservable, and the only way to confirm whether it has occurred is to compare the treatment of black and white clients with similar social and economic characteristics. If white clients receive systematically more favorable treatment, then one can conclude that discrimination has taken place.

Differences in the treatment of white and black homeseekers are measured by means of a housing audit. Separate teams of white and black "auditors" are sent to randomly selected realtors to pose as clients seeking a home or apartment. The auditors are trained to present comparable housing needs and family characteristics and to express similar tastes. After each encounter, the auditors fill out a detailed report of their experiences, and the results are tabulated and compared to determine the nature and level of discrimination (Yinger 1986, 1989).

Local fair housing organizations began to carry out such studies at the end of the 1960s, and these efforts revealed that discrimination was continuing despite the Fair Housing Act. A 1969 audit of realtors in St. Louis, for example, documented a pattern and practice of discrimination that was sufficient to force four realty firms to sign a consent decree with the U.S. Department of Justice in which they agreed to desist from certain biased practices (Saltman 1979). Likewise, a 1971 audit study carried out in Palo Alto, California, found that blacks were treated in a discriminatory fashion by 50 percent of the area's apartment complexes; and a 1972 audit of apartments in suburban Baltimore uncovered discrimination in more than 45 percent of the cases (Saltman 1979).

More recent audit studies suggest that racial discrimination persisted into the 1980s. In Chicago, for example, realtors continued to use a variety of exclusionary tactics to keep blacks out of white neighborhoods. In one 1983 study, suburban realtors showed homes to 67 percent of white auditors but only to 47 percent of black auditors (Hintzen 1983). Another study done in 1985 revealed that whites were offered financial information nearly twice as often as blacks (Schroeder 1985). One developer working in Chicago's south suburbs refused to deal with blacks at all: blacks were *always* told that no properties were available, whereas 80 percent of whites were shown real estate (Bertram 1988). In the same study, realtors told 92 percent of whites that apartments were available, but they gave this information to only 46 percent of blacks. Audit studies of other metropolitan areas reveal similar levels of racial discrimination. According to Yinger's (1987) review of studies carried out in metropolitan Boston and Denver during the early 1980s, the chance that black homeseekers would receive unfavorable treatment compared with whites on any given real estate transaction ranged between 38 percent and 59 percent. Through various lies and deceptions, blacks were informed of only sixty-five units for every one hundred presented to whites, and they were shown fewer than fifty-four units for every one hundred shown to whites.

In 1987 Galster (1990a) wrote to more than two hundred local fair housing organizations and obtained written reports of seventy-one different audit studies carried out during the 1980s, twenty-one in the home sales market and fifty in the rental market. Despite differences in measures and methods, he concluded that "racial discrimination continues to be a dominant feature of metropolitan housing markets in the 1980s" (172). Using a conservative measure of racial bias, he found that blacks averaged a 20 percent chance of experiencing discrimination in the sales market and a 50 percent chance in the rental market.

Studies have also examined the prevalence of "steering" by real estate agents in different urban areas. Racial steering occurs when white and black clients are guided to neighborhoods that differ systematically with respect to social and economic characteristics, especially racial composition. A study carried out in Cleveland during the early 1970s found that 70 percent of companies engaged in some form of racial steering (Saltman 1979). An examination of realtors in metropolitan Detroit during the mid-1970s revealed that, compared to whites, blacks were shown homes in less expensive areas that were located closer to black population centers (Pearce 1979).

Galster (1990b) studied six real estate firms located in Cincinnati and Memphis and found that racial steering occurred in roughly 50 percent of the transactions sampled during the mid-1980s. As in the Detroit study, homes shown to blacks tended to be in racially mixed areas and were more likely to be adjacent to neighborhoods with a high percentage of black residents. White auditors were rarely shown homes in integrated neighborhoods unless they specifically requested them, and even after the request was honored, they continued to be guided primarily to homes in white areas. Sales agents also made numerous positive comments about white neighborhoods to white clients but said little to black home buyers. In a broader review of thirty-six different audit studies, Galster (1990c) discovered that such selective commentary by agents is probably more common than overt steering.

These local studies, however suggestive, do not provide a comprehensive national assessment of housing discrimination in contemporary American cities. The first such effort was undertaken by the U.S. Department of Housing and Urban Development (HUD) in 1977. The study, which covered forty metropolitan areas with significant black populations, confirmed the results of earlier local audits. Discrimination clearly was not confined to a few isolated cases. Nationwide, whites were favored in 48 percent of transactions in the sales market and in 39 percent of those in the rental market (Wienk et al. 1979). In the past, housing researchers have reported "net discrimination scores" from the 1977 HUD survey. These scores are obtained by subtracting the percentage of cases in which blacks were favored from the percentage in which whites were favored. Recent research has shown, however, that this procedure understates the real incidence of discrimination for a variety of technical reasons (see Yinger 1991a, 1991b). The figures reported here are gross discrimination scores, or the percentage of encounters in which whites were favored, which still tend to understate the amount of discrimination, but not as severely as do net scores.

The 1977 HUD audit survey was repeated in 1988. Twenty audit sites were randomly selected from among metropolitan areas having a central city population of more than 100,000 and a black percentage of more than 12 percent. Real estate ads in major metropolitan newspapers were randomly sampled, and realtors were approached by auditors who inquired about the availability of the advertised unit; the auditors also asked about other units that might be on the market. The Housing Discrimination Study (HDS) covered both the rental and sales markets, and the auditors were given incomes and family characteristics appropriate to the housing unit advertised (Urban Institute 1991). The typical advertised unit was located in a white, middle-to-upper-class area, as were most of the real estate offices; remarkably few homes were in black or racially mixed neighborhoods.

Even after controlling for the neighborhood's social and economic composition, race was a strong predictor of whether a unit was advertised in the newspaper (Turner et al. 1991). Galster and his colleagues found a similar bias in real estate advertising in Milwaukee from 1981 to 1984 (Galster et al. 1987). Compared with homes in white areas, those in racially mixed or black areas were much less likely to be advertised, much more likely to be represented by one-line ads when they appeared, and much less likely to be favorably described. Real estate companies apparently do a poor job of marketing homes in racially mixed neighborhoods, thereby restricting white demand for integrated housing and promoting segregation.

The HDS provides little evidence that discrimination against blacks has declined since 1977. Indeed, the earlier HUD study appears to have understated both the incidence and severity of housing discrimination in American cities (Yinger 1991a, 1991b). According to HDS data, housing was made systematically more available to whites in 45 percent of the rental market transactions and 34 percent of the sales market transactions. Whites received more favorable credit assistance in 46 percent of sales encounters and were offered more favorable terms in 17 percent of rental transactions. When housing availability and financial assistance were considered together, the likelihood of experiencing racial discrimination was 53 percent in both the rental and sales markets.

The sales audits also assessed the frequency of racial steering—the systematic guiding of black clients to black or mixed neighborhoods and of whites to white neighborhoods. When this form of discrimination was considered as well, the likelihood of discrimination rose to 60 percent (Yinger 1991a). Since these figures refer to the odds on any single visit to a realtor, over a series of visits they cumulate to extremely high probabilities—well over 90 percent for three visits. In the course of even the briefest search for housing, therefore, blacks are almost certain to encounter discrimination.

In addition to measuring the incidence of discrimination (that is, the percentage of encounters where discrimination occurs), the HDS study also measured its severity (the number of units made available to whites but not blacks). In stark terms, the severity of housing discrimination is such that blacks are systematically shown, recommended, and invited to inspect far fewer homes than comparable whites.

Among advertised rental units, the likelihood that an additional unit was shown to whites but not blacks was 65 percent, and the probability that an additional unit was recommended to whites but not blacks was 91 percent. The HDS auditors encountered equally severe bias in the marketing of nonadvertised units: the probability that an additional unit was inspected only by whites was 62 percent, and the probability that whites alone were invited to see another unit was 90 percent. Comparable results were found in urban sales markets, where the severity of discrimination varied from 66 to 89 percent. Thus, no matter what index one considers, between 60 percent and 90 percent of the housing units made available to whites were not brought to the attention of blacks (Yinger 1991b). Thus, blacks' access to urban housing is substantially reduced.

The 1988 HDS audit also found severe discrimination in the provision of credit assistance to home buyers. For every one hundred times that agents discussed a fixed-rate mortgage, eighty-nine of the discussions were only with whites; of one hundred times that adjustable-rate loans were mentioned, ninety-one percent of the discussions excluded blacks (Yinger 1991b). Blacks see fewer homes and get fewer recommendations, and they receive much less information about financing.

Although these audit results are compelling, they do not directly link discrimination to segregation. They show that discrimination and segregation both exist and persist across time, not that they are causally connected. But several studies have been carried out to document and quantify the link between discrimination, prejudice, and segregation.

Using data from the 1977 HUD audit study, Galster (1986) related cross-metropolitan variation in housing discrimination to the degree of racial segregation in different urban areas. He not only confirmed the empirical link between discrimination and segregation; he also discovered that segregation itself has important feedback effects on socioeconomic status (see also Galster and Keeney 1988). Discrimination not only leads to segregation, but segregation, by restricting economic opportunities for blacks, produces interracial economic disparities and further discrimination and segregation.

Galster has also shown that white prejudice and discrimination are connected to patterns of racial change within neighborhoods. In a detailed study of census tracts in the Cleveland area, he found that neighborhoods that were all white or racially changing evinced much higher rates of discrimination than areas that were stably integrated or predominantly black (Galster 1987, 1990d, 1990e). Moreover, the pace of racial change was strongly predicted by the percentage of whites who agreed that "white people have a right to keep blacks out of their neighborhoods." Areas with a high degree of racist sentiment experienced systematic white population loss after only a few blacks had entered, and the speed of transition accelerated rapidly after the areas became only 3 percent black. In contrast, tracts where whites expressed a low degree of racist sentiment showed little tendency for white flight until the composition was about 40 percent black.

These studies confirm a strong link between levels of prejudice, discrimination, and the degree of segregation that blacks experience. The accumulated evidence thus suggests that black segregation in American urban areas is caused by white racial prejudice and discrimination, which has not moderated significantly in recent years. Rather than declining in significance, race remains the dominant organizing principle of U.S. urban housing markets. When it comes to determining where, and with whom, Americans live, race appears to overwhelm other considerations.

COMPARISONS WITH HISPANICS

Compared with African Americans, relatively few studies of prejudice and discrimination against Hispanics have been conducted, and there are no studies that examine attitudes and behaviors concerning Asians. Hakken (1979) found that discrimination against Hispanics in the rental housing market of Dallas was as likely as that against blacks, and similar results were reported by Feins and colleagues for Boston (Feins et al. 1981; Feins and Holshouser 1984). James and Tynan (1986) replicated these results in a study of Denver's sales market, but they found a substantially lower probability of discrimination against Hispanics in the rental market. In addition, despite the relatively high *likelihood* of discrimination in home sales, the *severity* of discrimination against Hispanics was not great: the average number of housing units offered to Hispanics was not significantly different than the number offered to non-Hispanic whites (James and Tynan 1986).

Discrimination against Hispanics appears to have a racial basis. Hakken (1979) found that dark-skinned Hispanics were more likely to experience discriminatory treatment than blacks, whereas light-skinned Hispanics were less likely. Consistent with this finding, Massey and Denton (1992) found that Mexicans who identified themselves as mestizos (people of European and Indian origins) were less likely to achieve suburban residence than those who identified themselves as white. The extent of the racial effect is even greater among Caribbean Hispanics, and particularly Puerto Ricans, where the racial continuum runs from European to African. Denton and Massey (1989) showed that those who identified themselves as black were as segregated as U.S. blacks; those who said they were white displayed low to moderate levels of separation. Caribbean Hispanics who said they were of mixed black-white origins were in between, but much closer to the high level of black segregation. The degree of segregation experienced by racially mixed Caribbean Hispanics was generally greater than that experienced by racially mixed Mexicans, suggesting greater white antipathy toward Africans than toward indigenous peoples.

The most complete and systematic data on the treatment of Hispanics in urban real estate markets comes from the HDS (Yinger 1991a, 1991b). The study found that the overall incidence of housing discrimination was greater for Hispanics than for blacks in the sales market (42 percent versus 34 percent), but less for Hispanics than blacks in the rental market (32 percent versus 45 percent). This result replicated the results of James and Tynan (1986) in Denver. Also in keeping with the findings of James and Tynan was the fact that the severity of discrimination in the sales market was considerably lower for Hispanics than for blacks: the marginal probability that an additional housing unit was denied to blacks was 88 percent, but it was 66 percent for Hispanics. As in earlier research, racial factors figured prominently in the treatment of Hispanics in the HDS: dark-skinned Hispanics were much more likely to experience discrimination in the sales market than light-skinned Hispanics (Yinger 1991a). Paradoxically, therefore, recent research on discrimination involving Hispanics reaffirms the conclusion that race remains the dominant organizing principle in U.S. urban housing markets.

CONCLUSION

Putting together recent trends in segregation with evidence on the persistence of white prejudice and discrimination leads to four basic conclusions. First, the residential segregation of African Americans continues unabated in the nation's largest metropolitan black communities, and this spatial isolation can in no way be attributed to class.

Second, although whites accept open housing in principle, they have not yet come to terms with its implications in practice. Whites still harbor strong antiblack sentiments, and they are unwilling to tolerate more than a small percentage of blacks in their neighborhoods. This prejudice apparently extends to dark-skinned Hispanics.

Third, discrimination against blacks—and dark-skinned Hispanics—is remarkably widespread and continues at very high levels in urban housing markets. Through a variety of deceptions and exclusionary actions, black access to housing in white neighborhoods is systematically reduced.

Finally, white biases and discrimination apparently do not extend to Asians or light-skinned Hispanics, at least not to the same degree. In no metropolitan area are Asians and Hispanics hypersegregated: despite the recent arrival of large numbers of immigrants and rapid rates of population growth, they display levels of segregation and isolation that are far below those of African Americans.

These results underscore the barriers that African Americans still face in trying to achieve equality in the United States, for housing markets distribute not only shelter, but also jobs, schooling, wealth, safety, and health. If people are denied access to housing on the basis of skin color, they are blocked from these other benefits as well, and a principal mechanism of social mobility is blocked. In a very real way, barriers to spatial mobility are barriers to social mobility.

The lack of full access to housing markets means that incentives for hard work, saving, and sacrifice are decisively undercut for the black middle class, and poor African Americans are forced to live under conditions of intensely concentrated poverty (Massey 1990). Given the central role that residence plays in determining one's life chances, current residential patterns suggest the need to incorporate racial segregation more fully into theories about the origins of the urban underclass.

Chapter 3 The Politics of Black-Korean Conflict: Black Power Protest and the Mobilization of Racial Communities in New York City

Claire Jean Kim

On January 18, 1990, Ghiselaine Felissaint stopped at the Family Red Apple Store in Flatbush, Brooklyn, to buy some fruit. An altercation ensued between Felissaint, a Haitian-born home care worker, and Bong Ok Jang, the Korean-born store manager. Felissaint claimed that Jang and two other employees unjustly accused her of shoplifting and kicked and beat her when she refused to open her bag. Jang claimed that Felissaint offered two dollars in payment for three dollars' worth of fruit and threw a green pepper at the clerk, setting off a scuffle in which no blows were exchanged. Drawn by the commotion, passersby in the predominantly Caribbean immigrant neighborhood gathered in front of the store. As the crowd grew, demanding the merchant's arrest, Jang sought refuge in another Korean-owned grocery across the street, which thus became embroiled in the conflict. Thus began the Red Apple Boycott of 1990. Over the next thirteen months, this spontaneous neighborhood protest developed into an organized retail boycott and picketing campaign of considerable magnitude. Hundreds of blacks—including African Americans, Haitians, and other Caribbean immigrants—boycotted, picketed, marched, and rallied in Flatbush during this period to protest the mistreatment of blacks by both the Korean merchant in question and the broader society.[1] The Red Apple Boycott, which attracted international as well as national attention, firmly impressed the phenomenon of black-Korean conflict on the American imagination well before the Los Angeles rebellion of 1992. Challenging Mayor David Dinkins's rapturous description of the city as a "gorgeous mosaic" of racial and ethnic groups, it also left an indelible imprint on politics in New York City.

Black-Korean conflict has become a familiar form of racial disharmony in many major U.S. cities. Since the early 1970s, Korean immigrants have established dominance over specific small business niches in American cities, particularly green groceries in New York and liquor stores in Los Angeles, often owning and operating stores in poor black neighborhoods.[2] Tensions between Korean merchants and black customers have at times led to overt conflict— from altercations to organized protests such as the Red Apple Boycott to the targeted destruction of Korean-owned stores during the Los Angeles uprising of 1992. Unprecedented levels of immigration indeed augur an increase in such conflicts between native-born racial minorities and immigrants of color.[3] Black-Korean conflict symbolizes this new face of contemporary racial conflict, reminding us that race in America is not just about black and white.

This chapter is a study of the Red Apple Boycott of 1990.[4] Most analyses of black-Korean conflict are grounded on the middleman minority theory (Bonacich 1973) and argue that the structural juxtapositioning of Korean merchants and blacks in the American economy provokes the latter to scapegoat or vent their frustrations on the former. Although this approach illuminates the structural backdrop against which black-Korean conflicts unfold, it cannot account for either the timing of such events or the precise mechanisms by which they occur. Indeed, in order to explain a sustained, organized protest campaign such as the Red Apple Boycott of 1990, one must examine not only the underlying political-economic structural arrangements but also the strategic or purposive agency of the protesters—how they perceived, interpreted, and took action against those arrangements. In this chapter, I argue that the Red Apple Boycott was not an isolated eruption of black frustration but rather a purposive protest campaign designed to mobilize the black community in New York City against patterns of racial domination in American society. I show that the boycott was in fact part of a new black power movement that arose in New York City during the mid-1980s in response to the ongoing exclusion of blacks from economic and political power. Circumventing conventional political channels, which were effectively closed off to them during this period, movement leaders sought through protests to build a new power base in the streets. I pay special attention to the phenomenological aspects of both the boycott and the larger movement, using concepts from the literature on social movement theory. Despite the conventional wisdom about "the declining significance of race" (W. Wilson 1980), this chapter shows that race-based activism is alive and well and that it represents a direct response to ongoing racial domination within American society.

I first critique the middleman minority theory and examine alternative approaches to explaining black-Korean conflict. I then use concepts drawn from social movement theory to analyze the new black power movement and the Red Apple Boycott of 1990. In the final section, I discuss this chapter's conclusions and the questions that it raises for students of race and American society.

BEYOND UNREASON: APPROACHES TO BLACK-KOREAN CONFLICT

The middleman minority theory dominates the academic literature on black-Korean conflict (Min 1996; Ong, Park, and Tong 1994; Jo 1992; Cheng and Espiritu 1989; Light and Bonacich 1988). In Edna Bonacich's (1973) initial formulation, the structural juxtaposition of the middleman minority and the masses prompts the latter to vent their frustrations regarding the system on the former.[5] This behavior is irrational insofar as it spares elites (who manage and benefit from the system) from direct challenge, thereby reinforcing the status quo. For the past generation, the middleman minority theory has inspired important research on the structural aspects of black-Korean conflict; most writings on this type of conflict tinker with but do not fundamentally revise this framework.

Yet the theory's crude determinism and neglect of strategic or purposive agency ultimately render it incomplete. Since the theory ignores the dynamic mechanisms by which collective actions actually unfold, it cannot explain why black-Korean tensions lead to overt conflict at certain times and not others. Much of the literature it has inspired fails to distinguish everday tensions from full-scale collective actions, thus lumping together phenomena that are characterized by strikingly different degrees of organization and purposiveness. On the whole, this literature asserts—without support—that all black-Korean conflict is irrational and unproductive—the contrary opinions of black participants notwithstanding. The mainstream media coverage of the Red Apple Boycott reflected this view. Appearing on ABC's "Like It Is" during the boycott (October 21, 1990), New York assemblyman Al Vann chastised the mainstream media for prejudging the protest without asking the following critical questions: "Why are there brothers and sisters who are willing to invest that kind of time and energy to try and close down a store? What motivates them? What is the history in that?" Lacking any conception of purposive agency on the part of the masses, the middleman minority theory and its academic and journalistic offshoots provide no answer to these questions.[6]

The rational action approach (M. Olson 1965), in contrast, does provide theoretical tools for addressing the purposive aspect of collective action. The rational action paradigm has shaped a generation of research on collective action generally and racial and ethnic mobilization specifically (Olzak and Nagel 1986; Banton 1983; McAdam 1982; Tilly 1978; Lipsky 1968). Contrary to the collective behavior paradigm that it replaced, the rational action approach problematizes collective action. That is, it sees collective action as requiring explanation since it is inherently costly to its participants, who are individual rational economic actors engaged in preference-maximization and cost-benefit analysis. If the collective behavior school holds that collective grievances arising from system strain automatically generate collective action, the rational action approach holds that grievances are ubiquitous and that collective action can only arise when the selective incentives provided by leadership overcome the so-called free rider problem, making individual participation cost-efficient (Oberschall 1973). Emphasizing resources, organization, and leadership, the rational action approach privileges the role of strategic agency in collective action. Unlike the middleman minority theory, therefore, it can both distinguish black-Korean tensions from overt conflicts and explain why the latter arise only in certain instances.

The main problem with the rational action approach, however, is its exceedingly narrow conception of rationality. Critics have pointed out that the notion of rationality as individual preference-maximization is too abstract and decontextualized to apply to real-life collective action (Ferree 1992). Indeed, many social movement scholars agree that the rational action approach responds to the structural and social-psychological determinism of the collective behavior paradigm by going too far in the direction of pure, unconstrained choice. These scholars have generated the alternative notion of strategic agency as socially embedded—or shaped by the actors' specific social location, community context, and collective identity and beliefs (Morris and Mueller 1992). This alternative notion suggests a few more questions for Al Vann's list: Why did participants in the Red Apple Boycott view their actions as meaningful, whereas most observers viewed them as irrational and counterproductive? How did collective identity shape the boycott leaders' strategic and tactical choices? How did the boycott leaders in turn act to reinforce this sense of collective identity? As I show below, the notion of purposive agency as a socially embedded process helps us explain black-Korean conflict while avoiding both the structural determinism of the middleman minority theory and the reductionism of the rational action approach.

NO JUSTICE, NO PEACE: THE NEW BLACK
POWER MOVEMENT IN NEW YORK CITY

The Red Apple Boycott of 1990 was perhaps the most memorable episode of black-Korean conflict in the city's history, but it was not the first. Boycotts of considerable magnitude occurred in 1980 (Harlem), 1984 (Harlem), and 1988 (Bedford-Stuyvesant, Brooklyn). They were all part of the resurgence of black activism that took place in New York City from the mid-1980s through the early 1990s—what I call the new black power movement.[7] Still, the Red Apple Boycott surpassed its precedents in magnitude, publicity, and impact. I first examine the new black power movement as a whole, focusing on the political and economic conditions under which it arose, the community beliefs that shaped its agenda, and its leaders' efforts to construct a "master frame" by which to mobilize support and reinforce collective identity within the black community. Snow and Benford (1992, 137) define a collective action "frame" as "an interpretive schemata that simplifies and condenses the 'world out there' by selectively punctuating and encoding objects, situations, events, experiences, and sequences of actions within one's present or past environments." A "master frame" is the overarching frame that connects a cycle or cluster of related protests (Tarrow 1992); "framing" is the process by which activists generate frames. These concepts, drawn from social movement theory, help us conceive of purposive agency as a socially embedded process. I then examine the Red Apple Boycott, focusing on the boycott leaders' framing efforts, their opponents' counterframing efforts, Mayor Dinkins's evolving response, and the boycott's overall consequences for New York City.[8]

During the 1980s, the black community in New York City confronted worsening economic conditions and a lack of political avenues by which to address them.[9] Global economic restructuring, national economic policies, and post–fiscal crisis austerity programs all aggravated income inequalities during this period, especially harming blacks, who were overrepresented among the city's poor.[10] From 1977 to 1989, moreover, Mayor Edward Koch actively pursued policies that benefited his two major constituencies—the corporate sector and middle-class, outer-borough ethnic whites—at the expense of the (especially black) poor. By dismantling the antipoverty apparatus, cutting public wages, and pursuing "progrowth" investment and tax policies, Koch exacerbated the economic polarization driven by national and international processes. With an eye to reelection, Koch also used various institutional and rhetorical weapons to demobilize or coopt black opposition and stymie minority political empowerment (Mollenkopf 1992). By 1989, his apparent invulnerability to minority challengers prompted the political scientist John Mollenkopf to call New York City "the great anomaly" (1990).

The new black power movement arose as a strategic response to this vise of economic deterioration and political exclusion. It did not leap like Athena from Zeus's head, fully formed, but was built haltingly by numerous activists over several years. The movement developed in two discernible but overlapping stages. During the first—the mobilization and consolidation of leadership—a number of community leaders and activists (mostly veterans from the black power and civil rights movements of the 1950s and 1960s) committed themselves to launching a new protest movement and elaborated a master frame to articulate the movement's agenda. Ranging from moderate machine politicians to pan-Africanist revolutionaries, this diverse leadership group was brought together by a series of campaigns for district, citywide, and national offices during the 1980s. Although these campaigns achieved only limited success in the electoral arena, they helped to launch the new movement by formalizing ties among black moderates and radicals and imparting an urgent common purpose to both.[11] The movement's key slogan—"No Justice, No Peace!"—expressed this urgency.

Complex and fluid, the emergent leadership structure enabled cooperation between black moderates and radicals without compromising the autonomy of either. This structure consisted of concentric circles of power—with radical activists at the center and moderates in the outer rings. The December 12th Movement, a coalition of radical activists formed in the mid-1980s, occupied the core.[12] Members of this group organized and led numerous protest campaigns while more moderate individuals and organizations often played supportive roles. In order to maximize the movement's appeal within the black community, movement leaders elaborated a black power master frame that played to a common denominator of shared beliefs in black power, omitting the more radical calls for revolution and black nationhood found in the December 12th Movement's literature. Set out in speeches, flyers, and slogans, the black power master frame exhorted blacks to come together and resist racial domination—particularly as embodied by Mayor Koch. It was both rooted in and reinforcing of a black collective identity. The new black power movement thus arose from a specific social location or community context. Just as it reactivated and recombined veteran personnel from the earlier black power movement, so did it draw on and reinvigorate long-standing black power beliefs and practices within the black community.[13] As a historically informed strategic response to worsening structural conditions, the movement was a socially embedded process.

During the second stage of the movement—the mobilization of racial community among blacks—activists organized a series of grassroots protest campaigns (some ad hoc, some planned) under the rubric of the black power master frame. The most common precipitant of a protest was an incident of racially motivated violence against a black person. Movement leaders made protests, but not exactly as they pleased. Social location shaped tactical decisions about when, where, and how to protest in two ways. First, blacks' subordinated position in the urban political economy meant that points of contact between blacks and other groups (Jewish teachers, Korean merchants) were natural sites for conflict. Second, the historical disempowerment of the black community meant that its standard repertoire of collective actions (Tilly 1978) included many reactive, disruptive tactics intended to challenge power at its capillary points (blocking bridges, disrupting airport traffic, boycotting stores).[14] Movement leaders were not standing in a Rawlsian original position, deliberating behind a veil of ignorance. To the contrary, they operated (as socially embedded actors) within the resources, opportunities, and constraints of a historically specific context. As Frances Fox Piven and Richard A. Cloward write: "Popular insurgency does not proceed by someone else's rules or hopes; it has its own logic and direction. It flows from historically specific circumstances: it is a reaction against those circumstances, and it is also limited by those circumstances" (1979, xi).

A deadly incident that occurred in Howard Beach, Queens, in 1986 was the spark that set the second stage of the new black power movement ablaze. On December 20 a group of white teenagers attacked four black men in Howard Beach, a predominantly white area in Queens. One Caribbean-born black man, Michael Griffith, was chased onto a highway, where he was hit by a car and killed. It was a random incident of racially motivated violence: the assailants did not know their victims. When Mayor Koch later complained that the black community was overreacting to the incident, he missed the point. The Howard Beach incident became a flash point for the new movement precisely because it was not an isolated incident but rather the most recent in a series of racially motivated killings of black people in New York City. By framing the incident this way, activists transformed it into a rallying point for the new movement. One year and a day after the deadly Howard Beach attack, a racially mixed jury convicted three of the four defendants of manslaughter. A few weeks later, activists organized the first of many "days of outrage," consisting of a march, speeches, and a citywide, one-day boycott of nonblack-owned businesses. More than 4,500 people marched from Brooklyn to Koch's home in lower Manhattan during this event.

Then, just as the Howard Beach furor began to die down, another killing sparked a second wave of protests in the summer of 1989. A group of forty white teenagers attacked four black youths in Bensonhurst, a predominantly white neighborhood in southern Brooklyn. Sixteen-year-old Yusef Hawkins, who was there to shop for a used car, was fatally shot. The resonance with Howard Beach was unmistakable, and the movement was carried forward. From incident to incident, activists achieved something more enduring than physical mobilization: they helped to "rearticulat[e] Black collective subjectivity" (Omi and Winant 1986, 85), encouraging blacks to see themselves *as* blacks, as members of a unified racial community. The adoption of pan-African symbols and concerns signaled the movement leaders' special interest in recruiting Caribbean and African immigrants into this community.[15]

In 1989 the new black power movement achieved its major proximate goal— replacing Koch with the city's first black mayor.[16] In order to defeat Koch in the Democratic primary, David N. Dinkins, a moderate out of the Carver Democratic Club in Harlem, had to walk a tightrope. He needed to motivate black voters to turn out without alienating white and Latino voters.[17] Since race-based appeals furthered the former task but hampered the latter, Dinkins waged a dual campaign, appealing to blacks through the black media and to nonblacks through the mainstream media (Arian et al. 1991). The new black power movement made a decisive contribution to both facets of the Dinkins primary campaign. On one hand, movement leaders campaigned on Dinkins's behalf within the black community. During the Bensonhurst protests in the weeks leading up to the primary election, they excoriated Ed "Bull" Koch and exhorted blacks to express their outrage about the killing in the voting booth. Because their reputations as critics of the system gave their endorsement weight, activists succeeded in translating community mobilization into electoral clout on behalf of Dinkins. On the other hand, by raising the specter of increased racial strife, the movement pushed reluctant white voters to support Dinkins, the self-proclaimed racial mediator, rather than Koch, the unabashed racial provocateur. After defeating Koch in the primary, Dinkins defeated Republican Rudolph Giuliani to become the first black mayor in the city's history.[18] Herbert Haines writes: "Radicals may thus provide a militant foil against which moderate strategies and demands can be redefined and normalized, i.e., responded to as 'reasonable'" (1988, 3). Dinkins's victory—which was also the movement's victory—marked a zenith in cooperation between the city's moderate and radical black leaders. It was an alliance that proved difficult to maintain.

A Protest Grows in Brooklyn

On January 18, 1990, just seventeen days after Dinkins's inauguration, the Red Apple Boycott began. For the leaders of the new black power movement, the presence of an ally in Gracie Mansion did not vitiate the continuing need for community mobilization. The black power master frame of the movement articulated numerous long-term aims beyond electing a black mayor—including the enhancement of racial solidarity and pride and the pursuit of meaningful political and economic empowerment. Yet Dinkins's inauguration transformed the political context so that the movement's critics acquired new leverage against it: the mayor himself. As an elected official who had won office on a platform of racial harmony, Dinkins's interests and imperatives now emphatically diverged from those of his recent allies. The Red Apple Boycott exposed and exacerbated this structural tension.[19] During the conflict, the mainstream media, the Korean American community, and other boycott opponents forced Dinkins off the tightrope that he had walked during the campaign, compelling him to intervene against the boycotters. Although it began as its precedents had, the Red Apple Boycott became, owing to the transformed political context, a pivotal event for both the movement and the new administration.

The Consolidation of the Boycott Leadership

The Red Apple Boycott began as a spontaneous neighborhood protest against the alleged abuse of Ghiselaine Felissaint, not as a planned movement campaign. Nevertheless, questions about who would lead it and toward what end were settled within the first few weeks. The consolidation of the boycott leadership and the resolution of the boycott's direction took place in two stages. During the first stage, Haitian activists, who were first to arrive on the scene, molded the spontaneous gathering in front of the two stores into an ongoing boycott and picketing campaign seeking justice for Felissaint. They framed the protest primarily as a Haitian concern—a community's defense of one of its own. Using word of mouth, social networks, the pulpit, Haitian newspapers, and especially the local Haitian-operated radio station, Radio Soleil, they mobilized support among

Haitian immigrants in and around Flatbush. Flatbush is home to the largest Haitian community in New York City (an estimated 500,000 to 750,000). Despite the national-origin emphasis of this initial boycott frame, Haitian activists eventually worked together with African American groups to form the Flatbush Coalition for Economic Empowerment (FCEE), an ad hoc group charged with organizing the boycott. Its name notwithstanding, the FCEE's primary focus was the precipitating incident itself; its avowed goal was to ensure Jang's arrest and successful prosecution.

Then, in early February, the Red Apple Boycott took on a more radical aspect. During this second stage of leadership consolidation, December 12th activists molded the neighborhood-based, Haitian-oriented protest into a full-fledged movement campaign with pan-African intonations and citywide significance. Just how December 12th activists first became involved in the conflict is unclear, but the results of their assumption of leadership are not.[20] They formed another ad hoc group, the Flatbush Frontline Collective (FFC), to displace the FCEE and to reorient the boycott toward a more radical agenda. They articulated a new boycott frame that, consistent with the black power movement's master frame, challenged the larger context of racial domination as well as the specific merchant's alleged mistreatment of Felissaint. Finally, eschewing any negotiations with Korean merchant representatives, they issued three unconditional demands: a formal apology from Jang, his arrest and prosecution, and the closing of the two stores.[21] As the FFC gained attention and support, it drew the FCEE's more radical members (both African American and Haitian) away, eventually rendering the latter group defunct.

The FFC's organizational structure was fluid, decentralized, and complex— to some extent, a microcosmic reflection of the wider movement's leadership structure. Robert Sherman, a staff worker at the City Commission for Human Rights, noted the diffusion of leadership tasks (*New York Times*, 16 July 1990): "It's a very grass-roots style of protest. Word spreads by word of mouth and identifying a single leader is difficult. There are a number of leaders and the landscape is always shifting." As the boycott progressed, a rough division of labor emerged between December 12th activists and other Haitian and African American activists. The former handled much of the strategic work, such as framing and planning major rallies to punctuate key events; the latter did much of the tactical work, such as turning people out to stand on the picket line day after day. This flexible structure, which permitted diverse activist groups to work together while preserving the autonomy of each, undoubtedly facilitated the protest's longevity.

Framing and the Mobilization
of Racial Community

By 1990, the retail boycott frame was a developed part of the movement's repertoire of available collective action frames (Tarrow 1992).[22] The leaders of the Red
Apple Boycott adopted this standard frame with few adjustments. Elaborated
through speeches, flyers, and slogans, this frame articulated two key ideas: first,
that the abuse of black customers by nonblack merchants was symptomatic of
racial domination in the broader society, and second, that the black community
should mobilize, boycott, picket, and otherwise use its collective economic
power to compel change in the merchants' behavior as well as in the broader society. In other words, solidarity in thought and deed was the answer to the problem of racial domination.

Of course, this frame's roots ran deeper than those of the black-led boycotts
of the 1980s. Like the black power master frame into which it fit, it derived from
established collective beliefs within the black community—in this case, from
the venerated ideal of community control (Altshuler 1970). *Community control*
describes a group's control over neighborhood institutions such as schools,
banks, and stores. The historical segregation of blacks into mostly black neighborhoods and the unique permeability of the latter to external capital and state
authority have rendered community control an important index of self-determination and political and economic empowerment for many blacks (Logan
and Molotch 1987). Calls for community control among blacks peaked during
the 1960s but originated as early as the late 1800s. Indeed, the ideal was expressed
through both the century-old exhortation to "buy black," or patronize black-
owned stores, and the "don't buy where you can't work" campaigns of the 1920s
and 1930s, which pressured white merchants in black areas to hire black clerks.

Activists framed the Red Apple Boycott so as to emphasize its connection to
the historically embedded notion of community control. One flyer put out by
the FFC stated simply: "The question for Black folks to consider is this: 'Who
is going to control the economic life of the Black community?'" (February 1990).
As if in response to its own question, the FFC set up and operated a sidewalk
produce stand called the African People Farmers' Market (APFM) on Satur-
days—just a block or so from the two boycotted stores. Flyers celebrated the
APFM as "controlled by AFRICAN people for AFRICAN people," exhorted
blacks to "buy black," and reminded them that "whatever will be done for us
must be done by us." At a public hearing sponsored by the New York City Human Rights Commission in June 1990, one activist explicitly connected the boy-

cott to the absence of community control in black neighborhoods: "No one will spend six months on a boycott line for nonsense. We have a reason to be out there. The reason is, that time and time again, the Koreans have been disrespectful to the community and to African people in the community as a whole. . . . One thing about our community, the dollar goes around one time in Flatbush. You go to Bensonhurst, you go to Bay Ridge, any other community that is non-African, you will find out the dollar goes around three times. In this community . . . the dollar . . . goes into the hands of the Korean merchants and it goes out of the community."[23] This portrayal of Korean merchants as exploitative interlopers rather than as fair competitors expressed the activists' conviction that the playing field for blacks and Koreans was far from level. In their view, Korean merchants participated in and benefited from a system of racial domination—a fact that accounted for both their prosperity and their allegedly habitual disrespect toward black customers. It was this perceived linkage between the merchants (the proximate targets) and the system of racial domination (the ultimate target) that made the Red Apple Boycott legitimate and fair in the eyes of its organizers and participants.

The boycott frame motivated ordinary people to participate by enhancing their personal identification with Felissaint as a victim of racism. Snow and Benford (1992, 1988) call this process—by which activists persuade potential supporters that the frame's broad interpretive claims make sense of and render coherent their individual experiences, orientations, and outlooks—"frame alignment." The fact that the precipitating incident was quotidian in nature, or embedded in the daily round, facilitated the task of frame alignment. Most blacks in New York City have either been personally mistreated by a Korean merchant or have a friend or family member who has been.[24] These experiences strongly enhanced black people's receptivity to the boycott frame. As one boycotter said with reference to Felissaint: "It could have been my wife, one of my own relatives" (*New York Newsday,* 24 January 1990).

Boycott leaders also framed developments in the conflict so as to reinforce the participants' sense of a common purpose and fate. For instance, they shifted their focus during the boycott from the precipitating incident to the system's efforts to shut down the protest. A January 1990 flyer called on blacks to "boycott merchants who disrespect and don't support the community"; several months later, a flyer pointed out that "the racist power structure of New York City is attempting to deny the African community their constitutional right to protest and demonstrate its legitimate concern and outrage." Thus participation, which depended on some degree of racial identification, also tended to strengthen it.

At times, the reinforcement of racial community was less benign. Blacks who shopped in the two stores were denounced by picketers as Aunt Jemimas, Uncle Toms, and "Negroes," as if the picket line demarcated the boundary of racial community and those who crossed it were race traitors. The boycott leaders' race-based definition of community was contested by a few black groups, such as CORE (the Congress of Racial Equality) and UMMA, a Flatbush Muslim Patrol group. Proffering a place-based definition of community, these two groups helped organize "the 6:30 Shoppers," a small group of Flatbush women who opposed the boycott and routinely crossed the picket line. As one 6:30 Shopper put it: "Sonny Carson can't tell me how to be black!" (based on a personal interview with the author).

By emphasizing the common experience of racial oppression rather than exhorting adherence to specific radical or revolutionary beliefs, the boycott leaders cast their mobilizing net as widely as possible. In this way they attracted supporters with divergent beliefs, grievances, and aims into one collective action—including Haitian immigrants, who continued to participate even after December 12th activists assumed the main leadership role. Throughout the boycott, activists wooed Haitian support, addressing all "African" or "black" people and citing Haitian as well as African American and Caribbean heroes (for example, one flyer urged participation "in the spirit of Malcolm X and Jean-Jacques Dessalines"). Haitians responded by pursuing national-origin mobilization—as they had begun to do at the start of the boycott—in tandem with broader racial mobilization. Linguistically and culturally distinct from African Americans and from other Caribbean-origin immigrants, Haitian immigrants strongly self-identify as Haitians. Yet Americans' perception and treatment of them as black people and their own beliefs about popular resistance have made them a natural constituency for radical black activism (Woldemikael 1989). In the Red Apple Boycott, they participated both as Haitians and as blacks.

Like the rest of the new black power movement, the Red Apple Boycott was primarily directed toward the black community. Distrustful of mainstream journalists, boycott leaders rarely gave them anything more than sound bites— charges of unbridled publicity mongering notwithstanding. But they actively solicited support among black people via black-oriented television programs, radio talk shows, weeklies, and community appearances. It is well known among scholars and activists that black-oriented appeals often alienate other groups, especially whites (Eisinger 1976; Aberbach and Walker 1970). Still, the boycott leaders underestimated three things: the magnitude of the opposition the boycott would generate, Dinkins's unique vulnerability to political pressure, and the boycott's ultimate dependence on Dinkins's neutrality. With a black mayor in Gracie Mansion, the movement's alienation of third parties, or "reference publics" (Lipsky 1968), would come at a steep price—for the mayor and for movement leaders.

Counterframing: The Korean American Community's Response

The Red Apple Boycott provoked an unprecedented countermobilization within the Korean American community in New York City.[25] During the movement's three previous boycotts, Korean merchant advocates had chosen to pursue behind-the-scenes negotiations with boycott leaders. That strategy had yielded limited benefits but had done nothing to prevent future boycotts. The Red Apple Boycott prompted Korean American community leaders to draw a line in the sand. Alleging a black conspiracy to drive Korean merchants from the city, these leaders—whose previous advocacy work had earned them both visibility within the community and familiarity with the local political system—organized and demanded official intervention in the conflict. Leaders of the Korean Association of New York, the Korean Produce Association, and the Korean American Small Business Service Center played key roles.

Korean American leaders "counterframed" the boycott to mobilize the Korean American community and other "reference publics" against it. Via social and business networks, the pulpit, the Korean-language media (especially the daily newspaper, *The Korea Times*), and the mainstream media, they declared the boycott to be illegitimate and unfair. Acknowledging the problem of antiblack racism, Sung Soo Kim of the Korean Small Business Service Center nevertheless stated: "Koreans are being scapegoated for a problem they neither created nor contributed to" (*New York Newsday*, 13 February 1990). This scapegoating narrative, which the mainstream media also favored, suggested the violation of cherished notions of the American Dream and of the hard-working Asian "model minority." The American Dream posits that anyone who works hard can prosper—that the playing field is indeed level—and the model minority myth points to the "success story" of Asian Americans.[26] Both notions support Kim's claim that Korean merchants are innocent, hard-working immigrants who happened to get caught in a racial crossfire—rather than greedy agents of racial domination. An article in *The Korea Times* elaborated this perspective (28 August 1990): "When we thought that our hard work was finally paying off after years of hardship, we face a great crisis. As a result of having been more diligent and frugal than any other ethnic group, we have established our-selves in a short period of time. Now that our children do well in school and we can afford to relax, an unexpected challenge hits us all. The boycotts and protests—though Blacks claim that they are aimed at specific shops and shop-owners—are clearly aimed at all diligent and successful Koreans whom they envy and dislike. Blacks are jealous of Koreans for leading a comfortable life and sending their children to good colleges while Blacks live in poverty. They suffer an inferiority complex."[27]

Reminding Korean Americans that they needed political power to protect their economic and social gains, community leaders urged mobilization, soli-darity, and active political participation. Korean Americans from all over the metro region donated tens of thousands of dollars a month to keep the two boy-cotted stores open.[28] Their exhortations echoed those made by black activists with a crucial difference: Korean American leaders made claims that resonated with dominant beliefs in order to win general support and compel official ac-tion on their behalf; black leaders made claims that challenged dominant beliefs in order to highlight and confront patterns of racial domination in American society. In any case, the Korean American community proved responsive to these appeals, in deed as well as opinion.

The Korean American demand for official intervention focused squarely on the new mayor. Sung Soo Kim wrote Dinkins several letters during the boycott, reminding the mayor of his campaign promise to safeguard the "gorgeous mo-saic" of racial and ethnic groups and urging him "to translate [his] vision of har-mony to reality" (personal communication, January 24, 1990). When direct ap-peals failed, Korean American leaders brought suit against the city and the New York Police Department to compel them to enforce a court order limiting the boycott. They also lobbied for intervention at the state and federal levels. Yet their community's small size and embryonic political networks limited its clout. After months of unsuccessful lobbying, members of the newly formed Civil Rights Committee of the Korean Association of New York organized an un-precedented rally in front of City Hall on September 18, 1990, to demand that Dinkins personally intervene in the conflict. The rally drew approximately 10,000 Korean Americans from across the metropolitan region. One commu-nity leader explained: "The [Red Apple Boycott] has exhausted our patience. The only choice we have now is to demonstrate in order to accelerate the actions of the city government" (*The Korea Times*, 4 August 1990). Although organizers self-consciously framed the rally as a "civil rights demonstration" or "peace con-vention" to avoid the appearance of attacking the mayor or the boycotters, their demand for intervention was clear and effective. Coupled with intensifying mainstream media criticism, the rally finally compelled Dinkins to act.

The Containment of Dissent: The Mainstream
Media and the Mayor

Mainstream media coverage of the Red Apple Boycott implied a double standard.[29] Mayor Koch's lack of involvement in previous boycotts had escaped scrutiny, yet the media demanded Mayor Dinkins's personal intervention in this one. Dinkins's earlier self-description as a racial mediator allowed the media to apply this double standard while disavowing any racial motive. Indeed the mainstream media depicted the boycott, which they unanimously condemned, as "a test of the very image that helped elect him as New York's first black mayor— that of a healer who could hold together the fractious city he calls a gorgeous mosaic" (*The New York Times*, 13 May 1990). Reluctant to criticize the movement that helped him win office, Dinkins initially adopted a position of public neutrality, aggressively pursuing behind-the-scenes negotiations.[30] Pressure from the mainstream media, other officials, and the Korean American community, however, eventually compelled him to intervene. Since he was presumed to favor blacks, Dinkins had to cross the picket line himself to demonstrate his "impartiality." The mayor's agonizing journey from neutrality to intervention provides a unique window onto the politics of race in New York City and the constraints facing black elected officials everywhere.

Overall, the mainstream media depicted the Red Apple Boycott as a morality play, recasting the scapegoating claim in pointedly racial mythological terms. The boycotters were the underclass scapegoating the model minority and destroying its American Dream. The media's interpretation largely ignored Haitian participation in the boycott. Perhaps conflict between a native minority group and an immigrant group made for a better morality play than that between two immigrant groups. The CBS news magazine show *48 Hours* billed the boycott as "an American Dream turned nightmare" (12 July 1990): footage showed the Korean merchants recounting their immigrant dreams in empty stores and black protesters chanting angrily outside while "New York, New York" played in the background. Indeed, the media pronounced the Korean merchants wholly innocent of any responsibility for black disempowerment, positing if not elaborating an objective calculus for ascertaining such responsibility. A few journalists expressed sympathy with the boycotters' "frustrations" but dissented from the targeting of Korean merchants. Most, however, dismissed the boycotters' stated grievances and attributed their actions to anti-

Korean racism or the habit of blaming others for their problems or both. A *New York Post* editorial summarized this mainstream media counterframe (24 May 1990):

> We have condemned the anti-Korean boycott in Flatbush virtually since its onset for one overriding reason: It's clear the four-month-long and still-continuing campaign—judging from the rhetoric and fliers used by the boycotters themselves—has been motivated chiefly by racism. Racism is always wrong. And the effort by black racial agitators to deny hard-working immigrants the opportunity to make a living seems to us a direct challenge to the American dream. . . . [The Koreans] labor long hours to make small businesses succeed; they pay taxes; their children excel in school, even when the parents don't speak English; they disdain welfare; and while they don't have an easy time getting bank loans, they often help each other with small start up loans. These immigrants, in other words, help subsidize the city. . . . [I]t seems to us that those whose constituencies are most dependent on public expenditures—on the subsidies and social programs that are funded by tax dollars—should be particularly alert to the consequences of anti-Asian racism.

As the conflict wore on, the media's efforts to criminalize the boycott leaders intensified. One editorial in *The Daily News* described the boycott leaders as "opportunists [who were] using racial scapegoating to advance their own fortunes" (20 September 1990). Another in *The New York Post* suggested that the "rabble rousers" had staged the precipitating incident in order to extort money from the merchants and avoid responsible employment (29 August 1990). An editorial in *The New York Times* titled "Racial Boycotts, Then and Now: From Brown Shirts to Brooklyn" carried this trend to its logical conclusion, likening the boycotters to Nazis (13 October 1990).

Unrelenting criticism from nearly every corner of officialdom quickly rendered Dinkins's neutrality a political liability. City council members, state senators and assembly members, the Brooklyn borough president, the Kings County (Brooklyn) District Attorney's office, community board members, a New York State Supreme Court justice, and many others chastised the mayor for his inaction and urged him to intervene in the conflict.[31] Alvin Berk, chair of Community Board 14 (which includes Flatbush), wrote to Dinkins: "You will be remembered as the mayor who presided over the beginning of the end" (personal communication). Caught on the same tightrope as the new mayor, most black elected officials remained silent about the boycott and the mayor's handling of it.

The mayor's reluctant odyssey from neutrality to intervention was marked by three crises and accompanying crescendos in public criticism. The first crisis concerned the enforcement of State Supreme Court Justice Gerald S. Held's court order of May 3, which required the boycotters to remain at least fifty feet away from the store entrances. When attorneys for the boycott leaders tried and failed to overturn the order, Dinkins refused to enforce it and appealed the decision. His stated rationale was, first, that the police should not be deployed in civil matters, and, second, that enforcement of the order would provoke violence. Dinkins's reluctance to alienate black supporters, his belief in the right to protest, and his hesitation to authorize police action against nonviolent black protesters doubtless informed his decision not to enforce the court order. When the mayor's critics accused him of failing to uphold the law—going beyond their previous charges of indecision and pandering—he responded with an unusual televised speech, in which he stated that he thought the boycotters were "making a mountain out of a molehill" (11 May 1990). It was his first public criticism of the protest. Although the speech angered many of Dinkins's former allies in the new black power movement, it purchased him a brief respite from media criticism—just as the appointment of a mayor's committee to study the boycott had done the month before.

The August 31 release of "Report of the Mayor's Committee Investigating the Protest Against Two Korean-Owned Groceries on Church Avenue in Brooklyn" sparked the second crisis. Acknowledging grievances on both sides of the conflict, the report urged a negotiated settlement and recommended a handful of programs to foster racial sensitivity and black entrepreneurship. Its central finding that the protest was not "race based" or essentially racist in motivation protected the boycotters from prosecution under a state law prohibiting such protests but also provoked outrage among the boycott's critics. Kings County District Attorney Charles Hynes (whom the report criticized) claimed that the report was "universally rejected by everyone in the free world" (*New York Newsday*, 8 November 1990). Columnist Murray Kempton called it "a specimen of the portentous nonsense you have to read not to believe" (*New York Newsday,* 31 August 1990), while an editorialist for another paper described it as "a tangle of clichés wrapped around a core of nonsense" (*The Daily News,* 2 September 1990). Like Dinkins's ongoing attempt to placate different constituencies, the report's attempt to reconcile two opposing perspectives pleased no one.

The Korean American rally at City Hall on September 18 generated the third and final crisis. When Dinkins attempted to address the crowd, he was heartily booed off the platform. Months of media criticism, the public derision of the report, and the evident outrage of nearly 10,000 Korean Americans and their supporters finally forced Dinkins's hand. On September 19 he promised to enforce the court-ordered fifty-foot zone. Two days later, he personally crossed the picket line and made purchases in the two boycotted stores. The mayor's actions pushed the protest toward its denouement. When the police compelled the picket line to relocate across the street from the store entrances—in compliance with the court order—the number of picketers slowly dwindled. Furthermore, shoppers from across the city, inspired by the mayor's example, began to visit Flatbush and patronize the two stores. Although it took months to wind down, the Red Apple Boycott never regained its momentum. By February 1991 it was over.

Dinkins's capitulation to his critics was too little, too late. It ultimately alienated blacks without appeasing angry whites and Korean Americans. If the mayor's former allies in the movement accused him of turning on black people, the media accused him of coddling them. Although his critics speculated openly about his character flaws, Dinkins's problem was, at bottom, a structural one. During periods of racial conflict, his position as a black mayor in a divided, majority nonblack city became untenable, a situation aggravated by the media's skillful playing of the race card. If the mainstream media's general charge is to contain dissent and "inculcate and defend the economic, social, and political agenda of privileged groups that dominate the domestic society and the state" (Herman and Chomsky 1988, 298; see also Cottle 1992), it clearly fulfilled this charge in the case of the Red Apple Boycott.

Political Consequences of the Boycott

Critics charged that the boycott gave its participants a brief symbolic high but did nothing to improve their material situation. In fact, many argued that the boycott harmed black people by distracting them from a more constructive, policy-oriented agenda and alienating potential white and Korean American allies. Of course, discrete policy reforms—which the boycott leaders neither pursued nor achieved—are not the only, or even most important, index of social change.[32] Viewing racial empowerment as an ongoing process rather than an endstate, black activists themselves saw the boycott as a success insofar as it furthered the new black power movement's aims of mobilizing the black community, enhancing its sense of racial solidarity, and challenging racial domination. The boycott's main outcome—the promotion of race-based mobilization in local politics—was long-term and cumulative with that of other movement campaigns. Whether seen as lamentable or glorious, the growing organization of collective identity, interest, and political action according to race has had a decisive impact on politics in New York City—from the election of Mayor Dinkins, to

the recruitment of Haitian immigrants into black protest politics, to the political awakening of the Korean American community, to the anti-Dinkins backlash in 1993. Some of these ramifications were intended by movement leaders;
others were not.

The Red Apple Boycott mobilized the black community both directly
(through the picket line) and indirectly (by generating a second, offshoot
protest). The thirteen-month protest attracted the active participation of hundreds and perhaps thousands of blacks, who adjusted their shopping practices,
paused at the picket line on the way to and from work, and attended Saturday
afternoon rallies held by December 12th activists. The boycott also reinforced a
sense of collective identity among other blacks who sympathized with but did
not join the boycotters. Although it is difficult to know precisely how many
blacks supported the boycott in thought or deed, table 3.1 shows responses to a
New York Newsday-Gallup telephone poll of June 15, 1990.

As might be expected, these data indicate that more blacks (27 percent) supported the protest than did whites (6 percent). The data also suggest that both
the boycott leaders and their critics were culpable of self-serving hyperbole, since
the former claimed that most blacks supported the boycott and the latter
claimed that only a handful did. Still, it is likely that the poll understates black
support. For one thing, the poll was taken five months after the boycott began,
and public support appears to have peaked at the start and then steadily faded.
Also, my personal interviews revealed that blacks held highly complex attitudes
toward the Red Apple Boycott. Many interviewees, for instance, sympathized
with the protesters' grievances but criticized some aspect of their actions. This
poll has too few possible responses to capture such ambivalence. Indeed, if all of
the black respondents who answered "don't know" are presumed to have had at
least some sympathy with the protesters, 61 percent of respondents could be said

Table 3.1
Percentage of Support for Red Apple Boycott, by Race or Ethnicity[a]

	Boycotters	Merchants	Don't know	Haven't heard enough
Blacks	27%	37%	34%	2%
Whites	6	68	22	4
Asians	12	58	27	3

Source: *New York Newsday*–Gallup telephone poll, June 15, 1990.
[a]Question: "Whom do you sympathize with in the boycott situation?"

to have sympathized with the boycott. Note that the relatively high rate of Asian support for the boycott (12 percent) reflects a lack of racial solidarity among the city's Asian groups.[33]

The Red Apple Boycott gave rise to a second protest campaign against the local community board for Flatbush-Midwood: Community Board 14.[34] Three months after the boycott began, board chairman Alvin Berk's denunciations of the boycott leaders prompted a handful of them to launch a parallel protest demanding greater black representation on the community board. Although whites comprised only 38 percent of the district population in 1990, the chair, the district manager, and thirty-nine of the fifty appointed board members were white. The fact that racial and demographic change had outpaced political change in Flatbush over the last twenty years indeed rendered the area fertile ground for both the boycott and the community board protest.[35] The latter, which lasted for almost two years, eventually secured a significant increase in the number of black board members.

The Red Apple Boycott also brought Haitian immigrants into the racial fold, encouraging them to see themselves as black people. As we have seen, Haitians mobilized simultaneously on racial and national-origin bases during the boycott. Events leading up to the election of Jean-Bertrand Aristide in Haiti also galvanized the city's Haitian community during this period. But the boycott compelled Haitian immigrants (many of whom considered themselves exiles) to shift some of their attention from homeland politics to local affairs, where race perhaps mattered more than national origin. In the spring of 1990, the Haitian activist Guy Victor recounted, he and some colleagues protested the federal Food and Drug Administration's ban on Haitian blood products at the United Nations in Manhattan and then went en masse to stand on the picket line in Flatbush (personal interview with the author). During the former action, they were Haitians; during the latter, blacks. Pan-African solidarity turned out to cut both ways. After the August 1991 coup in Haiti, many movement leaders attempted to influence U.S. policy toward Haiti in order to protect both the deposed president and the growing numbers of refugees.

Race-based mobilization begets more race-based mobilization as groups organize to compete with or defend themselves against other organized groups. Thus the Red Apple Boycott sparked the political mobilization and development of the city's Korean American community. Although many Koreans living in New York remained focused on the politics of their homeland—Illsoo Kim (1981, 228) described the Korean Consulate General as "the informal government of New York's Korean community"—the boycott drove home the necessity of pursuing local political power. In a letter to Dinkins, Sung Soo Kim wrote (January 31): "Korean Americans are a first generation immigrant community, with little knowledge of and access to the often confusing American political system. In the past, we have thus often taken no action when confronted with ethnic conflicts. . . . We can no longer afford to be so passive" (personal communication). As noted above, the September rally in front of City Hall marked the apogee of this mobilization as well as the community's baptism into pressure politics. The Civil Rights Committee of the Korean Association of New York and the Coalition for Korean Voters, two groups that formed in response to the boycott, continue to conduct civil rights advocacy and voter registration today.[36]

Finally, the Red Apple Boycott prompted a showdown between Mayor Dinkins and movement activists that damaged both. If the boycott furthered the movement's aim of promoting black mobilization, it also occasioned Dinkins's political crisis and highlighted the ultimate limits of black political unity—its organizers' intentions notwithstanding. His Republican-Liberal challenger, Rudolph Giuliani, turned "the Korean boycott" into a prominent campaign issue during the 1993 mayoral race, arguing that it demonstrated Dinkins's inability to lead and his favoritism toward blacks.[37] Giuliani's strategy was highly effective. On November 2, 1993, he narrowly defeated Dinkins in one of the most racially polarized votes in the city's history. Color lines proved much more important than party lines. Giuliani won 75 percent of the white vote and only 5 percent of the black vote. In this putative bastion of liberalism, Dinkins became the first black mayor of a major U.S. city to lose his first reelection bid (Arian et al. 1991). Jennings (1992, 23) recently posed the question: "Does Black nationalism mean that Black mayors and elected officials will have an easier time managing cities, or because they are Black, will more difficult problems be posed to these elected officials as a result?" This chapter points to the latter conclusion. It is a paradox of American politics that radical black activism helps black mayors get into office but complicates the task of governing once they are there.

CONCLUSIONS AND QUESTIONS

Black-Korean conflicts such as the Red Apple Boycott of 1990 are conventionally misread as unreasoned racial strife. The problem is circular: because we presume that black actions against Korean merchants are irrational, we do not subject them to types of analysis that would illuminate their strategic or purposive aspects. In this chapter, I have applied social movement theory to one such protest, emphasizing that the strategic agency of the collective actors was socially and historically embedded. This approach dereifies racial conflict, exposing the underlying community-level political dynamics that fuel it and give it meaning. It is equally applicable to racial conflict between other groups, such as blacks and Jews or blacks and Latinos.

This chapter's implications extend beyond black-Korean conflict to the related topics of contemporary black activism and immigrant politics. Noting that works on black politics focus overwhelmingly on conventional political behavior, Jennings (1992), Bush (1984), and others have urged scholars to pay more attention to radical forms of black activism, which continue to play a crucial role in black political life. This study of the new black power movement indeed suggests that radical activism is intersecting with conventional black politics in new and important ways in American cities. This finding challenges received conceptual dichotomies (for example, separatist versus integrationist) as well as the "from protest to politics" framework popular in analyses of black politics (Tate 1993; Browning, Marshall and Tabb 1990, 1984). In addition, this chapter suggests that the politics of immigrant communities are powerfully shaped by, and should be studied in the context of, both black-white conflicts and conflicts between immigrant groups. Although it is often noted that immigration from the Caribbean, Asia, and Latin America augurs increased conflict between native minorities and immigrants of color, it is less often noted that it augurs the same *between* immigrant groups of color—as between Haitians and Koreans in the Red Apple Boycott. Contrary to the impression given by some single-community studies, then, immigrant politics neither develop in a vacuum nor follow a fixed trajectory. Rather, they vary according to the local political and economic context and the specific geography of racial and ethnic groups.

If this chapter answers certain questions, it raises many more. When will radical black activism experience another resurgence in New York City? Will the Korean American community's growing political clout reduce the incidence of black-Korean conflict? How will the predicted growth of the Latino community alter current patterns of urban racial conflict? When will black immigrants ally themselves with African Americans, and when will they opt for ethnic mobilization alone? In what ways will global economic restructuring continue to distribute its burdens unequally among groups, aggravating racial inequities? Can groups contest these global processes? How and with what degree of success? Are cross-racial coalitions possible despite group differences in material interests and the deep resonance of racial appeals? Will the nation's turn to the right—reflected in the retreat on racial issues and rising xenophobia during the

1980s and 1990s—compel native minorities and immigrants to forge a united front, or will it drive them further apart? In 1903, W. E. B. Du Bois wrote: "The problem of the twentieth century is the problem of the color line" (1989, 13). It seems clear today that the problem of the twenty-first century will be the problem of *multiple* color lines. As immigration, global restructuring, and political developments continue to transform American society, the significance of race will surely change—and perhaps deepen—but there is every indication that it will not decline.

Chapter 4 Educating Immigrant Children: Chapter 1 in Changing Cities

Michael Fix and Wendy Zimmermann

This chapter focuses on the degree to which limited-English-proficient (LEP) children receive services under Chapter 1, the largest single grant program for elementary and secondary schools. The $6.8 billion federal program provides support for supplemental compensatory education aimed at economically disadvantaged children who are performing poorly in school. Along with Project Head Start, it was enacted as part of the war on poverty in the 1960s, and together these programs are the cornerstones of the federal government's commitment to educating disadvantaged children. Historically, Chapter 1 has focused on the reading, writing, and mathematics skills of children in elementary school. The program's reach is extraordinarily broad: it now serves one in nine school-age children in the United States.

We raise three equity-related policy issues concerning LEP children's participation in Chapter 1. First, are Chapter 1 services reaching the large number of immigrant children in the nation's schools who have limited English proficiency? These children frequently live in concentrated poverty and perform poorly in school. In short, they seem to present the profile of students who have a strong equitable claim and, perhaps in some instances, a right to benefit from Chapter 1. Second, what are the implications for native-born populations of serving LEP immigrants? Have urban school districts, which are frequently arenas of ethnic political conflict, found ways to serve new populations without displacing old ones? Or does participation in Chapter 1 represent a zero-sum game, with either new claimants being excluded from services or historical beneficiaries being displaced? Although much has been written about competition between native and immigrant populations for jobs and for political power, less attention has been paid to competition for public services. Third, where immigrant children are being served, what barriers to access do they encounter? Another way to state these issues might be: What claims do immigrant and LEP students have to Chapter 1 resources, and to what extent have they exercised those claims or rights? What social costs flow from the exercise of those rights, and who bears them? What social benefits flow from different ways of satisfying the claims of LEP students to Chapter 1 resources?

In this chapter, we use both national data and local case-study approaches to examine the participation of LEP children in the Chapter 1 program. We first review national data on trends within the child population theoretically eligible to participate, including the number of poor children, their spatial concentration, and their academic achievement. We also review these data to determine the degree to which LEP children are represented in the program.

We then go beyond these national data to examine the participation of LEP students in Chapter 1, using case studies conducted in four urban school districts in the fall of 1992. This approach was driven, in large part, by the absence of national-level or even state-level data to address the central questions in our study.

We thus decided to build on Urban Institute research on immigrant policy in four cities: Boston, Houston, Oakland, and Washington, D.C. Each city is characterized by high, recent growth in immigration, a large African American student population, and significant local African American political representation and power. As a result, we hypothesized, these sites would clearly portray the play of ethnic tensions—to the extent that they exist—around the issue of the distribution of Chapter 1 resources.

When we began, we posited that the entry of large numbers of immigrants into urban schools could lead to five possible outcomes regarding the distribution of Chapter 1 funds:

1. exclusion of LEP or immigrant children from Chapter 1 services;
2. displacement of established beneficiaries by immigrants;

3. provision of a *reduced* level of Chapter 1 services to an expanded student population composed of both established and immigrant LEP children;
4. replacement of the native poor by immigrant LEP children as they fill slots left vacant by natives moving out of the central city; or
5. expansion of Chapter 1 to serve both new children and established beneficiaries.

It can be argued, though, that these scenarios represent an incomplete conceptualization of possible outcomes because they fail to take into account the level of services and benefits that natives would have received in the absence of immigration. If no new immigration had occurred, would per-pupil expenditures in Chapter 1 have risen as sharply as they did? Would Congress have increased funding for Chapter 1 over the past ten years as much as it has? Although the answers to these questions are highly speculative, they must be acknowledged in any thorough examination of the issue of competition for public resources.

Even though we focused rather narrowly on four urban school districts, we were still forced to take an opportunistic approach to data collection and analysis. We relied heavily on administrative records (such as applications to the state or federal government for Chapter 1 funds), data supplied to us by the school districts, and the invaluable mass of documents that have accompanied legal action concerning these issues in two of the sites, Oakland and Boston. We found that school districts rarely kept systematic data on the number of LEP students receiving Chapter 1 services. In this regard our recent data are probably more reliable than the historical data needed to portray trends over time.

The data analysis was supplemented by in-person and telephone interviews with Chapter 1 staff and administrators, the staff and administrators of district bilingual and multilingual departments, principals in selected Chapter 1 schools, community activists, and public interest lawyers. This exploratory study has a number of limits. One is definitional. To some degree, the study is premised on a high presumed correlation between LEP students and students who are foreign-born or immigrants. There are, of course, problems with using English proficiency as a proxy for immigrants; many Puerto Ricans—who are not immigrants—have limited English, as do some native-born students, whereas many immigrants from the Caribbean, Canada, and Europe are English-speaking. Furthermore, the definition of limited English proficiency varies by state, district, period, and assessment method (Council of Chief State School Officers 1991), and the collection of data on LEP participation in Chapter 1 is in its infancy. For the 1988–1989 school year, only twenty states and the District of Columbia reported the number of LEP students served by Chapter 1. In the following year, all but three states did so (Westat 1991, 1992). We have made no effort to normalize definitions and have largely taken the available school district data as provided. However, the extremes represented by the four school districts we examined—they served either most or just a few LEP students—reduced, to some extent, the possible analytic problems.

The study is also limited in that it seeks only to answer several basic threshold questions that bear on the access of LEP children to Chapter 1 services. In so doing, the study raises but does not answer a series of more difficult and perhaps more important questions that bear on the quality of the instruction received and its impact on the academic performance of LEP and non-LEP children. Indeed, given the level of variation among schools it is difficult to determine what "being served" by Chapter 1 really means across schools and districts.

CHAPTER 1: CHANGING PURPOSES, CHANGING SERVICES

A number of features of Chapter 1 are especially pertinent to serving LEP children. To begin, it should be stressed that the purpose of Chapter 1 has been to overcome poor children's educational disadvantage by providing them with supplemental remedial services. Over the past twenty-five years, this has usually meant removing students from the regular classroom to provide them with "pullout" remedial instruction (Slavin 1991). The supplemental character of Chapter 1 is important to LEP children and is often misunderstood. It means that remedial instruction offered by Chapter 1 should be available to students who are taught in bilingual, English as a second language (ESL), or sheltered English classes, as well as to students taught in regular English-language classes. Put differently, the receipt of bilingual or ESL instruction delivered as a child's basic education does not make him or her ineligible for Chapter 1 services. In some districts, though, it is mistakenly believed that bilingual or ESL instruction is a substitute for Chapter 1.

Misunderstanding of the complementarity of Chapter 1 and language programs of instruction is due in part to historical practices in many urban school districts—practices that led to the racial and ethnic identification of certain programs in terms of their administrators, teachers, and students. As one high-level school administrator told us: "Bilingual education and the Emergency Immigrant Education Act were for the browns, Chapter 1 was for the blacks, and the magnet programs and special education were for the whites."

The provision of services to LEP children within Chapter 1 has been restricted in several ways, at least two of which are attributable to the law itself. In the first instance the law has been read to bar the inclusion of such students: "Children receiving services to overcome . . . limited English proficiency shall also be eligible to receive services under this part, if they have needs stemming from deprivation and not related solely to . . . limited English proficiency" (U.S.C. sec. 1014(d)(1)) In practice, disentangling the origins of poor academic performance from limited English proficiency is quite difficult, partly because of the limited availability of, and lack of uniformity among, native-language assessment tools. Indeed, the Commission on Chapter 1 (1992), along with the Stanford Working Group (1993), has recently called for the elimination of this constraint.

The second way in which the program has been constrained relates to the type of services that can be provided to LEP students under the law. Our work suggests that some districts' officials believe that they are barred from providing remedial instruction under Chapter 1 in a language other than English or in an ESL setting. The source of this belief is a provision in the law intended to ensure that school districts do not use their Chapter 1 funds to supplant state and local expenditures required to provide language services to LEP children who meet federal or state standards. The net effect of these constraints has been, on occasion, to deter the delivery of meaningful educational services to LEP children in the program.

Changes in the basic character of Chapter 1 are also influencing the extent to which LEP children are served and how they are served. As Slavin (1991, 587), an expert on educating the disadvantaged, has written: "For more than 25 years, Title I and Chapter 1 have primarily provided remedial services to children who are falling behind in basic skills by removing them from their regular classes for separate instruction. . . . Chapter 1 is still a remedial program serving individual children." Analysts have found that programs that adopt this approach typically provide twenty-four to thirty minutes of instruction a day, five days a week.

The law's 1988 reauthorization introduced a number of reforms that were intended to move the program beyond this traditional paradigm. From the perspective of LEP children, perhaps the most important of such reforms have been new, liberalized rules permitting schools with 75 percent or more poor students to administer schoolwide programs. Such programs allow schools to use their Chapter 1 funds more flexibly—to improve the overall instructional program within the school, and hence to serve all children, not just those deemed eligible for Chapter 1 by dint of test results. From Congress's perspective, the purpose of schoolwide programs has been to spur very poor schools to undertake fundamental educational change. This approach and other reforms, such as site-based management, reduce schools' emphasis on targeting and cost accountability and may make it easier to serve—and to credibly claim to have served—LEP students. Yet most principals who have introduced schoolwide projects report that they have not adopted new instructional or teacher-training strategies. Instead, they have often taken advantage of Chapter 1 resources to reduce class size, a reform that may not meet the needs of LEP children (U.S. Department of Education 1993).

Trends in child poverty, concentration of poverty, and subject matter proficiency should influence the level and distribution of Chapter 1 expenditures. Data constraints have compelled us to report a number of these trends from the vantage point of ethnicity and race, rather than language proficiency. Although ethnicity is not an especially good proxy for immigrant status or language capacity, as noted above, a significant portion of the Asian and Hispanic populations in this country are foreign-born or have limited English proficiency. In 1990, 20 percent of Hispanics under age nineteen were foreign-born. Also, more than 75 percent of the LEP population is composed of Hispanics and Asians: 59.4 percent of the total LEP population speaks Spanish, and 17.3 percent speaks an Asian or Pacific Islands language. Analyzing national trends in poverty and program participation makes clear in broad terms how Chapter 1's beneficiary populations are changing, with Hispanic participation rising significantly, black participation rising modestly, and white participation declining.

Child Poverty

The principal focus of Chapter 1 is on counteracting the educational disadvantages related to poverty. Overall we find that, with regard to the growth, incidence, and number of children affected, child poverty is growing most rapidly among Asians and Hispanics; the incidence of poverty is highest among blacks, followed by Hispanics and then LEP students. The absolute number of black children in poverty remains higher than the number of Hispanic and Asian children.

As table 4.1 indicates, the number of Hispanic and Asian children in poverty exploded during the 1980s, rising by 70 and 123 percent, respectively. Indeed, the growth in Hispanic child poverty accounted for almost one-half of the total growth in the number of poor children during the decade. An examination of

Table 4.1

Children Under Age Eighteen in Poverty by Race or Ethnicity, 1979 and 1989

	1979	1989	Percentage Change
Whites	6,193,000	7,599,000	22.7
percentage of total	(59.7)	(60.4)	
Blacks	3,833,000	4,375,000	14.1
percentage of total	(36.9)	(34.7)	
Hispanics[a]	1,535,000	2,603,000	69.9
percentage of total	(14.8)	(20.7)	
Asians	165,000	368,000	123.0
percentage of total	(1.6)	(2.9)	
Total	10,377,000	12,590,000	21.3

Sources: U.S. Department of Education, National Center for Education Statistics (1991, table 19); Bureau of the Census CPS (P-60), Nos. 168, 181; Children's Defense Fund, *Child Poverty in America* (1991).

[a]Persons of Hispanic origin may be of any race.

poverty rates by race and ethnicity reveals that in 1990, 43.7 percent of all black children were poor, compared with 36.2 percent of Hispanic and 14.8 percent of white children (Johnson 1991, 7). The share of children in poverty rose for all groups during the 1980s. In 1990 the share of all LEP children who were poor was 35 percent, unchanged from 1980.

Educational disadvantage has been closely correlated to concentrated poverty, that is, to schools in which a large share of the student body is poor. Overall, concentrated poverty seems to be growing only among Hispanics and Hispanic children, whereas the absolute number of children in concentrated poverty remains higher among blacks, and LEP and language-minority children are far more concentrated in schools with high poverty rates than are native English speakers (Johnson 1991; Barro 1991).

These changes in poverty go hand in hand with ethnic concentration. Taking a very broad measure of concentration—enrollment in the nation's large urban school districts—reveals striking rates of growth during the 1980s for both Hispanics (45 percent) and Asians (75 percent); see table 4.2. At the same time, there has been a sharp drop (25 percent) in the share of the large-city school population that is white and a modest decline (5 percent) in the share that is black.

Table 4.2
School Enrollment by Race or Ethnicity, 1980 and 1990

	1980	1990	Percentage Change
Black	44.3%	42.1%	−5.0
White	33.4	25.0	−25.0
Hispanic	18.4	26.5	+45.0
Asian	3.4	5.9	+75.1
Other	0.5	0.5	0

Source: Council of the Great City Schools, *National Urban Education Goals* (1992).
Note: Data are for the nation's forty-seven largest urban school districts.

Indeed, at the start of the 1980s, non-Hispanic whites represented almost twice the share of cities' school populations as Hispanics' share (33.4 percent and 18.4 percent, respectively). But by the end of the decade, Hispanics had surpassed the non-Hispanic white population in big-city schools (26.5 percent and 25 percent). Viewed broadly, then, Hispanics and to a lesser extent Asians replaced whites in central-city schools during the 1980s.

Other measures also shed light on the trend toward increased concentration of child poverty. Between 1976 and 1988, Hispanics witnessed a rise in the share of children living in high-poverty areas—areas in which 20 percent or more of the population is poor—while the share of black and white children in such areas declined; see table 4.3. Despite the fact that Hispanics alone experienced an increase in the percentage of children living in concentrated poverty, a larger overall percentage of black children lived in such areas in 1988 than did Hispanics; 52.7 percent of all children living in high-poverty areas were black, whereas 40.6 percent were Hispanic. These trends toward increasing concentration of Hispanic poverty are even more pronounced in our four case study sites.

Language-minority and LEP students are more likely to attend schools with high concentrations of poor students than are native-born English speakers. In high-poverty neighborhoods, 11 percent of students participate in bilingual instruction, compared with less than 1 percent in low-poverty schools. Thus, to the extent that future Chapter 1 allocations target districts and schools with high concentrations of poverty, increasing numbers of LEP students will be served by Chapter 1 (U.S. Department of Education 1993).

Table 4.3
Distribution of Children in Central Cities and in Poverty Areas, 1976 and 1988

		1976	1988
All children under 18		100	100
	Central city	26.9	30.4
	Poor areas[a]	20.9	18.9
	Poor children[b]	46.1	46.8
Whites		100	100
	Central city	21.5	25.0
	Poor areas[a]	12.7	12.3
	Poor children[b]	32.7	32.6
Blacks		100	100
	Central city	56.9	56.3
	Poor areas[a]	54.0	52.7
	Poor children[b]	70.7	71.1
Hispanics		100	100
	Central city	46.8	53.9
	Poor areas[a]	33.9	40.6
	Poor children[b]	51.3	57.5

Source: House Committee on Ways and Means, *1992 Green Book: Overview of Entitlement Programs* (1992, table 65).
[a]Poverty areas are those in which 20 percent of the population was identified as below the poverty level according to the latest census.
[b]Percentage of poor children in each group who live in poverty areas.

Academic Achievement and Progress

Besides being poor and living in areas of concentrated poverty, another measure of eligibility for Chapter 1 services is academic achievement. Overall, with regard to measures of academic achievement and progress, black nine-year-olds scored marginally lower on national proficiency tests than other children, but they have shown greater gains over the course of the past two decades than have either Hispanics or whites. At the same time, Hispanics continue to drop out of school at far higher rates than do blacks, whose dropout rates declined sharply through the 1980s.

Low achievement is typically gauged by below-average scores on nationally normed tests. Perhaps the most widely accepted measure of academic competence is the National Assessment of Educational Progress (NAEP), with five levels from rudimentary to advanced. As table 4.4 indicates, average scores achieved by white, black, and Hispanic nine-year-old children in reading and mathematics between 1975 and 1990 were uniformly on the "basic" or second lowest level. And although blacks and Hispanics have recorded larger gains than whites in both subjects over the past twenty years, blacks' basic skills remain marginally lower than those of Hispanics, whose scores, in turn, are somewhat lower than those of whites.

We have less information on the educational progress of LEP students, since they usually remain untested because of their language skills (McDonnell and Hill 1993). Moreover, there is no national reporting and aggregation of results of the achievement tests given by school districts that measure achievement in languages other than English.

The roughly comparable achievement levels reported by the NAEP mask sharp ethnic differences when it comes to dropping out of school. The share of blacks aged sixteen to twenty-four who were dropouts fell sharply during the 1980s (from 19.3 percent to 13.2 percent) and is now about the same as the share

Table 4.4
Trends in Average Subject-Matter Proficiency for Nine-Year-Old Children, 1977–90

	1973–75	1980–82	1986–88	1990	Percentage Change, 1973–90
Reading					
Whites	217	221	218	217	0.0%
Blacks	181	189	189	182	0.5
Hispanics	183	190	194	189	3.3
Mathematics					
Whites	225	224	227	235	4.4
Blacks	190	195	202	208	9.5
Hispanics	202	204	205	214	5.9

Source: U.S. Department of Education, *Trends in Academic Achievement* Skill levels: rudimentary (150); basic (200); intermediate (250); adept (300); advanced (350). (November 1991).

of whites (12 percent). Hispanics, however, remain much more likely to be dropouts than do either whites or blacks (32.4 percent).

Overall Spending and Participation

But how have these trends in child poverty and achievement translated into spending and participation in Chapter 1? When viewed in its entirety, real spending on Chapter 1 fell during the 1980s. If one looks at spending and participation within Chapter 1 for the decade from 1979–1980 to 1989–1990 (the last year for which there is a complete count of participants), several trends become apparent (table 4.5). First, real spending over the decade fell slightly (by 8.2 percent), but participation levels rose modestly (by 3.2 percent). As a result, funds per participant fell during the period by 11 percent. In short, a declining number of dollars were being distributed to an expanding number of children. But if one looks at changes in the program from the lowest point of funding in 1982–1983 through 1989–1990, one sees that spending increased 23 percent, participation rose 19 percent, and funds per participant increased 2 percent.

Rising appropriations, then, are being used to serve more students instead of providing more intensive services to recipients. One result is that Chapter 1 has received a declining share of total education expenditures for participants, falling from 21 to 17 percent. These trends toward favoring increased participation over more concentrated services were also found in the case study sites.

Hispanic and Asian Participation

Over the course of the past decade, the share of Hispanic and Asian students receiving Chapter 1 services grew rapidly while black participation rose moderately and white participation fell; see table 4.6. A simple comparison of the share of all children who are poor by race and ethnicity and of Chapter 1 participation reveals that the two are strikingly symmetric; see table 4.7. This balance is even more striking when one compares the racial and ethnic composition of children who are poor *and* low achieving with the composition of the Chapter 1 population. Only the Asian population appears to be overrepresented in the program using this comparison. Although a larger share of poor black and Hispanic children (61 percent and 47 percent, respectively) are low achieving than are whites (38 percent), a significantly larger share of all poor, low-achieving students are white because of their larger absolute number.

Table 4.5
Chapter 1: Funding and Participation, 1979–1980 to 1992–1993

| | Appropriation | | Participation | | | Total per-Pupil Spending, Elementary-Secondary (in 1991–92) |
	1991–92 $ Billions[a]	Annual Growth (%)	Millions	Annual Growth (%)	Per-Student Funding (in 1991–92 $)	
1979–80	4.729	—	5.162	—	916	3,718
1980–81	4.188	−11.4	5.076	−1.7	825	3,618
1981–82	3.735	−11.8	4.619	−9.0	809	3,708
1982–83	3.544	−5.1	4.448	−3.7	797	3,853
1983–84	3.693	4.2	4.573	2.8	808	3,992
1984–85	3.883	5.2	4.713	3.1	824	4,211
1985–86	4.049	4.3	4.740	0.6	854	4,419
1986–87	3.774	−6.8	4.733	−0.1	797	4,575
1987–88	4.090	8.4	4.951	4.6	826	4,685
1988–89	4.330	5.9	5.047	1.9	858	4,912
1989–90	4.342	0.3	5.328	5.6	814	
1990–91	4.902	12.9	—	—		
1991–92	5.558	13.4	—	—		
1992–93	5.944	6.9	—	—		

Sources: U.S. Department of Education, *National Assessment of the Chapter 1 Program: The Interim Report,* 1992; *A Summary of State Chapter 1 Participation and Achievement Information: 1989–90* (prepared for the U.S. Department of Education), 1992.
[a]Adjusted for inflation.

From a national vantage point LEP students are proportionally represented in Chapter 1. State data, however, reveal great variation in the degree to which LEP students are served by the program at the state (and hence district) level. For example, in 1990–1991 only about 10 percent of Florida's LEP population was served by Chapter 1, whereas more than 50 percent of California's was served. Closer examination of the data reveals that California's and Texas's LEP populations account for 82 percent of all LEP participants in Chapter 1 but only about 57 percent of all LEP students. In California, LEP students make up 34 percent of the Chapter 1 population, and in Texas they make up 21 percent. These two

Table 4.6
Race and Ethnicity of Chapter 1 Participants, 1980–90

Participants	1979–80		1989–90		Percentage Change
	Number	Percentage	Number	Percentage	
White (not Hispanic)	2,324,433	53.3	2,162,953	43.3	−6.9
Black (not Hispanic)	1,371,304	31.5	1,445,326	28.9	5.4
Hispanic	490,289	11.2	1,140,542	22.8	132.6
Asian	82,396	1.9	159,270	3.2	93.3
Total[a]	4,359,711	100.0	4,992,998	100.0	14.5

Source: Westat, *A Summary of State Chapter 1 Participation* (1992).
Note: The total number of participants reported by race and ethnicity differs from the total number of participants reported by states.
[a]Figures do not include participants in Peurto Rico. Native Americans are included in the total but not in the racial-ethnic categories.

states' high rates drive up the national rate of participation in Chapter 1 by LEP students (U.S. Department of Education 1993).

In sum, national data indicate that LEP students are not underrepresented in Chapter 1. But when we disaggregate these data by state and, as shown below, by city, we find substantial variation from place to place. This suggests a need to examine LEP participation in Chapter 1 at the district level.

Table 4.7
Race and Ethnicity of Poor Children and of Chapter 1 Enrollees, 1989–90

	Percentage of All Poor Children	Percentage of All Poor, Low-Achieving Children	Percentage of Chapter 1 Enrollees
White (not Hispanic)	40.7	43.8	43
Black (not Hispanic)	33.7	29.5	29
Hispanic	20.7	21.6	23
Asian	2.9	1.5	3
LEP	11.0		12

Sources: U.S. Census 1980; Current Population Survey 1989; Westat, Inc.; National Center for Education Statistics, National Educational Longitudinal Survey.

FOUR URBAN SCHOOL DISTRICTS

The portrait of a national program that seems to adjust to demographic trends masks what appears to be substantial variability at the local level, as well as the degree to which the allocation of Chapter 1 resources represents contested political and institutional terrain.

Our exploration of Chapter 1 and demographic trends in Boston, Houston, Oakland, and Washington, D.C., shows several patterns. In general, Hispanic and Asian poverty rates rose far more rapidly during the 1980s in these four cities than did either white or black poverty rates. Concentrated poverty among Hispanics exploded during the decade in each of the four sites; still, the number of blacks in concentrated poverty was roughly twice that of Hispanics in all four cities. The population of LEP students in each city's school system either expanded substantially or, in Houston, remained at an already high level.

In these four cities, Chapter 1 resources have been extended to limited-English-proficient populations when legal or political pressure has been brought to bear; when it has not, LEP enrollment has lagged. The trend of expanding the number of Chapter 1 beneficiaries has meant that increased enrollment of Hispanics, Asians, and LEP students has not led to any apparent direct displacement of blacks in the four sites examined.

Inclusion of LEP students has contributed, along with other factors, to a reduction in the per-pupil allocation of Chapter 1 dollars, however. The effects of new LEP students in Chapter 1 coincide with broad increases in the population of non-LEP students in the program. This expansion has been driven by a switch from an individual pullout approach to a schoolwide service delivery strategy and by the entry into the program of large numbers of Hispanics and blacks who do not have English-language deficiencies. The broad expansion in recipient populations raises questions about what being served by the program actually means.

Immigrant and LEP Populations

Despite the fact that only one of the four cities examined is usually associated with large-scale immigration (Houston), each had comparatively high levels of immigration over the past decade. Indeed, by 1990, a higher share of both Boston's and Oakland's populations was foreign-born than was Houston's. And in each of the four cities, a majority of the foreign-born had arrived during the past decade, demonstrating a rapid demographic transformation.

Not surprisingly, these trends altered the ethnic composition of the four school districts, where, between 1987 and 1990 alone, the Hispanic population grew from 16 to 25 percent. At the same time, both the white and the black student populations declined in three of the four cities. The change in the Asian population was more mixed, rising rather sharply in two (in Boston, by 12 percent; in Oakland, by 18 percent) and declining in two (in Houston, by 7 percent; in Washington, by 5 percent).

In the 1980s the LEP population grew by more than 300 percent in Oakland, Boston, and Washington. In Houston, the only site where the number did not rise dramatically, the school system already enrolled 37,000 LEP students in 1980, a population three-fourths the size of the entire Oakland Unified School District.

Such students now make up a sizable share of each district's total school population. One-quarter of Oakland's and more than one-third of Boston's total populations are now LEP students—proportions that exceed even Houston's and that certainly depart from our own preconceptions as to the representation of immigrant and LEP children in these school districts.

Trends in Poverty

We found sharply divergent patterns between the studied cities and the nation as a whole with regard to trends in child poverty. In the northeastern cities, Washington, D.C., and Boston, the total number of poor children decreased by 31 and 22 percent, respectively, over the course of the decade, in large part because of population declines in the central city. In both places the number of poor Asian and Hispanic children rose while the number of poor black and white children fell.

In Houston and Oakland, as for the nation as a whole, the number of poor children grew rapidly during the 1980s—by almost 20 percent in Oakland and by 64 percent in Houston. In each case very large proportional increases in the Asian and Hispanic child poverty rates were recorded. At the start of the 1980s, there were more than two poor black children in Houston for every poor Hispanic child. By the end of the decade, poor Hispanic children outnumbered poor black children despite a 27 percent rise in the number of poor black children.

The 1990 census shows that in Boston, Oakland, and Houston, more than 20 percent of poor children have limited English proficiency. At the same time, about 40 percent of all LEP children in each of those cities are poor. Their substantial share of the poverty population and high poverty rates underscore the legitimacy of LEP students' claims to Chapter 1 resources.

Poverty among foreign-born, recently arrived immigrants and among Hispanics and Asians has grown increasingly concentrated in each of the four sites. Given that Chapter 1 is intended to counteract concentrated poverty, this is perhaps the most striking finding of this study.

Analysis using the Urban Institute's underclass database reveals that the rate of growth in the foreign-born population in concentrated poverty (census tracts in which 40 percent or more of the population is below the poverty line) far outpaced that of the native-born population in all sites except Boston, where the two were roughly equivalent. In Washington, D.C., the share of the foreign-born population living in concentrated poverty rose by 282 percent, in Houston by 515 percent, and in Oakland by 240 percent during the 1980s. The data also suggest that a high proportion of recent immigrants are living in concentrated poverty.

Another demographic transformation of the central-city poverty population is the high, consistent pattern of growing concentration of poverty among Hispanics. This population grew by 222 percent in Washington, by 70 percent in Boston, by 788 percent in Houston, and by 330 percent in Oakland during the 1980s. The implications of this growth for the implementation of Chapter 1 appear to us to be profound. Despite the explosive growth in concentrated poverty among Hispanics and Asians, however, the absolute numbers of blacks living in concentrated poverty in each of these four cities was far higher than the numbers of Hispanics and Asians.

Participation of LEP Students in Chapter 1

We turn now to the question that is the central focus of this chapter: To what extent does the growing number of LEP children in these four cities, many of whom presumably are poor, receive Chapter 1 services? The case studies suggest that LEP children are proportionately represented in Chapter 1 programs when the size of the language-minority population reaches the critical mass necessary to exert political influence or when the parents of LEP children sue the school district. Thus, LEP children have not participated in the Chapter 1 program in Washington and, until recently, in Boston. They have, however, been largely integrated into compensatory education programs in Houston and Oakland. This suggests something of a regional phenomenon. If these cities are representative of their regions, then in the West and the Southwest, where LEP school populations are larger and better established, the distribution of resources under this federal grant program has been targeted differently than in the East, where the LEP population is usually smaller and more diverse. Indeed, there is a national trend toward serving LEP students in Chapter 1 when they are present in large numbers and excluding them when they are not, according to the Prospects study. We begin with the least inclusive district (Washington), then move along a continuum to what is arguably the most inclusive (Houston).

WASHINGTON, D.C.

Washington, D.C., has the smallest LEP population of the four cities, but it is growing quickly. Unlike each of the other cities, Washington, until recently, had felt little political or legal pressure to integrate LEP children in special programs other than bilingual education.

Washington has also lagged behind the other cities in this study in its efforts to collect data on LEP students, despite the need to do so to satisfy federal requirements. Indeed, it was not until October 1991 that the city conducted its first home language survey, which counted the language-minority students in the system. Similar surveys had been conducted for ten years or longer in each of the other three cities. Without a clear sense of the size and location of the language-minority population, there was little appreciation for their needs or how they could best be met.

Our research suggests that the low representation of LEP students in Chapter 1 is explained by several factors. First, the parents of many immigrant students do not sign the free-lunch forms used to count Chapter 1–eligible children because the forms are too burdensome, because they are badly translated or not translated at all, or because of a general fear of government forms. As a result, some schools in which LEP students are concentrated are not eligible for Chapter 1 funds, and others receive fewer funds than they could be entitled to. In addition, receipt of Chapter 1 services historically has been contingent on low scores on the California Test of Basic Skills and on being held back a grade level. According to school policy, the test was not administered to LEP students because of their limited language ability, and LEP students were initially placed in classes according to their age. With no alternative test in the students' native languages and no way to know if they were in fact behind grade level, LEP students ended up being excluded from Chapter 1.[1]

Limited representation of LEP children in the program is also explained in part by the unusual institutional arrangements in that city. In Washington, the Chapter 1 program is, for the most part, a separate program in the school system, with its own administrators and instructional staff. Its teachers answer to its administrators, not to school principals. It has been claimed that this unit operates largely independently and that its leadership has viewed the education of LEP students as the responsibility of the system's Language Minority Affairs Branch. Some have also observed that the principal vehicle of instruction employed by Chapter 1 in the district—pullout remedial instruction using computer programs in English—does not lend itself to teaching LEP children.

In the spring of 1993, the school district formed a task force on Chapter 1 and language-minority students specifically to address the issue of LEP students' inclusion in the program. As a result of the precedent set by a lawsuit in Boston (see below) as well as pressure from the Language Minority Affairs Branch and the community, the district appears poised to take steps to incorporate LEP students in Chapter 1 programs.

BOSTON

Boston, like Washington, historically has not served LEP students in its Chapter 1 program. In the 1990–1991 school year, for example, LEP students constituted 23 percent of the total enrollment of the Boston Public Schools but only 4 percent (576 children) of recipients of Chapter 1 services. As in Washington, the test (Metropolitan Achievement Test) that was used to determine program eligibility was typically not given to LEP students.

In 1991, however, the Boston Public Schools were the target of a lawsuit that called for Chapter 1 services to be distributed to LEP students in a manner that would reflect their representation among the educationally disadvantaged (*Boston Master Parents Advisory Council et al. v. Boston Public Schools,* USDC Mass, C.A. No. 91—11725-Z). The plaintiffs largely prevailed, and the school system signed a consent agreement that would reallocate a share of Chapter 1 resources to LEP students.

The school system's response to the lawsuit has been striking, to say the least. Between 1990 and 1992, the number of LEP students counted as Chapter 1 recipients rose from 576 to 9,506, and the LEP share of total Chapter 1 recipients rose from 4 percent to 43 percent (see Boston Public Schools 1993). Under Boston's revised regulations, all students who score below the 46th percentile on the tests used to determine eligibility for Chapter 1, as well as all children who do not take the tests, are eligible for the program.[2]

This jump in LEP enrollment happened in large part because the Boston public schools altered their approach to delivering Chapter 1 services from an individual, remedial approach to a schoolwide strategy. This approach follows the main reform trend in the field of Chapter 1: to provide comparatively unconstrained resources to schools in which 75 percent of the students are poor. Chapter 1 funds no longer must be spent only on the subset of a school population that is eligible for Chapter 1 but can also be used to benefit all students in the school.

The Boston experience raises questions about the degree to which LEP students (or other special-needs populations, for that matter) are actually being served, as opposed to simply being counted within schoolwide programs. Will the schoolwide strategy turn out to be a catalyst for educational reform? Or does it simply represent a new accounting method that is intended to deflect legal and political pressure? Indeed, is it fair to count all students in a schoolwide Chapter 1 program as "served"? The Boston school system has considered counting only students who would have been served under the pullout system. As more schools provide schoolwide services, the issues of how to count the number of participants, how to interpret expenditures per pupil, and what instructional reforms to adopt within schoolwide programs become issues for the Chapter 1 program nationally.

OAKLAND

Oakland reflects the demographic transformation of California. Of the city's student population, 30 percent is language minority and 25 percent is not proficient in English. It is unusually diverse, being composed of comparatively even shares of Mexicans, Central Americans, Chinese, Laotians, and Cambodians. As in Boston, the experience in Oakland confirms the power of legal action to spur the distribution of Chapter 1 resources to LEP children: virtually the entire eligible LEP population is served by the school district's compensatory education program. The universal extension of service results from (1) earlier litigation (*Zambrano v. Oakland Unified School District*) intended to ensure that LEP students were provided with a program of quality bilingual education, (2) the ongoing and often contentious implementation of the settlement agreement reached in that suit, and (3) the way in which recipients of Chapter 1 services are counted in Oakland (and all of California).

The focus of the litigation was on ensuring that the Oakland school district recruit and hire a sufficient number of bilingual-education teachers to meet the state requirement that all students needing native-language instructional services receive them. We believe that the issues raised by the case, along with the attention it focused on the needs and rights of LEP students, contributed to the proportional inclusion of LEP students in the district's compensatory education programs. In short, *Zambrano* can be viewed as having prepared the ground for the equal distribution of compensatory education services in Oakland.

To grant the claim that virtually all poor LEP children in Oakland receive Chapter 1 services, one has to accept a rather broad formulation of Chapter 1 that includes compensatory education services supported not just under the federal program but also under the state Education Impact Assistance Program. Recipients of services under both programs are pooled for reporting purposes in California.

Although district officials see LEP students as being eligible for compensatory education services, they feel constrained about the type of services that they can provide with different streams of funding. Specifically, they avoid using Chapter 1 funds to provide LEP students with remedial or supplementary ESL or native-language instruction and instead use state funds to provide such services. At minimum, this approach complicates program administration.

As one outcome of the *Zambrano* settlement agreement, Oakland has begun to test students in their native languages to determine their basic skill levels. Tests are given in six major languages. Ironically, this may reduce the number of LEP students eligible for Chapter 1 services. Historically, all LEP children in a low-income school who were deemed to be educationally disadvantaged were eligible for Chapter 1. If these tests reveal that a student is performing at grade level in his or her native language, however, then he or she becomes ineligible for compensatory education.

HOUSTON

Houston reflects the force of political rather than legal pressure to include LEP children in Chapter 1. In 1987, more than 10,000 LEP students, or 32 percent of the total LEP population, received Chapter 1 services. By 1991, 19,400, or 49 percent, of all LEP students were receiving services.

The political story here is one of numbers. From 1987 to 1992 the school system went from being a majority black district to a majority Hispanic district. In 1990 the school system's first-grade cohort was 65 percent Hispanic, a development that had been predicted for the year 2000. Only Houston of the four cities examined began the decade with both a large number and a large share of LEP students in its school system: it enrolled 37,000 LEP students in 1980 and 38,000 in 1990.

These changes have had important institutional effects. In 1989, for example, the Chapter 1 program was removed from the Houston Independent School District's Division of Curriculum and Instruction and placed under the control of the Superintendent for Multilingual Education in what is now called the Division of Multilingual and Compensatory Education. This has tended to give the program much more of an orientation toward LEP and language-minority students. Reflecting the size and influence of the district's Hispanic population, the achievement tests that are used to determine eligibility for Chapter 1 services are administered in both Spanish and English in Houston.

Effects of Demographic Change

We posited that one possible outcome of demographic change would be either the exclusion of newcomers from Chapter 1 or the displacement of established beneficiaries from the program. As we look across the four case study cities, we see no evidence of displacement. The small LEP population in Washington, along with the historical absence of either political or legal pressure, has meant that LEP students can be viewed as having been underserved by, and in large part, excluded from the program. Correlatively, this has meant that there has been no displacement of traditional beneficiary groups.

In the other three cities, legal and political pressure has been met or anticipated by the broad inclusion of LEP students within Chapter 1. Thus, the Oakland, Houston, and Boston school districts have adjusted to claims of legal or political entitlement by expanding their Chapter 1 programs without displacing established beneficiaries. This comports with the national trends observed earlier of broadening the base of Chapter 1 recipients rather than increasing allocations per participant. By expanding the number of beneficiaries, the most politically difficult questions of ethnic competition have been deflected.

This expansion has been accomplished, in part, by shifting from an individualized service delivery approach to a schoolwide model, permitting schools to rapidly increase the number of students they claim to serve under Chapter 1 without substantial new resources. In Houston, for example, enrollment in Chapter 1 almost doubled between 1987 and 1992, growing from 32,000 to 59,000. In Boston, reported enrollment in the program nearly doubled in one year, going from 13,248 in 1990–1991 to 22,210 in 1991–1992. The share of both LEP and non-LEP students enrolled in schoolwide programs is substantial in both Houston and Washington and encompasses virtually the entire Chapter 1 population of Boston.

In sum, the inclusion of LEP students and other new populations does not appear to displace native blacks. In Boston, for example, there was a 13 percent rise in the number of blacks receiving Chapter 1 services during the 1980s, despite a decline in the number of blacks in poverty during that decade. And in Houston, the distribution of Chapter 1 resources in the public schools remains closely calibrated to the racial and ethnic breakdown of the school district's population as a whole, despite a dramatic rise in Hispanic poverty. (We were unable to conduct this kind of analysis in Oakland because the racial and ethnic breakdown of Chapter 1 recipients was not readily available.)

The entry of LEP students into Chapter 1 does not appear to have led to the direct displacement of established beneficiary groups. But what are the implications of the entry of LEP students into Chapter 1 for per-pupil expenditures and the intensity of services that are delivered? Given the limits of the data that we collected, we can only say that the participation of LEP students in Chapter 1 has had small or no effects on expenditures in Washington but has contributed to reduced per-pupil spending in Boston and Houston. (Again, data limitations do not permit this kind of analysis for Oakland.) It is difficult to determine, however, what share of the reduction in per-pupil spending is due to increased numbers of LEP students and what share is due to a general expansion in Chapter 1 enrollment and to the shift to schoolwide services, in which all students in a school are counted as served.

An analysis of the estimated change in dollars allocated per participant (a rough approximation for per-pupil spending) shows that allocations have risen in Washington, where Chapter 1 enrollment has fallen over time and where LEP students are as yet the least fully integrated into the Chapter 1 program. In Boston, per-pupil allocations rose during the 1980s, before many LEP students were included in Chapter 1 and while funding to the school district was increasing. Following implementation of the court settlement and the concurrent broad expansion in schoolwide programs, however, Chapter 1 participation rose rapidly—from 13,000 in 1990 to 35,000 participants in 1992 (270 percent)— and per-pupil allocations fell sharply. In Houston, the inclusion of LEP students in Chapter 1 and an increase in the number of schoolwide programs also dramatically lowered per-pupil allocations between 1987 and 1991. It must be emphasized, however, that these figures assume that all participants in Chapter 1 receive equivalently intensive services. We have no way of knowing whether that is the case or whether the established beneficiary populations continue to benefit disproportionately from the program. It should also be emphasized that these reductions in per-pupil allocations are the result of including low-achieving LEP students who are, and have been, eligible for Chapter 1 but who were previously excluded from the program.

The shift from an individualized approach to instruction to a schoolwide approach begs the question: Has the arrival of newcomer populations effectively hastened a potentially important reform of Chapter 1? Or has it simply led to new, and perhaps somewhat inflated, counts of program beneficiaries? We cannot answer these questions on the strength of this small-scale study. But we can make several observations on developments within the four sites visited and recommend further study of the implications of a shift to schoolwide Chapter 1 programs for special-needs populations.

Proponents of schoolwide programs, such as Robert Slavin, argue that they can represent an important reform of Chapter 1 when used for effective staff development. Slavin contends that the payoff from improving teacher skills is likely to be higher than that associated with providing low-achieving children with an hour or two of remedial instruction per week, in part because under a pullout approach the removal of a child from the classroom can not only disrupt the flow of the student's day, it can also have a stigmatizing effect. From an administrative perspective, being forced to parcel out Chapter 1 resources—from pencils and paper to field trips—only to Chapter 1 students is difficult and inefficient. For these and other reasons the shift to a schoolwide approach could be positive for both LEP and other students.

But it is not at all clear that the movement to schoolwide instruction will meet the distinctive educational needs of disadvantaged LEP children. In Boston, for example, one school administrator told us that the real incentive to adopting a schoolwide approach was "relief from regulatory compliance." And although Boston has responded to the court decree by hiring twenty additional teachers to provide native-language and ESL instruction to LEP children under Chapter 1, on a school-level basis this change does not necessarily translate into appropriate services for all LEP students. In one school, for instance, there is only one native-language Chapter 1 teacher for nearly three hundred Chapter 1–eligible LEP students.

In Houston, serving LEP children in schoolwide programs (or even in individual pullout programs) is complicated by the larger problem of finding and paying bilingual teachers. We were told that the Houston school district does not hire certified bilingual teachers for the Chapter 1 program because of regulatory constraints on paying the kind of salary supplement that is routinely offered to bilingual teachers to recruit them to the district.[3]

Our interviews with staff and administrators in the four districts did not provide evidence that important curricular or other innovations designed to meet the needs of LEP students had been systematically introduced in their Chapter 1 programs. (We did not study differences in individual schools, however, and were able to learn only about general, districtwide patterns.) From an instructional standpoint, the most common uses to which Chapter 1 funds were put, when they were used to serve LEP students, were to purchase instructional materials in Spanish and to hire bilingual aides. Whereas the former is unarguably a valuable way to spend Chapter 1 dollars, the merits of the latter are currently the subject of debate in education circles.

This is not to say that schoolwide programs cannot lead to highly innovative strategies for assisting LEP and newcomer students. In Albuquerque, New Mexico, for example, one school used its Chapter 1 funds to improve collaborative planning among teachers and increase parental involvement. To accomplish the latter, the school set aside a classroom and created a parent center where the Chapter 1 parents could make phone calls, do laundry, learn computer skills, and the like.

IMPLICATIONS FOR REAUTHORIZATION OF CHAPTER 1

In this section we draw some implications for the reform of Chapter 1 of the results we have reported.

The delivery of appropriate remedial and other instruction both in and outside the context of Chapter 1 depends on reliable assessment instruments. With the exception of Spanish, however, we found that school districts were attempting to cobble together their own native-language tests in languages ranging from Portuguese to Lao, often unaware whether a suitable test was available in another school district or state. Given the expanding diversity and numbers of immigrants, and the scale economies of developing and later distributing such tests, there is a strong argument for expanding the federal role in this area. If such tests do not exist, they could be centrally developed for the most commonly spoken languages. Where they do exist, consideration might be given to distributing them more broadly.

We have shown that the LEP population is growing especially rapidly in the nation's urban schools. We have also shown that there is a notable increase in the number and share of the foreign-born who are now living in areas of concentrated poverty in the four studied cities. These findings suggest that further concentrating Chapter 1 funds in disadvantaged neighborhoods and schools in the nation's central cities would greatly benefit the foreign-born, Hispanic, LEP, and, to a lesser extent, Asian populations. The growing share of children in concentrated poverty who have limited English proficiency also underscores the importance of adapting Chapter 1 services to the needs of newcomer populations.

Chapter 1 is currently distributed through a two-part formula based on two different poverty indicators. One (basic grants) allocates aid according to the number of low-income children in a state. The other (concentration grants) allocates aid on the basis of the concentration of low-income children in a state. Concentration grants represented only 8.3 percent of total Chapter 1 outlays in fiscal 1990 (Barro 1991). One strategy for concentrating Chapter 1 funding in disadvantaged schools or communities would be to allocate a greater share of total Chapter 1 spending to concentration grants. Another would be to combine basic and concentration grants and allocate a single stream of funds to school districts with the greatest concentration of poverty.

As Barro also points out, the choice of the metric used to distribute such aid has powerful effects on the jurisdictions that emerge as winners and losers. One approach to adjusting the formula that appears to reward urban districts, as well as the states that have absorbed the largest numbers of immigrants over the past decade, is to raise the threshold level of the share and number of children in poverty in an individual community. These changes would tilt funding toward large, urbanized areas, with more aid going to California and Massachusetts (Barro 1991, 4–35).

Because Chapter 1 uses the decennial census to allocate funds, Chapter 1 dollars for the 1992–1993 school year were allocated mainly on the basis of the national distribution of poor children in 1980. This distribution does not reflect the high level of immigration that took place over the intervening decade. More important, the general approach of allocating resources on the basis of census data fails to account for the kind of rapid, concentrated growth often associated with immigration. Indeed, through the 1980s and 1990s, the states that have been penalized most by this counting strategy have been California and Texas—the states that have absorbed the largest numbers of immigrants and that together enroll 82 percent of all LEP participants in Chapter 1.

Severing the link between the Chapter 1 allocation formula and the decennial census count of poor children begs the question of what alternative data might be used. One such measure would be the number of children receiving support under Aid to Families with Dependent Children. This is an especially inappropriate measure for new immigrants, however, many of whom are barred from or rarely receive these payments. Another commonly advanced alternative measure is the number of students receiving free or reduced-price lunches. As Barro (1991) points out, though, there are numerous problems with this strategy. One is that it would introduce a new, looser standard, because poverty thresholds for free or reduced lunches are set at 130 or 185 percent of the dollar figure that demarcates the poverty line.

One promising approach that has been advanced by the Census Bureau would be to use the tax and social security records that are now used to annually update the bureau's population estimates. This information, when supplemented with data from other sources, such as Food Stamp Program record files, could help to identify trends in income and poverty status over time across different local jurisdictions (Ruggles 1993).

Our research has shown that school districts often do not serve LEP students in Chapter 1 unless they are pushed to do so through political or legal channels. This finding suggests that some monitoring to ensure that LEP students receive a proportionate share of Chapter 1 services may be advisable. This recommendation holds both for traditional programs and, especially, for schoolwide programs, in which it is difficult to tell what "being served" really means. Finally, we see a need for further study of the services received by LEP students in schoolwide programs and for the broad dissemination of models of effective schoolwide programs for LEP children. Schoolwide programs could also help school districts overcome the fragmentation of resources used for the education of LEP children, which has also been noted in other reports and studies (Westat 1991, 1992; Stanford Working Group 1993). This fragmentation is most noticeable in the lack of coordination among Chapter 1, bilingual education, and migrant education programs at the school, district, and state levels.

EPILOGUE: 1998

At the time this chapter was originally drafted, the Chapter 1 program and the Elementary and Secondary Education Act were poised to be reauthorized. In 1994, Congress undertook a massive overhaul of the law, shifting its focus from remedial education to high standards and high achievement.[4] Not only has the remedial, "pull-out" character of instruction typically offered under the program changed, but the new law made clear that special accommodations were to be made for assessing and educating LEP children. That said, we believe that the issues of competitive dilution in allocating education funding, and the failure of many schools to meet the needs of immigrant and LEP students, persist, not just in the Title 1 program but in elementary and secondary education generally.[5]

Chapter 5 Immigrants, Puerto Ricans, and the Earnings of Native Black Males

Thomas J. Espenshade

The United States is in the midst of a second great wave of immigration that rivals in size the immigration to this country in the first decade of the twentieth century. The number of foreign-born individuals living in the United States grew by more than 50 percent between 1980 and 1990, reaching a total of 21.6 million at the last census—up from 14.1 million in 1980. At the same time, the proportion of the U.S. population born in other countries—a proportion that had fallen to a historic low of 4.7 percent in 1970—since then climbed steadily, to nearly 9 percent by 1990 (Kennedy 1992). By 1997, the foreign-born population in the United States totaled 25.8 million persons, or 9.7 percent of the civilian noninstitutional population (Schmidley and Alvarado 1998).

What are the consequences for American society of such a large and concentrated wave of immigrants? To be sure, hardly any aspect of our culture remains untouched, whether one considers the food we eat, our styles of dress, the music we listen to, the mix of languages we speak, or the religions we practice. Despite America's celebrated history as a nation of immigrants, whenever sizable numbers of migrants arrive, they evoke deeply rooted feelings about their effects on the labor market (Abowd and Freeman 1991; Borjas and Freeman 1992). The current flow has grown so large that it is raising concerns among some natives that major action might be necessary to protect American workers. Blue-collar workers fear that new immigrants are taking their jobs and contributing to higher unemployment; others worry that immigrants lower the wages and working conditions of American workers (Espenshade and Calhoun 1992).

The occupational distribution of recent immigrants has shifted toward the low-skilled end of the scale in the past two or three decades (Greenwood and McDowell 1986). This results largely from the changing national origin mix of the immigrant flow, rather than from declining skill levels within particular racial or ethnic immigrant groups (Borjas 1991; LaLonde and Topel 1991a). These trends raise questions about the effects of recent immigration on the least-skilled members of the native-born work force.

While the volume of U.S. immigration and the proportion of immigrants with few or no skills were growing, income distribution was exhibiting increasing inequality. Earnings inequality remained relatively stable throughout the 1970s but then grew rapidly in the 1980s (Levy and Murnane 1992). After 1979 the declining education premium reversed direction, and there was also a collapse in the wages of younger high school graduates and dropouts. Part of the collapse reflected an inward shift in the demand for low-skilled workers, arising from increased import competition in U.S. markets. Murphy and Welch (1988) and Borjas, Freeman, and Katz (1992), for example, argue that rising levels of foreign imports reduced the demand for domestic low-skill U.S. labor because imports were more intensive in unskilled labor than were exports. In addition, however, an increased volume of immigration contributed a supply-related explanation for the increase in the earnings premium associated with formal education because immigrants have less formal education, on average, than native-born Americans (Levy and Murnane 1992). Thus, because recent immigrants are now a significant fraction of less-educated workers in many cities, it is reasonable to ask whether declines in the real earnings of the least skilled workers in the U.S. economy are related to the effects of immigration (Butcher and Card 1991).

As Smith and Welch (1989) have shown, black males in the United States have since 1940 been making considerable economic progress—both in absolute terms and relative to white males. In 1940 the typical black male worker earned 43 percent as much as a white male; by 1980 the relative wage gap had decreased to 73 percent. Overall, gains occurred all along the income distribution, and a substantial black middle class developed over this period. The one notable exception is black males in the bottom 10 percent of the income distribution, who have generally failed to share in these overall gains.

These considerations have prompted many economists to propose that native-born blacks are perhaps more likely than any other class of worker to be adversely affected by U.S. immigration (Muller and Espenshade 1985; Morris 1985; Greenwood and McDowell 1986; LaLonde and Topel 1991b). This chapter explores this hypothesis further by bringing state-level information to bear on the question of how immigrants influence the earnings of native black males. Its major conclusion is that 1980 census data from New Jersey fail to provide any evidence that variations in the concentration of immigrants in local labor markets are associated with the annual earnings or weekly wages of native blacks, once controls for other relevant factors have been introduced. On the other hand, the chapter does find that the presence of Puerto Ricans in New Jersey lowers the wages and earnings of native blacks. The next section briefly reviews the existing literature on immigrants' effects on the earnings and employment of native black workers. Following that the data and general methodological approach are described. Results are discussed next, and then the chapter's main findings are summarized.

EFFECTS OF IMMIGRATION: FINDINGS AND BELIEFS

Historical evidence suggests that immigrants once had a direct negative effect on the wages and working conditions of less-skilled native workers (Williamson 1982). Indirectly, however, immigrants may have boosted natives' wages by enabling the United States to capitalize on positive economic returns to scale that were thought to exist in the U.S. economy at least until about 1920. Hill (1975) estimated that, during the period from 1840 to 1880, the existence of a 10 percent scale economy would have been sufficient to cause immigration over the same interval to raise per capita income by about 3 percent. Others have noted that long swings in black internal migration were associated with long swings in white immigration. For example, when blacks and recent immigrants were close labor market substitutes, black rural-to-urban migration fluctuated inversely with the main immigration flows to larger urban areas (Reder 1963; Thomas 1973). Reder (1963, 227) argued that immigration jeopardized employment opportunities for native workers: "A greater flow of immigration will injure labor market competitors with immigrants; these are, predominantly, Negroes and

Puerto Ricans." For many decades prior to 1900, most black migration occurred within the South, but the sharp reduction in European migration in the 1920s radically altered this pattern. The major South-North black migration that was under way by 1910 picked up momentum after 1940. Because prevailing wages were higher in the North, there were direct wage gains to migration. Between 1940 and 1980, black South-North migration raised average black wages between 11 and 19 percent and represented one of the most important factors accounting for a smaller black-white wage differential during this period (Smith and Welch 1989).

Much of the rhetoric in the contemporary period would lead one to conclude that recent immigrants and native blacks are still strong labor market substitutes. According to Graham and Beck (1992, 215): "While the massive immigration provides cheap labor that benefits a well-to-do portion of Americans, it depresses living conditions for the working classes in ways that disproportionately harm black citizens." These authors believe that immigration has contributed to the deteriorating economic and social conditions of inner-city blacks and that large numbers of African Americans have been displaced from jobs owing to the importation of low-skilled foreign workers.

Wieck (1992, 217) agrees that the problems of unskilled U.S. workers have been exacerbated by unskilled immigrants: "Illegal workers often live in crowded, marginal housing, and bid down the wage scale in local markets. This competition for low-paid jobs feeds the rage of native blacks and Hispanics in neighborhoods like South Central Los Angeles." Without supporting their views, other authors also believe that illegal immigration was partially responsible for the Los Angeles riots in May 1992 because blacks have lost to new immigrants (Francis 1992; Luttwak 1992).

Although the available ethnographic data are limited, there is some support for the hypothesis of labor market competition between immigrants and native blacks. Tienda and Liang (1992) claim that there is growing evidence that immigrants compete with domestic workers. Their review of evidence from the Chicago Urban Poverty and Family Life Study suggests that increased competition with immigrants has contributed to the labor market exclusion of blacks. Field studies conducted in Houston in 1983, 1985, and 1990 at different phases of the business cycle also suggest considerable job displacement of Americans and legal immigrant workers by illegal immigrants (Huddle 1992a, 1992b). Harrison (1992) cites as an example the fact that in Los Angeles building maintenance workers were once predominately black but are now mostly Mexican immigrants. In a contrary finding, however, Portes and Zhou (1991) show how immigrant industries not only facilitate the social and economic integration of Asians but also can generate jobs for inner-city blacks. In contrast, however, most econometric analyses of large-scale census or sample survey data do not substantiate the hypothesis of strong adverse effects from immigration on either the earnings or the employment opportunities of low-skilled native workers in general or native blacks in particular.

In research that has examined employment effects, the reported estimates of aggregate labor supply elasticities are relatively small. Borjas and Heckman (1979) suggest that uncompensated wage elasticities for prime-age males lie in a relatively narrow range—between -0.07 and -0.19—and that compensated elasticities fall between 0.04 and 0.20. These labor supply elasticities refer to the percentage change in the quantity of labor supplied for a 1 percentage point change in the wage rate. "Compensated elasticities" refers to elasticities holding income (or wealth) constant, whereas "uncompensated" refers to the case where total income is allowed to vary as the wage rate varies. In both cases, however, reported labor supply elasticities are close to zero, suggesting that labor supply is relatively unresponsive to changes in the wage rate. These estimates imply that the effect of immigration on domestic employment levels is small (Greenwood and McDowell 1986).

Johnson (1979) projected that employment levels among low-skilled domestic workers would fall only slightly with immigration, although the effects were more likely to be concentrated in recessions and among minority youth. Johnson (1980) found evidence for a labor market displacement rate of about 10 percent. Grossman (1984) used a two-sector labor market model to examine the effects of illegal immigrants: If wages paid to domestic unskilled workers are fixed at the minimum wage level, which is assumed to be higher than the market clearing wage, then more immigration implies greater unemployment of native unskilled workers.

Altonji and Card (1991) found that the degree of competition between immigrants and less-skilled natives varies by race and sex and is greatest for black females and least for black males. The overall results, however, suggest only a modest degree of competition. Immigrants generally are not sufficiently concentrated in the industries that employ less-skilled natives to have large effects. For example, Altonji and Card estimated that a 1 percentage point increase in a city's share of immigrants generates approximately a 1 percent increase in the supply of labor to industries in which less-skilled natives are employed. They conclude that there is essentially no effect of increased immigration on the participation or employment rates of less-skilled natives.

Muller and Espenshade examined the effect of Mexican immigration on black Americans in southern California. Comparative trends in labor force participation rates and unemployment rates over the period 1970–82 in Los Angeles, the state of California, and the United States for black teenagers, black adults, and all persons suggest that blacks generally, and black teenagers especially, do not appear to have been harmed by immigration. In regression analyses using 1980 census data for 247 metropolitan areas across the United States and a smaller sample of 51 cities in California, New Mexico, Texas, and Arizona, black unemployment rates were not increased—and perhaps were lowered— by a rise in the proportion of Mexican immigrants in a local labor market.

In considering the effect of immigrants on the wages of less-skilled native workers, one observes large differences across cities in relative growth rates of wages for low- and high-paid workers, but these differences bear little or no relation to the size of immigrant inflows (Butcher and Card 1991). Consequently, there is little indication of negative wage effects of immigration, either in cross-sectional analysis or over time within cities. Even for workers at the bottom end of the wage distribution (that is, in the 10th percentile), there is no evidence of a significant decline in wages in response to immigrant inflows. Work by Grossman (1982) supports these findings.

Similar conclusions were reached by LaLonde and Topel (1991a, 1991b). They found that increased immigration has had relatively small effects on recent immigrants. For example, a doubling of the rate of new immigration to the typical standard metropolitan statistical area (SMSA) "reduces the wages of new immigrants by only 2.4 percent" (301). Effects on the wages and earnings of young black and Hispanic natives are so small as to be "economically negligible." There are essentially no effects on employment and unemployment in the sense that all of the effects of immigration on annual earnings come through its effects on wages. Overall, these authors conclude that any adverse effects of current immigration flows on U.S. labor markets and on native welfare will be small because most of the consequences will be felt by other immigrants.

Borjas (1984) used 1970 and 1980 census data to examine the impact of immigrants on the earnings of the native-born population. He found that male immigrants did not adversely affect—and indeed may have augmented—the earnings of any male native group. The beneficial effects of immigrant males were especially strong for black males, both young and old. In other words, black men were not the group most negatively affected by the entry of male immigrants into the labor market (Borjas 1985). Borjas did find, however, that women and men are strong substitutes in production, and the negative effect of females is particularly evident for older black males. But further disaggregation of these results showed that it is native-born, not foreign-born, women who have the most negative effects. In any case, the magnitude of the effects that Borjas estimated do not appear to be large: the earnings of older and younger white males would increase by less than 0.01 percent, and the earnings of black men would increase by less than 0.1 percent in response to a 1 percent rise in the supply of male immigrants.

Altonji and Card (1991) concluded that there is a negative effect from immigration on native wages, but the specific estimates depend on the group being studied and on one's methodological approach. An inflow of immigrants equal to 1 percent of the population of an SMSA reduces average weekly wages of less-skilled natives by about 1.2 percent. Least-squares estimates imply a more modest decline in the neighborhood of 0.3 percent.

Regional studies conducted in the American Southwest also generally fail to find negative wage effects of immigration. Bean, Lowell, and Taylor (1988) estimated the earnings effects on native workers from undocumented Mexican migration and concluded that the presence of a sizable undocumented population actually increased the earnings of other groups, although the magnitude of the effects was small. McCarthy and Valdez (1986) found that the negative labor market effects of immigrants in California have been minor and mainly limited to lower wages for native-born Hispanic workers. In a sample of U.S. cities, Muller and Espenshade (1985) found that increasing the proportion of Hispanics in a local labor market has a statistically significant negative effect on black family income, but the influence is not quantitatively important. For instance, raising the share of Hispanics from 5.0 to 7.5 percent equates to a fall in average black family income from $15,818 to $15,733—just $85 (in 1980 dollars). In the Southwest sample, raising the proportion of Mexican immigrants increases average black family income, but the effect is not statistically significant.

A LOCAL STUDY: NEW JERSEY BLACK MALES

Data and Methods

With few exceptions, studies of the labor market consequences of U.S. immigration have used national data. Immigrants are not uniformly distributed throughout the population, however, and some researchers *believe that this is* the reason why econometric work has failed to detect strong immigrant effects at the aggregate level (Smith and Newman 1977). One might rather expect that the largest effects would be for workers who are good substitutes for new immigrants not only in terms of skill level but also of location (Lalonde and Topel 1991a).

This chapter reports on a study of New Jersey, a state that ranked sixth in the nation in both 1980 and 1990 in the number of foreign-born residents (behind California, Texas, Florida, New York, and Illinois). Immigration accounted for 57 percent of the state's population growth between 1980 and 1990, in comparison with 34 percent for the entire country. Foreign-born residents in New Jersey numbered nearly 1 million in 1990, 12.5 percent of the state's 7.7 million residents. This was an increase from 1980, when there were approximately 750,000 foreign nationals, 10.3 percent of New Jersey's population of 7.4 million. By contrast, foreign-born persons comprised 6.2 and 8.7 percent of the U.S. population in 1980 and 1990, respectively. Roughly 40 percent of New Jersey's foreign-born population in 1990 had entered the United States since 1980, suggesting that the pace of immigration to the state was not slowing.

Few states in the nation experienced the dramatic shifts in racial and ethnic composition between 1980 and 1990 that New Jersey did. The white population stayed constant at 6.1 million, a decline from 83 to 79 percent, between 1980 and 1990, whereas the black population increased by 12.1 percent. During this decade, the Hispanic population grew by 50 percent and made up nearly 10 percent of the state's 1990 population; the Asian population increased by 162 percent—up from 104,000 in 1980 to 273,000 (New Jersey State Data Center 1992a).

The New Jersey study focused on the consequences of immigration for the earnings of black males. Data are drawn from the 5 percent microdata sample and pertain to native-born black males who were resident in New Jersey and aged 16–64 at the time of the 1980 census. Sample individuals were included in the analysis if they were members of the civilian labor force in 1980, had positive earnings (defined as the sum of wage and salary income and self-employment income from farm and nonfarm activities) in 1979, reported both their industry and occupation categories, and were not living in group quarters or enrolled in school in 1980. The resulting sample contains 7,160 cases.

The two response variables of major interest are annual earnings (defined above) and weekly wages, calculated as 1979 annual earnings divided by the number of weeks worked in 1979. All dollar quantities are measured from the 1980 census and are unadjusted for subsequent inflation. Distributions for the response variables are skewed to the right, with means of $13,358 and $294, respectively. Many black males reported working less than a full year.

The general strategy was to examine the determinants of black male annual earnings and weekly wages in New Jersey to see whether the concentration of immigrants in local area labor markets is negatively associated with the response variables after controlling for other individual and area-level determinants of earnings opportunities.

New Jersey has twenty-one counties. The 1980 census public-use microdata samples identify nineteen counties or county groups (formed by combining Hunterdon and Warren Counties into one group and Cape May and Salem Counties into another), and the study treats each of these nineteen county groups as a distinct local labor market. For each one, the following variables were calculated: the civilian (male, female, and total) unemployment rate, the size of the civilian labor market (the number of male, female, and total employed persons aged 16–64 in the civilian labor force), immigrants' share of the local labor market (defined as the percentage of employed persons aged 16–64 who are foreign-born), and the Puerto Rican share of the labor market (the percentage of employed persons aged 16–64 born in Puerto Rico). I chose to focus on Puerto Ricans because of their numerical significance in New Jersey. In the 1990 census, for example, 9.3 percent of New Jersey's population consisted of persons of Hispanic origin; 42 percent of these were Puerto Rican (New Jersey State Data Center 1992a), and 50 percent of the Puerto Rican population was born in Puerto Rico (New Jersey State Data Center 1992b). These contextual variables were then attached to the individual records for black males according to their county of residence.

The heaviest concentrations of immigrants in New Jersey occur in the five northeastern counties (Hudson, Passaic, Union, Essex, and Bergen) across the Hudson River from New York City and Staten Island. These counties—especially Hudson and Passaic—also include relatively high concentrations of Puerto Rican workers. Puerto Rican concentrations are also relatively high in Cumberland County, which is more rural and depends on Puerto Rican and other farm workers to harvest crops, and in Atlantic County, which is home to the tourist trade in and around Atlantic City. The greatest number of observations is drawn from Essex County, which includes Newark and the Oranges. Other New Jersey cities with large black populations include Jersey City (Hudson County), Patterson (Passaic County), Elizabeth (Union County), Trenton (Mercer County), and Camden (Camden County).

Additional explanatory variables pertaining to the individual demographic and socioeconomic characteristics of black males were also included in the analysis. Among these are the sample person's education (years of schooling completed), years of work experience (age minus education minus six), marital status, ethnicity, disability status, occupation (classified into ten categories), and industry (divided into eighteen groups), together with whether children under age eighteen are present in the household.

In modeling the dependence of annual earnings and weekly wages on a set of predictor variables, the analysis proceeded sequentially by including first the share of immigrants in the local labor market and then adding other groups of variables. In this way, I was able to concentrate on the importance of immigration as it affects the labor market opportunities of black males and to see whether the importance of this factor is diminished when other relevant explanatory variables are included.

Analysis and Results

In order to begin to explore the relation between immigrant concentrations in New Jersey labor markets and the earnings opportunities of native black males, I grouped the 7,160 observations by county of residence and computed indices of typical annual earnings and weekly wages for males within each county. These indices were then compared with the percentage of each county's employed labor force consisting of the foreign-born. If immigrants harm the earnings of black males in a particularly strong way, one should expect to find in these simple comparisons a negative relation between immigrant shares and both the earnings and wages of black males.

The results of several of these computations show that mean and median annual earnings and weekly wages of native-born blacks are lowest in counties such as Essex, which contains the city of Newark, and Hudson, in which in 1980 nearly one-third of the workforce was foreign-born. Reviewing the raw data thus gives the clear impression that black male earnings and wages are negatively associated with immigrants' share of a county's population. This impression is corroborated by the weighted (linear) correlation coefficients between black male earnings and immigrants' share. In each case, the correlation is negative, ranging from -0.19 to -0.40. At first glance, then, crude correlations seem to support the hypothesis that the presence of immigrants negatively affects the ability of black males to earn a livelihood.

These simple correlations are not all that one would want to know, of course, because there are presumably numerous other factors that may also affect earnings and wages, and one needs to control for them before concluding that immigrants have a net adverse effect. These other factors include the individual-level demographic and socioeconomic characteristics of black males, as well as the values of contextual variables reflecting general labor market conditions in each county. In the regression analysis, which incorporates the additional relations into a general linear model and estimates the resulting regression coefficients using ordinary least-squares (OLS) estimation, the two response variables were reformulated as the natural logarithms of annual earnings and of weekly wages. I estimated a series of successively expanded models for each response, beginning with a specification that included the immigrant share in each county as the sole predictor and then adding other predictors.

EARNINGS

When earnings are regressed on the immigrant share by itself, the regression coefficient is negative and statistically significant at the .05 level. The magnitude of the estimated effect suggests that a 1 percentage point increase in the fraction of the local workforce consisting of foreign-born persons is associated with an expected decline of about 0.4 percent in the annual earnings of New Jersey's black males. Although the effect is statistically significant, it is not large in absolute terms. When evaluated at the mean annual earnings of $13,358, a 0.4 percent decline corresponds to $53 per year (before taxes).

The negative effect of immigration is reduced when education (measured as the number of years of schooling completed) is included, and the effect becomes statistically insignificant after the further incorporation of years of work experience (age minus education minus six) and related higher-order terms. The industries in which black males are employed are introduced in the analysis through a set of seventeen indicator variables.[1] When industry variables are included, the net effect of immigrant share is once again negative and significant. One explanation for this reemergence of an effect for immigration is that immigrant share and industry variables are correlated. Specifically, immigrants are concentrated in the parts of New Jersey in which blacks are also employed in the higher-paying industries, so that immigrant share masks the (positive) effect of industry composition before the latter variables are explicitly included. The effect of immigrant share is apparently unaltered when nine indicator variables for occupation are introduced.[2] Adding variables for marital status (whether married and whether divorced), the presence of children in the household, and whether the sample person has a work-related disability maintains the significance of immigrant share.

Up to this point, each of the variables included beyond immigrant share pertains to individual characteristics of black males. In the final models, I incorporated two additional factors to capture overall labor market conditions: the county's male unemployment rate and the share of each county's employed workforce consisting of males born in Puerto Rico.[3] When the male unemployment rate is added, the effect of immigrant share is reduced only slightly. Removing the unemployment rate and adding the Puerto Rican male share in the labor market converts the effect of immigrant share from negative to positive, but it is statistically insignificant. When the unemployment rate is added back in, the effect of immigrant share is weaker than in any other specification, and it is also statistically insignificant. The conclusion I draw from the analysis is that the concentration of immigrants in local labor markets in New Jersey has no detectable effect on the annual earnings of black males, once the influence of other potentially important predictors is included.

The full model estimates are shown in table 5.1. The immigrant share is represented by the variable "immtot." The education variables, including linear, squared, and cubic terms, imply increasing returns to education through the completion of high school and diminishing returns thereafter.[4] The return to experience is also positive but diminishes with additional years of experience. With the exception of agriculture, most industries offer higher pay than construction (the reference group). Moreover, workers in service, laborer, and "other" occupations are among the most poorly paid. Marital status matters a great deal. Married black males have 42 percent higher average earnings than their never-married counterparts (everything else being the same), and being divorced carries a 21 percent earnings premium compared with never-married blacks. Males with a work disability suffer a 28 percent decline in annual earnings, and there is apparently a 5 percent earnings penalty associated with the percentage of children in the household.

The results from the two contextual variables are the most interesting. First, slack labor demand, reflected in higher local unemployment rates, reduces black male annual earnings. Each 1 percentage point increase in the male unemployment rate is associated with an expected additional 1.6 percent decline in annual earnings. Second, the Puerto Rican male share of the workforce is also negatively and significantly related to black earnings. Each 1 percentage point increase in the Puerto Rican male share is associated with an average additional decline in

Table 5.1
OLS Model for the Logarithm of Annual Earnings of Black Males in 1979

Predictors	Coefficient	Standard Error	t	P>|t|
immtot	.0003585	.002197	0.163	0.870
educ	−.1804611	.0370602	−4.869	0.000
educ2	.0202191	.0036284	5.572	0.000
educ3	−.000524	.0001101	−4.758	0.000
expernce	.0491355	.0031734	15.483	0.000
exper2	−.0007618	.0000637	−11.959	0.000
indagr	−.4244811	.1675679	−2.533	0.011
indmin	.1257656	.2559828	0.491	0.623
indfoo	.0653876	.0615568	1.062	0.288
indche	.2407689	.0554486	4.342	0.000
indpap	.2368882	.0607508	3.899	0.000
indmet	.252195	.0626717	4.024	0.000
indmac	.2362413	.0614166	3.847	0.000
indeqp	.4610137	.0730276	6.313	0.000
indoth	.072164	.0802424	0.899	0.369
indtrn	.3743981	.0507369	7.379	0.000
indcom	.2685524	.0576645	4.657	0.000
indwhl	.2265246	.0592512	3.823	0.000
indret	.0573082	.0527768	1.086	0.278
indfir	.1830117	.0674704	2.712	0.007
indrep	−.0514173	.0582913	−0.882	0.378
indent	.0212785	.0691259	0.308	0.758
indadm	.0824048	.0495588	1.663	0.096
occpro	.2878088	.0509964	5.644	0.000
oocmgr	.2600938	.0521329	4.989	0.000
occsal	.1010842	.0630697	1.603	0.109
occclr	.0713803	.0440195	1.622	0.105
occsrv	−.1322303	.0421029	−3.141	0.002
occrep	.1007403	.0382517	2.634	0.008
occtrn	.0243077	.0407851	0.596	0.551
occlab	−.1622051	.0424866	−3.818	0.000
occoth	−.3057521	.139499	−2.192	0.028
married	.4250899	.0304344	13.967	0.000
divorced	.2130353	.0358647	5.940	0.000
wkdisabl	−.2817214	.0472216	−5.966	0.000
children	−.0520782	.0227415	−2.290	0.022
unempm	−.0155835	.0074832	−2.082	0.037
prmale	−.0399759	.0193826	−2.062	0.039
cons	8.551397	.1457457	58.673	0.000

Source: 1980 census data.
$R^2 = 0.238$ $N = 7160$

annual earnings of 4 percent. This earnings loss is nontrivial and leads to the unanticipated conclusion that black males and males born in Puerto Rico are possibly close labor market substitutes in New Jersey. Thus, although there is no evidence in this study that immigrants lower the earnings of black males, Puerto Ricans and blacks may be in direct labor market competition.

WEEKLY WAGES

The approach was repeated for the response variable log of weekly wages. The effect of immigrant share is not reduced by the inclusion of any individual level characteristic or by the male unemployment rate. In each of the relevant specifications, the effect of immigration is negative and statistically significant at the .01 level, and the magnitude of the effect suggests that each 1 percentage point increase in immigrants' share of the labor market is associated with an expected decline of roughly 0.4 percent in weekly wages, or about $1.20 when evaluated at the weekly mean of $294.

The inclusion of Puerto Rican males in the analysis, however, reverses the conclusion. When this variable is added, the effect of immigrant share is essentially zero, and it is not close to being statistically significant by any conventional standard. Once again, one must conclude that there is no labor market competition between immigrants and black males. When other factors affecting the wages of blacks are introduced into the analysis, the contribution of immigration to explaining variation in black male wages is nonexistent.

Table 5.2 contains the detailed regression results to support this conclusion. The same set of predictor variables as in table 5.1 is used here. Most of these predictors are associated with wages and with annual earnings in the same way. Some of the exceptions are concentrated in such industry categories as retail trade, business repair, entertainment, and administration, all of which exhibit lower weekly wages than construction work, although there were no significant differences in terms of annual earnings. In comparison with annual earnings, the wage penalty associated with children has disappeared, and unemployment has a smaller effect on weekly wages than on annual earnings. The measured effect on wages of the Puerto Rican male share of the labor market is roughly of the same order of magnitude as its effect on annual earnings, however. A 1 percentage point increase in the male Puerto Rican component of the workforce is associated with an average 4.6 percent decline in black male weekly wages. This effect is statistically significant and reinforces the conclusion about labor market competition between blacks and Puerto Ricans.

Table 5.2
OLS Model for the Logarithm of Weekly Wages of Black Males in 1979

Predictors	Coefficient	Standard Error	t	P>|t|
immtot	.0000951	.0018462	0.052	0.959
educ	−.116864	.0311436	−3.752	0.000
educ2	.0125045	.0030492	4.101	0.000
educ3	−.0002897	.0000925	−3.130	0.002
expernce	.030103	.0026668	11.288	0.000
exper2	−.0004779	.0000535	−8.927	0.000
indagr	−.2987112	.1408157	−2.121	0.034
indmin	.1921812	.2151152	−0.893	0.372
indfoo	.0738602	.0517293	−1.428	0.153
indche	.0500668	.0465962	1.074	0.283
indpap	.0389777	.0510519	0.763	0.445
indmet	.0465124	.0526662	0.883	0.377
indmac	.0436077	.0516114	0.845	0.398
indeqp	.2748631	.0613688	4.479	0.000
indoth	−.0114867	.0674317	−0.170	0.865
indtrn	.1476996	.0426368	3.464	0.001
indcom	.0449111	.0484584	0.927	0.354
indwhl	.0094172	.0497917	0.189	0.850
indret	−.1083696	.044351	−2.443	0.015
indfir	−.0652552	.0566988	−1.151	0.250
indrep	−.1539887	.0489851	−3.144	0.002
indent	−.1311751	.0580899	−2.258	0.024
indadm	−.099739	.0416467	−2.395	0.017
occpro	.2553513	.0428549	5.959	0.000
oocmgr	.2355644	.0438099	5.377	0.000
occsal	.114942	.0530006	2.169	0.030
occclr	.0428454	.0369918	1.158	0.247
occsrv	−.0637984	.0353811	−1.803	0.071
occrep	.0903014	.0321449	2.809	0.005
occtrn	.0676913	.0342737	1.975	0.048
occlab	−.0759451	.0357036	−2.127	0.033
occoth	.1161832	.117228	−0.991	0.322
married	.2786091	.0255755	10.894	0.000
divorced	.1417694	.0301389	4.704	0.000
wkdisabl	−.0994731	.0396826	−2.507	0.012
children	−.0144712	.0191108	−0.757	0.449
unempm	−.0107637	.0062885	−1.712	0.087
prmale	−.0460659	.0162882	−2.828	0.005
cons	5.155199	.1224774	42.091	0.000

Source: 1980 census data.
$R^2 = 0.172$ $N = 7160$

Effects that predictor variables have on annual earnings may be mediated by effects on either weekly wages or weeks worked. Table 5.3 shows the results of a tobit regression model for the number of weeks worked during 1979, fit to the full set of predictors.[5] The effect of immigration is again statistically insignificant. Most of the industry composition variables are strongly positive and significant. Government administration workers, for example, are expected to work an additional 12.5 weeks annually compared with construction workers. Coefficients on other industry variables are equally large or larger, reflecting the seasonal nature of much construction work. The presence of children exerts a negative and significant (at the .10 level) effect on weeks worked, although it had little effect on weekly wages. This result means that the 5 percent earnings penalty associated with children comes about largely through a loss of somewhat more than a week's work if children are in the household and not because the weekly pay rate is reduced. One interpretation of this finding is that it reflects black fathers' involvement in child care, which reduces their annual weeks worked.

As noted above, higher local unemployment rates reduce black male annual earnings by about 1.5 percent for each 1 percentage point increase in the unemployment rate. Some of this effect is transmitted through lower weekly wages, but another significant portion comes about through a reduction in weeks worked. Each 1 percentage point increase in local male unemployment is associated with an expected decline in annual weeks worked of more than one-half week. Finally, the Puerto Rican male share variable is statistically unrelated to weeks worked. This suggests that the reduction in annual black male earnings associated with an increase in the proportion of Puerto Rican males in the local labor market can be attributed to an adverse effect on the wages of black men and not to any decline in work effort as reflected in weeks worked. In other words, the evidence uncovered for labor market competition between black and Puerto Rican males manifests itself more in the form of competition for wages than for employment.

CONCLUSIONS

The results of this study support two major conclusions. First, there is no evidence that immigrants affect black males one way or the other in local labor markets in New Jersey. Numerous individual-level characteristics of blacks and several factors reflecting aggregate labor market conditions are associated with black males' earnings and wage opportunities, but the fraction of the labor mar-

Table 5.3
Tobit Model for the Number of Weeks Worked by Black Males in 1979

Predictors	Coefficient	Standard Error	t	P>|t|
immtot	−.0160138	.0647206	−0.247	0.805
educ	−3.580428	1.119039	−3.200	0.001
educ2	.4460716	.1093291	4.080	0.000
educ3	−.0136664	.0033187	−4.118	0.000
expernce	1.045039	.091947	11.366	0.000
exper2	−.0141629	.0018563	−7.630	0.000
indagr	−1.075148	4.486271	−0.240	0.811
indmin	18.18966	7.871334	2.311	0.021
indfoo	10.17148	1.739161	5.848	0.000
indche	13.42386	1.599724	8.391	0.000
indpap	12.05542	1.720677	7.006	0.000
indmet	15.25201	1.856396	8.216	0.000
indmac	15.54078	1.828046	8.501	0.000
indeqp	9.128834	2.078539	4.392	0.000
indoth	8.827957	2.271619	3.886	0.000
indtrn	14.73005	1.453306	10.136	0.000
indcom	16.75868	1.7037	9.837	0.000
indwhl	14.20819	1.710028	8.309	0.000
indret	11.62237	1.487545	7.813	0.000
indfir	16.73997	2.030813	8.243	0.000
indrep	8.693452	1.637161	5.310	0.000
indent	8.609722	1.935374	4.449	0.000
indadm	12.57707	1.408076	8.932	0.000
occpro	1.001608	1.536297	0.652	0.514
oocmgr	5.177924	1.639261	3.159	0.002
occsal	.3470891	1.881277	0.184	0.854
occclr	3.52608	1.334504	2.642	0.008
occsrv	−1.393701	1.238144	−1.126	0.260
occrep	2.023299	1.14487	1.767	0.077
occtrn	−2.197926	1.202475	−1.828	0.068
occlab	−3.400701	1.223469	2.780	0.005
occoth	−8.169063	3.850184	−2.122	0.034
married	6.814	.8746907	7.790	0.000
divorced	2.68196	1.039326	2.580	0.010
wkdisabl	−9.494058	1.314387	−7.223	0.000
children	−1.108514	.6698375	−1.655	0.098
unempm	−.5461619	.2220526	−2.460	0.014
prmale	.3175098	.5699141	0.557	0.577
cons	36.44016	4.362619	8.353	0.000

Source: 1980 census data.
Log Likelihood = −14914.482   N = 7160   Pseudo R^2 = 0.0333
$chi^2(38)$ = 1027.94   Prob > chi^2 = 0.0000

ket consisting of foreign-born workers is not among them. There is a statistically insignificant association between these immigrant shares and black male annual earnings, weekly wages, and annual weeks worked.

These findings are consistent with other state-level investigations (for example, Muller and Espenshade 1985, conducted in California). They are also consistent with summary assessments by LaLonde and Topel (1991a, 297), who concluded that U.S. immigration has had a "negligible impact on U.S. workers' wages and employment prospects" and that recent immigration will not have serious long-term effects on the U.S. labor market. They also parallel the results of Greenwood and McDowell (1986, 1769), who found that "the effects of immigrants on the employment and wages of indigenous workers appear to be small."

Second, the study uncovered preliminary evidence for labor market competition between native-born black males and males born in Puerto Rico but living in New Jersey. The analysis has shown that each 1 percentage point increase in the share of Puerto Rican males in New Jersey local labor markets is associated with an additional average 4 percent decline in black male annual earnings. This effect is quantitatively large and statistically significant. The reduction in annual earnings is entirely the result of a reduction in weekly wages paid to black male workers; there is no effect of Puerto Ricans on the annual weeks worked by blacks.

The evidence for wage competition between Puerto Ricans and blacks in New Jersey is preliminary and deserves further investigation. But it is not inconsistent with other findings by Borjas (1984) that Hispanic immigrant men are more substitutable with native-born men than are non-Hispanic immigrant men. Borjas's research implies that the entry of Hispanic immigrants into the labor market may have had less beneficial consequences for native men than the entry of non-Hispanics. Although persons born in Puerto Rico are not immigrants in a legal or administrative sense, they do possess many of the language and socioeconomic characteristics of Hispanic immigrants. Therefore, the conclusion that Puerto Ricans appear to jeopardize the wages and earnings of black males in New Jersey to a substantially greater extent than immigrants to the state may not be very surprising.

Chapter 6 Labor Market Dynamics and the Effects of Immigration on African Americans

Frank D. Bean, Mark A. Fossett, and Kyung Tae Park

Postwar increases in immigration and the inclusive attitudes that brought them about were rooted at least to some extent in conditions that emerged out of the U.S. postwar economic expansion. From the end of World War II to the early 1970s, the United States experienced rising economic prosperity and increasing affluence. Levels of productivity were high and wages and personal incomes rose (Landau 1988; Levy 1987; Kosters 1991). Not by coincidence, the country in 1965 eliminated the restrictive and discriminatory national origins criteria for the admission of immigrants that were embodied in the 1924 National Origins Quota Act and had been ratified in the 1952 McCarran-Walter Act. Adopted in their place were more inclusionary family reunification criteria, reflecting the domestic policy emphases of the era on improving civil rights and the foreign policy emphases on establishing better relations with newly independent third-world countries (Bean and Fix 1992; Cafferty et al. 1983). As a result of such policies in general and the family reunification provisions in particular, legal immigration began to rise substantially (Reimers 1983, 1985). At about the same time, because of the termination of the Bracero (Mexican agricultural labor) program in 1964 and because of growing demand for inexpensive labor, undocumented (mostly Mexican) immigration began to increase (Massey 1981). Unlike the "old" immigrants, who were mostly European in origin, the "new" immigrants (both legal and undocumented) came mostly from third-world Hispanic and Asian countries (Bean and Tienda 1987).

Although immigration steadily increased throughout the postwar period, beginning in the mid-1970s the social and economic conditions undergirding the trends and policy reforms slowly started to change. Growth in real wages began to level off (Levy 1987, 1998), unemployment began to rise (Reischauer 1989), and calls for immigration reform began to emerge (Bean, Telles, and Lowell 1987). Frequently, these calls consisted of restrictionist outcries against the new immigrants, often stated in the form of unsubstantiated claims about the pernicious nature of immigrants and their harmful effects on the country.

During the 1980s a growing body of social science research challenged those beliefs: it found little factual basis for claims that immigration was generating substantial negative economic and social effects. In fact, the research tended to show that immigrants were assimilating socioeconomically within a reasonable period of time, were not exerting very large labor market effects on the wages and unemployment of natives, and were not consuming more in the way of public benefits than they were paying in taxes (Chiswick 1978; Bean, Telles, and Lowell 1987; Borjas and Tienda 1987; Simon 1989; Butcher and Card 1991). Although some research raised questions about the degree to which the skill levels of immigrants might be declining both within and across countries of origin (Borjas 1990; Lalonde and Topel 1991a), the evidence tended to support the general conclusion that immigration was not generating large positive or negative effects on the wages or unemployment of native workers.

Given that real wages continued to stagnate after the early 1970s, however, especially among low-skilled American workers (Levy 1998; Kosters 1991), and that unemployment remained at levels that were relatively high during the 1980s and early 1990s, the question of the labor market effects of immigration has remained an important policy issue, particularly for native African Americans. This concern is given impetus by research indicating that immigration has contributed to an increase in the earnings gap between low-skilled and high-skilled American workers since the early 1970s (Borjas, Freeman, and Katz 1992; Smith and Edmonston 1997), which suggests that African Americans especially might be adversely affected. As is true for other groups, however, the empirical research has found that the labor market effects of immigration on African Americans appear to be small (Muller and Espenshade 1985; Borjas 1986; Stewart and

Hyclak 1986; Bean, Lowell, and Taylor 1988; Borjas 1987; DeFreitas 1988, 1991; Taylor et al. 1988; Altonji and Card 1991; and Lalonde and Topel 1991a). In a review of research on the issue, Reischauer (1989, 120) concluded that "careful and sophisticated analyses by a number of social scientists provide little evidence that immigrants have had any significant negative impacts on the employment situation of black Americans."

This chapter reexamines the issue of the labor market consequences of immigration for African Americans. Such consequences depend both on the scale and nature of immigration and on the structure and vitality of the labor markets within which the members of both immigrant and native groups seek employment, higher pay, and improved working conditions. As both immigration and the context within which it occurs change, so too may the labor market effects of immigration. As noted above, immigration patterns to the United States continue to evolve, increasing in volume and shifting in terms of the origins of the immigrants. Also changing are the conditions under which the labor market incorporation of newcomers takes place. In addition to recent patterns of U.S. immigration, this chapter outlines certain features of the overall U.S. economy that are likely to influence patterns of the incorporation of immigrants, as well as certain structural features of local labor markets that may affect the nature of immigration's effects. We consider several dimensions of the issue: why previous research suggesting that immigration causes few labor market effects on African Americans is inconclusive; the changing economic context within which immigration is occurring; several hypotheses about how certain structural features of local labor markets may mediate the consequences of immigration; and an empirical illustration of how consideration of one aspect of local labor market dynamics suggests modifications in recent conclusions about the effects of immigration on African Americans.

QUESTIONS FROM PREVIOUS RESEARCH

The research to date generally finds that immigration has little effect on African Americans, but these findings are open to question for several reasons. First, even though national-level econometric studies of labor market competition between immigrants and native minorities have shown little evidence of substitution of immigrant for native workers, local area and case studies have frequently produced findings showing appreciable labor market competition (Waldinger 1986; Bailey 1987; Tienda and Stier 1990; Bach and Brill 1990; U.S. Department of Labor 1989). Such apparent anomalies do not necessarily indicate contradictory results: the local area and case studies have not followed displaced workers for sufficiently long periods of time to discern what eventually happens to them (many displaced workers may ultimately end up better off than they were before). But the persistent tendency of such studies to show apparent effects reinforces the possibility that there is more to the dynamics of labor market relationships involving immigrants and native minorities than the national-level studies have so far revealed.

Second, the data and analyses have not been sufficiently detailed to indicate which labor force groups benefit and which are harmed by immigration. Although more evidence about the aggregate impact of immigration on the labor market outcomes of native groups (including African Americans) exists now than a decade or so ago, research about the labor market consequences of immigration is still relatively limited. Immigrants are geographically concentrated and generally have fewer skills than natives (Bean and Tienda 1987; Jasso and Rosenzweig 1990), which suggests the value of examining more disaggregated effects of immigration on low-skilled native African Americans and Hispanics living in areas that have received large immigration flows.

Third, much of the research conducted to date is based on data collected during the 1970s or in 1980. (In a few instances, analyses have used data collected during the 1980s.) The question is whether similar results would obtain for periods of greater immigration and slower growth in job opportunities. Given that these are precisely the conditions that emerged in the late 1980s and early 1990s, the issue of the "degree to which the labor market can absorb immigrant workers without imposing undue hardships on existing workers" (Morris 1985, 54) has continued to attract the attention of policymakers. In particular, negative effects may not emerge except under conditions of high unemployment or stagnant economic growth.

From 1970 to 1980, African American unemployment rose from 6.9 to 13.2 percent, compared with an increase of 4.5 to 7.1 percent in the overall population; from 1980 to 1990, unemployment decreased from 13.2 to 11.3 percent among African Americans, compared with a decrease from 7.1 to 5.5 overall (U.S. Department of Labor 1971, 1981, 1991). Among young unskilled African Americans, the unemployment rates were even higher. Given Freeman's (1990) finding that unskilled black workers benefit from tight labor market conditions, it is reasonable to think that the adverse labor market effects of immigration on African Americans will depend on the condition and structure of the labor markets within which both immigrants and African Americans seek employment. This possibility is reinforced by the historical observation that black economic opportunities in and migration to northern industrial cities increased during the 1920s and 1950s, when cheap immigrant labor was scarce (Simon 1989; Kuznets 1977).

Fourth, the extent to which immigrants compete with other social groups for jobs and wages depends on the degree to which local labor market outcomes are affected by area race relations. The sociological and demographic literature repeatedly finds that relative racial group size affects the degree of social and economic competition between minority and majority groups (Blalock 1967; Frisbie and Neidert 1977; Tienda and Lii 1988; Olzak 1992). The greater the concentration of African Americans, the more likely African Americans are to experience unfavorable labor market outcomes such as lower earnings and higher unemployment. This result holds implications for studies that seek to estimate immigration's effects.

Historically, African Americans have tended to migrate from the South to the industrial Midwest during periods of low immigration. More recently, immigrants have tended to concentrate in cities in the Southwest and in coastal cities containing relatively small numbers of African Americans but relatively large numbers of Hispanics. Thus, the relative sizes of the foreign-born and the African American populations are inversely related across cities in the United States, whereas those of the foreign-born and the Hispanic populations are positively related.[1] Cities with relatively small African American populations, in which blacks would be expected to experience more favorable labor market outcomes, would therefore also tend to contain relatively large foreign-born populations. If the effect of immigration on African Americans is negative, then the effect of relatively large numbers of foreign-born persons would worsen African American labor market outcomes. In short, under such circumstances the effects of the relative concentrations of African Americans and immigrants will offset one another and be confounded in research that does not systematically include both variables in statistical models designed to estimate the effects of immigrants on the wages and unemployment of African Americans. In summary, there are several reasons to regard the findings of previous research on the labor market effects of immigration on African Americans as inconclusive.

CHANGING TRENDS IN IMMIGRATION AND JOB GROWTH

Any examination of whether the labor market effects of immigration might be affected by external contextual factors must start with a consideration of the trends in immigration and in labor force growth. It has already been noted that immigration to the United States has increased substantially in recent years. And legal inflows remained high during the 1990s: the 1990 immigration bill left virtually intact the family unification provisions of previous law while providing for both increased immigration on the part of persons meeting certain skill criteria and the legalization of sizable numbers of family members of persons previously legalized under the 1986 Immigration Reform and Control Act, or IRCA (Bean and Fix 1992). It thus guaranteed that legal immigration levels during the 1990s would be higher than those of the 1980s, perhaps by as much as 40 percent. Supplementing legal immigration will be inflows of undocumented migrants and refugees, which also appear likely to be higher than those of the 1980s. Although one intention of IRCA was to reduce illegal immigration to the United States, the evidence indicates that although the law initially exerted a slight dampening effect on undocumented flows, illegal immigration has now reached the high levels characteristic of the years immediately preceding IRCA's enactment (Bean, Passel, and Edmonston 1990; Donato, Durand, and Massey 1992). Also, the turbulent events in Eastern Europe and the Balkans, together with the continuing turmoil in the Middle East, virtually ensured that the 1990s would witness still further worldwide increases in the number of refugees, with likely rises in pressures to admit additional refugees to the United States.

Do these changes mean that immigration is approaching levels that make the labor market absorption of immigrant workers difficult? Many observers have noted that the percentage of foreign-born persons in the U.S. population, even though it rose during the 1970s and 1980s, remained substantially below the percentage foreign-born in the early part of the twentieth century (Passel 1986; Simon 1986; Borjas 1990; Portes and Rumbaut 1990). In other words, although large in absolute terms, relative to the size of the population, immigration during the 1970s, 1980s, and early 1990s remained below the levels occurring early in the twentieth century (see chapter 1). Interestingly, however, because of higher fertility among the earlier generations of native-born persons, and because a larger share of early-twentieth-century immigrants eventually returned to their countries of origin than appears for more recent immigrants to be the case, net immigration in the early 1990s accounted for roughly the same fraction of population growth as it did then—about 35 percent (Easterlin 1982; Passel and Edmonston 1992). But whether measured in terms of absolute numbers, in terms of the percentage of foreign-born people in the population, or in terms of the contribution of net immigration to population growth, the recent volume of immigration does not exceed the immigration to the United States that occurred during the first twenty years of the twentieth century.

More directly relevant to the issue of labor market effects, Borjas and Tienda (1987) have examined immigration growth relative to the rate of growth in the civilian labor force. They find that given the magnitude of immigrant flows during the period 1951–80, even if all those admitted entered the labor force, immigrants would have composed at most 33 percent of the increase in employment during the 1950s, 27 percent during the 1960s, and 20 percent during the 1970s. Rates of aggregate unemployment averaged around 4.0 percent in the 1950s and around 6.5 percent in the 1980s. Borjas and Tienda also point out that only about one-half of all immigrants admitted to the country entered the labor force on arrival during this period. Thus, however measured, the rate of labor force growth during this period exceeded the rate of growth in immigration.

The economic circumstances of the 1950s, 1960s, and 1970s thus seem to have been more than sufficiently healthy to absorb the numbers of immigrants arriving at the time. During the 1980s, however, several trends reversed. The rate of growth in immigration continued to increase while the rate of growth in the labor force began to decline. From 1980 to 1990, the growth rate in the U.S. labor force dropped to 17 percent, from 27 percent during the 1970s. By contrast, the growth rate in the number of new immigrants jumped to 63 percent during the 1980s, from 35 percent during the 1970s. Thus, the number of immigrants coming during the 1980s accounted for 36 percent of the growth in the labor force, compared with 20 percent during the 1970s; see table 6.1.

These changes raise questions concerning how the immigration experience of the late 1980s and early 1990s compares both with other post–World War II years and with the early part of the twentieth century. That is, how does the volume and growth of immigration compare with growth in the size of the economy, now and early in the century? The examination by Borjas and Tienda

Table 6.1
Percentage Change in Civilian Labor Force and in Immigrants as a Component of Labor Force Changes by Decade, 1950–90

	Civilian Labor Force	Immigrants Relative to Labor Force Growth
1950–1960	12%	33%
1960–1970	19	27
1970–1980	27	20
1980–1990	17	36

(1987) of growth in immigration relative to growth in the labor force represents one of few attempts to address the issue. Easterlin (1982) has broadly discussed the implications of immigration for growth in the economy, pointing out that at the simplest level of analysis, aggregate production clearly rises in direct proportion to increases in immigration but that the challenging problem is unraveling its effects on per capita output. To the extent that immigrants differ from the general population in characteristics that enhance production (higher proportions working, younger age structures, perhaps greater motivation), the effect on economic output would be favorable. To the extent that their characteristics decrease production (lower education, less knowledge of English), the effect would be negative. In either case, the effects are not likely to be large because immigrants are still a relatively small fraction of the population, and the characteristics of legal immigrants are not enormously different from each other or from those of natives (Sorensen, Bean, Ku, and Zimmermann, 1992).

During the first ten years of the century, when immigration reached the highest levels of any decade in the nation's history (and with respect to a population base less than one-half the current base), the size of the economy grew faster than either population or inflation. For example, from 1900 to 1910, the average inflation and population-adjusted growth rate was 2.8 percent. In other words, the economy expanded 2.8 percent faster than did the population after adjusting for inflation. In the 1950s, this differential was 1.6 percent; in the 1960s, 2.5 percent; in the 1970s, 1.8 percent; and to 1988, 2.0 percent. From 1989 to 1992, it was −0.1 percent. It is difficult to say how long the current economic trends will continue. But because of IRCA's legalization programs and because the Immigration Act of 1990 increased the possibilities for legal immigration, it is likely that the rate of growth in immigration will continue to increase. Because labor market opportunities vary with the business cycle, the question of the labor market effects of immigration on African Americans warrants reassessment in relation to factors that structure the context of economic opportunities within which immigration exerts its labor market influence.

MEDIATING STRUCTURAL FACTORS

In addition to occurring within a context shaped by macrolevel economic factors, the effect of immigration on any native-born group, including African Americans, is also affected by patterns of structure and change in local labor markets. The aspect of labor market structure that has received the most attention is the relative concentration of immigrants in an area. Different disciplinary theoretical traditions envision this variable working in different ways, and both economic and sociological-demographic theories have been applied to the study of the effects of immigrant group concentration on the labor market outcomes of other groups, including African Americans. Economic theories provide a framework within which to analyze the consequences of immigration, but they do not predict whether increasing immigration will have positive or negative impacts (Borjas 1984, 1989, 1990). For economists, ascertaining labor market effects is thus an empirical matter that requires determining the extent to which immigrants are substitutes or complements to the native-born in the labor market. Immigrants might either compete with native-born workers (substitute for natives) or enhance their productivity (complement natives), perhaps by concentrating in jobs and sectors in which, for various reasons, U.S. workers are not available (Borjas 1990; Bach and Meissner 1990).

Various empirical approaches have been used to estimate substitution and complementarity effects on labor market outcomes (Borjas 1990; Bean et al. 1987). Within the framework of these approaches, the labor market outcomes of one labor input group (such as native blacks) are generally viewed as a function of the relative concentration and change in size of other labor input groups (such as immigrants). Findings of worsened labor market outcomes for such groups as African Americans, outcomes associated with increasing immigration, indicate substitutability; findings of improved outcomes indicate complementarity.

One way in which immigrants might function as a complementary source of labor is illustrated in the case of undocumented immigrants. Because of their willingness to fill low-paying, often temporary, jobs at the base of the social hierarchy (Piore 1979; King, Lowell, and Bean 1986), undocumented immigrants may fill an economic role that would otherwise be difficult to fill. Their ready availability and flexibility may enhance economic expansions and cushion the shocks of cyclical changes in the economy (DeFreitas 1988). Although the wages that undocumented workers receive have been found to be a function of their education and experience and the duration of their job-specific training (Massey 1987), it is the economic niches they occupy and the employment conditions they are often willing to accept (in contrast to those that are acceptable to documented immigrants or natives), as well as the potential increases in productivity and demand for goods and services that may accompany these, that lead to the possibility that such workers may complement native workers.

Sociological-demographic theories have provided bases for predicting the presence and magnitude of competition between immigrants and other groups, including native-born African Americans, in local labor markets. During the

1970s and 1980s the nation shifted from a manufacturing-based to a more information- and service-based economy, with these changes affecting some cities more than others (Sassen 1990). It is well documented that these shifts have been particularly hard on African Americans, especially in the Northeast and the Midwest (Holzer and Vroman 1991; Wilson 1987). Moreover, regions and cities vary considerably, not only in their pattern of restructuring (Kasarda 1985, 1989) but also in the extent to which they are the destination of immigrants (Waldinger 1989a). That cities such as New York and Chicago during the 1980s experienced both net outmigration *and* the influx of large numbers of immigrants (Fix and Passel 1991) suggests that no single perspective on structure or change is likely to fully encapsulate the dynamics affecting the employment and earnings prospects of different racial and ethnic groups in urban areas.

Theories about spatial and skills mismatches, industrial and occupational restructuring, and job queuing point to factors affecting the likelihood that different groups will compete in the labor market. Originally formulated as an explanation of structural unemployment (Holzer and Vroman 1991), the spatial mismatch hypothesis has more recently been invoked to explain the emergence of underclass areas in inner cities (Wilson 1987; Kasarda 1989). The hypothesis links the development of urban poverty and the growth of such areas to the decline of manufacturing jobs and their movement to the suburbs. Less-educated, inner-city African Americans, because they lack the resources to relocate to the suburbs or to travel to jobs located there, suffer a "mismatch" between the location of employment and residential opportunities that impairs their economic well-being. All else being equal, the greater the inflow of low-skilled immigrants into cities, the greater any negative effects associated with mismatch. Conversely, any negative effects of low-skilled immigration on native-born African Americans can be expected to be most severe in areas of relatively greater mismatch.

Although the spatial mismatch hypothesis points to some of the structural circumstances under which job competition and displacement between low-skilled immigrants and natives might be exacerbated, mismatch notions by themselves do not provide very satisfactory explanations of urban population change and economic competition because they provide little basis for understanding why large numbers of immigrants have moved into cities that have also experienced manufacturing declines. The perspective of urban economic restructuring, with its emphasis on the globalization of the economy and the growth of the service sector (Sassen 1988, 1989, 1990), provides more in the way of an answer.

Some cities that have experienced declines in manufacturing have also witnessed substantial increases in service jobs. Large postindustrial cities with substantial international business service sectors have generated large numbers of
both new high-status, high-paying jobs and new low-status, low-paying jobs
(Waldinger 1986, 1989a). In short, the economic restructuring perspective, by
focusing on the growth of services in their most advanced form, emphasizes increased demand for both high- and low-skilled labor. Because low-skilled immigrants have been willing to take the low-level, often unstable jobs, the economic restructuring hypothesis is better suited to explain both the decline in
black manufacturing employment and the increase in immigrant employment,
at least as these have occurred together in certain cities.

When manufacturing jobs held by African Americans decline and such workers must look elsewhere for employment, do low-skilled African Americans
compete with low-skilled immigrants for expanding low-level service jobs, or is
there sufficient growth in the demand for such employment to accommodate
the needs of both groups? One view, which has been termed the job queuing hypothesis, following the work of Lieberson (1980), postulates that ethnic groups
are arranged in a hiring preference queue. Employers move down the queue until all of the members of higher-ranked groups have been hired. Thus, when demographic change causes the size of the preferred white group at the top of the
queue to shrink, a vacancy chain is set in motion that results in nonwhites moving up as replacements for whites. As the supply of white replacement labor diminishes, opportunities for immigrants and for blacks who have lost manufacturing jobs increase.

More generally, the overall labor market effect of low-skilled immigrants on
blacks and Hispanics in a given city may depend on the change in the number
of low-skilled manufacturing jobs, the degree of movement of low-skilled manufacturing jobs to the suburbs, the growth in low-skilled service jobs, and the
change in the supply of low-skilled jobs resulting from declines in the size of preferred groups that are higher in the job hierarchy. These factors vary across local labor markets. In some, their relative balance will be such that immigrants
and low-skilled minorities can be absorbed more easily as replacement labor and
as holders of new jobs in the service sector; in others, their relative balance will
be such that competition and displacement are more likely to result.

Other aspects of urban sociodemographic structure may also mediate the degree of economic competition between low-skilled immigrants and low-skilled
natives. The extent to which immigrants compete with other social groups for
jobs and wages depends on the degree to which hiring patterns are structured

by race, ethnicity, and discrimination. As Tienda (1989, 131) notes, "how Mexican origin is used to define and maintain job queues has implications for the ethnic composition of labor demand and the role of national origin and/or immigrant status in matching Mexican origin workers to specific jobs. Thus, the idea that jobs are 'ethnically typed' explicitly acknowledges that vacancy competition is not a random process. It is systematically ordered by national origin."

To the extent that the jobs typically held by particular racial, ethnic, and immigrant groups are structurally separated from one another, the groups are less likely to compete. Immigrants are less likely to exert negative economic effects on African Americans and other native groups if historical hiring patterns have channeled workers in these groups into industries that are different from those in which immigrants work. The degree of economic competition between immigrant and other groups should thus vary inversely with the degree of industry segregation. Also, complementarity may be hypothesized to be enhanced by the combination of industry and occupation segregation. In particular, immigrants who live in cities with low industry segregation but high occupational segregation (meaning that they tend to work in *different* occupations in the *same* industry as the native-born) are especially likely to function as a complementary labor supply.

An example of the way in which industry segregation may cushion the effects of immigration was observed by Muller and Espenshade (1985) for blacks in Los Angeles in the 1970s. To a considerable extent, the potentially negative effects of the substantial immigration there were mitigated by the high African American employment in public-sector jobs (about 30 percent in 1980), positions to which immigrants, partly because of their lack of language skills and education, had less access. Moreover, as immigration increased, the demand for public-sector employment to provide services to the immigrants increased, thus creating additional employment opportunities for blacks. In general, the size of the public sector and the representation of blacks in public-sector employment, as well as the degree of separation between native blacks and immigrants in other industries, are factors that are hypothesized to mediate any negative labor-market consequences of immigration for native workers.

AN EMPIRICAL ILLUSTRATION

Do the labor-market effects of immigration on African Americans differ depending on varying local and national characteristics? In this illustrative analysis, we investigate the degree to which general employment opportunities in

U.S. metropolitan statistical areas (MSAs) condition the effects of immigrant concentration on African American unemployment rates, using census data for 256 MSAs in 1980 and 180 MSAs in 1990. We excluded areas with fewer than five hundred men in the labor force in 1980 in order to improve reliability of the measures of unemployment, which are based on sample data.[2] We also excluded three areas with extreme values for key variables.[3] We also conducted logit analyses of the unemployment rate, using the natural logarithm of the ratio of unemployed to employed men.

The independent variable of central interest is the percentage of the metropolitan area population that is foreign-born. We also examined the foreign-born population originating in North America and South America. This population is more recent in origin and is composed primarily of economic migrants with relatively low skills, a group that seems especially likely to compete directly with African Americans for jobs. Several variables were also included as controls. One of the most important is the unemployment rate for non-Hispanic white men (Anglos). Employment data for nonblack, non-Hispanic men were obtained by subtraction, and unemployment rates for this group were computed separately. This variable measures the strength of demand in the local labor market. Thus, the effects of the measures of the foreign-born population on African American unemployment rates are estimated net of the general demand for labor.

Population growth over the previous decade, measured by expressing the 1980 or 1990 population as a percentage of the 1970 or 1980 population, was also included as a control for longer-term metropolitan economic vitality. The percentages of African Americans and Hispanics in an area's population were included as controls for intergroup competition, based on the consistent finding that relative outcomes for blacks on socioeconomic factors are inversely associated with the relative size of the black population (Blalock 1967; Dowdall 1974; Farley 1987) and that interethnic competition is further heightened by the presence of multiple minorities (Frisbie and Niedert 1977). Other controls are the welfare benefit rate (measured using the natural log transformation, ln, of the average monthly family benefit for Aid to Families with Dependent Children, or AFDC), the percentage of the labor force in durable goods manufacturing, the percentage unionized of the state nonagricultural labor force, and the mean socioeconomic status of occupations in the local area based on Nam-Powers socioeconomic status (SES) scores (Nam and Terrie 1986).[4]

Descriptive statistics for the variables included in the analyses are shown in table 6.2. The average non-Hispanic white unemployment rate was 5.6 percent and the average African American rate 12.6 percent in 1980, and the rates were

Table 6.2
Descriptive Statistics and Correlations for Black Male Unemployment and Other
Selected Characteristics for 256 U.S. Metropolitan Areas in 1980

	Dispersion				Percentiles		
	Mean	S.D.	IQR	IDR	10th	50th	90th
Unemployment rate, black males	12.57	4.77	5.68	12.10	7.16	11.82	19.25
Unemployment rate, non-Hispanic white males	5.56	2.16	2.85	5.47	3.05	5.25	8.52
Percentage population growth, 1970–1980	15.72	16.78	19.61	37.23	−0.44	11.75	36.78
Percentage black	11.64	9.45	12.85	25.10	2.10	8.45	27.20
Percentage Hispanic, native-born	3.67	6.84	2.41	10.10	0.35	1.05	10.45
Percentage foreign-born	4.43	4.01	3.75	8.31	1.09	3.11	9.39
Percent foreign-born Western Hemisphere	1.35	2.11	1.31	3.12	0.15	0.58	3.27
Female labor force share	42.89	2.13	2.61	5.54	39.93	42.97	45.48
Ln AFDC average monthly benefits per family	5.36	0.45	0.69	1.24	4.65	5.44	5.89
Percentage LF durable goods manufacturing	14.30	8.40	11.94	21.90	5.18	12.45	27.09
Mean Nam-Power's SES for total employed CLF	49.91	2.79	3.68	6.76	46.68	49.79	53.44
Mean education for black males 25+	3.36	0.47	0.63	1.22	2.79	3.33	4.01

4.7 percent and 13.6 percent, respectively, in 1990. It is noteworthy that the percentages of Hispanics, total foreign-born, and Western hemisphere foreign-born are low and, in the case of the latter two variables, have somewhat small standard deviations. The restricted range of variation in these variables increases the difficulty of finding large effects associated with their influence on the African American unemployment rate.

Table 6.3 shows the regression results for the same cities in 1980, and table 6.4 shows the results for 1990. It is worth noting, first, that the control variables behave as would be expected. In particular, the higher the unemployment rate of

Table 6.3

Selected Regressions Investigating Effects of Minority Composition and Immigration on Unemployment for Black Men in U.S. Metropolitan Areas in 1980

Independent Variables	(1)	(2)	(3)	(4)
Unstandardized Regression Coefficients (b's)				
Unemployment rate, non–Hispanic white males	1.487[a]	1.206[a]	1.492[a]	1.363[a]
MSA population growth, 1970–80	−0.021[c]	−0.021[c]	−0.021[c]	−0.021[c]
MSA percentage black	0.110[a]	0.110[a]	0.113[a]	0.106[a]
MSA percentage Hispanic, native-born	0.080[a]	0.082[a]	0.078[b]	0.083
MSA percentage foreign-born, total	−0.051	−0.488[a]	—	—
Percentage foreign-born * NHW male unemployment	—	0.081[a]	—	—
MSA percentage foreign-born, Western Hemisphere	—	—	−0.056	0.734[b]
Percentage foreign-born WH * NHW male unemployment	—	—	—	0.129[b]
Percentage union in state nonagricultural labor force	0.091[a]	0.094[a]	0.093[a]	0.099[a]
Log state AFDC average monthly benefit per family	0.446	0.171	0.241	−0.164
Percentage MSA labor force in durable goods manufacturing	0.085[a]	0.106[a]	0.085[a]	0.100
Means Nam-Power's SES for employed MSA labor force	−0.055	0.024	−0.063	−0.013
Constant	0.312	−0.956	1.585	1.703
T Ratios for Regression Coefficients				
Unemployment rate, non–Hispanic white males	12.873	8.303	12.906	10.455
MSA population growth, 1970–80	−1.784	−1.781	−1.768	−1.811

(continued)

Table 6.3 (continued)

Independent Variables	(1)	(2)	(3)	(4)
MSA percentage black	5.122	4.999	5.060	4.752
MSA percentage Hispanic, native-born	2.704	2.835	2.318	2.479
MSA percentage foreign-born, total	−0.916	−3.228	—	—
Percentage foreign-born * NHW male unemployment	—	3.100	—	—
MSA percentage foreign-born, Western Hemisphere	—	—	−0.522	−2.151
Percentage foreign-born WH * NHW male unemployment	—	—	—	2.092
Percentage union in state nonagricultural labor force	2.722	2.866	2.784	2.980
Log state AFDC average monthly benefit per family	0.685	0.265	0.407	0.265
Percentage MSA labor force in durable goods manufacturing	3.579	4.358	3.572	4.045
Mean Nam-Power's SES for employed MSA labor force	0.817	0.336	−0.928	−0.180
R^2	0.7296	0.7398	0.7290	0.7338
F Ratio	73.77	69.67	73.53	67.53
Number of cases	256	256	256	256
Standard deviation of dependent variable	4.7702	4.7702	4.7702	4.7702
Standard deviation of residuals	2.5253	2.4822	2.5282	2.5110

a, b, c denote probability is less than 0.01, 0.05, or 0.10, respectively (two-tailed test).

Table 6.4

Selected Regressions Investigating Effects of Minority Composition and Immigration on Unemployment for Black Men in U.S. Metropolitan Areas in 1990

Independent Variables	(1)	(2)	(3)	(4)
Unstandardized Regression Coefficients (b's)				
Unemployment rate, non–Hispanic white males	1.924[a]	1.907[a]	1.912[a]	1.850[a]
MSA population growth, 1980–90	−0.024	−0.024	−0.023	−0.024
MSA percentage black	0.152[a]	0.151[a]	0.151[a]	0.148[a]
MSA percentage Hispanic, native-born	0.052	0.051	0.055	0.054
MSA percentage foreign-born, total	−0.074	−0.092	—	—
Percentage foreign-born * NHW male unemployment	—	0.004	—	—
MSA percentage foreign-born, Western Hemisphere	—	—	−0.110	0.273
Percentage foreign-born WH * NHW male unemployment	—	—	—	0.034
Percentage union in state nonagricultural labor force	0.193[a]	0.192[a]	0.193[a]	0.191[a]
Log state AFDC average monthly benefit per family	0.218[a]	0.219[a]	0.219[a]	0.220[a]
Mean Nam-Power's SES of employed MSA labor force	−0.049	−0.047	−0.078	−0.072
Constant	0.729	−0.809	1.517	1.320
T Ratios for Regression Coefficients				
Unemployment rate, non–Hispanic white males	7.821	6.132	7.777	6.579
MSA population growth, 1980–90	−1.358	−1.355	−1.322	−1.360

(continued)

Table 6.4 (continued)

Independent Variables	(1)	(2)	(3)	(4)
MSA percentage black	4.014	3.958	3.986	3.880
MSA percentage Hispanic, native-born	1.092	1.084	1.068	1.036
MSA percentage foreign-born, total	−1.203	−0.462	—	—
MSA percentage foreign-born, Western Hemisphere	—	0.094	—	—
Percentage foreign-born WH * NHW male unemployment	—	—	−1.035	−0.733
Percentage union in state nonagricultural labor force	—	—	—	0.456
Log State AFDC average monthly benefit per family	2.686	2.662	2.690	2.648
Percentage MSA labor force in durable goods manufacturing	0.260	0.270	0.090	0.140
Mean Nam-Power's SES for Employed MSA Labor Force	3.642	3.632	3.641	3.651
Constant	−0.453	−0.423	−0.744	−0.378
R²	0.5582	0.5582	0.5572	0.5578
F Ratio	23.86	21.35	23.77	21.31
Number of cases	180	180	180	180
Standard deviation of dependent variable	5.2310	5.2310	5.2310	5.2310
Standard deviation of residuals	3.5679	3.5783	3.5718	3.5801

a, b, c denote probability less than 0.01, 0.05, or 0.10, respectively (two-tailed test).

non-Hispanic whites and the greater the percentage of African Americans in the metropolitan population, the higher the unemployment rate of African Americans. Also, the controls for industrial structure, AFDC payments, and unionization behave as predicted and generally show t-ratios greater than twice their standard errors.

Second, the percentages of the metropolitan population that are made up of either immigrants in general or Western-Hemisphere immigrants (mostly Latino) in particular have no statistically significant additive effects on African American unemployment. When the measures of the relative sizes of the immigrant groups are interacted with the Anglo unemployment rate (our measure of the tightness of the labor market), however, such interaction variables do have negative effects. The weaker the local labor market, the more larger concentrations of immigrants tend to raise African American unemployment. Conversely, larger concentrations of immigrants lower African American unemployment in strong labor markets. Stated differently, the weaker local labor demand is, the higher the relative numbers of immigrants raise African American unemployment. Specifically, if the non-Hispanic white unemployment rate had been 4 percent, a change of 10 percentage points in the relative number of immigrants would have lowered the black unemployment rate by 1.6 percentage points in 1980 and by 0.8 of a percentage point in 1990. But if the non-Hispanic white unemployment rate had been 8 percent, an increase of 10 percentage points in the relative number of immigrants would have increased black unemployment by 1.6 percentage points in 1980 and lowered black unemployment by 0.6 of a percentage point in 1990. In general, the weaker the local labor demand and the more "loose" the local labor market, the more adverse the impact of immigration on African American unemployment.

CONCLUSIONS

This analysis of 1980 and 1990 census data to ascertain the extent to which a sharpened focus on areas with limited employment opportunities might reveal negative effects on African American unemployment suggests that it does. Increasing numbers of immigrants in places with weak labor demand tend to raise African American unemployment. These results may help to explain in part why previous research has not found much in the way of negative effects on the labor-market outcomes of African Americans. Previous studies have not examined variation in the tightness of labor markets that are likely to influence intergroup labor-market competition. When this is taken into account, we find that negative effects emerge under the condition of relatively slack local labor demand. Additional research offers the promise of pinpointing still further the circumstances under which increasing immigration may be associated with more favorable or less favorable labor-market outcomes among African Americans.

Chapter 7 Political Representation and Stratified Pluralism

Thomas E. Cavanagh

In analyzing the representation of white ethnic groups, it has been customary to use a framework I term *responsive pluralism,* which emphasizes the response of political elites to newly mobilized political forces that are demanding recognition. A key tenet of responsive pluralism is that all votes are equal and fungible. In other words, political elites—those with power—will entertain the possibility of a coalition with any group that possesses votes. In return for these votes, the elites will make available a stream of public goods in the form of patronage, symbolic recognition, and social services.

But for minorities, the situation is more complex and considerably less flattering to America's preferred conception of its political traditions. Simply put, minorities have often faced constraints on their participation in the American polity due to their social and legal status. This situation has resulted in what I term stratified pluralism. As members of racial or other categories, they have often been defined out of the realm of full citizenship as it is usually understood in a democracy.

Blacks in particular could not vote for a long time so candidacies for office were not feasible. It was not until the democratic rights of citizenship were formally recognized by the polity that racial minorities could even compete as players in the electoral arena. Moreover, racism further hampered minority advancement even after the vote had been granted. In some cases, white voters simply refused to vote for minority candidates; in others, the elites themselves made it clear that they wished to limit or prevent minority representation. Minority votes were considered less desirable than white votes, and they were therefore less fungible as a commodity to be exchanged for public goods. Minorities were often incorporated into a dominant coalition only if a race-oriented agenda was abandoned by the minority leaders. As a consequence of stratified pluralism, widespread and efficacious minority officeholding has been the exception rather than the rule in U.S. history.

A group trying to elect representatives to office must use the electoral process to convert its demographic raw materials into positions of authority in government: in effect, the group tries to translate numbers into power. There is nothing automatic or mechanical about this process of conversion. It is conditioned by at least five distinct factors, each of which can intervene to prevent a group from being represented in office in relation to its proportion of the population: enfranchisement, mobilization, spatial concentration, favorable districts, and coalitions.

Enfranchisement. As noted, America's racial minorities generally did not enjoy the right to vote on a uniform national basis until quite recently. The lack of citizenship continues to keep substantial segments of the Latino and Asian populations out of the electorate. The regulation and enforcement of the franchise has historically been a potent factor depriving minorities of political representation.

Mobilization. Even within the population eligible to vote, there have been substantial fluctuations in registration and turnout, especially at the local level. To a considerable extent, these fluctuations are responses to a particular political situation: for example, a viable minority candidate for mayor will often spur intense organizational efforts to sign up new voters and get them to the polls (Cavanagh 1991; see Chapter 9 of this book).

Spatial concentration. The geographic patterns of the minority population produces substantial regional variations in minority representation. African American elected officials, like the African American population, are most numerous in the South and in northern urban areas; most Latino officials are found in the Southwest and Florida, with small clusters in the New York and Chicago areas; and Native American and Asian American representatives are found almost exclusively in the West. Within a given locality, the higher the degree of residential segregation, the more likely a minority group is to enjoy the critical mass of potential voters necessary to elect one of its number to a legislative or city council post—assuming that districting arrangements are favorable. The difficulty faced by nonwhite candidates in attracting white votes, however, has made it difficult for such candidates to win statewide office outside of Hawaii, with its large Asian American majority.

Favorable districts. Even where minority voting is widespread, incumbent politicians have frequently resorted to racial gerrymandering to create district lines unfavorable to the election of minority candidates or used at-large representation to prevent the creation of minority-majority districts. Celebrated examples include the dispersion of the Mexican American population of East Los Angeles among a half-dozen or more county council and state legislative districts and the widespread shift from district to at-large systems in the South following passage of the Voting Rights Act (VRA) of 1965. Since passage of the 1982 revisions to the VRA, the federal government has moved toward a posture of "affirmative gerrymandering," or the creation of minority-majority districts wherever they are feasible (see Chapter 8 of this book).

Coalitions. Even assuming a favorable environment with regard to the first four factors, minority officeholding often hinges on the ability of nonwhite candidates to form coalitions with sectors of the white electorate. Even in cities with black majorities (such as Atlanta, New Orleans, or Washington), white voters have sometimes served as a pivotal swing bloc determining which of two black candidates would be elected to a mayoralty or congressional seat. More commonly, minorities have to compete in a white-majority environment, and success in such environments will be increasingly important in determining whether the cadre of minority officeholders can expand beyond the small nucleus of minority-majority localities and legislative districts.

Only a handful of Minority Office-Holding Election Successes have ever been elected to key executive posts. Charles Curtis, a Republican who served as vice-president under Herbert Hoover, was a Kaw Indian who had lived in a tepee on the Kansas plains as a child (Miniclier 1993); he remains the only nonwhite ever elected on a national ticket. At the state level, L. Douglas Wilder became the only African American ever elected governor when he won the Virginia election of 1989. Two Latino Americans have served as governors of New Mexico: Toney Anaya, elected in 1974, and Jerry Apodaca, elected in 1982. There has also been a Mexican American governor of Arizona (elected in 1982), and a Cuban American, Robert Martinez, was elected governor of Florida in 1986. Hawaii has had two governors of Asian ancestry: George Ariyoshi, a Japanese

American elected to three terms beginning in 1974, and John Waihee III, a native Hawaiian who was elected in 1986.

Minorities have had little more success in winning the other major statewide race, that for a U.S. Senate seat. There have been only four black senators, and two of those (Hiram Revels and Blanche Bruce of Mississippi) served during Reconstruction. Edward Brooke, a Republican from Massachusetts, was elected in 1966 and reelected in 1972; Carol Mosely Braun, a Democrat from Illinois, became the first black woman senator when she was elected in 1992. Only three Latino Americans have served in the Senate, all from New Mexico: Octaviano Larrazolo, who was elected to an unexpired term of four months in 1928; Dennis Chavez, who served from 1935 to 1962; and Joseph Montoya, who served from 1964 to 1977. There have been five Asian American senators, all but one from Hawaii: Hiram Fong (1959–1977), Spark Matsunaga (1977–1991), Daniel Inouye (since 1963), and Daniel Akaka (since 1991); the one non-Hawaiian was S.I. Hayakawa, elected from California in 1976, who served one term.

Given their numbers in the population, Native Americans have been surprisingly numerous in the Senate. In addition to Charles Curtis of Kansas, who was elected to four terms prior to becoming vice-president, Senator Robert Owen, a Cherokee from Oklahoma, was elected to three terms starting in 1907, and Ben Nighthorse Campbell, a Cheyenne from Colorado, was elected in 1992. Two other nineteenth-century senators are reputed to have had Native American ancestry, although conclusive documentary evidence is lacking: Hiram Revels, the first black senator from Mississippi, and Matthew Stanley Quay of Pennsylvania.

With the exception of Native Americans, minority representation in the House of Representatives has grown steadily since the early 1950s; see table 7.1. In this century, most of the pioneering victories came in districts with a black population majority (such as Chicago's South Side, Harlem, Philadelphia, and Detroit) or a Mexican American majority (in the southern parts of Texas and California). In recent years, however, African Americans have been increasingly successful in winning seats in white-majority districts (Swain 1993). The first Asian American elected to Congress was Dalip Singh Saund, a Californian who was born in Amritsar, India, and served from 1957 to 1963; all Asian American representatives have been elected from Hawaii or California.

The minority presence in the House of Representatives was greatly expanded by the 1992 elections: the key factor was political, not demographic, change. The 1982 amendments to the VRA mandated the creation of minority-majority districts wherever they were mathematically feasible, and the results of this

Table 7.1

Minorities in Congress, 1951–99

	Black		Latino		Asian		Native American	
	House	Senate	House	Senate	House	Senate	House	Senate
1951	2	0	1	1	0	0	1	0
1953	2	0	1	1	0	0	0	0
1955	3	0	1	1	0	0	0	0
1957	4	0	0	1	1	0	0	0
1959	4	0	0	1	2	1	0	0
1961	4	0	1	1	2	1	1	0
1963	5	0	2	0	1	2	1	0
1965	6	0	3	1	2	2	1	0
1967	6	1	3	1	2	2	1	0
1969	10	1	4	1	2	2	1	0
1971	13	1	5	1	2	2	1	0
1973	16	1	5	1	2	2	1	0
1975	17	1	5	1	3	2	0	0
1977	17	1	4	0	2	3	0	0
1979	16	0	6	0	2	3	0	0
1981	18	0	7	0	3	3	0	0
1983	20	0	10	0	3	2	0	0
1985	20	0	11	0	3	2	0	0
1987	22	0	11	0	4	2	1	0
1989	23	0	10	0	4	2	1	0
1991	25	0	10	0	3	2	1	0
1993	39	1	17	0	4	2	0	1
1995	40	1	17	0	3	2	0	1
1997	39	1	17	0	3	2	0	1
1999	39	0	19	0	5	2	0	1

Sources: Data on African Americans from Swain (1993, table 2.4); data on other groups compiled by the author from archival sources, with the assistance of the Congressional Research Service and the Bureau of Indian Affairs.

Note: Totals include only full voting members of Congress, that is, representatives and senators. Other categories, such as nonvoting delegates and commissioners in the House of Representatives, are excluded.

procedure were dramatic in the round of redistricting following the 1990 census. The number of black representatives from the rural South reached its highest level since Reconstruction. Overall, as a result of the 1992 elections, African American representation increased from twenty-five to thirty-nine in the House, and the number of Latino Americans jumped from ten to seventeen.

Since that date, however, the growth of minority representation in the House has been minimal.

State legislative seats are an especially useful benchmark for comparing minority representation because they comprise relatively small constituencies of uniform size within each state. In 1993, across the country as a whole, 6.9 percent of state legislators were black, slightly more than one-half of their 12.1 percent share of the population in the 1990 census. The underrepresentation of other minorities was even more pronounced: 2.2 percent of state legislators were Latino Americans, compared with their 9.0 percent share of the population; 0.8 percent were Asian Americans, compared with their 2.9 percent share of the population; and 0.4 percent were Native Americans compared with their 0.8 percent share of the population.

Breaking down the figures by state, one finds only isolated cases where the proportion of legislators approximates the proportion of minorities in a given state; see table 7.2. Hawaii, with its large Asian American majority, is the only place where one could argue that a nonwhite group is substantially overrepresented relative to its share of the population: Asian Americans comprise 73.7 percent of the legislature and 61.8 percent of the population. At the other extreme, five southern states are more than 25 percent black in population, but only Mississippi has comparable representation, with 24.1 percent blacks in the state legislature. Among the more noteworthy anomalies, only 0.8 percent of California legislators are Asian American, compared with 9.6 percent of the population, and only 0.7 percent of Oklahoma legislators are Native American, compared with 8.0 percent of the population. In contrast, Maine reserves two nonvoting seats in the legislature for representatives of the Penobscot and Passamaquoddy tribes, who comprise less than 1 percent of the state population.

Percentages are less meaningful in evaluating elected officials in local governments—which includes county, municipal, regional, and special district governments—because local government constituencies (unlike state legislative seats) vary greatly according to population. Although there is a scattering of officials from all four minorities across almost every state, the same regional concentrations emerge. Over one-half of all black officials serve in the South, and the other groups are even more concentrated. A single state, Texas, accounts for more than one-third of all Latino officials, with virtually all of the rest located in California, New Mexico, Arizona, and Colorado. Most Native American representatives are found in Alaska (where they account for more than one-half of all elected officials) and Oklahoma. Asian American officials are similarly

Table 7.2

Percentage Minority State Legislators by State, 1993

	Black		Latino		Asian		Native American	
	Legislature	Population	Legislature	Population	Legislature	Population	Legislature	Population
Northeast								
Connecticut	6.4	8.3	2.1	6.5	—	1.5	—	0.2
Maine[a]	—	0.4	—	0.6	—	0.5	—	0.5
Massachusetts	4.0	5.0	2.0	4.8	—	2.4	—	0.2
New Hampshire	0.5	0.6	—	1.0	—	0.8	—	0.2
New Jersey	10.0	13.4	—	9.6	—	3.5	—	0.2
New York	12.3	15.9	5.2	12.3	—	3.9	—	0.3
Pennsylvania	6.7	9.2	0.4	2.0	—	1.2	—	0.1
Rhode Island	6.0	3.9	0.7	4.6	—	1.8	—	0.4
Vermont	1.1	0.3	—	0.7	—	0.6	—	0.3
Midwest								
Illinois	11.3	14.8	3.4	7.9	—	2.5	—	0.2
Indiana	7.3	7.8	0.7	1.8	—	0.7	—	0.2
Iowa	0.7	1.7	—	1.2	—	0.9	—	0.3
Kansas	3.6	5.8	2.4	3.8	—	1.3	—	0.9
Michigan	9.5	13.9	—	2.2	—	1.1	—	0.6
Minnesota	0.5	2.2	1.0	1.2	—	1.8	0.5	1.1
Missouri	8.1	10.7	—	1.2	—	0.8	—	0.4
Nebraska	2.0	3.6	—	2.3	—	0.8	—	0.8

(continued)

Table 7.2 (*continued*)

	Black		Latino		Asian		Native American	
	Legislature	Population	Legislature	Population	Legislature	Population	Legislature	Population
North Dakota	—	0.6	—	0.7	—	0.5	0.7	4.1
Ohio	11.4	10.6	—	1.3	—	0.8	—	0.2
South Dakota	1.0	0.5	—	0.8	—	0.4	2.9	7.3
Wisconsin	6.1	5.0	—	1.9	—	1.1	—	0.8
South								
Alabama	17.1	25.3	—	0.6	—	0.5	—	0.4
Arkansas	9.6	15.9	—	0.8	—	0.5	—	0.5
Delaware	4.8	16.9	—	2.4	—	1.4	—	0.3
Florida	11.9	13.6	8.1	12.2	0.6	1.2	—	0.3
Georgia	16.9	27.0	—	1.7	—	1.2	0.4	0.2
Kentucky	2.9	7.1	—	0.6	—	0.5	—	0.2
Louisiana	22.2	30.8	—	2.2	—	1.0	—	0.4
Maryland	16.5	24.9	—	2.6	—	2.9	—	0.3
Mississippi	24.1	35.6	—	0.6	—	0.5	—	0.3
North Carolina	14.7	22.0	—	1.2	—	0.8	0.6	1.2
Oklahoma	3.4	7.4	—	2.7	—	1.1	0.7	8.0
South Carolina	14.7	29.8	—	0.9	—	0.6	—	0.2
Tennessee	11.4	16.0	—	0.7	—	0.7	—	0.2
Texas	8.8	11.9	17.7	25.5	—	1.9	—	0.4
Virginia	7.9	18.8	—	2.6	—	2.6	—	0.2
West Virginia	0.7	3.1	—	0.5	—	0.4	0.7	0.1

West

Alaska	1.7	4.1	—	3.2	—	3.6	16.7	15.6
Arizona	4.4	3.0	10.0	18.8	—	1.5	3.3	5.6
California	7.5	7.4	8.3	25.8	0.8	9.6	—	0.8
Colorado	4.0	4.0	9.0	12.9	—	1.8	—	0.8
Hawaii[b]	—	2.5	—	7.3	7.3	61.8	—	0.5
Idaho	—	0.3	1.0	5.3	—	0.9	—	1.4
Montana	—	0.3	—	1.5	—	0.5	2.0	6.0
Nevada	4.8	6.6	3.2	10.4	—	3.2	—	1.6
New Mexico	—	2.0	40.2	38.2	—	0.9	—	8.9
Oregon	3.3	1.6	—	4.0	2.2	2.4	—	1.4
Utah	—	0.7	1.0	4.9	—	1.9	—	1.4
Washington	1.4	3.1	2.7	4.4	2.0	4.3	—	1.7
Wyoming	—	0.8	1.1	5.7	—	0.6	—	2.1
Total	6.9	12.1	2.2	9.0	0.8	2.9	0.4	0.8

Sources: Data on state legislators from National Council of State Legislatures; population data from 1990 Census of Population and Housing, Summary Tape File 1-C.

[a]The Maine legislature includes two Native Americans who serve as nonvoting tribal representatives. They are not included in the totals.

[b]Native Hawaiians have been classified as Asian Americans.

Table 7.3

Minority Local Elected Officials by State, 1987

	Total[a]	Black	Latino	Asian	Native American
Northeast	95,302	984	271	30	28
Connecticut	7,497	151	29	5	—
Maine	5,993	14	7	1	2
Massachusetts	12,418	55	24	5	5
New Hampshire	5,305	1	3	—	—
New Jersey	7,875	287	49	10	4
New York	22,138	314	88	7	14
Pennsylvania	26,425	152	31	1	2
Rhode Island	846	9	1	—	—
Vermont	6,805	1	39	1	1
Midwest	184,108	1,594	531	44	275
Illinois	33,012	502	80	10	1
Indiana	9,685	87	28	1	5
Iowa	15,840	20	25	1	—
Kansas	13,015	56	47	8	11
Michigan	17,159	340	37	2	29
Minnesota	16,737	14	49	1	46
Missouri	13,440	206	32	2	6
Nebraska	11,125	14	41	3	32
North Dakota	12,100	17	47	1	56
Ohio	18,000	304	68	5	8
South Dakota	7,117	15	16	—	25
Wisconsin	16,878	19	61	10	56
South	86,763	5,231	1,933	20	363
Alabama	3,518	388	8	—	1
Arkansas	7,273	431	21	—	12
Delaware	827	31	2	2	—
District of Columbia	325	240	—	—	—
Florida	4,060	210	49	—	5
Georgia	5,651	614	15	1	2
Kentucky	6,206	105	28	—	1
Louisiana	4,015	536	13	1	1
Maryland	1,399	102	4	1	—
Mississippi	4,237	531	14	1	—
North Carolina	4,647	420	—	—	21
Oklahoma	7,301	181	74	5	301
South Carolina	3,211	462	15	—	1

(*continued*)

Table 7.3 (*continued*)

	Total[a]	Black	Latino	Asian	Native American
Tennessee	6,182	167	—	1	—
Texas	22,673	596	1,689	7	18
Virginia	2,799	182	—	1	—
West Virginia	2,439	35	1	—	—
West	52,901	458	1,969	254	1,044
Alaska	1,273	4	5	1	715
Arizona	2,539	36	257	5	78
California	15,943	324	741	144	41
Colorado	6,035	16	254	12	6
Hawaii	69	—	3	38	—
Idaho	3,635	—	23	11	16
Montana	4,014	5	18	3	64
Nevada	814	11	9	—	3
New Mexico	1,615	20	565	—	38
Oregon	6,790	13	40	17	20
Utah	2,143	1	11	6	2
Washington	6,253	27	33	14	47
Wyoming	1,778	1	10	3	14
Total	419,074	8,267	4,704	348	1,710

Source: Recalculated by the author from data presented in U.S. Bureau of the Census (1990, tables 18, 19).
[a]Totals do not include officials not reported as to race.

concentrated in California and Hawaii. Table 7.3 shows the number of minority local officials for all states for 1987.

APPOINTED OFFICIALS

Racial minorities have been members of the president's cabinet only since the 1960s, when civil rights legislation, social movements, and electoral mobilization converged to put minority issues on the national agenda. Most of the minority appointments have been African Americans; there have been four Latinos; there has never been an Asian American or a Native American in the cabinet.

Prior to the Clinton Administration, black appointees were traditionally consigned to a sort of cabinet ghetto of domestic social policy portfolios. Robert Weaver, the first black member, served as secretary of the Department of Housing and Urban Development (HUD) during the Johnson Administration; William Coleman was appointed secretary of the Department of Transportation by Gerald Ford; Patricia Roberts Harris headed HUD and later the U.S. Department of Health and Human Services (HHS) under Jimmy Carter; Samuel Pierce was secretary of HUD under Ronald Reagan; and Louis Sullivan was secretary of HHS under George Bush. Bill Clinton broke new ground by appointing Hazel O'Leary as secretary of the Department of Energy, Mike Espy as secretary of the Department of Agriculture, Ronald Brown as secretary of the Department of Commerce, and Jesse Brown as secretary of Veterans Affairs. Thus, Clinton greatly expanded the range of departments for which black appointments were considered, making Clinton's the first administration in which more than one African American has headed a cabinet department at any time. Another pattern of note has been the tradition of appointing a person of color as U.S. ambassador to the United Nations, a gesture obviously intended to improve relations with the Third World. Andrew Young and Donald McHenry served in this position under Carter, Edward Perkins under Bush, and Bill Richardson under Clinton.

The Latino presence in the cabinet is especially new. Lauro Cavazos, the first Latino member, became secretary of the Department of Education in 1988 under Reagan, and Manuel Lujan became secretary of the Department of Interior under Bush in 1989. In line with his campaign rhetoric, Clinton stressed the theme of diversity by appointing two Latinos to the cabinet: Henry Cisneros as secretary of HUD and Federico Pena as secretary of Transportation.

The statistical patterns with regard to executive officeholding are quite similar to those for elected officials: African Americans have made far more progress than Latinos, who in turn have made far more progress than Asian or Native Americans; see table 7.4. Looking first to executives in the federal government, the black share rose rapidly from 1.65 to 5.0 percent during the 1970s then stagnated during the Reagan years, and increased again under President Clinton. Clearly, this time series is sensitive to national politics: the Reagan Administration did not increase black representation in the senior federal ranks either because the president and his advisors found it difficult to recruit blacks sufficiently conservative to participate in policy-making or because they felt little obligation to a constituency that explicitly disapproved of Reagan policies.

Other minority groups are much more scarce in the senior ranks of the federal government. Latinos rose from 0.32 percent of the total in 1970 to 1.10 percent in 1980, 1.36 percent in 1988, and 2.50 percent in 1996. Asian American appointments increased at a steady pace—from 0.27 percent in 1970 to 0.53 percent in 1980, 0.82 percent in 1988, and 1.82 percent in 1996—but they

Table 7.4
Federal Executives by Race, 1970–96

	Total	Black	Latino	Asian	Native American
1970	5,586	1.65%	0.32%	0.27%	0.09%
1972	5,712	2.54	0.58	0.40	0.21
1974	5,385	2.92	0.65	0.46	0.19
1976	6,987	3.15	0.86	0.59	0.24
1978	6,598	3.55	0.76	0.42	0.30
1980	8,419	5.00	1.10	0.53	0.43
1982	7,803	4.28	1.61	0.65	0.63
1984	9,030	4.15	1.16	0.74	0.41
1986	8,867	4.17	1.21	0.82	0.37
1988	9,181	4.26	1.36	0.82	0.50
1990	10,118	4.73	1.52	0.87	0.59
1992	14,867	4.45	1.89	1.21	0.56
1994	14,594	5.93	2.21	1.44	0.56
1996	15,024	6.44	2.50	1.82	0.59

Source: Unpublished data from Office of Personnel Management.
Note: Executives are defined as grade GS-16 or above from 1970 to 1990 and all senior pay
levels after 1990.

remain quite scarce. Even more scarce are Native Americans, who constituted only 0.09 percent of federal executives in 1970, rising to 0.43 percent in 1980, 0.50 percent in 1988, and 0.59 percent in 1996.

Asian American appointments increased at a steady pace, from 0.27 percent in 1970 to 0.53 percent in 1980 and 0.82 percent in 1988, but they remain quite scarce. Even more scarce are Native Americans, who constituted only 0.09 percent of senior federal executives in 1970, rising to 0.43 percent in 1980 and 0.50 percent in 1988.

Breaking down the racial percentages by agency reveals a very interesting picture; see table 7.5. Minorities are most represented in the social service and civil rights agencies most identified with the concerns of minority constituents. Thus, more than one-half of the executives of the Equal Employment Opportunity Commission are minorities, and one also finds relatively large percentages at HUD, Education, and HHS. Other departments have minority leadership for mission-specific reasons: the Small Business Administration because of its minority contracting programs; the Labor Department because of its regulation of affirmative action programs; the Agency for International Development because of its heavy involvement in Africa; the Justice Department because of civil rights policy; Veterans Affairs because of the high black share of enlisted forces; and the Transportation Department because of the concentration of minorities in transit-dependent big cities. The Interior Department is distinctive because of the heavy representation of Native Americans (15 executives of 276), due to its management of Indian reservations. The agencies with the lowest minority leadership tend to be related to diplomacy, finance, scientific technology, or national security—the most prestigious branches of the federal civil service.

For administrators at the state and local level, the time-series trends are somewhat different; see table 7.6. The black percentage has fluctuated in recent years, holding steady around 5.70–5.84 percent between 1975 and 1980, increasing to 10.18 percent by 1990, and receding slightly to 9.89 percent in 1993. The proportion of Latino officials has risen steadily, from 1.58 percent of the total in 1975 to 3.72 percent in 1993. The representation of Asians Americans has grown most rapidly, albeit from a very small base: from 0.47 percent in 1975 to 1.44 percent in 1993. The least progress has been made by Native Americans, who went from 0.23 to 0.43 percent of the total from 1975 to 1993.

The sensitivity to political trends is especially notable with regard to federal judicial appointments. Thurgood Marshall was the first African American to serve on the Supreme Court, appointed by Johnson in 1967. When Marshall retired in 1991, Bush replaced him with Clarence Thomas, a black conservative who had forcefully opposed affirmative action policies during his tenure as chairman of the Equal Employment Opportunity Commission under Reagan.

As the controversy over the Thomas appointment suggests, civil rights policy has been a key point of contention between the two major parties in recent years. Even so, it is still startling to note that African Americans comprised 14.3 percent of Carter's judicial appointments and a remarkable 24.0 percent of Clinton's, compared with only 1.8 percent under Reagan, the lowest of any president since passage of the Voting Rights Act. Clearly, the dearth of black judges agreeing with Reagan's civil rights policies discouraged black appointments during the Reagan years. Clinton has also appointed more Latino judges than any other president (8.8 percent), with Carter again second (6.2 percent); interestingly, Reagan's 4.0 percent Latino share was more than double his black percentage of judicial appointments (table 7.7). There has not yet been a Latino or Asian American appointment to the Supreme Court, although the increasing importance of the Latino electorate makes it probable that a Latino will make it to the Court in the not-too-distant future.

Table 7.5

Minorities in Senior Executive Service by Agency, 1989

	Total	Minorities (%)
Equal Employment Opportunity Commission	37	56.8
Department of Housing and Urban Development	106	19.8
Education Department	70	18.6
Department of Health and Human Services	555	12.6
Small Business Administration	41	12.2
Labor Department	258	10.5
Agency for International Development	39	10.3
Justice Department	293	9.9
Interior Department	276	9.8
Veterans Affairs Department	256	9.0
Transportation Department	362	8.8
Treasury Department	516	7.8
Agriculture Department	313	7.0
Nuclear Regulatory Commission	206	6.8
U.S. Information Agency	45	6.7
State Department	121	6.6
General Services Administration	125	6.4
Office of Personnel Management	63	6.3
Air Force[a]	195	6.2
Commerce Department	401	6.0
Energy Department	495	5.7
Navy[a]	442	4.1
National Aeronautics and Space Administration	508	3.9
Army[a]	310	3.9
Environmental Protection Agency	243	3.7
Total	7,705	7.5

Source: Recalculated by the author from data in Equal Employment Opportunity Commission (1991, table I-14).

[a]Parts of the Defense Department.

Making sense of these numbers requires a more systematic analysis of how stratified pluralism has operated in practice. How has the legal environment structured the citizenship rights and political opportunities of each of these minority groups? How have they interacted with dominant whites in the context of a system of political subordination? And to what extent do America's minorities coalesce or compete with one another in the electoral arena?

Table 7.6

State and Local Officials and Administrators by Race, 1975–93

	Total	Black	Latino	Asian	Native American
1975	190,947	5.84%	1.58%	0.47%	0.23%
1980	205,472	5.70	2.31	0.71	0.38
1986	259,771	8.78	2.84	1.09	0.40
1990	299,461	10.18	3.37	1.26	0.39
1993	273,394	9.89	3.72	1.44	0.43

Source: Unpublished data from Equal Employment Opportunity Commission.
Note: Includes full-time administrators only.

**MIGRATION, CITIZENSHIP,
AND ENFRANCHISEMENT**

Although the specific institutional mechanisms of inequality have varied across race, time, and space, the formal characteristics of inclusion and equality have not generally applied to African Americans, Latino Americans, Asian Americans, or Native Americans until quite recently. The circumscription of citizenship and the deprivation of the franchise obviated even the possibility of officeholding. As a consequence, political activity was frequently channeled into social movement and protest activity.

The European "invasion of America" began with the dispossession of the original inhabitants, the American Indians. Then, as land came under white ownership, attention turned to attracting the labor needed to exploit the land. Thus, the frequent absence of political representation for minorities was essentially a

Table 7.7

Federal Black and Latino Judicial Appointments, 1963–96

	Years	Black	Latino	Total
Johnson	1963–68	4.8%	1.8	165
Nixon	1969–74	2.6	0.9	228
Ford	1974–76	4.6	1.5	65
Carter	1977–80	14.3	6.2	258
Reagan	1981–88	1.9	4.1	368
Bush	1989–92	6.5	4.3	185
Clinton	1993–96	18.7	7.1	198

Sources: Henry et al. (1985, table 10); Goldman and Slotnick (1997, tables 3 and 6).

by-product of institutional arrangements established for obtaining cheap labor. The exclusion from officeholding was merely one aspect of a comprehensive system of social, legal, and economic subordination.

The most extreme case, of course, is that of African American slavery. But even after the Civil War brought about the abolition of slavery, unfree labor retained its convenience for the propertied interests. By the turn of the century, most of the former black slaves and their descendants had been reduced to sharecropping, tenant farming, or wage peonage in the South, and their political and civil rights had been abrogated through the imposition of the Jim Crow laws.

In the western states, Chinese and Japanese immigrants were employed as gang labor in the construction of the railroads or as field laborers in the sugar and pineapple plantations of Hawaii. And Latinos in the Southwest were imported as migrant workers to harvest cotton and agricultural crops. Most of these immigrants were considered short-term laborers rather than permanent settlers, so they received little encouragement to put down social or political roots.

Asian American immigrants faced an additional complication: under the terms of the Naturalization Act of 1790, only whites were eligible to become naturalized citizens of the United States. The naturalization laws were broadened to make persons of African descent eligible in 1870, making Asians the only group remaining ineligible for citizenship. Chinese immigration was banned altogether by the Chinese Exclusion Act of 1882. The prohibition on naturalization was lifted for the Chinese in 1943 and for Asian Indians in 1946. Filipinos were in a particularly complex situation: following the Spanish-American War they were eligible for naturalization as residents of a U.S. territory, a right that was removed in 1933 and restored in 1946. Not until the passage of the McCarran-Walter Act in 1952 were racial restrictions on naturalization completely removed (Hocking 1980). Asian immigration was still severely restricted by the national origin quotas, which remained in force until 1965.

The situation of minority immigrants was starkly different from that of European immigrants with regard to the rights of citizenship, representation, and incorporation in the polity. It has never been a requirement under the Constitution that a person be a citizen in order to be eligible to vote. In fact, the right to vote was held out as an enticement to attract white immigrants to the newly settled territories of the Great Plains and mountain states during the middle of the nineteenth century (Porter 1918, 113). Between 1840 and 1898, a total of eighteen states adopted laws permitting aliens to vote provided they declared their intent to apply for citizenship (Piven and Cloward 1988, 87 n. 58).

What changed this situation was the "reform" movement that began to dominate state politics around the turn of the century. Literacy tests and registration requirements were adopted in order to impede voting by the uneducated lower class, who were thought to provide the raw material for political corruption (Rosenstone and Hansen 1993, 205 n. 84): "The exact nature of the 'problem' differed from place to place—in the North it was European immigrants; in the West it was Chinese and Japanese; in the Southwest it was Mexicans; in the South it was blacks—but the political coalitions that advanced registration were remarkably similar: middle class, white, native stock, often the era's 'progressives.'" In addition, the strong nativist currents stirred by World War I resulted in most states' making citizenship a prerequisite for suffrage (Harris 1929; Piven and Cloward 1988, ch. 3).

By the time these actions were taken, the European immigrant groups (and especially the Irish) had already achieved a secure foothold in urban politics. In fact, the restrictions were a *response* to the political progress and influence enjoyed by these groups. In the case of blacks, Latinos, Asians, and Native Americans, however, legal circumscriptions had foreclosed their ability to participate in the polity in the first place. In sum, the entry of these minorities into the polity proceeded against a much harsher legal and economic backdrop than that which white ethnic groups faced as they sought political inclusion.

The high point of nativist agitation was reached with the Immigration Act of 1924, which established 1890 as the base year for calculating immigration quotas—in order to tilt the influx toward northern and western Europe and away from the southern and eastern Europeans who had predominated since that date. One result was to create a sudden shortage of cheap labor. The mining, railroad, and agricultural interests in the rapidly growing areas of the Southwest began to recruit unskilled laborers from Mexico, as did Midwestern farm owners. The recruitment of noncitizens in the Southwest was later formalized through the *bracero* program, which enabled hundreds of thousands of Mexicans annually to cross the border for poorly paid seasonal employment between 1942 and 1964 (Acuna 1988, 142, 262–66).

Although they were shut out of the political system, the minority immigrants did have one recourse: their children could become citizens because any person born on American territory is automatically an American citizen, regardless of the parents' legal status. Thus, beginning with the second generation, the immigrant communities were enfranchised once they reached voting age. It was only a matter of time until these heretofore ignored constituencies would then produce their own leaders who would aspire to office.

African Americans

Perhaps the key point to emphasize in the history of African American politics is the cyclical nature of black incorporation in and exclusion from the polity. The evils of slavery were followed by a very rapid, albeit short-lived, improvement in civil and political status. Blacks were granted the right to vote by the Fifteenth Amendment. During Reconstruction, numerous African Americans were elected to office, including two U.S. senators, twenty-one Congressmen, dozens of state legislators, and hundreds of local officials. By the end of the nineteenth century, however, blacks had been effectively disfranchised throughout the South through the use of poll taxes, literacy tests, white primaries, and outright violence, and the tradition of black officeholding had been reduced to ashes.

The disruption of immigrant flows during World War I encouraged the recruitment of black agricultural laborers from the South to the factories of northern cities, a process that was accelerated by the shut-off of European immigration in the 1920s, the acute labor shortages of World War II, and the mechanization of agriculture in the postwar period. As a consequence, for the first half of this century, black officeholding was generally confined to a small number of black-majority districts in Congress, state legislatures, and city councils in a handful of northern cities. The writer W. E. B. Du Bois (1948, 239) could locate only ten black city council members and two black state legislators serving in 1917. The total number of black elected officials had increased to thirty-three by 1941 and to eighty-two in 1951 (Jaynes and Williams 1989, 238–41).

The modern history of black electoral politics dates from the passage of the Voting Rights Act in 1965, which finally guaranteed the franchise to southern blacks. Ensuing years brought forth huge increases in the number of black elected officials. The national total rose from 280 in 1965 to 1,469 only five years later, with an especially dramatic increase in the South from 87 to 703 during those years (Jaynes and Williams 1989, 238). The rate of growth has slowed appreciably since that time; according to the Joint Center for Political and Economic Studies (personal communication), the national total reached 4,890 in 1980 and 7,335 in 1990.

The African American population today is highly concentrated in urban areas. Consequently, black officeholding is primarily an urban phenomenon. Until Mike Espy was elected to represent the Mississippi Delta in 1986, all of the black members of the House of Representatives in this century had represented urban districts. The urban focus has been most visible in the election of black mayors in major cities, beginning with Carl Stokes in Cleveland and Richard

Hatcher in Gary in 1967. By 1989, when David Dinkins was elected mayor of New York, African Americans had held the mayoralty of all three of America's largest cities at some time during the previous decade, a record unparalleled by any ethnic group since the heyday of Irish American machine politics several decades earlier.

Latinos

The immigrant status of the Latino population poses a major barrier to political mobilization even today. Many immigrants tend to see themselves as "sojourners" rather than permanent American residents and thus are slow to take an interest in American politics (Fuchs 1990). Because almost one-third of voting-age Latinos are noncitizens, registration and turnout rates tend to be extremely low in comparison to those of whites or African Americans (see Chapter 9 of this book). But among citizens of voting age, Latino turnout is generally comparable to black turnout (Pachon 1985).

The history of Latino American elected officials is similar to that of black elected officials in its cyclicality: an early peak in the middle of the nineteenth century, a trough due to civic exclusion later on, and a renewed period of incorporation beginning in the 1960s. Just as the African American political elite was extinguished in the post-Reconstruction South, the Mexican American political elite was similarly driven from power after the American military conquest of the Southwest.

There were approximately 75,000 persons of Hispanic ancestry in the Southwest at the time the United States acquired these territories following the Mexican-American War. These residents were granted American citizenship by the Treaty of Guadalupe Hidalgo in 1848 (see Acuna 1988; del Castillo 1990; Garcia 1974). Once the territories were absorbed by the United States, however, the new population of Anglo inmigrants wasted no time in establishing their dominance of local politics. Because Latinos have comprised at least one-third of New Mexico's population for more than a century, the state has long been the most favorable one for Latino American politics. In the years prior to statehood, there was usually a Latino American majority in the territorial legislature, and the voters frequently elected a Latino delegate to Congress. Anglos, however, monopolized virtually all of the key appointive offices, such as the territorial governorship and judgeships. After New Mexico became a state, it gradually became traditional to elect Latino Americans to the lieutenant governorship, one U.S. House seat, and one U.S. Senate seat (Padilla and Ramirez 1974).

In the rest of the Southwest, political relations between Anglos and Latinos generally exhibited much more conflict. Following American annexation, Latino political representation very nearly disappeared outside of New Mexico, save for a few counties in southern Colorado. In California, the state government encouraged white squatters to take over land held by Mexicans. A mixture of violence, expensive title litigation, and a heavy state property tax virtually wiped out the old Mexican landowning class, which had served for generations as the social and political elite, and the tradition of Mexican officeholding had virtually disappeared by the 1880s. There was no Latino representation in the California state legislature from 1913 to 1962 or on the Los Angeles city council between 1881 and 1949 (Acuna 1988; Padilla and Ramirez 1974).

Because the Mexican American population is less urbanized than the black population, there have been relatively few high-profile Latino mayors in the Southwest. The first "breakthrough" election in a major city was that of Raymond Telles as mayor of El Paso in 1957. Unquestionably, the most significant Latino political leader of recent years is Henry Cisneros, who was elected mayor of San Antonio in 1981 and served several highly successful terms before retiring. Federico Pena became the first Latino mayor of Denver in 1983 and survived a host of controversies to win reelection in 1987. Both Cisneros and Pena were appointed to President Clinton's cabinet.

Despite these successes, the contemporary relation of Mexican Americans to the broader political culture is decidedly ambivalent. Mainstream election campaigns are often dismissed as "fiesta politics," providing a fleeting attention to the Latino population at election time but little sustained follow-up. In addition, the "pull" or magnet factor that encourages immigration gibes uneasily with attempts to mobilize votes based on feelings of group deprivation (Pachon 1985, 248). Or as Joel Kotkin (1992) argues, newly arrived immigrants are unlikely to adopt politics that idealize the countries they came to California to escape.

The Puerto Rican community in New York dates back to the late nineteenth century. In 1917 the Jones Act—passed over the objections of Puerto Rico's legislature—granted American citizenship (albeit with limited constitutional protections) to inhabitants of Puerto Rico. Migration to the mainland increased rapidly thereafter; the Puerto Rican population in New York City swelled from about 35,000 at the end of World War I to almost 100,000 in 1927. The largest migration occurred immediately after World War II and was orchestrated by the government of New York City and the Commonwealth Office of Puerto Rico.

On the island, the sugar companies were consolidating their holdings into large plantations, thereby displacing thousands of small farmers, and at the same time cheap labor was needed for the factories and service industries in New York. Thus, the mainland acted as a kind of safety valve for the surplus labor created through modernization of the island economy. By 1949 there were at least 250,000 Puerto Ricans in New York (Jennings 1977, 30–41).

The new migrants often saw themselves as commuters between the island and the mainland, so they were generally slow to register to vote in New York. Political mobilization was further hindered by the reluctance of the Democratic machine to enlist them; the existing white ethnic leadership in areas such as the South Bronx was afraid of being displaced. The most important Puerto Rican politicians, such as Herman Badillo, have flourished through establishing personal organizations outside of machine control (Jennings 1977).

In the Miami area, the Latino American population is largely Cuban in origin. Although there has been a small Cuban-American community in South Florida since the late nineteenth century, the bulk of the migration dates from the Cuban revolution, consisting for the most part of middle-class refugees from Castro's communist regime. During the 1960s, the Cuban emigrés generally saw themselves as temporary residents, biding their time until the fall of Castro would make a return possible. By the early 1980s, however, many Cubans had begun to become naturalized citizens and accept the United States as their permanent home. Economic progress led to rapid political progress. Florida elected a Cuban American governor, Bob Martinez, in 1986, and Miami elected its first Cuban mayor, Xavier Suarez, in 1987, after Maurice Ferre, a Puerto Rican, had served three terms.

The Cuban experience differs significantly from that of the other minority groups considered in this chapter: they were generally accorded a hero's welcome as ideological opponents of communism. Their entrepreneurial skills have enabled them to avoid the welfare-class stereotype that has hobbled other minorities in the United States, and their physical appearance in the eyes of whites was often seen as differentiating them from blacks and even from Mexican Americans.

Asian Americans

The first major breakthroughs in Asian American representation occurred in Hawaii after it became an American territory in 1900. Native Hawaiians dominated the electorate and the political system well into the twentieth century. In the territorial legislature of 1901, fully 73 percent of the members were Hawaiian. The Hawaiian bloc comprised more than half of the electorate through 1922 and retained a majority of elective and judicial positions as late as 1927 (Fuchs 1961). Yet this political dominance would not endure.

During the last half of the nineteenth century, white settlers seized control of Hawaii's plantation economy. Finding that European laborers refused the harsh work in the pineapple groves and sugar cane fields, the planters imported several successive waves of Asian laborers and devised an elaborate caste structure in which occupational position was stratified along racial and ethnic lines. Workers could not move from one plantation to another without a discharge certificate, effectively tying them to one employer—a system reminiscent of the restrictions hampering the mobility of black sharecroppers in the rural South. By pitting newcomer groups against earlier arrivals, it was possible to keep wages extremely low and prevent the organization of a unified labor movement (Fuchs 1961; Takaki 1989, ch. 4).

The major threat to Hawaiian political influence emanated from the large community of Japanese imported as plantation workers. As the *nisei* (second-generation Japanese, who were born into American citizenship) attained voting age, the Japanese proportion of the electorate surged from 8 percent in 1926 to 25 percent in 1936, when they surpassed Hawaiians to become the largest single ethnic voting bloc. Shut out of landowning and access to capital for small businesses, "the Japanese tended to emphasize a class strategy of unionization, politics and collective action" (Takaki 1989, 179).

Following World War II, Japanese Americans formed an alliance inside the Democratic Party with the International Longshoremen's and Warehousemen's Union, which had organized the multiracial workforce of the plantations and the docks during the war and now saw an opportunity to seize political control from the sugar interests (Fuchs 1961, chs. 13–14). Japanese Americans have dominated the politics of the islands since the 1954 territorial elections, when they captured almost one-half of the seats in the legislature.

On the mainland, Asian American officeholding is still something of a novelty. The most prominent successes have come in California. In the 1970s, along with S. I. Hayakawa's election to the U.S. Senate, Robert Matsui and Norman Mineta were elected to the U.S. House, and March Fong Eu began serving as secretary of state. More recently, Michael Woo became the first Asian American elected to the Los Angeles City Council in 1985. Asian Americans may just now be reaching a kind of takeoff point in officeholding, analogous to that of African Americans in the late 1960s and Latinos in the 1970s. Unfortunately, this new-found political prominence may also be ushering in some of the dynamics of racial stereotyping, backlash, and polarization that have often accompanied black and Latino political advances. In Monterey Park, California, the rapid growth of the Chinese immigrant population enabled Lily Lee Chen to become the first Chinese American woman mayor in the United States in 1983. But her tenure was marked by a bitter controversy over city council moves to require the use of "English only" on store signs in response to the proliferation of Chinese-owned businesses. The 1986 city council election was marred by openly racist campaigning: "[U]nder the caption 'Chen's Laundry,' grotesque caricatures of her washing dollar bills against a backdrop of banks with names in Chinese characters had been widely circulated" (Fong 1994, 122).

As with Mexican Americans and Puerto Ricans, the recency of immigration is one force that mitigates against effective Asian American political involvement. Thus, voter registration and turnout tend to be quite low among recently arrived immigrants. Case studies of Asian American officeholders have generally shown an emphasis on "recognition politics," the advancement of Asian professional elites into positions of influence in city government, and concerns about servicing and funding organizations in the Asian American community rather than a broader thrust for social and economic equality (Lau 1991; Lee 1980).

The Chinese were the first Asian group to enter the United States in large numbers, lured by the gold mining companies during the California Gold Rush. The construction of the transcontinental railroad spurred further importation of contract laborers during the 1860s. Their presence stirred up tremendous resentment from white laborers, prompting the passage of discriminatory laws. Beginning in 1872, California adopted a series of laws depriving aliens (primarily Chinese) of the right to own land. The 1879 California state constitution prohibited the hiring of Chinese immigrants. As noted above, the influx was shut off altogether by the federal government's Chinese Exclusion Act of 1882. Lacking the protections of citizenship and deprived of employment opportunities, the Chinese began to cluster in big-city slums known as Chinatowns, where they could devise a self-contained economy of small businesses to support one another (Hocking 1980; Kwong 1987; Takaki 1989, ch. 3).

Political life was carried on with virtually no connection to the broader society. The key organizational structures were the *huiguan*, or associations organized according to the migrants' regions of origin in China. These mutual aid societies provided housing and charity, served as credit and employment agencies, collected debts, and resolved disputes. In San Francisco, the *huiguan* were coordinated by the Chinese Six Companies, an elite group of merchants who settled interdistrict quarrels and spoke on behalf of the Chinese community in dealings with white businesses and the city government (Takaki 1989, 119). This same structure arose in New York's Chinatown in the form of the Chinese Consolidated Benevolent Association, which ruled through a consensus of the major factory owners, merchants, landlords, and press magnates (Kwong 1987, ch. 5).

In recent years, this Chinese American leadership has begun to lose its hold over the most recent generation of American-born offspring. Several studies have noted an emerging division between the insular traditional elite of business owners and a new social service elite of young professionals in government agencies and community organizations. The social service elite takes its inspiration from the civil rights movement, is actively involved in electoral politics and broader community affairs, and defines its identity in Asian American terms. There is also a young entrepreneurial elite with economic roots in finance and trade that expresses conservative political values but mimics the outreach-oriented tactics and style of the social service elite (Fong 1994; Nee and Nee 1972; Wong 1982). Thus, the long-standing insularity of Chinese American politics is beginning to evolve into something that resembles more conventional interest group politics.

Native Americans

The traditional culture of Native Americans did not recognize European-derived distinctions between political and religious or social authority. Among the Indians, "government" was not a tangible institution but rather a community ritual based on consensus and deference to elders, whose forms and procedures varied from circumstance to circumstance. "Authority" in such a setting was generally temporary and decision-specific. In order to expedite the management of Indian reservations, the Bureau of Indian Affairs (BIA) has attempted to augment a system of tribal government with regular meetings and elections. These procedures coexist uneasily with more traditional forms of authority in many tribes today (O'Brien 1989).

Although the Indian nations were formally accorded the status of sovereignty under Anglo-American jurisprudence, in practice such legal niceties were ignored whenever military or economic necessity made them inconvenient. For much of this century, the federal government has sought to assimilate Native Americans and terminate the distinctive legal rights associated with tribal membership. It is only in recent years that Native American claims to land ownership and use, and legal autonomy in general, have been seriously considered and enforced by the courts (Olson and Wilson 1984; Wilkinson 1987; Wunder 1994).

Citizenship came to Native Americans piecemeal. Individuals became citizens as a result of military service, the allotment of tribal lands, or acculturation into the mainstream society. All Native Americans were granted American citizenship through the Indian Citizenship Act of 1924. The franchise, however, has traditionally been considered a right extended by the several states rather than the federal government, and as late as 1938, there were seven states in which Native Americans were still not permitted to vote. The last two holdouts, New Mexico and Arizona, only extended the franchise to Native Americans following court rulings in 1948. Political participation remained extremely low, however; scattered data from reservations suggest that perhaps one-third of Native Americans were voting during the Eisenhower period (Peterson 1957). At present, most state and local governments appear to do little either to encourage or discourage voter participation by Native Americans.

Access to the government of the broader society has been carefully filtered through the control of the reservation system by BIA. This agency is often enlisted as an intermediary whenever Native Americans wish to request services or pursue their interests in dealing with other federal agencies. The local BIA representative is not accountable to the tribal government at all but to the Interior Department, lodging ultimate authority in political structures beyond Native American control. Thus, voter participation has been hampered by the belief that the tribal governments and the BIA, rather than mainstream elected officials, are the only political actors relevant to their lives (Cornell 1988).

THE DYNAMICS OF PROGRESS AND REACTION

In a system of responsive pluralism, because all votes and voters are equally valued, the political system is, in effect, colorblind; political leaders will be as responsive to a given number of minority citizens as they would be to the same number of white citizens. It is fungibility that ensures responsiveness, and in so doing, plays a major role in legitimating the regime in the eyes of all of its citizens.

Yet this model seems intuitively wrong as a description of the way the American political system actually operates. It is naive in the sense that it ignores the very real differences in the responsiveness of political elites to equally numerous subgroups of the electorate. Clearly, there is an important class dimension that must be considered.

There is just as clearly a racial or ethnic dimension here, which is correlated with class but also independent of it to some degree. The preferences of one hundred members of a black church congregation will not be weighted as heavily as those of one hundred white chamber of commerce diners; very probably, they will not even be weighted as heavily as those of one hundred members of a white church congregation. African Americans seated at the chamber of commerce banquet table are likely to be given more of a hearing than others of their race outside the hall. *Votes* may be equally weighted at the ballot box, but *voters* are quite unequal in their capacity to see their candidates elected or their preferences enacted into law.

Thus, formal equality does not guarantee responsiveness. In the American context, the result is a political system in which influence is stratified by race and class. To some extent, the inequality of social and economic resources is reified and even amplified in the political sphere. Differing levels of education, occupation, and income translate into differing levels of voter turnout, civic competence, and campaign funds.

The legacy of legal and social stratification can affect the attitudes of officeholders, who may be more interested in representing their white constituents than the citizenry as a whole. Or political elites may fear that responsiveness to a bloc of minority voters will cost them an even larger bloc of support from hostile whites. In a highly charged racial context, voters are far from interchangeable; adding minority votes to a coalition may result in a net overall loss of electoral support. Thus, in a system of stratified pluralism, votes are not fungible, and the system is not colorblind in its operations.

A regime of "responsive pluralism" is only truly responsive to the groups that have been included within its definition of the citizenry. All other groups are allowed to participate in the governance of the polity only within the parameters set by the dominant majority. The model of stratified pluralism recognizes this inequality of status and the many ways in which its perpetuation is desired by the white electorate and reflected in elite political behavior.

Nonetheless, America's minority groups have made a great deal of progress in recent years with regard to officeholding. In at least two respects, enfranchisement and districting, the federal government has been quite aggressive in altering the prevailing rules of the game to assist in the quest for minority representation. It is important to recognize that the concept of stratified pluralism denotes a dynamic, not a static, system.

Although altering the racial pecking order is possible, it is politically difficult, and it invariably provokes a negative reaction (backlash) from a significant segment of the white electorate. We can envision a kind of developmental sequence that does not fit a straight-line model of racial succession but rather can be viewed as the dynamics of progress and reaction. In political forces that result, the negative reaction of whites tends to be weighted more heavily by political elites than the aspirations of minorities.

The clearest example of this process can be seen in the dramatic shift in the political allegiance of the South since the passage of the Civil Rights Act of 1964 and the Voting Rights Act of 1965. The widespread enfranchisement of African Americans and their growing influence in the Democratic Party triggered a wholesale defection of whites to the Republican Party beginning with the 1964 presidential election. The subsequent growth of GOP loyalty among southern whites is due to a number of factors, some of which (such as conservative religious values and an anticommunist foreign policy) have little or nothing to do with race per se (Cavanagh 1985). But the backlash to the civil rights movement's fight to overturn the long-standing hierarchy of racial subordination was undoubtedly the key factor that enabled the Republicans to establish a major beachhead in southern politics for the first time in the twentieth century.

The legacy of this period lives on in the peculiar position of African Americans in contemporary presidential politics. Blacks consistently cast roughly one out of every four votes received by the Democrats' presidential candidates. Their reward for this loyalty has been insistent criticism that the party is perceived as "too black" in its public image and too responsive to distinctive African American concerns on such subjects as affirmative action and welfare spending. Black participation in the Democratic coalition, in short, is perceived by the dominant school of political analysis as more of a liability than an asset. According to this line of argument, the visibility of black influence on policy priorities has driven more supposedly "desirable" constituencies, such as southerners, blue-collar whites, and the suburban middle class, to the Republican party, giving them a semipermanent presidential majority. (The most influential proponents of this position are Carmines and Stimson [1989] and Edsall and Edsall [1991].) Traditional white elites in the Democratic party have used this argument to justify a virtual abandonment of the fight against discrimination and poverty that lured many African Americans into the party.

Similar dynamics operate with even greater clarity at the local level. During the era of ethnic political machines, the Irish grudgingly made way to incorporate Italians, Jews, Poles, and other groups in their governing coalitions through ticket balancing and other gestures (Erie 1988; McNickle 1993). But the growth of a black constituency was generally greeted with alarm and resistance. In Chicago the Democratic machine cultivated white ethnic support through the pursuit of openly discriminatory policies in the administration of schools and housing, while allowing and even encouraging the atrophy of black voter par-

ticipation and political influence (Kleppner 1985). This is clearly a world far removed from the log-rolling clubhouse politics of the old white ethnic machines,
in which the votes of newly arrived groups were actively solicited and converted
into candidate slating and other public goods. Indeed, attempts to place ethnic
and racial politics in the same framework are thoroughly wrong-headed both
conceptually and empirically, for the simple reason that ethnic and racial politics are not different aspects of the same phenomenon but rather are *inversely* related. That is, the political and cultural identifications that distinguish white
ethnic groups lose virtually all of their salience when other minority competition begins to dominate electoral politics; as race becomes important, ethnicity
becomes irrelevant, and so does party identification.

In general, the tendency of white elites and white voters to resist minority political aspirations is seen most spectacularly when African American candidates
run for mayor in big cities. The campaign of Maynard Jackson in 1973 was confronted by the lament, "Atlanta's too young to die!" The Chicago mayoral election of 1983, in which Irish and Polish Democrats backed a Jewish Republican
over an African American Democrat, is perhaps the ultimate example of this
phenomenon. Race, in other words, clearly won out over both partisanship and
ethnicity as a determinant of the vote. Harold Washington's opponent in that
Chicago contest warned the city to turn back the black insurgency "Before it's
too late!" The symbolism of overturning the existing system of racial stratification has encouraged a level of hysteria in many of these contests that is unparalleled in contemporary mainstream American politics.

Of course, the transition from a biracial to a multicultural environment has
increased the challenges facing all of the players in contemporary urban politics.
Ironically, Latino and Asian Americans are now experiencing the same frustrations encountered by African Americans during earlier periods when they first
began challenging the entrenched ethnic machines of the frost belt. No sooner
have black politicians begun to taste some of the fruits of power than they find
themselves anxiously facing the aspirations of a new generation of outsiders re-
sentful of a legacy of exclusion.

One strategy that has been proposed to defuse such tensions is to downplay
issues of racial identity in favor of a more class-oriented call for economic redistribution. Whatever its ideological merits, this strategy faces at least two serious
operational limitations. First, African Americans at the grass-roots level have become increasingly embittered in recent years, especially in inner-city communities, and it can be difficult to mobilize them politically without some overt appeal to sentiments of racial pride. Second, class appeals may not be much more

palatable to the white middle class than racial and ethnic appeals, given the continuing fervent opposition to any new public initiatives requiring tax increases. Given such difficulties, black candidates seeking office in a white-majority environment generally downplay both racial issues and appeals for economic redistribution in favor of a bland, nonthreatening posture favorable to business and development interests. This strategy, known as "deracialization," has proved increasingly successful at the ballot box and may well be the major avenue for increasing black officeholding beyond its current strongholds in black urban areas. But it has also raised serious questions concerning the adequacy and legitimacy of the substantive representation being provided to the African American community (see Persons 1993).

It is tempting to imagine that the long history of minority subordination has created the potential for cross-racial unity to assert minority interests—a "rainbow coalition," in the vivid if controversial phrase of Jesse Jackson's 1984 presidential campaign. To the extent that stratified pluralism has placed minorities at an economic disadvantage, it might seem reasonable to expect a shared desire for a more redistributive political agenda. Indeed, virtually all major minority politicians today are Democrats. In Congress during the 1990s, only two African Americans, two Latino Americans, one Asian American, and one Native American were Republicans. The patterns are similar among state legislators: as of 1993, only 7 of 514 blacks, 20 of 161 Latinos, 2 of 54 Asians, and 1 of 41 Native Americans were Republicans (National Conference of State Legislatures, personal communication 1993). With the conspicuous exception of Cuban Americans in Florida, it is difficult to find a major nonwhite voting bloc with a recent pattern of Republican allegiance.

Although the shared experience of subordination may produce a common party identification in state and national politics, it does not necessarily unite America's ethnic racial minorities in the electoral realm at the local level. The distinctive aspects of each group's history frequently militate against any common ground. Indeed, given the advantages enjoyed by whites in the system of stratified pluralism, the minorities have sometimes sought to draw invidious distinctions among each other in the hope of bettering their positions.

CONCLUSION

As a matter of sheer arithmetic, it would seem inevitable that population trends will produce a less overwhelmingly white corps of elected and appointed officials in the increasingly multicultural United States of the twenty-first century.

If representation is a zero-sum game, in other words, one might simply expect to find losses of white representation and corresponding increases in minority representation.

Of course, the world is not so simple. Political incumbents rarely yield power gracefully and voluntarily. White political elites will no doubt find ways to delay the inevitable by coopting new minority allies as they appear and exploiting tensions among the various minority groups. The Republican strategy to cultivate Latino Americans as an "offset" to blacks is one example of these dynamics in action. The forthcoming entry of Korean Americans into electoral politics may be explosive, given the current strong animosity between them and African Americans in many of the country's urban areas (see Chapter 3 of this book).

But an even more fundamental question is how much any of this really matters in the allocation of who gets what in the polity and the society. Black politicians have been increasingly troubled in recent years by the seeming intractability of social and economic problems to their political efforts. Because most of these officials have come to power in cities ravaged by several decades of economic decline, resources have not generally been available to pursue a redistributive agenda on behalf of the predominantly lower-income black constituency. Affirmative action programs and minority contracting have made possible a sort of pork barrel for the African American middle class, but the benefits have yet to trickle down to the grass roots of the community (see Reed 1988).

When the pluralist school of political science was in its heyday, it was considered an article of faith that political and socioeconomic elites were distinct and that high socioeconomic status did not automatically translate into political influence. This position has lost credibility in recent years, not least because its assumptions of equal political responsiveness were shown to be so untrue for racial and ethnic minorities. Yet the current frustration of black political elites may demonstrate that there was, in an ironic sense, some validity to the pluralists' vision.

Political and economic elites are indeed distinct. That is precisely why political officeholding seems to afford so little leeway in solving social problems. With most of society's allocation decisions controlled by the private sector, public officials must resort to coaxing, cajoling, and financial incentives to induce investment decisions that are beneficial to their constituencies. Even in big cities where whites have "lost control" of electoral politics to African Americans, the direction of the economy generally remains in white hands.

Thus, in a sense, the pluralists had it right all along. The economy and the polity are indeed run by separate elites. But the pluralists (as well as their critics) misconceptualized the dynamics of influence. As the growing frustration of minority officeholders demonstrates so vividly, the essential problem is not that economic elites are able to dominate the polity but rather that political elites evidently lack the capacity to redirect the economy. And no amount of minority representation is likely to alter this reality any time soon.

Chapter 8 Legislative Redistricting and African American Interests: New Facts and Conventional Strategies

Bruce E. Cain

The Voting Rights Act (VRA) has promoted the electoral progress of the African American community in at least three distinctly different and important ways since its enactment in 1965. Initially and most dramatically, the ban on literacy tests, poll taxes, and other obstacles to enfranchisement led to the registration of more than one-half million new southern black voters within two years of its enactment. In subsequent years, section 5 preclearance review successfully prevented southern jurisdictions from adopting voting schemes that would have diluted the potential electoral influence of newly enfranchised black voters. Most recently, the Justice Department and minority voting rights advocates have used section 2 (as amended in 1982) to force both southern and nonsouthern jurisdictions into adopting electoral systems with lower thresholds of representation for minority candidates and into drawing redistricting plans that better respect the contours of African American neighborhoods.

Since 1965, various congressional amendments and judicial decisions have incrementally but considerably altered the act's focus. During this time, there have also been dramatic changes in the demographic and political conditions of many cities because of immigration patterns. The first change—the act's evolution from enfranchisement to dilution—has been much debated in recent years and needs little further elaboration here (see, for example, Thernstrom 1987; Butler 1985; Grofman and Davidson 1992). The less frequently discussed but equally important question is what the shifting urban demographic context means for African Americans with respect to voting rights specifically and political power generally. The latter is the focus of this chapter.

Simply put, my thesis is that immigration has changed African American politics in important ways. The old, essentially biracial urban context has given way to multiracialism, significantly complicating the application of the VRA to redistricting. By so doing, it has raised questions about the role that the act and legislative redistricting will have in promoting future African American political interests.

This chapter looks at the issues of vote dilution for the African American community in the context of this increasingly multiracial urban setting. It begins with the question of whether the VRA implicitly assumes an African American model of vote dilution and, if so, whether that model is appropriate for Latinos and Asians. It then looks at the zero-sum political problems that arise when various "protected" groups have competing claims to representation in a particular geographic area. Finally, it looks at how the complications introduced by multiracialism have fueled a debate over the limits of a districting strategy as a means of gaining and preserving African American political power.

THE VOTING RIGHTS ACT AND THE
CHALLENGE OF MULTIRACIALISM

The concept of political progress for African Americans through the extension and enforcement of voting rights is fairly straightforward. It begins with the assumption that the influence of the African American community depends on its electoral strength: white and black incumbents alike are more likely to be responsive to African American needs if they depend on the support of black voters to get elected. Election rules specify important restrictions on the voting process: the qualifications of candidates, the eligibility of voters, the methods by which ballots are counted, the jurisdictional boundaries that define which voters vote for which candidates, and the like. In this sense, the translation of preferences within the African American community into support for specific candidates and ultimately into public policies is mediated by rules and institutions.

In theory, "fairer" rules and institutions should lead to more responsive representatives and policies.

The Act from 1965 to 1990

The central purpose of the VRA is to prohibit institutions and practices that deny African Americans and other protected groups "an equal opportunity to elect a representative of their choice." The act explicitly defines "fairness" as "equal opportunity" rather than "proportionate division," but in practice the latter is often used as an indicator of the former. The actual determination of fairness is an empirical matter (a test)—an institution or practice is unfair if in a particular behavioral and demographic context it leads to the systematic exclusion or severe underrepresentation of a protected group. The facts of a voting rights case are therefore especially critical because a group may have a valid claim against a particular form of election or redistricting arrangement in one context but not in another.

Since its enactment the act has focused on two types of procedural unfairness. The first was voting requirements, such as poll taxes and literacy tests, that had been used extensively to disenfranchise potential African American voters in the post-Reconstruction South. Their discriminatory effects were twofold: literacy tests and poll taxes required knowledge or resources that most African Americans and poor southern whites did not possess, and they were typically administered so arbitrarily that local voter registrars could exclude virtually anyone they chose to reject (Kousser 1974, 1984, 1992). Poll taxes and literacy tests infringed on the right to vote per se.

The second type of procedural unfairness involved institutional obstacles that infringed on a more subtle voting right—the right to an undiluted vote (Butler and Cain 1992). A number of southern jurisdictions reacted to the prospect of enhanced African American electoral power by inventing ingenious ways to dilute or minimize that power. Some majority-white cities altered their boundaries to exclude minority African American neighborhoods. Others adopted at-large election schemes that enabled the white electorate to outvote the black minority in all districts or gerrymandered district boundaries to divide black neighborhoods. These actions did not impair the ability of African Americans to vote per se, but they did seriously mitigate the impact of the African American vote.

Beginning with *Allen v. State Board of Elections* (393 U.S. 544, 1969), voting rights cases increasingly dealt with issues of vote dilution rather than disenfranchisement (Grofman, Handley and Niemi 1992). The Supreme Court attempted to limit its intervention to cases of intentional discrimination in *Mobile v. Bolden* (446 U.S. 55, 1980), but in 1982 the VRA was amended to change the standard of proof from intention to effect. The Court upheld this shift in *Thornburg v. Gingles* (478 U.S. 30, 1986). The consequence of these changes in the law and its interpretation has been a rapid expansion during the last decade of the Justice Department's and the Court's activities in vote dilution issues.

The Act's Assumptions

Given the particular history of the Voting Rights Act, it is not surprising that the problems it addressed and the institutional remedies it imposed were tailored closely to the African American experience. That is, the act implicitly assumes a southern African American model of political facts. Many of those assumptions do not apply to nonsouthern urban settings or to other racial groups, however. This discrepancy raises questions about the appropriateness and adequacy of tests and remedies established under the act for urban politics in the 1990s. This point is illustrated in table 8.1, which presents the basic assumptions of the VRA and how they relate to the three major racial and ethnic groups in the United States.

AN ELIGIBLE MAJORITY

The first, and in many ways most central, assumption is that a protected group has a large (that is, at least a majority) core population that is eligible to vote but has been prevented from doing so by institutional barriers. This key assumption is true only for African Americans. The appallingly low participation of southern blacks prior to 1965 was caused primarily by institutional barriers, not by demographic factors such as disproportionate age ineligibility or high rates of noncitizenship. And the assumption is still generally true today, despite the growth of the foreign-born Caribbean black population in certain urban areas and the elimination of the most blatant discriminatory practices. Most African American neighborhoods still have relatively low ratios of noncitizens to citizens because black immigration, in contrast to Asian or Latino immigration, reached its peak earlier in the nineteenth century and has never been substantial since the Civil War. The Voting Rights Act provided African Americans with a remedy for procedures that operated unfairly against their predominantly native-born, age-eligible population.

Demographic factors are certainly not irrelevant to the difficulties of achieving full African American participation—in particular, below-average levels of education and income and high residential mobility have tended to suppress

Table 8.1

Assumptions and Applicability of the Voting Rights Act to Various Groups

	Applicability to		
	African Americans	Latinos	Asian Americans
Large core of age-eligible, unregistered citizens	Yes	Large population but high rates of noncitizenship and age ineligibility	Small but growing population; high rates of noncitizenship
History of discrimination	Yes	Yes, in older communities	Some, for example, Japanese, Chinese
Politically cohesive	Yes	Specific nationalities	Specific nationalities
Geographically concentrated	Yes	Dispersed outside core barrios	Varies by nationality and generation
Biracial voting (polarization)	Yes in the South, complex elsewhere	Generally no	Generally no

African American voting rates—but higher-than-average rates of noncitizenship and age ineligibility are more lethal electoral liabilities than below-average socioeconomic characteristics. The latter can be overcome with a great deal of organizational effort to mobilize the vote; no amount of increased political effort or consciousness can overcome ineligibility due to age or noncitizenship.

For these reasons, the issue of political participation for Latinos and Asians is more complicated than it is for African Americans. Many Asian and Latino communities have relatively high rates of noncitizenship and age ineligibility, creating enormous discrepancies between their shares of the population and their shares of the citizen voting-age population. For instance, in 1993 Asian and Latino groups in the city of Oakland proposed an Asian American plurality city council district that was 35 percent Asian in population but only 17 percent eligible and a Latino district that was 38 percent Latino in population but only 20 percent eligible. For another example, the ninth council district in Los Angeles in 1991 was more than 66 percent Latino in population but only 9 percent Latino in registered voters. The VRA can be used to remedy institutional biases, but it obviously cannot affect underparticipation caused by high rates of ineligibility.

The eligibility issue has forced the courts and the relevant jurisdictions to consider special factors when deciding whether Latino and Asian plaintiffs have a valid voting rights claim. Informal redistricting norms that have been developed in cases involving African Americans—such as the so-called 65 percent rule (under which a district must have a 65 percent African American population in order for it to have a fair opportunity to elect a representative of its choice)—are inadequate in cases involving large immigrant communities (Brace, Grofman, Handley, and Niemi 1988). Because of the age distribution and noncitizenship, a proposed Latino or Asian district might need to be 75 percent or more Latino or Asian in order for candidates from the protected communities to have a realistic chance of winning. Remedies that change rules, district or other boundaries, or procedures for Asians or Latinos without taking sufficient account of the group's demographic characteristics will only appear to address the problem of underrepresentation; they will inevitably fail in the actual results.

Apart from problems of implementing the VRA, Latino and Asian immigration has raised the controversial and divisive philosophical issue of whether ineligible nonvoting populations should receive the same voting rights protections that the predominantly native-born black population receives. In theory, the act could have been designed as a right of representation that intended to protect "communities of interest" constituted by minority neighborhoods. This would have been consistent with the American practice of counting population, not voters, for apportionment purposes. The right explicitly referred to, however, is "the opportunity to elect a representative of their own choice." The question thus becomes whether the existing institutions are denying a protected group its rightful *electoral* opportunity. Had it been designated a community-of-interest or a representational rather than a voting right, citizenship and voter eligibility issues would have been avoided. As the act stands, however, a court needs some basis for determining whether particular groups have valid voting claims. Hence the considerations of citizen, voting-age population.

A HISTORY OF DISCRIMINATION

A second assumption in the Voting Rights Act is that the protected group has a political history of discrimination and can show a persistent pattern of electoral frustration. The act was initially designed to remedy a long-standing problem of systematic electoral discrimination against African Americans. It furthered the enfranchisement goals of the Fourteenth and Fifteenth Amendments, but, as discussed above, it also extended equal protection into the realm of vote dilution and "fair representation." Plaintiffs in a case must establish that minority candidates have tried to run for office and failed to win on a number of occasions—in other words, that there has been a history of electoral failure. Moreover, a number of the secondary criteria in the overall circumstances considered as tests refer to such factors as demonstrating a history of official discrimination in electoral procedures and public policy, proving that lower levels of education, employment, and health services are due to the lingering effects of discrimination, or finding evidence of racial appeals to voters in past campaigns.

Since the African American community has a relatively long, uninterrupted and well- documented political history, these tests are well suited to voting rights claims by African American plaintiffs. And since racism toward African Americans has been so open and ingrained in American culture, the historical record showing discrimination and even intent is usually clear, especially in the South. But the record is not always so clear for other protected groups.

To be sure, there has been historical discrimination against Latinos and Asians—immigration quotas, restrictions on land ownership, and the like. But a very large percentage of the growing Latino and Asian populations is foreign-born, and many of the immigrants have no personal or family connection to the discrimination of the earlier period. Certainly this can be said of the Koreans, Central Americans, and Indo-Chinese whose presence in the United States was minimal prior to World War II. But even for groups with many second- and third-generation members, such as Mexican Americans and Chinese Americans, the presence of so many new immigrants raises questions about historical claims that do not arise with predominantly native-born populations.

Changes due to immigration and migration also alter potential electoral opportunities and legal liabilities under the Voting Rights Act. In areas where it is only possible to create 45 percent Latino population seats at the beginning of a decade, it might be feasible to create a 70 percent Latino seat by the end of the decade. These novel demographic conditions raise new questions. When are there enough potential voters of a given race or ethnicity in an area to create obligations under the VRA? Is a remedy really necessary—for instance, is there any evidence as yet of white voter polarization against a given group during the relatively short time it may have been in the United States? If there are not enough potentially eligible voters, or if the community has never tested the electoral waters with a credible candidate, then plaintiffs might have to go through a couple of electoral cycles in order for these conditions to be met.

Urban multiracialism does not neatly fit into the simple generalizations of southern biracialism. Some urban racial minorities have been more successful than others in winning white support. Thus, to assume white voting polarization against Asian Americans, for instance, is problematic because Asian American candidates have been very successful in winning white votes in such states as California and Hawaii. Or, in some instances, the political frustration of one minority group is caused at least partially by bloc voting against it by another protected group.

POLITICAL COHERENCE

The third assumption of the Voting Rights Act is that protected groups are politically coherent. This premise is most clearly embodied in the *Gingles* criterion, which requires members of a racial or ethnic group that is seeking protection under the act to operate as a single political entity, exhibiting common political goals and actions. Here again, an African American model underlies the premise: the fact that African Americans are a cohesive political force is sufficiently common in the United States that it can generally be taken for granted. African American identity is not heavily fractured along national or tribal lines, and a combination of partisan and ideological factors reinforce African American political coherence. Most blacks identify with the Democratic Party, and their political attitudes are highly liberal, even in the black middle class (Uhlaner 1991; Carmines and Stimson 1989). Recent work has called attention to class and generational differences within black public opinion, but compared with other racial and ethnic groups, African Americans exhibit the highest level of political coherence (Jackson 1991). In contrast, nationalism creates substantial divisions for some of the new immigrant groups (see Chapters 9 and 10 in this book). Among Latinos, for instance, there are important differences in the political attitudes, party identification, and voting behavior of Cubans, Puerto Ricans, and Mexican Americans. The recently conducted National Latino Political Election Survey (NLPES) found that Latinos were more likely to think of themselves in national than in such pan-ethnic terms as Latino or Hispanic (de la Garza et al. 1992). Voting rights litigation involving Latinos to date has not been forced to deal with this problem to any major degree because Latino residential patterns tend to follow nationality lines—Cubans are concentrated in Florida, Mexican Americans in the Southwest, and Puerto Ricans in northeastern cities. On the basis of the NLPES data, however, one might predict that if there is greater intermingling of these different Latino groups, pan-ethnic cohesiveness may become a serious issue for Latino Americans in the future in terms of making claims under the VRA.

Nationality differences are even more pronounced in the Asian American community. A 1984 statewide survey of California Asians found evidence of significant attitudinal and partisan differences among Koreans, Japanese, Filipinos, and Chinese (Cain and Kiewiet 1984). A more recent study of Asian voting behavior in the Bay Area uncovered important nationality differences in the support for an Asian American candidate for statewide office (Tam 1992). Since the Asian groups tend to be more equal in size and to live in closer proximity to one another than the Latino groups, the tension between national and racial identity is fairly critical. A voting rights claim for a specific nationality group, such as the Koreans or the Japanese, is more likely than an "Asian" claim to pass the political coherence test but then fail with respect to the size requirement because a group must be sufficiently large to constitute a majority of a district. In contrast, a claim for a pan-Asian coalition is less likely to pass the coherence requirement but more likely to satisfy the size requirement. This dilemma is why there has been no successfully litigated Asian voting rights claim to date.

GEOGRAPHICAL DEFINITION

The fourth assumption of the Voting Rights Act is that protected groups live in geographically well-defined areas. This premise arises from the requirements for single-member district remedies that the courts typically impose on jurisdictions that are in violation of the act. A district system will remedy underrepresentation in a racially polarized situation only if a group is geographically concentrated in sufficiently large numbers to constitute a majority of the potential voters in a district. If a particular racial or ethnic minority group has the requisite size but is dispersed throughout a jurisdiction, a district solution provides no relief: instead of being a minority in one at-large district, the group becomes a minority in a number of single-member districts, exchanging one form of electoral failure for another.

When a protected group is sufficiently concentrated in a given area, it is possible to draw district lines that optimize their electoral potential. And to the extent that there is tolerance for contorted shapes, carefully crafted district lines can compensate for moderate geographic dispersion. A review of voting rights cases suggests that the courts have adopted a fairly flexible definition of compactness (Grofman, Handley, and Niemi 1992). In response, many jurisdictions in the 1990 round of redistricting adopted noncompact districts in minority areas in order to avoid or settle potential voting rights litigation. The decision in *Shaw v. Reno* (113 S. Ct. 2816 [1993]), however, indicates that the Court will not tolerate extremely noncompact districts.

The applicability of the geographical concentration assumption even in this loosely defined sense varies enormously across both groups and locales (see Chapter 2 of this book). The purest cases of well-defined geographic concentrations are black neighborhoods in cities such as New York, Boston, Chicago, and Los Angeles. At the other end of the continuum, rural southern black populations tend to be located in dispersed pockets, requiring sprawling and wildly noncompact district solutions. Latino neighborhoods are a mixture. Some are concentrated barrios, especially in urban and farming areas, but suburban Latino pockets are often dispersed and integrated. Geographic dispersion in the Asian community varies with the degree of assimilation: it is particularly high in the Japanese American community and relatively low in the Korean and Chinese populations.

The geographic concentration requirement becomes more of an issue for all groups as the goal shifts from using the Voting Rights Act to remedy exclusion to maximizing minority representation to the greatest feasible degree. Typically, the core minority neighborhoods are the first areas to get voting rights protection, but as the focus shifts to creating additional opportunities, the pressure to resort to more exotic district shapes mounts. More than any other assumption, compactness has been altered by the realities of implementation to accommodate the evolving goals of the act.

RACIAL POLARIZATION

The final implicit assumption of the Voting Rights Act is there are clear patterns of voting polarization along racial or ethnic lines. Prior to 1965 in the South, blacks were politically dominated by a white majority. The empirical issue was relatively simple: Could candidates supported by the black community expect any support from white voters? The tests required in order to prove this were also relatively simple—either homogeneous precinct analysis (that is, looking at the voting patterns for white and black candidates in majority black and white population precincts) or statistical bivariate correlations and regressions. There was little or no need to be concerned with class differences or the effect of other racial and ethnic groups on voting support patterns (Lupia and McCue 1990).

In the contemporary urban environment, the context is multiracial and often more subtly polarized. The original rationale behind examining voting polarization patterns in voting rights cases was that the need for a remedy stems from the coincidence of both institutional and behavioral hurdles: a minority can be consistently frustrated from achieving fair representation if the dominant racial group votes as a bloc *and* if the voting procedure or districting arrangement favors the majority. But when the electorate is divided into several racial and ethnic groups, the possibilities of cross-group support greatly complicate the calculus of polarization. From a measurement perspective alone, multiracialism changes the statistical analysis from bivariate to multivariate tests. But more important, it raises a number of troubling implementation issues: What if the minority is blocked by a coalition of white and nonwhite voters? Can a coalition of minorities claim voting rights protections, or are they only reserved for single ethnic and racial groups? The courts must provide answers to these questions with little or no guidance from the Voting Rights Act.

Separate from the complications of having multiple racial and ethnic groups, the assumption of clear patterns of polarized voting can also break down in other ways. One is that racial attitudes are often not homogeneous throughout a city. Polarization may be evident in certain white neighborhoods of a city and absent in others. Such a pattern is important because a majority minority strategy where there is no polarization can actually diminish a group's share of representation by leaving potentially supportive white voters out of minority districts and reducing the size of the voting pool from which minority districts can be drawn. In contrast, areas where polarization exists may need voting rights protections in order to create or preserve minority representation.

The possible existence of neighborhood differences in polarization levels also raises delicate and increasingly subtle questions about the need for voting rights protection. For instance, if a city contains only a few extreme neighborhoods that are dominating the analytic data on polarization, does it make sense to characterize the whole city as racially polarized? Or, to take another example, if there are wide socioeconomic variations among neighborhoods, can one be sure that race, rather than class, is causing the seemingly polarized voting pattern?

Implications

I do not mean to imply that the complications of applying the VRA caused by multiracialism are irresolvable. Rather, I want to argue two points. First, like a scientific model that increasingly encounters empirical anomalies, the breakdown of the law's underlying assumptions destroys its parsimony. Simplicity in understanding of when and where the act applies is lost, leading to misunderstanding and confusion. Second, support for the VRA among the public and the press seems to weaken as the facts of recent cases are less like the circumstances that led to the act's passage in 1965.

From this standpoint, it is a virtue that the VRA is applied on a case-by-case basis and that the specific facts of each case are carefully considered. To date, the courts have paid close attention to the empirical issues, ruling against minority plaintiffs in situations in which the *Gingles* criteria have not been met (for example, *Romero v. City of Pomona* [883 F.2d 1418, 9th Cir. 1989] and *Latino Political Action Committee v. City of Boston* [784 F.2d 409, 1st Cir. 1986]). But the disadvantage of the case-by-case approach is that because violations are determined by facts, and because voting rights considerations are numerous and increasingly subtle, it is hard to know with certainty in advance whether a jurisdiction has an obligation under the Voting Rights Act, especially when it involves immigrant communities. More frequently than not in multiracial urban areas, jurisdictions find themselves on the legal frontier without firm guidelines to assist them in their decisions. In *Garza v. County of Los Angeles* (918 F.2d 763, 9th Cir. 1990), a case involving the dilution of the votes of Latinos in the redistricting of the Los Angeles Board of Supervisors, the court could have tried to address a number of these questions about how to apply the VRA in the context of the new mulitracialism, but instead chose to base its decision on a finding of intentional discrimination, leaving the questions unanswered.

CONGRESSIONAL REDISTRICTING IN THE 1990S

Given the potential complications of an increasingly multiracial political world, it is valuable to look at recent experience to see how voting rights protection has helped or hindered the cause of African American empowerment. I focus on the congressional redistricting after the 1990 census for two reasons. First, redistricting is the only procedural way that African Americans can increase their representation in the U.S. House of Representatives. Whereas some state and local governments continue to use various at-large and multimember systems that can under certain circumstances dilute black voting strength, congressional elections are held in single-member districts only. Vote dilution in congressional elections is therefore restricted to situations in which African American voters have been unfairly partitioned into separate districts. Because the VRA can be used by protected groups to force jurisdictions to align their district lines more optimally, congressional redistrictings are the purest case of electoral empowerment through the application of the act.

Another advantage of studying congressional redistrictings is that they proceed at a more rapid pace after a census than other legislative redistrictings due to the requirements of Article 1, Section 2, of the U.S. Constitution. Thus, one can say more at the present time about developments in congressional redistricting than about redistricting at any other level.

Table 8.2 provides a summary of the states in which minority voting rights figured significantly during the 1990 congressional redistricting. This table lists the state, the type of minority representation issue at stake, whether the geographical area in question was rural, urban or suburban, the race and party of affected incumbents, whether to this point there has been any litigation on these matters, and the state's minority percentages. It is possible to make some generalizations from this matrix about how African Americans fared in this latest round of congressional redistricting.

New Black Districts

First, African Americans are still gaining congressional districts as a result of the VRA, either directly (through changes in district plans due to formal review by the courts or by the Justice Department) or indirectly (through the actions of jurisdictions trying to avoid litigation or Justice Department review). There are

Table 8.2

States in Which Minority Representation Was an Issue in 1990 Congressional Redistricting

	Issue	Location	Incumbent Affected	Litigation	State Minority Population
Alabama	Creating black seat	Birmingham and environs	White Democrat	Yes	Black, 25%
Arizona	Adding Latino voters ro Latino incumbent district; splitting Hopi and Navaho communities	Phoenix and Tucson; northern Arizona	White Republican	Yes	Hispanic, 19% Native American, 5%
Arkansas	Creating black minority-influence seat	Disparate rural areas	White Democrat	Yes	Black, 16%
California	Creating Latino seats; preserving black seats	Los Angeles primarily, but also central valley	White Democrat	Yes	Hispanic 26% Asian, 9% Black, 7%
Florida	Creating black and Latino seats	Miami; south Florida	White Democrat	Yes; federal panel drew district lines	Black, 13% Hispanic, 12%
Georgia	Creating second and third black majority districts	Augusta and Savannah; southwest	White Republicans, and White Democrat	No, but Justice Department rejected two prior plans	Black, 27%
Illinois	Preserving two black districts; creating new Latino seat	Chicago	White Democrat	Yes; federal court–approved map	Black, 15% Hispanic, 8%
Louisiana	Creating second black seat	Linked rural areas	White Democrat	No; Justice Department	Black, 31%
Maryland	Creating second black seat	Suburban Washington, D.C.	White Democrat	Yes	Black, 25%
Massachusetts	Creating black minority-influence seat	Boston	White Democrat	Yes, but only concerning Massachusetts's total of seats number	Hispanic, 5% Black, 5%
Michigan	Preserving two black seats	Detroit	White Democrats	Yes	Black, 14%

State	Action	Location	Incumbents	Approved?	Population
Minnesota	Creating black minority-influence seat	Minneapolis	White Democrat, White Republican	Yes	Black, 2%
Mississippi	Preserving existing black seats	Western Mississippi along river delta	Black Democrat incumbent (Espy)	No; Justice Department approved	Black, 35%
Missouri	Preserving black district	Urban and suburban St. Louis	White Democrat (female)	No	Black, 11%
New Jersey	Creating second majority minority Hispanic, 10%	Hudson County (urban)	White Democrat	No (Commission)	Black, 13%
New York	Creating second Latino seat; preserving existing black seats	New York City	White and Black Democrats	No; Justice Department approved	Black, 14% Hispanic, 12%
North Carolina	Creating two new black seats	rural; Durham, Greensboro, Charlottesville, Winston-Salem	Two white Democrats	Yes	Black, 22%
Ohio	Creating minority-influence seat; "packing" minority voters in small number of state house districts to reduce influence in adjacent districts	Cleveland, Columbus	Black Democrat	No; yes	Black, 11%
Pennsylvania	Preserving black district	Philadelphia	White Democrat	Yes	Black, 9%
South Carolina	Creating new black seat	South and central rural and urban areas	White Democrat	Yes	Black, 30%
Tennessee	Preserving black seat	Memphis	Black Democrat	No	Black, 16%
Texas	Creating two new Latino and one new black seat	Houston, San Antonio and southern Texas, Dallas	None (most incumbents protected)	Yes; federal court approved	Hispanic, 26% Black, 12%
Virginia	Creating new black seat	Part of Richmond and suburbs and rural areas east of Richmond	White Republican	No; Justice Department approved	Black, 19%

currently thirty-nine African Americans in the House of Representatives: all but two represent majority nonwhite districts, and twenty-two represent majority black populations. With the completion of the 1990 round of redistricting (including court and Justice Department reviews), there were eleven new black majority congressional districts.

Second, all of the gains in majority black districts are in the southern and border states. In a few states—such as South Carolina, North Carolina, Virginia, Florida, and Alabama—they are the first majority black districts in the modern era. In others—such as Georgia, Louisiana, Maryland, and Texas—they represent additional black majority districts. African Americans also picked up a few so-called minority-influence districts in states such as Arkansas and Massachusetts—districts in which blacks constitute a significant minority but not a majority of the electorate.

Several of the new black districts stretch conventional norms and expectations of compactness, linking far-flung black communities together into new black majority districts. A good example of this phenomenon is North Carolina's first congressional district, which ties together rural eastern North Carolina with African American neighborhoods in Durham. The Justice Department approved the district but commented that its convoluted form was probably not necessary, implying that the preservation of Democratic Party interests rather than the geographical dispersion of black communities per se caused the district's shape to be irregular (*Congressional Quarterly* 1991, 3726). The district was invalidated by the U.S. Supreme Court in *Shaw v. Reno* (113 S. Ct. 2816 [1993]).

But despite the sometimes creative efforts of state legislators to minimize the impact of voting rights adjustments on incumbents, new minority districts often have adverse consequences for white incumbents, especially but not always white male Democrats. Sometimes Republican incumbents are affected by these efforts: for instance, to help make way for a new black district in Virginia, two Republican incumbents, Thomas J. Bliley and George F. Allen, were placed in the same district; in Georgia, Newt Gingrich's district was carved up to help create an Atlanta-based black majority district.

Prior to the release of the census data, there was much discussion about a new Republican voting rights strategy: Republicans would turn vigorous enforcement of the VRA to partisan advantage, using their control of the Justice Department (which is responsible for section 5 pre-clearance and for section 2 litigation) to force the formation of minority districts at the expense of white democratic incumbents. From this strategic perspective, there were notable successes for the Republicans. For example, Tom McMillan lost his district in Maryland to make way for a new black district, as did Ben Jones in Georgia. But, unfortunately for Republicans, Democrats controlled the redistricting process in most of the states in which the issue of new black majority districts arose. In Texas and Virginia, for instance, the Democrats were able to form new districts with convoluted lines that simultaneously protected party interests and satisfied the VRA. The November 1992 elections brought a great deal of turnover in the Congress, and the fact that some incumbents had been running in newly redrawn boundaries may have contributed to this outcome, but there was no major partisan advantage for either party.

Even in states where the Democrats did not have control of the redistricting process by themselves, the VRA did not disadvantage them very much. Consider California, for example, where Democrats, Republicans, and, eventually, the Court Masters produced six different congressional plans (three by the Democrats alone), all of which would have passed Justice Department review but which varied widely in their projected partisan effects, largely due to differences in white suburban and rural districts that were not covered by the VRA. Although some of the white Democrat incumbents were moved further into the suburbs in order to preserve or create new black and Latino districts, no California Democratic incumbent lost in 1992.

New Demographic Realities

The creation of a new black or minority-influence district is the most dramatic voting rights outcome, but it may not be the most important one, especially during the upcoming round of 2001 redistrictings. Another important role for the VRA is that of protecting existing majority black districts from detrimental changes that might result from broad demographic changes. Two kinds of changes were particularly important in recent years. The first and most prevalent was the loss of representation by inner cities. Cities that declined in population either absolutely or proportionately, and states that lost congressional districts in the apportionment process, had to decide which seats to collapse and how to fill out the populations of the remaining districts. Protection of black majority districts under the VRA removed them from the list of districts that could feasibly be collapsed. As a consequence, no state reduced its number of black majority districts in 1992.

Although the VRA can be used to prevent retrogression in African American representation, it is not a prophylactic against all adverse political consequences for black incumbents. Saving an underpopulated inner-city district sometimes means picking up surrounding districts in the suburbs, or at least outside their inner-city bases. Examples of this were the changes in the districts of Gus Savage in Chicago, John Lewis in Atlanta, and Barbara-Rose Collins and John Conyers in Detroit. Sometimes the preservation of districts alters their character in important ways. For instance, in Savage's case, moving his district into middle-class black and white neighborhoods was partly responsible for Mel Reynold's primary victory.

Where black districts have population deficits, the VRA cannot be used to avoid the constitutional requirements of "one person, one vote." All districts must be equally populated within the normal bounds. The act's protection can only ensure that in the process of meeting the "equal population" constitutional mandate, there is no unnecessary "retrogression" in the district's racial composition. In 1990, the problem of underpopulation in inner-city black districts (districts with less than the target population for redistricting) was exacerbated by the census undercount. The Census Bureau acknowledged that its counts missed about 5 percent of the black population, causing black districts to be credited with less population than they had. The Census Bureau had anticipated this problem and worked during the decade preceding the 1990 census to develop a method of adjusting for the undercount in the minority communities. Unfortunately, the Commerce Secretary, Robert Mosbacher, overrode the bureau director's recommendation and prevented the use of the adjusted figures for redistricting (or any other) purposes.

The effect of the secretary's decision on black majority districts was to malapportion them in much the same way (although to a considerably lesser degree) that urban districts were malapportioned prior to the Supreme Court's decision in *Baker v. Carr* (369 U.S. 186 [1962]). Suburban and white districts were credited with a higher share of the population than they truly had, and urban, nonwhite areas were credited with less. Moreover, it meant that the burden of finding areas with additional people for underpopulated inner-city black majority seats was greater than it should have been.

Returning to table 8.2, the third and last generalization to be gleaned from it is that much of the congressional redistricting action after 1990, especially outside the South, concerned the creation of Latino districts. New Latino districts were constructed in California, Florida, Illinois, New York, and Texas, and in two states, Arizona and Florida, congressional seats held by Latino incumbents were made majority Latino.

The most troubling aspect of this development from the perspective of African Americans is that in at least two cases, Latinos and African Americans had legitimate claims to represent the same areas. The two cases are California and New

York. In California, the black population in eastern and south-central Los Angeles had been migrating west and was being replaced by Latinos. In the ten-year span between the 1980 and 1990 censuses, neighborhoods of African Americans had been replaced by Latinos, and African American incumbents such as Marvyn Dymally were representing districts with large and growing Latino populations. In New York, the dispersion of the city's Latino population over all five boroughs meant that Latino neighborhoods had to be taken from the districts of four black Democratic incumbents in order to create a second Latino seat.

When Latino neighborhoods are taken from districts represented by black incumbents, those districts have to pick up additional black neighborhoods or they have to take voters from adjacent census tracts containing white voters. The former concentrates black electoral strength suboptimally, and the latter raises the prospect of a new white voting bloc capable of winning a plurality in a multicandidate race. Either way, the political implication is that Latino gains may in certain situations come at the expense of black political representation or, at least, add risk to the electoral situation of vulnerable black representatives. This is most likely to occur in the multiracial cities than in the rural South and more likely at state and local levels of representation before it becomes widespread for congressional districts. For example, in Los Angeles the issue has been more salient for redrawing the city and school board districts than it was for the congressional districts.

It is also possible that the Asian population may begin to make competing claims for representation in the near future. For instance, the Koreans in Los Angeles and the Chinese in San Francisco made presentations to the California state legislature and to the relevant city and county authorities about what they wanted from the 1990 round of redistricting. To date, there are no Asian American majority congressional districts on the U.S. mainland (although there are Asian American congressmen), nor does it appear that there is sufficient population in any area at the present time under the *Gingles* criterion to support such a claim. Asians are a protected group, however, and assuming they can meet the requirements of the VRA, there may be more voting rights litigation from the Asian American community in the future.

From an African American perspective, the VRA has been (demonstrably) advantageous in hostile biracial situations. But in multiracial settings with no option to expand the existing number of representatives, the claims of one protected group can clash with those of another, creating a zero-sum voting rights struggle. In areas of demographic transition, jurisdictions can face an impossible choice: they can remove Latino or Asian neighborhoods from black incumbent districts in order to form new Latino or Asian districts, potentially causing retrogression in black representation, or they can retain these neighborhoods in the black districts, missing an opportunity to increase Latino or Asian representation. The VRA itself provides no clear guidance on this choice, forcing the conflict into the realm of pure politics.

The Electoral Strategy Revisited

Recent redistricting experiences have fueled a debate among some African Americans about the value and importance of the traditional voting rights electoral strategy. Conventional wisdom argues that incremental gains in African American representation through the creation of black districts contributes to the cause of African American empowerment. Once in office, it is argued, African American incumbents better represent the interests of the African American community than did their white predecessors. Recently, however, critics have challenged this conventional wisdom: one line of criticisms questions the electoral strategy on its own terms, the other questions its basic premises.

One key difficulty with the electoral strategy on its own terms is that there are only a finite number of potential black majority districts that can be drawn in the United States. As discussed above, all of the post-1990 black congressional districts were drawn in the South. In the rest of the country, the black share of the population is not growing as rapidly as that of the new urban immigrant populations or the white suburban population, so the main application of the Voting Rights Act is protective. The critical questions are whether there is going to be enough demographic raw material to create any substantial number of additional black majority districts in the year 2001, and if so, where? Unless the African American population share rises rapidly, in the 2000 census it is likely that the redistricting goal of the African-American community will be only preventive, not expansionist. The theoretical upper limit of descriptive representation (that is, representation of black communities by black representatives) is proportional representation—a share of descriptive representation equal to the black share of the population. In reality, due to the difficulty of trying to achieve proportionality through the mechanism of single-member districting, a more realistic expectation for minority groups is something below perfectly proportional shares (Rae 1967).

Thus, the first problem with a majority minority districting strategy is that there is a theoretical and empirical ceiling to how much descriptive representation can be achieved. For blacks, that ceiling already may have been realized, and the political demands of Latinos and Asians could further lower that ceiling. As the population share of other protected groups increases, their legitimate claims to representation may increasingly clash with the legitimate claims of the African American community. From the perspective of a descriptive representation strategy, the situation is a no-win one for African Americans. Taking low-voting, high-immigrant Latino or Asian neighborhoods out of black districts to create majority Latino or Asian seats could lead to retrogression in African American representation. But opposing that approach puts African Americans in the uncomfortable position of opposing additional representation for other underrepresented groups and of using the logic and rhetoric that had previously been used against African Americans by white opponents of the VRA.

The problem is resolvable if people are willing to compromise. It is extremely unlikely that the courts are going to be able to settle the issue, especially since the VRA offers no guidelines for distinguishing between the claims of competing ethnic or racial groups. Some political way of resolving the differences will have to be found, and it is likely to be difficult. In negotiations over the city council redistricting in Los Angeles, the city encouraged representatives from the Mexican-American Legal Defense and Education Fund and the NAACP to work out their differences in private and to present a joint proposal to city officials. But negotiations between the groups broke down. The Latinos wanted to create a new majority Latino district in downtown Los Angeles, pushing the African American districts out of the central city commercial areas and to the west. The African American community was unwilling to give up the downtown area and argued that the westward movement would excessively concentrate black neighborhoods, resulting in the loss of a black-influence district. In the end, the city enacted a compromise plan that the African American community endorsed and the Latinos opposed.

A similar situation occurred in the Oakland, California, redistricting in 1993. A task force of Asian Americans and Latinos presented a plan that would have linked Asian neighborhoods to an Asian plurality district. But the plan removed a black incumbent from a traditional black district in West Oakland, placed a white incumbent in her place, and doubled the number of white voters to a position of near parity with the black voters in the African American district. The logic of those who presented the plan was that African Americans already had their fair share of representation, that the white incumbent and her predominantly white constituents had to be placed into the previously majority African American district in order for Asian Americans to have a fair opportunity to elect a representative of their choice. As in Los Angeles, Oakland was forced to produce a compromise plan.

In both cases, the logic and language of legal entitlement seemed to get in the way of political settlement. All of the groups felt that they had a right to protection under the Voting Rights Act and that they should not be required to bargain away that right. If these cases are a glimpse of future redistricting conflicts in multiracial urban areas, they will be thorny issues to sort out, and in the end, unless the African American population grows significantly, the VRA will bring few if any new gains for African Americans and may require that they relinquish representation in some areas.

The other line of criticism of conventional voting rights strategies comes from an African American political scientist, Carol Swain (1993). Swain argues that forming coalitional rather than majority black districts is a more promising strategy and that nonblacks who represent significantly large black neighborhoods tend to have voting records that are very sympathetic to the black community. Swain argues for more coalitional districts that will leverage black political influence beyond the level that can be achieved through majority black districts alone. And even when such electoral strategies are unnecessary, governing coalitions may be necessary if African American representatives constitute a minority of those elected to office. Browning, Marshall, and Tabb (1986) distinguish between various levels of empowerment, arguing that membership in the dominant coalition is the essential last step. A narrowly focused redistricting strategy might result in more descriptive representation for any given minority group, but it does not guarantee membership in the dominant coalition once elected to office.

Guinier (1992) makes an even more radical critique of the majority minority districting strategy, arguing that it fails to take an adequately broad vision of political equality and empowerment, which would create equal status for members of minority groups as full participants in political decision-making so as to bring about fair results. Guinier, in essence, is looking for institutional changes in the way we select representatives and make policy, rather than legal remedies under the existing rules.

Swain's vision of coalitional politics and Guinier's vision of more fundamental empowerment are unlikely to supplant the majority minority electoral strategy in the near future, but as the VRA increasingly functions to protect the status quo for African Americans but fails to expand black political power, alternative visions and strategies become more appealing. For the time being, however, redistricting and the majority minority electoral strategy are likely to retain a central role into the twenty-first century.

Chapter 9 Political Activity and Preferences of African Americans, Latinos, and Asian Americans

Carole Jean Uhlaner

Thirty years ago a discussion of minority group members in American politics would have focused almost exclusively on the experiences of African Americans. Today attention is shared with one or more Latino and Asian American groups. The demographic change reflects not only natural increase but also substantial immigration from Asia and Central and Latin America. These new nonblack, nonwhite residents have the potential to profoundly affect U.S. politics. This effect could be either to dilute or to enhance the political influence of African Americans, depending on two key factors.

First, a group's rate of participation has the effect of either magnifying or diminishing its size. For example, if few members vote, their electoral impact will be slighter than their numbers suggest. Low naturalization rates further reduce electoral influence. To the extent that African Americans are more politically active than Latinos and Asian Americans, the latter groups' population percentages overstate their political impact. Second—and this is crucial—if groups form coalitions they can augment each other's power. For instance, the influence of African Americans will increase if Latinos support them. Group attitudes can provide evidence that coalitions have formed or are feasible. This evidence would include shared party identification and similar preferences on key issues or basic policy positions. Thus, in mapping out the impact of immigration on the political fortunes of African Americans, it is important to assess the relative participation rates of blacks, Latinos, and Asian Americans, their comparative party preferences, and the similarities and dissimilarities in their opinions on issues.

Of course, none of these racial or ethnic groups is homogeneous, despite the convenience of suggesting otherwise. The terms *Latino* and *Asian American* lump together people of various national origins, many of whom do not identify with the broader category. Given limitations in available data, this aggregation across national lines will be an unavoidable problem in discussing Asian Americans. In at least part of this chapter, however, the category "Latino" can be disaggregated by national origin. Moreover, recent immigrants differ from longer-term residents, and both differ from native-born Americans in a number of important ways. There are substantial numbers of Latino and Asian American immigrants, whereas few African Americans were born outside the United States. Finally, there are major differences within each of these racial or ethnic groups in sociodemographic characteristics, including income and education. Some apparent differences in political attributes between ethnic, racial, or national-origin groups may simply reflect differences by race or ethnicity in the distribution of these variables. If apparent differences between groups remain once demographic characteristics are controlled, then there might be political characteristics that are related to ethnicity or race. By making comparisons across ethnic and racial groups, and with non-Hispanic whites, we can assess which phenomena are particular to a group, which arise from a more general minority group experience, and which reflect processes that are common to everyone.

This chapter has three parts, addressing political participation rates, party identification, and issue preferences and the prospects for coalition. Within each of the sections, I first discuss some applicable theories. Next I present a comparative description of African Americans, Latinos, Asian Americans, and, usually, non-Hispanic whites, first as whole groups and then disaggregated, as sketched above, along lines of national origin, immigration status, and sociodemographic factors. I begin with a description of the data.

DATA

Some information was obtained from government documents and other published reports. In addition, two primary sources of survey data were used in my analysis. The first is the American National Election Studies (NES) for 1980, 1984, and 1988. Although the sample size of about two thousand in these studies limits the number of minority respondents, and the samples include only citizens, the studies have the compensating advantage of containing vote validation data. After the election, researchers accessed registration and voting records to verify respondents' reports of activity, since self-reports tend to inflate activity. The NES studies contain enough non-Hispanic whites, African Americans, and, especially in the later years, Latinos for analysis, but they have far too few Asian American respondents for year-by-year examination.

The second source is the 1984 survey of ethnic groups in California directed by Bruce Cain, Rod Kiewiet, and Carole Uhlaner and funded by the Seaver Foundation. The respondents included both citizens and noncitizens, with 574 Latinos (of whom 513 are of Mexican origin), 335 African Americans, 308 Asian Americans, and 317 non-Hispanic whites. Each group was sampled separately. (See Uhlaner et al. 1989; Cain et al. 1991.) Although California is only one state, it does have roughly 10 percent of the U.S. population, and it is one of the handful of states that have significant numbers not only of African Americans and Latinos but also of Asian Americans. Of course, it is not representative of the nation: for instance, the Latinos in California are preponderantly of Mexican ancestry; far fewer are of Cuban or Puerto Rican ancestry than in the East. Despite this caveat, California provides one of the better sites for study of minority group politics.

The most extensive study of Latino political behavior in the United States to date is the Latino National Political Survey. Despite its name, this study avoided treating Latinos as a homogeneous population. Instead, it sampled separately persons of Mexican, Puerto Rican, and Cuban origin. Material reported in de la Garza et al. (1992) provides descriptive information from the study that is used below.

POLITICAL ACTIVITY

Theory

Although voting has been downplayed by some as uninteresting because of the limited demands it places on the individual, its low likelihood of allowing an individual to be decisive, and the limited information it conveys, votes are collectively the most powerful political actions (Verba and Nie 1972, 106–114). Voting produces a definitive outcome. Voting is therefore the key to many citizenship and participatory rights, as has been well understood by the women,

African Americans, Latinos, and Asian Americans who fought at various times for the legal right to vote and for the removal of legally supported barriers to the exercise of that right (see, for example, Conway 1991, 98–107). Thus, voting turnout and the closely related (in the United States) act of registration to vote merit extended attention. A series of other participatory actions are also intended to affect electoral outcomes, by directly or indirectly influencing other people's votes. These include persuading others how to vote, donating money to candidates or their parties, and various ways of participating in campaigns (from wearing buttons to organizing rallies).

Some activities attempt to alter policies in a nonelectoral framework, outside of an attempt to change an election outcome. People who make their views known through direct contact with an official, a bureaucrat, or the media participate in this way. Another form of nonelectoral participation involves working together with other members of the public, for instance, through a voluntary association or an ad hoc group organized to accomplish some end, such as demanding street repair or changing the schools.[1]

There are a number of explanations of individual variations in political activity. The best-established empirical generalization is that participation rates increase with income and education levels or, combining these variables, socioeconomic status (SES). The effect is weaker for voting than for other forms of participation, but it is positive almost everywhere. It is especially strong in the United States. Second, many studies have shown that persons active in organizations, even those with no obvious political component, are more likely to be politically active. Political parties are a specific type of organization that is especially concerned with electoral politics; people who strongly identify with a party do tend to participate more.

Formal organizational membership does not appear to be necessary in order for a group to increase participation. Informal group affiliation suffices, especially when it takes the form of "group consciousness." Group consciousness exists when a person combines identity with a group with a sense of unfair treatment by the political system and with a sense that something can be done about the treatment (Miller, Gurin, Gurin, and Malanchuk 1981). This concept applies broadly. It characterizes, for example, workers inspired to vote to defend their class and women who vote out of feminist consciousness. The concept has particular relevance for understanding the political behavior of members of minority groups. Verba and Nie (1972, 157–64) found that in the United States in the mid-1960s, blacks with a sense of black consciousness participated well above the levels expected given their income and education. Minority groups can use group consciousness as the basis for an alternative path to participation, one where the importance of SES and individual participatory norms is attenuated by resources and norms derived from the politicized sense of the group (Verba, Nie, and Kim 1978; Shingles 1981; Guterbock and London 1983; Gurin, Hatchett, and Jackson 1989).

A second set of theories to explain participation focuses on the costs and benefits of action. This rational actor approach, first associated with Downs (1957) and related to Olson's work (1965), predicts that rational individuals would participate at rates far below those observed in the world and, except under rather restrictive circumstances, would not vote at all. Despite the limitations of an approach that yields such counterfactual conclusions, it has very usefully highlighted not only the assessment of costs and benefits but also the function of various internal and external factors in shifting their relative size. For example, from a rational actor perspective, the higher voting rates of the better educated reflect lower costs because they can process information (such as how to vote) in less time than other people do. A number of proposed solutions to the paradox of not voting hinge on the citizen's obtaining benefits from the act of voting itself ("consumption" rather than "investment" benefits, with the latter arising from the election outcome) and have, as a corollary, expanded our view of what benefits might arise from that activity (see Riker and Ordeshook 1968).

Adding group identity to the rational actor approach improves the theory (see Uhlaner 1989a, 1989b; Morton 1991). In this version, group leaders act as political entrepreneurs who increase turnout rates within their group by providing benefits to their members in return for voting. These benefits are typically consumption goods, and they may be provided by means of appeals to group loyalty and solidarity. One can derive the prediction that leaders will provide these benefits in amounts determined by the agreements they can obtain from a candidate to adopt preferred policies or other desired positions. The candidates make these offers in order to obtain higher turnout levels from a supportive group and thereby increase their probability of winning election. The individual citizen still votes because of consumption goods, but these now include the benefit of feeling good about fulfilling a duty to some group he or she identifies with. The overall level of turnout, however, reflects "rational" exchanges of turnout for policy. Enhancing a sense of group consciousness is likely to be a central element of leaders' attempts to increase the normative satisfactions from voting in order to fulfill a duty to the group.

This model of participation works better when groups are well defined, fairly stable in membership over time, and more or less homogeneous in political preferences with respect to the most important issues. Minority groups fit this description well when some attribute of the group corresponds to the lines of political conflict. One would then expect elites to use these mechanisms to increase activity and the model to be useful for understanding participation by members of these groups. In contemporary American politics, race has clearly served as an organizing principle, and one would expect the model to apply to the African American experience. Ethnicity has increasingly become a basis for political appeals, especially within the Latino community. Asian national origin, either collective or in terms of specific nationalities, does not yet seem to serve such a role, despite strenuous efforts by political leaders. Overall, though, group-based models are particularly applicable to discussions of participation by members of minority racial and ethnic groups.

Some authors have recently questioned the importance of group consciousness in accounting for the participation of African Americans by suggesting that the earlier conclusions were at least partially time-bound (see Tate 1991, 1161–64 for a summary). In their analysis of data collected in 1987, Bobo and Gilliam (1990) identify black empowerment (that is, the holding of local political office by African Americans) as a contextual factor that leads to greater participation by blacks through its effect on attitudes and on knowledge (385). They concluded, in contrast to earlier findings that the most participatory African Americans were those with high feelings of efficacy but low levels of trust (Guterbock and London 1983; Shingles 1981), that activity is highest among blacks with both high levels of trust and high feelings of efficacy: the "politically engaged." Tate (1991) finds some effect from group consciousness but sees it as no stronger than that from membership in black organizations or churches. She also places weight on contextual variables, namely, the stakes in the contest and the presence of a black candidate. Thus, although both the Bobo and Gilliam and the Tate arguments de-emphasize group consciousness, leaders can still play a powerful role.

Some additional considerations are particularly relevant to analysis of the political actions of members of ethnic and racial minority groups. African Americans, Latinos, and Asian Americans have all been subjected to legal barriers limiting their participation, especially as voters. Clearly such barriers decrease participation during the time they are in force and may affect the amount of participation even after they are removed.[2] More generally, members of minority groups face discrimination more often than the rest of the population. Discriminatory experiences either depress or increase activity. When discrimination is severe, individuals may respond by withdrawing from political life. On the other hand, discrimination may provide motivation for political activity to demand redress. Another effect of discriminatory experiences could be to encourage minority coalitions. These experiences, especially if shared by individuals from two groups, could serve as a basis for joint action. Discrimination could, however, diminish political cooperation if it creates conflict among groups for scarce resources or produces political withdrawal.

The fact that a substantial fraction of Latinos and Asian Americans are immigrants raises additional issues in analyzing their political activity and distinguishes these two groups from African Americans. First, many immigrants are not citizens and so cannot legally vote. Second, even naturalized immigrants tend to have characteristics that might depress their activity levels, often by limiting their knowledge of U.S. politics and their ability to acquire information. They tend to have a poorer command of English than native-born citizens do. The mere fact of having lived in this country for a shorter time can lead to more limited knowledge of U.S. politics. Some immigrants maintain very close ties to their country of origin and in some cases intend to return there, generally reducing the salience to them of U.S. politics. In addition, immigrants tend to be exposed to discrimination and to have lower socioeconomic levels. For all these reasons, immigrant Latinos and Asian Americans also differ in important ways from native-born persons of the same ethnic background.

Voting and Registration by Racial and Ethnic Groups

Comparison of African Americans, Latinos, and Asian Americans with each other and with non-Hispanic whites shows that they vary substantially in their rates of electoral participation. Table 9.1 presents both self-reported and verified rates of voting for these groups from several sources.

Several methodological comments are in order before discussing the substance of these data. The Current Population Survey (CPS) data are based on self-reports from very large samples (54,132 households providing information on 110,452 individuals in 1988 [Abramson and Claggett 1991, 187], for example), so the standard errors of the estimates are very small. The CPS data include both citizens and noncitizens in the denominator for calculating registration and turnout rates (Bureau of the Census 1989b). This introduces huge biases for Latinos, among whom roughly one-third of the voting-age population are not citizens (Bureau of the Census 1988). The CPS reports on the Hispanic population (Bureau of the Census 1988, 1989a) do, however, report rates of electoral participation separately for Hispanics who say they are citizens, and these are also shown. For non-Hispanics, including noncitizens in the denominator shifts the

Table 9.1
Voting Rates for Racial and Ethnic Groups

	CPS[a]				NES[b]							Calif[c]
					Self-Report			Validated				
	1980	1984	1988	1992	1980	1984	1988	1980	1984	1988		1984
White non-Latinos	60.9	61.4	59.1	63.6	73.1	76.0	72.4	60.8	64.8	62.2		76
					(1,181)	(1,610)	(1,368)	(1,238)	(1,775)	(1,493)		(317)
African Americans	50.5	55.8	51.5	54.0	67.7	65.4	59.7	49.7	46.5	39.2		80
					(161)	(214)	(216)	(159)	(245)	(263)		(334)
Latinos	29.9	32.6	28.8	28.9								44
												(574)
Latino citizens	44.1	48.0	45.9	48.3	52.1	62.1	66.7	42.9	43.6	49.4		60
					(59)	(115)	(135)	(56)	(149)	(158)		(387)
Asian Americans				27.3								48
												(308)
Asian American citizens				49.9								69
												(199)

[a]Self-report data from Bureau of the Census (1989a, 1989b, 1993). Cell numbers not given because they are very large.
[b]Data from American National Election Studies, 1980, 1984, 1988.
[c]Self-report data from 1984 California Survey (Cain et al. 1991).

rates down by less than 2 percent. Since the CPS reports do not provide break-downs by citizenship and race simultaneously, noncitizens are included in the denominator for non-Hispanic whites and blacks. Rates for people of Asian origin are not included in the CPS data before 1992. The tradeoff for the huge numbers in the CPS samples is the paucity of attitudinal and political variables, thus limiting their usefulness for further analysis. The NES figures include both subjects' responses as to their turnout and validated data. The NES national samples contain too few Asian Americans in any year to include them. The last column of data, from a 1984 survey in California, is based on self-reports. This study does have sufficient Asian Americans in the sample to permit analysis.

Although the NES validation data solve some problems, there is some question as to whether they can be taken at face value. A number of scholars have observed that the margin between black self-reports and black verified voting and registration is larger than that for nonblacks (for example, Abramson and Claggett 1991). This finding typically has been attributed to a greater propensity for black respondents to overreport their activity, but Presser, Traugott, and Traugott (1990) argue that this margin reflects problems in the verification process instead: African Americans are more likely to live in places where records are poorly kept or are difficult for researchers to access. If so, then the discrepancy between self-report and verification may reflect an error in the record rather than an exaggeration by the respondent. Because of this possibility, I have included both the self-report and the verified data.

In both of the national samples, voting rates for non-Hispanic whites went up from 1980 to 1984, dipped in 1988, and then, according to the CPS data, rose again in 1992 to a point above their 1980 level. Both sets of studies agree that African Americans voted at lower rates than whites throughout but differ slightly on the pattern. In the NES data African American turnout shows a steady decline from 1980 through 1984, whereas in the CPS data it rises and falls in the same pattern as for whites, although peak turnout for blacks occurs in 1984. According to the CPS data, the gap between non-Hispanic white and African American turnouts was about ten points, both at the beginning and the end of the period; according to the NES data, however, the gap widened substantially from 1980 to 1988. The CPS and NES data also differ as to how the relative rates for Latinos and African Americans changed over the decade. Both sets of data show that African Americans were more likely to vote than Latinos in 1980. According to the CPS, that relative ranking remained unchanged thorought 1992, despite some increase in Latino turnout. According to NES data, however, Latino voting rates rose steadily even as African American rates declined until, by 1988, Latino rates surpassed those of blacks. The CPS data from off-year (congressional) elections from 1982 through 1994 show a slight decline in non-Hispanic white and Latino voting rates and a steady decline since 1986 in black turnout. These CPS data thus support that conclusion that Latino voting participation rates are catching up to those of blacks, whereas the gap between white and black turnout has remained roughly the same or widened.

In contrast to the national situation, African Americans in California voted at a rate comparable to or higher than the rate for non-Hispanic whites, as shown in the last column of table 9.1. In 1984, 80 percent of blacks reported voting, versus 76 percent of non-Hispanic whites (or 81 versus 80 percent with noncitizens omitted). This result is not peculiar to these data, nor to 1984. The CPS data (Bureau of the Census 1989b) for 1988 show that 58.4 percent of California blacks voted in 1988, compared with 53.4 percent of California whites. A similar pattern holds in congressional elections: in 1986, 48.8 percent of California blacks voted versus 47.3 percent of non-Hispanic whites (Bureau of the Census 1987); in 1990, the CPS estimated the black voting rate to be only slightly lower than the white (42.0 versus 44.8 percent) and substantially less than the national difference, 39.2 versus 46.7 percent (Bureau of the Census 1991a). State-level data for 1984 are not readily available, but figures for the Pacific region show that blacks voted at a rate much closer to the non-Hispanic white rate—65.2 percent versus 66.4 percent (Bureau of the Census 1986)—than was true nationally, as shown in table 9.1. In light of Bobo and Gilliam's (1990) finding that black empowerment increases black participation, it is significant that both a long-term mayor of Los Angeles and the powerful speaker of the state assembly were African Americans. The electorate can see evidence of the feasibility of an African American winning high office.

Latinos and Asian Americans in California have lower turnout rates. When noncitizens are included in the denominator, as found in the standard CPS reports and in many journalistic accounts, the turnout rates for these groups are very low: 44 percent and 48 percent, respectively. Because these groups contain so many noncitizens, turnout rises substantially—to 60 and 69 percent, respectively—when calculated for citizens only.[3] These rates are still clearly below those for non-Hispanic whites and African Americans but by a significantly smaller margin. The first, lower, set of rates clarifies the number of Latinos or Asian Americans available to change election outcomes and influence candidates. The second set, however, is more useful for understanding the process of participation and predicting its course, especially when noncitizens are naturalized. Both sets of figures show that, in California, Latinos and Asian Americans

Table 9.2

Registration Rates for Racial and Ethnic Groups

	CPS[a]				NES[b] Self-Report			NES[b] Validated			Calif.[c]
	1980	1984	1988	1992	1980	1984	1988	1980	1984	1988	1984
White non-Latinos	68.4	69.6	67.9	70.1	74.7 (1,150)	84.0 (1,588)	81.5 (1,368)	73.3 (1,276)	76.5 (1,767)	73.1 (1,502)	82 (317)
African Americans	60.0	66.3	64.5	63.9	76.8 (168)	77.8 (212)	77.3 (216)	64.1 (170)	65.3 (245)	61.4 (264)	87 (335)
Latinos	36.3	40.1	35.5	35.0							53 (574)
Latino citizens	53.6	58.9	56.6	58.5	57.6 (59)	75.7 (115)	74.8 (135)	78.3 (58)	57.7 (157)	59.1 (159)	72 (387)
Asian Americans				31.2							55 (308)
Asian American citizens				57.0							77 (199)

[a]Self-report data from Bureau of the Census (1989a, 1989b, 1993). Cell numbers not given because they are very large.

[b]Data from American National Election Studies, 1980, 1984, 1988.

[c]Self-report data from 1984 California Survey (Cain et al. 1991).

were substantially less electorally active than African Americans. The 1992 CPS figures show voting rates for Asian American citizens just above those for Latino citizens, consistent with the California data. Nationally, blacks have traditionally been more active than Latinos, but that may have changed in 1988 as declines in black electoral participation met increases in Latino activity.

Comparable figures on registration are presented in table 9.2. The conclusions with regard to relative voting rates of African Americans and non-Hispanic whites carry over to these data on registration rates. The CPS data on registration also show the same patterns as the vote data for Latino participation. Both versions of the NES data, however, show less of a decrease in African American registration from 1980 to 1988 than was true of voting, and registration actually increased slightly from 1980 to 1984 while voting fell. The NES data also indicate little or no increase in Latino registration from 1984 to 1988 (after a substantial jump in the first part of the decade). The combined effect is that Latino registration rates just came close to African American rates by 1988 instead of passing them. Thus, for Latinos and African Americans, the changes in the last part of the eighties were more gradual for registration than for voting. The California data once again show participation for Latinos and Asian Americans at rates lower than for non-Hispanic whites and African Americans. The 1992 CPS figures agree with the California data that Asian Americans register at about the same rates as Latinos, but their relative ranking differs slightly in the two sets of data.

Disaggregation by National Origin

As noted in the introduction, the labels "Latino" and "Asian American" cover people of diverse national origins. In 1988, for example, 62 percent of the Latino population was of Mexican origin, with another 12 percent from Central and South America, 13 percent from Puerto Rico, slightly more than 5 percent from Cuba, and 8 percent of other Spanish origin (Bureau of the Census 1989a). These people do not necessarily think of themselves in terms of the blanket ethnic label. In fact, there is some evidence (de la Garza et al. 1992, 13–14) that only a minority of Latinos think of themselves as either Latino or Hispanic, with much the larger number preferring a national origin label. Anecdotal evidence suggests even less subjective political meaning for the category "Asian American." None of the available studies have sufficient cases to permit reliably disaggregating the Asian American category.[4] In both the NES and the California studies, however, Mexican Americans can be separated from other Latinos.

The top two sections of table 9.3 present NES data on voting and registration rates for Mexican Americans, Puerto Ricans, and persons of other Latino origin

Table 9.3
Voting and Registration Rates for Latinos by National Origin

	Self-Report			Validated		
	1980	1984	1988	1980	1984	1988
NES Data: Percent Who Voted						
Mexican	43	58	60	28	42	43
Americans	(28)	(85)	(62)	(29)	(107)	(67)
Puerto Ricans	67	73	50	50	20	32
	(9)	(11)	(14)	(12)	(15)	(19)
Other (incl.	64	75	77	67	63	58
Cuban)	(11)	(20)	(57)	(15)	(27)	(73)
NES Data: Percentage Who Registered						
Mexican	50	74	76	39	57	59
Americans	(32)	(85)	(62)	(31)	(107)	(68)
Puerto Ricans	75	90	57	50	53	42
	(12)	(10)	(14)	(12)	(15)	(19)
Others (incl.	61	75	79	67	63	64
Cuban)	(15)	(20)	(57)	(15)	(27)	(73)

Percentage of Citizens Reporting That They:

	Ever Registered to Vote	Were Registered to Vote When Interviewed	Voted for President in 1984	Voted for President in 1988
Mexican	77	65	55	49
Americans	(877)	(877)	(720)	(875)
Puerto Ricans	74	64	51	50
	(585)	(585)	(493)	(581)
Cuban Americans	82	78	72	67
	(312)	(312)	(267)	(312)
Non-Hispanic	90	78	n/a	70
Whites	(446)	(446)		(446)

Sources: National Election Studies, 1980, 1984, 1988; de la Garza et al. (1992: tables 8.13, 8.14, 8.17, and 8.23).
Note: Numbers of cases are in parentheses.

(primarily Cuban in these studies). This disaggregation produces very small numbers of Latinos of other-than-Mexican origin and so should be interpreted cautiously. The data suggest that Cuban Americans are the most electorally active and that the increase noted above in Latino voting and registration primarily reflects increased activity by Mexican Americans. The California study of ethnic minorities had 574 Latino respondents; since all but sixty-one of them were of Mexican origin, the turnout and registration figures for Mexican Americans only are virtually identical to those for the full sample.

The bottom part of table 9.3 shows data from the one source that has enough respondents to permit direct comparison of the participation rates of the three largest Latino populations, the Latino National Political Survey (LNPS). That study sampled Mexican Americans (1,546 respondents), Puerto Ricans (589), Cuban Americans (682), and non-Hispanic whites (438) who reside in the same sampling areas. Most of the field work was done in the second half of 1989. Table 9.3 compares the citizens only in these groups on their self-reported rates of registration at the time of the survey and of voting in the presidential election in 1988. The numbers agree with the NES data: Cuban Americans are the most electorally active of the three Latino groups, and Cuban voting and registration rates are essentially the same as those for the non-Hispanic white population and higher than the voting rates for African Americans. The figures also indicate that, at least by 1988, Puerto Rican and Mexican American citizens were registering and voting at about the same rates as each other. (There were too few Puerto Rican respondents in the NES for reliable conclusions.) If the LNPS marginals are comparable to those of the NES, then it also appears that Puerto Rican and Mexican American turnout and registration rates are roughly 10 percentage points less than those for African Americans.

Effects of Demographics and Attitudes

Further investigation is needed to determine whether the differences across ethnic and racial groups in voting and registration rates reflect some process related to race or ethnicity or are instead the spurious result of differences across the groups in such variables as education and income. The national NES data have too few Asian Americans for analysis, but they do allow one to investigate whether the registration and voting rates of African Americans and Mexican Americans reflect something in their racial or ethnic experience over and above the operation of sociodemographic factors, political factors, or political-psychological factors.

I used NES data and probit analysis to estimate models on six dependent variables: validated registration in 1980, 1984, and 1988 and validated turnout among those registered to vote in 1980, 1984, and 1988.

Table 9.4 reports the results for validated registration in 1980 to illustrate the procedure. The table includes probit coefficients and associated t-values from each model. The results from the other tables will be summarized. I estimated three models for each dependent variable. The first (I) includes only sociode-mographic variables, including income, education, age, unemployment, gender, race, and Mexican American ethnicity. The second (II) adds political measures: whether they belong to an organization allied with the group with which they most closely identify and the strength of their identification with a political party. The third (III) adds three psychological variables: interest in politics, political efficacy, and sense of citizen duty.[5] In all of the models, a statistically significant (as indicated by a large t-value) positive coefficient on "African American" means that blacks are more likely to register or vote than nonblacks who

Table 9.4
Probit Estimations of "Registered to Vote" in 1980 Using Validated Registration Data

Independent Variable	Model I Probit Coefficient	t	Model II Probit Coefficient	t	Model III Probit Coefficient	t
Family income	**.0008**	2.36	**.0007**	1.97	**.0008**	2.29
Education	**.098**	7.08	**.089**	6.21	**.061**	3.85
Age	**.027**	8.31	**.023**	6.90	**.019**	5.44
Old (over 70)	−.28	−1.55	−.25	−1.34	−.09	−.45
Out of work	0.51	.27	−.006	−.03	−.025	−.13
Male	**.14**	1.70	**.16**	1.84	.12	1.35
African American	.06	.42	−.04	−.26	.03	.19
Mexican American	**−.62**	−2.17	**−.65**	−2.18	**−.60**	−1.89
Belongs to organization			**.21**	1.97	**.21**	1.80
Strength of partisanship			**.16**	3.53	**.13**	2.67
Interest					**.18**	3.94
Efficacy					**.11**	3.08
Citizen duty					**.06**	2.69
Constant	**−1.93**	−7.88	**−1.45**	−5.38	**−1.92**	−6.58
Log likelihood at convergence	−614.1		−5.81.2		−522.8	
N	1185		1151		1098	

Boldfaced, underlined **coefficients** are significant at .05 in a two-tailed test.
Boldfaced **coefficients** are significant at .10 in a two-tailed test.

otherwise have the same characteristics (that is, taking account of the other variables included in the estimation). A significant negative coefficient means that African Americans are less likely to participate than are nonblacks after controlling for these variables. Significant positive and negative coefficients on "Mexican American" similarly indicate more or less likelihood of participation by them than by non–Mexican Americans with the same characteristics. If the coefficients are not statistically significant, then the differences we observe between members of these groups and non-Hispanic whites in registration and voting reflect the other characteristics considered in these models. In that case, race and ethnicity do not play an independent role over and above their influence on the other characteristics.

The results reported in table 9.4 show that the factors well known in the literature to increase registration worked as expected in 1980. People who were more likely to register were those with more education, higher income, stronger partisanship, more interest, more efficacy, and a stronger sense of citizen duty. Older people were more likely to register. Men were slightly more likely to register, until one takes account of attitudes. These results were substantively the same for 1984 and 1988, except that by 1988 gender made no difference.

The relations of most interest to us, however, are those between participation on one hand and race or ethnicity on the other. Table 9.5 gathers together the coefficients and t-values for the African American and Mexican American variables in each model. The labels "I," "II," and "III" refer to the model with demographic variables, the model that adds political variables, and the model that adds psychological variables, respectively. These results show that in all three elections African Americans were no more or less likely to register than non-Hispanic nonblacks who had the same characteristics on each of the included variables. This is true whether one accounts only for the demographics, accounts also for the political variables, or accounts for the psychological variables as well. After controlling for both political and psychological variables, however, the black dummy approaches significance (a t-value of 1.44) and is negative. That is, one could argue that after controlling for blacks' level of interest, efficacy, citizen duty, organizational membership, and partisanship, in 1988 they were perhaps slightly less likely to register than comparable whites. That the African American variable is clearly insignificant before introducing these other factors is evidently due partly to a high level of organizational and party involvement among blacks in 1988. For Mexican Americans the story goes in the opposite direction. In 1980 they were significantly less likely to register than comparable

Table 9.5
Effect of Race and Ethnicity on Registration and on Voting Among the Registered in 1980, 1984, and 1988 from Probit Estimations

Dependent Variable and Year Registered	Model Number[a]	N	African American		Mexican American	
			Probit Coefficient[b]	t	Probit Coefficient[c]	t
1980	I	1185	.06	.42	**−.62**	−2.17
	II	1151	−.04	−.26	**−.65**	−2.18
	III	1098	.03	.19	**−.60**	−1.89
1984	I	1755	.02	.21	−.17	−1.08
	II	1677	−.01	−.08	−.17	−1.07
	III	1662	−.02	−.18	−.20	−1.24
1988	I	1886	.03	.35	.12	0.70
	II	1600	−.14	−1.26	.06	0.31
	III	1593	−.16	−1.44	.02	.102
Voted if already registered						
1980	I	827	−.05	−.30	.12	.22
	II	814	−.01	−.77	.06	.10
	III	779	−.02	−.79	.16	.25
1984	I	1322	**−.35**	−2.62	−.08	−.36
	II	1269	**−.37**	−2.67	−.08	−.39
	III	1257	**−.41**	−2.88	−.09	−.41
1988	I	1317	**−.55**	−4.61	−.19	−.83
	II	1139	**−.63**	−4.56	−.31	−1.27
	III	1137	**−.63**	−4.49	−.32	−1.31

[a]See text for description of models.
[b]Coefficient on dummy variable coded "1" for African Americans in estimation.
[c]Coefficient on dummy variable coded "1" for Mexican Americans in estimation.
Boldfaced, underlined **coefficients** are significant at .05 in a two-sided test.
Boldfaced **coefficients** are significant at .10 in a two-sided test.

nonblack non-Hispanics; by 1984 the variable was at best borderline significant; and by 1988 they were clearly as likely to register as anyone else with comparable characteristics.

When the same analysis is done using self-reported rather than validated registration as the dependent variable (not shown here), African Americans are more likely to report registering in 1988 than non-Hispanic nonblack citizens (coefficient of .217 with a t-value of 1.87) in the model that has only demographic variables. When organizational membership and strength of partisanship are added to the model, the coefficient on African American weakens to a point beneath the level of statistical significance. African American self-reports of registration may have reflected heightened group and partisan mobilization. Taken together, these results suggest that in 1988 African Americans were more likely than other people with similar characteristics to report that they were registered but less likely in fact to register, subject to the caveat discussed above about the reliability of the validation measure. For Mexican Americans, also, analysis of the self-report data shows them more likely to register than non-Hispanic nonblack citizens (coefficient of .382 with a t-value of 2.02). This effect weakens with the introduction of the political and especially the psychological variables. Thus, Mexican Americans were, like African Americans, more likely to report registration in 1988 than were other people with similar characteristics while, in their case, being no more or less likely actually to register.

Registration is a required first step before voting in the United States and, as we have seen, one that not everyone takes. Among those who do register, who chooses to vote? Most of the registered do show up at the polls, but are there systematic differences between these people and those who do not vote? In particular, does race or ethnicity matter? Estimations similar to those reported in table 9.4 were done in each of the three years; the independent variables were the same, but the dependent variable was validated vote in the election that year, and the sample was restricted to those who had registered. Thus, these estimations indicate which factors are related to more or less voter turnout among those who are registered.

Education and interest provide the strongest predictors that a registered individual will vote. Beyond that, the particular factors that are significant vary somewhat across the three years (for example, income is significant in 1984, age in 1984 and 1988), but none go in surprising directions. Once again, the coefficients on the race and ethnicity variables are gathered and summarized in table 9.5.

In 1980, neither being African American nor being Mexican American had any independent effect on whether a registered citizen went to the polls or stayed home. The same statement holds for Mexican Americans in the two later elections as well. Thus, at the beginning of the eighties, Mexican American ethnicity, even after controlling for other factors, was associated with lower electoral participation because it was associated with lower registration rates. By 1988 this was no longer true; Mexican American ethnicity had no effect on registration and voting over and above the effects of the other variables.

Table 9.5 indicates a contrasting picture for African Americans. In both 1984 and 1988, registered blacks were significantly less likely to vote than were registered nonblacks. Thus, although race was irrelevant to registration and turnout at the beginning of the decade, by the end one could predict that a registered African American would be less likely to vote in the general election than a registered citizen of another race. It is worth reflecting on the contemporary political events. At the time of the 1984 and 1988 elections, Jesse Jackson's candidacy was widely thought to be a force to mobilize voters, especially minority voters and most especially African Americans. His candidacy throughout the primary season was believed to increase primary voting and registration rates. His absence from the general election ticket was thought by some, however, to lead at least some of his supporters to stay home, out of discouragement or in protest. The analyses above are consistent with the discouragement hypothesis since they not only show a relatively greater drop in black participation in 1988 but also indicate that the drop occurred more at the time of voting in November than at registration.

A more detailed analysis of these data, adding measures of black consciousness and attitude toward Jackson, suggests that both Jackson's candidacy and feelings of black consciousness led significant numbers of African Americans to vote in the primaries and to register (possibly in order to be able to cast a primary vote); see Uhlaner (1991a). Only black consciousness, however, seems to have produced general election votes. The evidence provides a tantalizing suggestion that Jackson's most fervent supporters may have stayed home in November.

Similar estimations of electoral participation using the 1984 California data also control for various socioeconomic and demographic characteristics (see Uhlaner, Cain, and Kiewiet 1989). These find that the differences in voting and registration rates between Mexican Americans and both blacks and non-Hispanic whites can be largely explained by demographic factors plus the respondent's facility in English and the length of time naturalized citizens have lived in the United States. For Asian Americans, however, these controls fail to account for their lower levels of electoral participation. Moreover, few of the usual variables are correlated with Asian American electoral participation. Most notably, higher levels of education do not correspond to higher rates of voting and registration. The only variables that do matter much are party identification and gender—Asian American men are more likely to register than are women. But saying that Asian Americans who strongly identify with a party are more likely to register and vote is almost tautological; it is saying that those who have developed a partisan political attachment also take political actions. Thus, the lower rates of Asian American registration and voting remain largely unexplained.

Perceived discrimination could affect rates of political activity, as discussed above. Three measures of perceived discrimination were available in the California data. In these data, perceptions of discrimination clearly lead to increased activity. When the measures are added to estimations that control for the demographic and immigration factors, they demonstrate a significant positive impact on the probability of voting, registering, working in groups, contributing money, contacting news media, and contacting elected officials (Uhlaner 1991c). This result also holds when strength of partisanship is controlled. Thus, all else equal, persons are likely to be more, not less, politically active if they have personally experienced discrimination, believe that Americans are prejudiced toward people like them, or believe that their group has fewer opportunities than others.

Immigration

When new immigrants join current residents there are two crosscutting impacts on the group's electoral situation. First, the group's potential electoral power obviously increases as it grows larger. Second, participation rates of the group will decrease in the short term. This is most obvious if the noncitizen immigrants are counted in the denominator in calculating registration and voting rates, as noted above. But even after the immigrants become citizens, registration and voting rates may remain depressed. In a probit analysis of the 1984 California ethnic data that controlled for ethnicity, demographic and socioeconomic factors, and identification of group-related problems, respondents whose primary language was not English were significantly less likely to vote. In addition, the larger the percentage of his or her life a respondent had lived outside the United States, the less likely he or she was to vote or to register (Uhlaner, Cain, and Kiewiet 1989).

Other factors that are not directly due to immigration but are distributed differentially also tend to decrease participation rates of immigrants. The most important of these is age: Asian and Latino immigrant populations tend to be young, and younger citizens are less active than older ones. A simulation model estimated that if Latino and Asian American citizens matched non-Hispanic whites in age structure and use of English as a primary language, their voting rates would come to within four to six points of non-Hispanic white rates (Uhlaner, Cain, and Kiewiet 1989). The reality, however, is that the population currently *is* young and contains substantial numbers of persons not comfortable in English. Thus, although immigrants add to the long-term political strength of these groups, they reduce the group's average political activity in the short-to-medium term.

Participation Other Than Voting and Registration

People can influence elections with actions other than voting, actions ranging from contributing money to working on a campaign. Outside of electoral politics, people can work collectively, as in a neighborhood association, or contact officials or news media in attempts to change policy. If rates of involvement in these activities also vary across racial and ethnic groups, that would be a further source of disparate influence on the political system. Table 9.6 presents data from the California ethnic study on the percentage of each group that engages in these other political activities. Since the Latino respondents are predominantly of Mexican origin, those of other national backgrounds are excluded from the data. In general, the smaller the number of people engaged in an activity, the smaller the differences across groups. The groups differ the most in their rates of contacting officials and working communally.

Unlike voting and registration, nonelectoral activities are open to noncitizens. Technically, they are also barred from contributing money to campaigns. As the data indicate, noncitizens were quite active, although less so than citizens (but the difference was small in the case of Asian American contacts with media). Almost 20 percent contacted officials; more than 10 percent contacted media or worked in groups. Virtually the same fractions of Mexican American citizens and noncitizens displayed posters and signs. The major difference between Asian American and Mexican American noncitizens was in the relatively greater propensity of the former to contact the news media and of the latter to display posters and stickers.

The importance of various factors in explaining participation can be assessed by a logit estimation. When models of participation by noncitizens were estimated (Uhlaner, Cain, and Kiewiet 1989, 212–14), once again the respondents who had lived in the United States for a larger percentage of their lives participated more, specifically by working in groups, contacting the news media, or contacting officials. After controlling for time in the United States, however, younger immigrants were more likely to participate, suggesting perhaps a

Table 9.6
Percentage Participation in Political Activities in California in 1984 by Ethnic
Group

Activity	Non-Hispanic Whites	Blacks	Mexican Americans	Asian Americans
Contributed money				
All	20%	17%	12%	18%
Citizens	—	—	14	24
Noncitizens	—	—	7	6
Displayed poster or sticker				
All	8	10	11	6
Citizens	—	—	11	4
Noncitizens	—	—	10	6
Worked on campaigns				
All	6	5	3	3
Citizens	—	—	4	4
Noncitizens	—	—	1	2
Attended political rally				
All	15	16	10	8
Citizens	—	—	12	11
Noncitizens	—	—	4	4
Contacted officials				
All	47	37	26	26
Citizens	—	—	29	31
Noncitizens	—	—	19	20
Contacted media				
All	22	20	18	25
Citizens	—	—	20	25
Noncitizens	—	—	13	23
Worked with community group				
All	33	38	20	24
Citizens	—	—	24	32
Noncitizens	—	—	12	11
Number of respondents				
All	317	335	513	308
Citizens	300	313	356	199
Noncitizens	14	4	137	84

greater willingness to try new things and reversing the otherwise almost-uni-
versal pattern of older people being more politically active. Respondents who
did not speak English or who were linked to the country of origin were less likely
to contact the news media, and persons from households with an unemployed
head were less likely to work in groups. Finally, among noncitizens, those who

identified some particular problem or concern related to their ethnicity were more active. Similar analyses for citizens found similar results. Naturalized citizens who had spent a greater fraction of their life in the United States were more likely to work in groups. Citizens whose primary language was not English were less likely than English speakers to work in groups or to contact officials.

Conclusion

Participation rates vary across racial and ethnic groups, with Latinos the least participatory and non-Hispanic whites the most. As we have seen, however, the picture is more complex than a simple summary would suggest. In California, for example, African Americans are the most politically active group. Latinos of Cuban origin are more active than those of Mexican or Puerto Rican origin. Moreover, some of the differences across groups reflect differences in demographic characteristics, such as income and education, plus immigration-related phenomena, such as years in the United States and command of English, although other participatory differences persist even after taking account of these factors.

Three points seem key in understanding these variations in participation. First, since some demographic factors such as age, education, and income are closely correlated with participation, demographic differences across groups will produce different rates of activity. This process accounts for a large part of the lower participation levels of Latinos and of African Americans outside of California. Paradoxically, a young age structure produces less participation now but indicates future group voting power, since it is a concomitant of an increasing population. The reduction in activity that reflects differences in socioeconomic circumstances, however, will persist if socioeconomic disadvantage continues. At least some of that disadvantage is likely to disappear for Latinos, however, if immigrants and their children experience the historically typical pattern of upward mobility. Their participation would then be expected to increase along with their education and income.

Second, factors specific to the immigration experience play a role in diminishing participation among groups with large numbers of immigrants, Latinos and Asian Americans in particular. For example, even with ballots and official publications available in other languages, much of the information about elections comes in English. People who are not comfortable in English have to expend more effort to learn about an election or issue. More generally, as people spend more of their lives in the United States, they incidentally absorb more politically relevant information. And, of course, noncitizens cannot be electorally active and are less participatory in other ways as well. These and related factors account for part of the difference in participation rates between Latinos and Asian Americans and the groups with few immigrants. They are also factors that suggest increased activity as immigrants live in the United States longer.

Of course, rates for the group as a whole may not rise if the numbers of new immigrants are large enough. In that case, as with the effect of age structure, although rates may stay low, absolute political weight would eventually increase (Uhlaner 1996, 70). Although these processes may appear inevitable, one key component, the decision to become a citizen, clearly is not (DeSipio 1996, 119–33). In particular, immigrants from Mexico become citizens later and in smaller proportions than immigrants from countries in Asia (Uhlaner, Cain, and Kiewiet 1989, 212). As a consequence, participation rates among Mexican-born citizens may be elevated since they are already self-selected as people with more attachment to U.S. politics; however, the overall impact of the group is diminished because not all eligible persons become citizens.

Although age structure, socioeconomic circumstances, and immigration-related variables account for almost all of the differences between Latino participation rates and those of non-Hispanic whites or African Americans, they do not explain the lower activity rates of Asian Americans or the higher activity rates of African Americans. For that, we must turn to a third set of factors: variations in how worthwhile political activity appears and, equally important, in how much incentive leaders have to encourage such activity. These variations occur not only across groups but also across time. The more worthwhile political activity appears to be and the more benefit is to be derived from encouraging it, the more participation one would expect. The one measure of such factors that was available in these data (whether a respondent in the California study identified a specific problem related to his or her ethnicity) did show increased activity. Participation rates by a minority or any other group are neither static nor insulated from politics. Events and leadership can increase activity, as they did for many years in the African American community (Tate 1991; Bobo and Gilliam 1990). Other combinations of events can lead people to stay home. The big increases in Mexican American registration and voting rates over just a few elections cannot be attributable to socialization or even simple economic mobility because those processes don't work that fast; leadership and organization can, however.

A number of components affect the apparent value of politics. These include historical experiences, a group's residential patterns, and the fit between a group's preferences and the political cleavage structure. Residential patterns are important to candidates and leaders: in a single-member district plurality system, that used in most elections in the United States, a group that is geographically concentrated is more politically valuable than one of equal size that is spread across electoral districts. In addition, a group is more valuable as it comes closer to forming a majority in some electoral district. A leader could not expect to win by appealing on a racial or ethnic basis to small or dispersed groups; one would expect these leaders to find alternative bases for mobilization.

African Americans tend to be highly residentially concentrated and are numerous enough to make up a substantial portion or majority of many districts. (See Chapters 7 and 8 in this book for discussions of the Voting Rights Act and Chapter 2 for information on residential segregation.) The history of the Voting Rights Act is the history of turning that theoretical possibility into actuality. Latinos are less residentially concentrated but still somewhat so and also numerous enough to figure in district-level calculations. Asian Americans, in contrast, tend not to concentrate residentially and are a far smaller fraction of the population, even if they and we ignore national origin differences. As a consequence, there are only a few districts where they weigh heavily. Thus, the interplay of absolute numbers and residential concentration, or the lack thereof, contributes to differences in the electoral usefulness of group-based politics.

Individuals differ in whether they see politics as useful for advancing their interests in the world, and these differences may well concentrate ethnically and racially, especially since leaders can endogenously influence them. Politics may appear useful to the extent that the political system handles problems or issues or dispenses benefits that matter. For African Americans concerned about citizenship rights, politics provided a logical arena for redress. Latinos interested in immigration law and Cuban Americans interested in U.S. policy toward their homeland can easily see the relevance of the political process to them. Irish Americans paid attention to urban politics, recognizing that they could use it for economic advancement through the mechanism of jobs disbursed by those who controlled the city government. Politics will be seen as less useful, however, when alternative paths to economic advancement are seen as more reliable. Anecdotal evidence suggests that Asian Americans rely on education as a surer path to economic mobility than political involvement. A person's view of the role of politics is partly determined by circumstances, but it is also an endogenous product of the activities of candidates and leaders. Whether a leader can make political action appear important to the concerns of a group depends partly on the initial relation between those concerns and the political agenda. It also depends heavily on the leader's skill in altering either the group's concerns or the political agenda so that they match more closely or at least are perceived to.

All of these factors contribute to the low levels of activity among Asian Americans. Mobilization is difficult. Asian American electoral participation may increase if events arise that leaders can use to generate political relevance for the ethnic group, whether defined by national origin or defined as Asian American. For now, even the category "Asian American" is of limited political relevance, and it would require high leadership skills to create a pan-Asian political community. African American activity rates are lowered by the group's age structure and socioeconomic circumstances, but mobilization has been successful and, despite some fluctuations, is likely to continue to be so. Latino participation is lowered by socioeconomic and immigration-related circumstances but can be increased by mobilization. The greatest changes in the near future are likely to come from changes in naturalization rates and in the salience of group-specific policies (as evident in the reaction to such measures as California propositions 187 and 209, which affected immigrants and affirmative action).

PARTY PREFERENCES

The impact of voter participation on the outcome of elections obviously depends on which party the members of these groups support. Voting choice in any particular election can depend on many things, but party identification tends, on average over the long term, to provide a reasonable indicator of voting choice. Moreover, people who have a party identification tend to differ from those who claim to be politically independent. Especially among populations in which U.S. politics may not be very salient (for example, recent immigrants), the strength of partisanship indicates involvement in electoral politics.

Theory

Many of the standard models of partisanship acquisition emphasize the role of early socialization and other formative psychological experiences in producing a party identification that serves as a longstanding, fairly stable orientation toward the political world (Campbell et al. 1960). An alternative view is that partisanship is a rational information-reducing mechanism that is continually updated by new information (Downs 1957; Popkin et al. 1976). Of course, even in the socialization model, party identification served a similar informational function, because it was the mechanism for summing up previous experience for use in making the current decision (compare the funnel of causality in Campbell et al. 1960). Fiorina (1981) developed a model that effectively combines these views. An individual begins with a set of partisan biases derived from parental influence and other preadult experiences. Subsequent party preference deviates from this bias by the sum of the individual's positive and negative information about the parties. As information accumulates, party preference may be modified.

It follows from both the original standard model and from Fiorina's that strength of partisanship increases with age, since partisanship is reinforced by later experiences and habit, as long as there is some stability in experiences and preferences. Converse (1969) clarified that chronological age is actually only a proxy for length of attachment to a party; he demonstrated the point in circumstances where party systems had been disrupted. As a corollary, in cases where a person experiences major life changes, then party preference and strength may change. Immigrants are a group of people for whom age does not reflect length of attachment. The party identification of immigrants would be expected to strengthen with length of time in the new political system. Since immigrants enter at many different ages, this means that there will be no systematic relation between chronological age and strength of partisanship. Instead, one must examine the relation of partisan strength to time in the United States.

Are there any prior biases or subsequently received party information that is likely to have a systematic effect on the partisanship of African Americans, Latinos, or Asian Americans specific to their racial or ethnic group? In other words, what aspects of a theory of partisanship might be specific to these groups taken together as "minorities" or to each separately?

One answer is that members of minority groups are more likely to experience discrimination. Since during the past few decades the Democratic Party has more often fostered the image of being sympathetic to the needs and concerns of the disadvantaged and of being more committed to redressing discrimination than has the Republican Party, one might expect accumulated experience to favor the Democrats. Cain, Kiewiet, and Uhlaner (1991) refer to this as the "minority group status" hypothesis.

Some members of minority groups do advance economically. Especially among immigrants, time in the country tends to produce upward mobility. Since advantaged groups have tended to support the Republican Party, the "economic advancement" hypothesis holds that members of minority groups who are better off would support Republicans. In particular, one would expect native-born and longer-resident immigrants to be more likely to support Republicans than recent arrivals among Latinos and Asian Americans. African Americans who have experienced upward mobility are similarly expected to be more likely to be Republican identifiers.

In addition to economics or minority group concerns, specific issues may lead to identification with one party or the other. Historically, African Americans supported the Republicans after the Civil War and then solidified their support for the Democrats in the wake of the civil rights legislation of the 1960s. Foreign policy concerns revolving around Communist governments have been of major concern to some Latino and Asian immigrant groups. The Republican Party has been seen as tougher on Communism; the "foreign policy concerns" hypothesis suggests that immigrants who left Communist regimes abroad (such as Vietnamese or Cubans) or whose home country faced a threat from a Communist regime (such as Koreans) would be more likely to support the Republicans. The corollary "domestic concerns" hypothesis is partially subsumed by the "minority group status" hypothesis to the extent that it involves the perception that the Democrats have been more supportive of affirmative action, economic redistribution, and related agendas; it suggests support for the Democrats. Because of the large proportion of Catholics among Latinos, the Republican Party has assumed that it would receive substantial Latino support because of the party's stand against abortion.

Data

Data on the party preferences of African Americans, Latinos, Asian Americans, and non-Hispanic whites consistently indicate that African Americans give the greatest support to the Democratic Party. More Latinos than African Americans support Republicans, but they are still substantially more likely to support Democrats than are non-Hispanic whites. For example, as shown in table 9.7, the 1988 NES survey found that more than 80 percent of African American respondents identify themselves as Democrats, compared with only 40 percent of non-Hispanic whites and 60 percent of Latinos. The 1984 California ethnic data also show African Americans identifying overwhelmingly with Democrats. That data set is the only one with sufficient numbers of Asian Americans to estimate their partisanship: they identify with Republicans substantially more than either Latinos or African Americans and slightly more than non-Hispanic whites.

In an attempt to get some indication of Asian American party preferences nationally, I merged data from the 1972 through 1988 National Election Studies (omitting 1974). I also used the General Social Survey (GSS) cumulative file for 1972–1991, merging the information on persons of Chinese, Japanese, and Filipino ethnicity across the years. In both cases, I present the data in table 9.7 for the entire period and also separately for the 1980s in order to make it more comparable to the 1984 data. Both sets of national data indicate less support for Republicans among Asian Americans than does the California data set. The Asian Americans were, however, clearly less supportive of Democrats than either Latinos or African Americans, especially during the 1980s. Thus, the qualitative conclusions about relative support for the parties remain the same.

Since the Latino category includes at least one heavily Republican group (Cuban Americans), it is useful to split the Latino group by national origin; table 9.8 presents these data. The 1989 Latino National Political Survey (LNPS) is the only reliable source for Puerto Rican and Cuban party preference. Puerto Rican partisanship is almost identical to that of the Mexican Americans. Both groups are more likely to identify with the Democrats (71 and 67 percent, respectively) than are non-Hispanic Anglos (53 percent). In contrast, Cuban Americans strongly support the Republicans; almost 70 percent identify with them and only 25 percent with the Democrats. The 1988 NES data show more Mexican Americans identifying with Democrats (77 percent) than were found in the LNPS data, but their rates of identification still clearly fall between those of

Table 9.7
Party Identification of Citizens by Race and Ethnicity

Group and Data Source	Democrat	Republican	Independent	N
NES, 1988				
Non-Hispanic whites	40%	11%	49%	1,520
African Americans	82	6	12	260
Latinos	60	14	26	160
NES Merged, 1972–88				
Asian Americans[a]	57	17	26	105
Asian Americans, 1980–1988 only	43	22	35	58
GSS Merged, 1972–91				
Asian Americans	43	26	32	172
Asian Americans, 1980–1989 only	38	25	37	84
California Ethnic Study, 1984				
Non-Latino whites	49	8	43	270
African Americans	89	5	5	308
Latinos	63	10	27	472
Mexican Americans	65	9	26	427
Asian Americans	42	10	48	248

Note: "Leaners" are included with identifiers; "Independent" is pure independent only.
[a]Defined as persons who name China, Japan, or the Philippines as the country they identify as their place of ethnic origin.

African Americans and non-Hispanic whites. The 1984 California data yield numbers almost identical to the LNPS's for Mexican American identification.

In order to examine partisanship among Asian Americans, I used the 1984 California data and the merged GSS data. Even so, there are only about fifty respondents from each national-origin group, so these figures should be considered suggestive. The California data include noncitizens. The GSS data are limited to citizens; merging the years may have obscured changes over time. In the California data, Filipinos and Japanese Americans are more or less evenly split between the two parties, rather like the non-Latino whites. In contrast, Chinese Americans and Korean Americans identify more strongly with the Republican Party. Vietnamese are also typically Republican identifiers. The GSS data show distributions roughly similar to those in the California data, although with somewhat fewer Republicans and more independents.

Immigration status and nativity may affect party choice, as discussed above. Table 9.9 presents the relevant data from the California ethnic study. Restricting the base to citizens evidently makes little difference, both for Mexican Americans and for Asian Americans. When the Mexican American and Asian American

Table 9.8
Party Identification for Latino and Asian American Citizens by National Origin

	Democrat	Independent	Republican	N
PS, 1989				
Mexican Americans	67%	12%	21%	811
Puerto Ricans	71	12	17	550
Cuban Americans	25	6	69	309
Non-Latino Anglos	53	7	40	436
NES, 1988				
Mexican Americans	77	10	13	69
California Ethnic Study, 1984				
Mexican Americans	69	8	23	427
Chinese Americans	35	13	52	52
Filipinos	48	10	42	40
Japanese Americans	44	12	44	59
Koreans	39	4	57	69
GSS Merged, 1972–91				
Chinese Americans	31	29	40	65
Filipinos	51	23	26	47
Japanese Americans	48	25	27	60

Note: "Leaners" are included with identifiers; "Independent" is pure independent only.

groups are divided according to whether the respondent was born in the United States or immigrated, however, differences do appear, with the native-born clearly more likely to identify with the Democrats. Among Asian American immigrants, party preference is the same whether or not the respondent is a citizen. Among Mexican Americans, however, immigrants who have naturalized are much more likely to choose a party and to choose the Democrats than are noncitizens.

The difference in partisanship between the native and the foreign-born could be due to some other factor that just happens to correlate with immigration status. The results in Cain, Kiewiet, and Uhlaner (1991) suggest otherwise. For Latinos, both greater time in the country and older age among the U.S.-born are positively associated with support for the Democrats, even after controlling for such variables as education, income, and language facility. This may represent a cohort effect, but the authors concluded that it was more plausible to interpret it as a learning effect. Uhlaner and Garcia (1998) also found support for a learning process in an analysis of all three national-origin groups included in the LNPS. For the Asian Americans, the difference between the U.S.-born and the foreign-born seems to be an artifact of composition. Asian Americans from countries that had either been taken over or threatened by Communist regimes were more likely both to be among the foreign-born and to support the Republicans. Time in the United States and age had little apparent independent effect.

The analyses in Cain, Kiewiet, and Uhlaner (1991) indicate that both the economic advancement and the minority group hypotheses are operating in the case of Mexican Americans. That is, they become more attached to the Democratic Party as they spend more time in the United States or grow older, and they become more attached to the Republican Party as they become wealthier. A similar situation probably holds for Puerto Ricans, with the added complication of accounting for differential attachment to Puerto Rico. Neither the minority group nor the economic advancement explanation accounts for Asian American party preference. At the time of these studies, however, the foreign policy hypothesis did seem to match the data. Chinese, Korean, and Southeast Asian immigrants were more supportive of Republicans, as were Cuban Americans. These effects are likely to fade over time. Already by the 1992 election, some young Vietnamese political leaders publicly shifted their support to Democrats, citing concerns with various new issues. Both the minority group and the economic advancement hypotheses are consistent with the pattern of African American support. As more blacks experience economic mobility, the hypoth-

Table 9.9
Party Identification by Immigration Status in the California Ethnic Study, 1984

	Democrat	Republican	Independent	N
Mexican Americans				
All	65%	9%	26%	427
Citizens only	69	8	23	325
U.S.-born	70	9	21	272
Foreign-born	56	10	33	147
Foreign-born citizens	67	2	31	45
Asian Americans				
All	42	10	48	248
Citizens only	43	10	47	191
U.S.-born	48	11	41	106
Foreign-born	38	8	54	137
Foreign-born citizens	38	8	55	80

esis predicts a shift in support toward Republicans, and African American leaders have made clear that black support cannot be taken for granted as issues shift.

ISSUE PREFERENCES

Do African Americans, Asian Americans, and Latinos share preferences on issues? To put it another way, how realistic is it to expect them to form a coalition? Although that is the way the question often is put in both popular and political discussion, doing so misses several points. First, none of these groups are monolithic. Second, leadership can influence members' issue preferences, especially in previously peripheral areas. Leaders can also make a peripheral area into one of more central concern. Third, expressed preferences on issues may well not represent considered opinions. The fact that certain survey responses are obtained may bear little relation to issue positions that matter politically.

A number of key issues in recent U.S. politics have been defined along racial or ethnic cleavage lines. And others that are not so explicitly defined nonetheless have differential effects on immigrants (for example, immigration and language policy) or on people of different economic circumstances. Since Latino and Asian American groups contain disproportionately large numbers of immigrants, and since racial and ethnic status is correlated with economic circumstances, immigration and economic issues have group relevance. At the same time, cleavages within the groups, along immigration status and economic lines, may well prove more important than those along racial or ethnic lines.

The 1984 California study asked a series of issue questions, many of which focused on matters of particular concern to immigrants. The study took place before final passage of the Immigration Reform and Control Act of 1986. Thus it is useful to look separately at the views of noncitizens, foreign-born citizens, and U.S.-born citizens. The immigration and language issues included amnesty for illegal immigrants, employer sanctions for hiring illegal immigrants, bilingual education, and bilingual ballots. Also included were a question each on classic "guns and butter" issues (increased funding for welfare and increased spending for defense) and a number of social issues (support for the Equal Rights Amendment, tax support for parochial schools, prayer in schools, banning federal funding for abortions, gun control, supporting the death penalty, restricting abortions or permitting choice). Of course, issues change over time, and, as just noted, their salience to the public can vary enormously and not exogenously. Nonetheless, examination of the responses on this set of issues provides some initial information on issue preferences.

Table 9.10 reports the percentage of respondents in each racial and ethnic group (including non-Hispanic whites) in favor of each issue (excluding respondents who had no opinion). Because four of the issues concern immigration, Mexican American and Asian American respondents were divided into the foreign-born and the native-born.[6] Compared with the other groups, African Americans tended to be Democrats who favored increased spending on welfare and opposed increased spending on defense. Along with foreign-born Mexican Americans, they were less supportive of the death penalty than the other groups. Foreign-born Asian Americans favored more spending on defense. Foreign-born Mexican Americans favored amnesty and opposed employer sanctions. Non-Hispanic whites and U.S.-born Asian Americans opposed bilingual education, bilingual ballots, and prayer in school and were prochoice. Native-born Asian Americans also opposed banning federal funding of abortions, and foreign-born Asian Americans were the group most favorable to gun control.

Persons who perceive disadvantages for minorities may well have different views on the issues. Thus, similar percentages were derived for respondents from each group who said "Blacks face fewer opportunities" and for those who said "Latinos face fewer opportunities." The results, not shown here, are more or less as one might expect. Non-Hispanic whites who saw either blacks or Latinos as disadvantaged took more "liberal" views on the issues and were more likely to be Democrats than other non-Hispanic whites. In contrast, African Americans who perceived structural inequities had views very similar to views of those who did not. They were, however, even more likely to be Democrats and far less likely to decline to state partisanship. Those who saw Latinos as disadvantaged were more supportive of bilingual ballots and less supportive of banning abortion funding. Native-born Mexican Americans were more supportive of amnesty, bilingual education, bilingual ballots, and gun control if they saw Latinos as disadvantaged. The views of foreign-born Mexican Americans changed little, except that they were more likely to be Democrats if they reported feeling that either group gets fewer opportunities than they deserve. Foreign-born Asian Americans who perceived blacks or Latinos as disadvantaged had more liberal views than other foreign-born Asian Americans across many of these issues, and they were more likely to be Democrats. The views of U.S.-born Asian Americans changed little with their perception of inequities, with the exception that those who saw blacks as disadvantaged were more in favor of employer sanctions, whereas those who perceived Latinos as disadvantaged were more opposed. Surprisingly, native-born Asian Americans who saw either black or Latino structural disadvantage were more likely to be Republicans.

In order to assess the prospects for coalition, the real question is how the position on the issues of each minority groups compares with the positions of the others. Therefore, for each issue, probit estimations were run to assess whether the differences of position between African Americans, Asian Americans, and Mexican Americans are significant. The dependent variable in each estimation was the percentage of respondents in favor, with those with no opinion on the issue excluded. There are six independent variables: native-born, naturalized citizen, and noncitizen Mexican Americans and the same three categories for Asian Americans. African Americans were the reference group and non-Hispanic whites were excluded from the analysis. Thus, if a coefficient is significant, it indicates that the members of that group had substantially different views on the issue than did African Americans. The pattern that emerges is mixed. All Mexican Americans and Asian Americans were more in favor of defense and less supportive of welfare spending than were African Americans. On a number of the social issues, there were no or few significant differences among the groups. Foreign-born Asian Americans were more supportive of gun control than anyone else. All groups except noncitizen Mexican Americans were more supportive of the death penalty than African Americans; all groups except foreign-born Mexican Americans were less in favor of prayer in school than African Americans. Asian American citizens and native-born Mexican Americans supported the ERA less than others of their ethnicity or than African Americans do.

Table 9.10

Issue Preferences by Ethnicity or Race and Birthplace

Issue and Party Identification	Non-Hispanic Whites	African Americans	U.S.-Born Mexican Americans	Foreign-Born Mexican Americans	U.S.-Born Asian Americans	Foreign-Born Asian Americans
Increase defense spending	36%	26%	36%	38%	36%	55%
Increase welfare spending	67	93	79	86	75	71
Amnesty for illegal immigrants	53	54	66	86	55	57
Employer sanctions	70	62	55	41	74	51
Bilingual education	46	71	73	79	49	61
Bilingual ballots	30	56	63	71	38	52
Support for the ERA	78	93	86	93	84	84
Private school tax credit	55	53	50	55	45	56
Prayer in schools	55	74	62	76	51	62
Banning of federal abortion funding	42	47	40	42	27	48
Gun control	51	50	55	54	54	69
Death penalty	83	61	78	64	89	81
Abortion choice	61	47	44	34	63	47
Democrat	42	82	61	44	43	30
Republican	37	5	18	26	37	42
Independent	7	5	8	8	10	7

Note: Data are those in favor as a percentage of those who have an opinion.

Attitudes on immigration and language issues reflected differences in the groups' situations. Mexican Americans favored amnesty far more than did either African Americans or Asian Americans. Noncitizens were opposed to employer sanctions more than anyone else, whereas U.S.-born Asian Americans favored them; others, including African Americans, were in between. Bilingual education was supported by Mexican-origin noncitizens and opposed by Asian American citizens; African Americans and Mexican American citizens held similar views. Thus, opinions on these issues were mixed, partly reflecting differences in immigration status but with substantial black support for the positions of many Mexican Americans and Asian Americans. Of course, views on even these specific issues may well have changed since 1984, and new issues have arisen. From these data, coalitions based on issues appear neither automatic nor far-fetched.

These differences in positions are for each group as a whole; however, a number of the significant differences in overall group opinion across race and ethnicity may reflect other factors, such as education, age, or attitudes, which happen to be correlated with race and ethnicity. One would like to compare people in each ethnic and racial group to those in others who share similar characteristics. Thus, a second series of probit models (not shown; see Uhlaner 1996, 54–62) estimated issue positions not only on the dummies reflecting ethnicity and citizenship or immigration status but also on control variables for other factors. The control variables were language, party identification, a number of demographic variables (religion, sex, homeownership, education, and age), and measures of perceived discrimination. The results indicate that some of the differences in issue preferences across groups reflect differences in language status, in perception of opportunities, and in demographics, especially religion, for the social issues. Even with the controls, none of the other minority groups were as supportive of welfare and other social spending programs as were African Americans. On "gun" issues, only the foreign-born Asian Americans stood out as hawkish. On immigration-related issues, ethnicity and length of time in the United States mattered. Citizens of every ethnicity favored employer sanctions more than did noncitizens. Thus, some of the apparent racial or ethnic differences reflect the operation of class- or immigration-related variables.

Directly comparable data on Latino subgroups are not available, but results from the Latino National Political Survey are of interest. These indicate that "the majority of Latinos believed that federal spending should increase, even if it necessitated an increase in their taxes" (de la Garza et al 1992, 89). Puerto Ricans were more supportive of spending in general than Mexican Americans or

Cubans, and especially so for welfare (89). Puerto Ricans and Mexican Americans were more supportive of spending for programs to help blacks than were Cubans or non-Hispanic whites (90). More than two-thirds of the citizens in all three groups "believed that there were currently too many immigrants coming to the U.S." (100). Surprisingly, even higher proportions of the noncitizens agreed (168).

Overall, foreign-born Mexican Americans appeared to have views on social issues that were closest to those of African Americans. On immigration-related issues, the views of African Americans appeared to be closest to those of Mexican American citizens, except on amnesty, for which they were closest to those of Asian American citizens. On defense, they were closest to those of U.S.-born Mexican Americans and Asian Americans, whereas on welfare they were divergent from those of all Mexican Americans and Asian Americans.

The implications of these findings for coalition are mixed. Perhaps the clearest lesson is that a coalition based on ethnic or racial groups alone would not succeed nearly as well as one that was sensitive to the differences in preferences related to differences in circumstances, especially class and immigration status. (See Chapter 10 of this book.)

CONCLUSION

Increased immigration can clearly increase a group's political impact. But many of the characteristics of immigrant communities have the paradoxical effect of decreasing their rates of activity in the short term while increasing their total political impact in the long term. For example, a young population tends to be less participatory. The youth typically arises from high fertility, however, leading to increased numbers and greater political power in the future. In analyzing the political future of ethnic and racial groups, it is important to pay attention to numbers *and* to rates of activity.

The future political impact of immigrants in particular and members of minority groups in general also depends heavily on the extent to which they become active in support of particular issues, candidates, or parties. The African American community already has well-honed organizational structures that have been very active in the past. Latinos are developing such structures, with evident success. Relatively little ethnically specific political organizing has occurred in Asian American communities; in fact, there is serious disagreement as to whether there is a politically relevant "Asian" community in contradistinction to people of various national origins. More important, ethnicity is not obviously a politically useful organizing principle for people of Asian origin, at least at the present time. Although cooperation across these particular ethnic and racial lines is not obvious, it is highly plausible and has at times occurred. What happens in the future will depend heavily on what leaders emerge and how they try to organize.

Chapter 10 Coalition Formation: The Mexican-Origin Community and Latinos and African Americans

John A. Garcia

The racial and ethnic mosaic of the United States has undergone significant changes in the past twenty-five years (see, for example, Bouvier and Graut 1994). Continued migration from Latin America and Asia has contributed to this change, as Hispanics and Asians have been the fastest-growing minorities in the past fifteen years (Valdieso and Davis 1988; O'Hare 1992). At the same time, African Americans are the largest minority group and have developed into an important force in American politics (Smith et al. 1991). This pattern is very evident in U.S. urban areas, particularly the largest central cities. As a result, political gains and competition have occurred between minorities and Anglos as well as between different minority groups (Mladenka 1989; McClain and Karnig 1990).

This chapter discusses the dynamics of coalition formation among minorities. Although issues of coalition formation have received significant attention from political scientists, only recently has attention been directed toward possible "rainbow coalitions" among minority communities (Henry and Munoz 1991). Such attention has focused on the competitive forces that make coalition formation between Latinos and African Americans difficult and tenuous, as well as the possible inducements to intergroup cooperation (McClain and Karnig 1990). This chapter examines the difficulty such coalitions face from intragroup fragmentation. I begin with a discussion of coalition formation within a specific Latino subgroup, that of Mexican origin, and then consider possible bases for coalitions between the Latino and the African American communities. The initial focus within the Latino community establishes the diversity comprising all minority groups and enhances our understanding of minority coalition formation in general by identifying mobilization processes that lead individuals and groups toward common political actions.

In the first section, I identify the Mexican-origin community as a diverse and differentiated population. The diversity existing within the Mexican-origin and larger Latino communities emphasize that collective efforts by these communities represent coalition formation. Drawing on Browning et al. (1984), who used the concept of political incorporation to suggest that successful coalitions including African Americans and Latinos require members with sophisticated organizational development and political experience, I use the concept of political integration—a process of incorporating members into a cohesive political community—to show that subcommunities within the Mexican-origin community have reached different levels of political integration. Common national origin and cultural values and patterns do not automatically guarantee a collective political aggregation and common agenda.

The conclusion is suggestive of the entire Latino community. Coalitional efforts involving Latinos require expanding the modes of political participation of individuals. Transcending passive participation to move Latinos to connect with organizations and be aware of leadership cadres is necessary.

The second section considers possible bridges between the Latino community and the African American community. The chapter explores three models of coalition formation: common interests, minority status (that is, discrimination), and common status goals. I find empirical evidence supporting the minority status model (that is, subordination and differential treatment) for each of the three major Latino subgroups.

DIVERSITY WITHIN THE MEXICAN
AMERICAN COMMUNITY

The Mexican-origin community can be divided into three segments or subcommunities: undocumented (or illegal) residents, permanent resident aliens, and the native-born population (Chicanos). One dimension that connects all segments of the Mexican-origin community is the immigration experience. That is, the Mexican-origin population includes people who are Mexican-born residents (permanent or sojourners) and members of the second (or later) generation in the United States. The experience or heritage of immigration serves as a cultural connection for all of them, but it differentiates them by their distance from that experience and by their legal status. Recent attempts to account for the rapid growth rate of the Mexican-origin population since the early 1970s indicates that almost one-third of the total growth was the result of net international migration and illegal migration (Browning and Cullen 1982).

The undocumented population, one of the three segments of the Mexican-origin community, can be roughly divided into two groups: temporary, circular migrants (or sojourners) and longer-staying migrants (settlers with families). Distinctions between the two groups are generally associated with gender differences (there are more females in the settler category) and a different attitudinal orientation toward life in the United States: accumulation of equity (homes, jobs) and greater attention to the education system and social service agencies are important among settlers. In U.S. labor markets, undocumented workers are usually employed in labor-intensive industrial and manufacturing firms, agriculture, and small businesses. The workplace serves as a major arena of economic and social intercourse between *indocumentados* and Chicanos.

The question of the legal status of the undocumented population reflects a sense of attachment to either the mother country or the host country, as well as the nature of formal interactions with agents of key U.S. institutions. Since the passage of the Immigration Reform and Control Act of 1986 and its amendments in 1990, the status of the undocumented has been further differentiated by amnesty for those who satisfied certain conditions (Sierra 1987). Being undocumented or granted temporary resident status defines a legal arrangement distinct from those of Mexican-origin permanent resident aliens or U.S.-born persons of Mexican origin.

The second subcommunity I identify are the permanent resident aliens. More than one million Mexican nationals permanently reside in the United States—about one-fifth of all permanent resident aliens in the country. During the 1970s, an average of 6,050 Mexican nationals were naturalized annually, with a high figure of 8,662 in 1978 (INS 1980). According to the 1980 census, approximately 40 percent of the Mexican-born population was naturalized, compared with an overall rate of naturalization of 63.6 percent for all foreign-born residents (SCRIP 1981). Mexicans have taken longer to indicate their intent and to meet all of the requirements for citizenship (North 1985). During the 1980s, organizations such as the National Association of Elected and Appointed Officials have worked to promote naturalization, and the rate has increased (Pachon et al. 1990).

Besides low rates of naturalization the resident aliens face issues of assimilation, acculturation, and integration into U.S. society. Do their experiences, expectations, lifestyles, and values substantially differ from those of Chicanos or *indocumentados?* One of the few systematic studies of Mexican nationals (de la Garza et al. 1992) examined core political values among Mexican immigrants (permanent resident aliens) and native-born Mexican Americans. With respect to economic individualism, patriotism, trust in government, and political tolerance, the Mexican immigrants reflect a strong loyalty to core American values. Certainly, the decision to make one's permanent home in the United States involves considerable equity accumulation in this system, but the unknown factor is the relevance of foreign-born status for political behavior.

The third segment of the Mexican-origin community is the Mexican American, or Chicano, component. This native-born segment has clear attachments to this country and their socioeconomic and political status can be compared with those of other ethnic groups in the United States. This segment can be characterized by its youthful population (Estrada et al. 1981), indigenous sociopolitical orientations (Acuna 1981), and involvement in organizational activities at the national level (Falcon et al. 1991; Sierra 1982). Thus, the Mexican American segment represents an ethnic group with an established political and economic presence in the United States (See Chapter 7 of this book). For Chicanos, ethnicity serves as a cohesive political force in participating in the U.S. political system. In order to understand the political involvement and internal coalitions of the Mexican-origin population, these three segments—undocumented immigrants, permanent resident aliens, and the native-born Chicanos—must be distinguished.

The Role of Political Integration

Political integration refers to the cohesiveness of the members of a political community (Lamare 1982; Wilson 1973) in terms of political values, beliefs, emotive traits, and activities (Almond and Verba 1965). Political integration into a society entails the development of a psychological attachment and a sense of satisfaction with the society as acculturation (that is, acquiring some degree of structural and identificational assimilation) occurs. For example, an immigrant community could adopt widespread acceptance of the society's prevailing beliefs, norms, and accepted political activities while continuing to maintain its ethnic identity.

In relation to the three subcommunities of Mexican-origin persons, particularly the undocumented, legal status entails different relations with political and social institutions in the United States. Decisions regarding access to the workplace, search and seizure practices of the U.S. Border Patrol, access to basic services, and protection from economic and social exploitation have a direct effect on the undocumented community. For the permanent resident alien segment, areas such as civic identity and assimilation, naturalization, political organizational involvement, partisan and electoral involvement (de la Garza and DeSipio 1993), participatory political attitudes (Kinder and Sears 1985; Uhlaner et al. 1991), and loyalty to the United States (de la Garza et al. 1991) constitute important interfaces with the political system. For both the undocumented and permanent resident alien subcommunities, the act of migrating to the United States generally involved an economic motive to improve one's condition. At the same time, immigrants may have been pushed by the insecurity or inadequacy of their social setting or by general dissatisfaction with their own economic and political system. Economic security and legal standing and rights are permanent concerns of these two subcommunities.

Political integration for the segments closest to the immigrant experience may well rest on the extent of the economic stability and mobility they achieve. The arena of the labor market is the entry point and potentially the site of political activities for the undocumented subcommunity. For permanent resident aliens, economic mobility potentially opens up more mainstream relationships outside the Mexican-origin community. Finally, political integration for the Chicano subcommunity focuses on their emergence as a legitimate collective force on the American political scene. Infrastructure building occurs in terms of organizations, resources, leadership, and an identifiable policy agenda. A strong level of identification with the political system serves as an impetus to engage in making political demands. Political integration for Chicanos deals with the process of political involvement and the outcomes of their activities.

These three subcommunities share commonalities (national origin, cultural patterns, language, immigration experience) but distinct political statuses. What is the pattern of their political participation, and where does the overlap occur that could stimulate shared interests and activities? Three measures of political integration are satisfaction, identification, and acculturation. Satisfaction involves the current evaluation of life in the United States, including satisfaction with one's job, standard of living, sense of well-being in the United States relative to Mexico, and desire to stay in the United States. The identification and acculturation measures include affective identification with the United States, interest in organizational involvement, participation as active consumers of American goods, and personal interactions with non-Mexicans. I suggest that in addition a measure of attachment, as well as a feeling of being a stakeholder in the United States, serves as an important prerequisite for each segment for any type of political participation.

My discussion of political involvement incorporates two stages. The first stage is passive participation, which entails having an interest in political events and actors in the United States, talking about political issues, personalities, and events, and keeping informed about the political system. It reflects the development of positive orientations toward the political system, as well as the exchange of formulated views with other people. The second stage is active participation, which entails extensive involvement in organizations and such political activities as campaigns, partisan work, direct contact with public officials, and attempts to influence policy choices.

Some degree of political integration is necessary to facilitate the movement to passive political participation and then to active participation. Several factors influence that movement: prior participatory patterns, particularly in one's country of origin; socioeconomic status, which indicates human capital skills and investment and is convertible into political activities; extent of positive identification with the United States; and, for the undocumented and permanent resident segments, the length of residence, which indicates extent of equity accumulated in the United States. For the native-born segment, generational distance from Mexico taps the same dimension as length of residence.

Differences in Political Integration

I suggest that the level and manifestations of political integration may be substantially different for Chicanos, permanent resident aliens, and the undocumented. Survey data from public opinion polls conducted by the Southwest Voter Registration and Education Project illustrate levels of political integration. These surveys, conducted in 1981 and 1982 in San Antonio and East Los Angeles, focused on political participation and attitudes. The respondents were Spanish-surnamed adults, and the categories of citizens and noncitizens in the survey correspond roughly to the Chicano segment and to the undocumented and resident alien segments (Mexicanos).

An indicator of passive participation is the level of awareness of the political system, events, and issues. Table 10.1 summarizes citizens' and noncitizens' use

Table 10.1
Media Sources of Information Among Mexican-Origin Citizens and Noncitizens

	Citizens (N = 276)	Noncitizens (N = 515)
Read the newspaper daily	70.5%	48.2%
Watch Spanish television		
Less than English	55.7	29.9
Same amount as English	22.2	44.5
More than English	22.2	25.6
Listen to English or Spanish local news		
English	76.2	12.4
Spanish	11.9	12.4
Both equally	11.9	15.3
Use these sources of information about global and national events		
Radio	20.4	22.5
Television	60.1	64.5
Newspapers	19.0	10.7
Use these sources of information about the local community		
Radio	15.5	22.8
Television	54.0	62.7
Newspapers	30.0	11.6
Other	0.4	3.0
Use these sources of information about the Mexican American community		
Radio	22.1	26.8
Television	43.0	58.5
Newspapers	32.3	11.8
Other	2.9	2.9

of a variety of media sources and news programming. Less than one-half (48.2 percent) of the noncitizens read a newspaper daily, whereas almost three-fourths (70.5 percent) of the Chicanos read a newspaper daily. With Spanish usage very dominant among the noncitizens, the unavailability of Spanish-language newspapers could be a contributing factor in this discrepancy. Twice as many noncitizens watched equal amounts of English- and Spanish-language television programming as their Chicano counterparts. In addition, the primary source of

Table 10.2
Discussion of Politics with Different Parties Among
Mexican-Origin Citizens and Noncitizens

Discusses Politics with	Citizens (N = 276)	Noncitizens (N = 515)
Friends		
Often	21.6%	12.7%
Sometimes	38.1	18.0
Seldom	18.7	18.9
Never	21.6	40.4
Family		
Often	26.0	19.3
Sometimes	37.7	34.9
Seldom	16.6	13.8
Never	19.7	32.0
Organization members		
Often	7.2	3.7
Sometimes	10.2	5.9
Seldom	8.0	3.7
Never	74.7	86.7
Spouse		
Often	30.7	26.4
Sometimes	22.4	27.3
Seldom	8.8	8.6
Never	37.9	37.7

news information for both segments was television, yet newspapers were a very important source for Chicanos as well.

Another aspect of passive participation involves the discussion of politics with other individuals (see table 10.2). If individuals are aware of political events, actors, and so on, then there is greater potential for active participation. Two-fifths (40.4 percent) of the noncitizens never discuss politics with friends, compared with one-fifth (21.6 percent) of Chicanos. Chicanos discuss politics more often with both family members and friends than do permanent resident aliens. Interestingly, comparable percentages of Chicanos and Mexicanos discuss politics with their spouses (30.7 percent and 26.4 percent, respectively). The vast majority of both noncitizens and Chicanos never discuss politics with members of organizations (86.7 percent and 74.7 percent, respectively).

The final aspect of passive political participation is political orientation, which is conducive to participation. Political orientation includes political trust and efficacy and support for electoral participation. Responses to four of the orientation factors examined in table 10.3 suggest that noncitizens demonstrate a greater attitudinal distance from the American political system than do citizens. More noncitizens see individuals as having little impact on government and consider public officials as not responsive. Interestingly, both Chicanos and Mexicanos view American politics as too complicated (68.8 percent and 75.9 percent, respectively). Both segments have internalized the value of voting, however. At the same time, Mexicanos express a greater sense of cultural proximity between politicians and "us" if the politician is a Mexican American.

On all these dimensions of passive participation, noncitizens display much lower levels of political awareness, interest, and understanding of the political system than do citizens. I have included one active participation activity—organizational involvement. In table 10.4, low levels of organizational involve-

Table 10.3
Political Orientation Among Mexican-Origin Citizens and Noncitizens

	Citizens (N = 276)	Noncitizens (N = 515)
Individuals have no say in government.		
Agree	28.7%	40.9%
Disagree	67.6	49.3
Public officials don't care what people think.		
Agree	43.0	53.3
Disagree	51.9	40.9
Politics is too complicated.		
Agree	68.8	75.9
Disagree	28.7	20.8
Voting is the only way to have a say in government.		
Agree	81.6	74.4
Disagree	15.8	17.9
Mexican American politicians care more about us.		
Agree	45.1	69.6
Disagree	46.5	22.7

Note: The responses do not add up to 100 percent because "don't know" responses are omitted.

ment are evident: only 39.1 percent of the Chicanos and 25.4 percent of the Mex-icanos belonged to at least one organization. Yet national studies (Verba and Nie 1972) indicate that 60 percent of all adult Americans belong to an organization. Multiple membership is a rare phenomenon among both segments, particularly Mexicanos (4.4 percent).

Political and civic organizational involvement is very uncommon. Not a single Mexicano belonged to a civic organization, and only 4.7 percent of the Chicanos did so. If Mexicanos belong to any organization, it is more likely to be a church-related group.[1] Organizational membership allows the introduction of political stimuli, development of organizational skills, and increased levels of political information. This preliminary profile of Chicanos and Mexicanos

Table 10.4
Organizational Activity of Mexican-Origin Citizens and Noncitizens

	Citizens		Noncitizens	
	N	(Percentage)	N	(Percentage)
Member of any organization				
Yes	201	(39.1)	70	(25.4)
No	314	(61.0)	206	(74.6)
Number of organizations of which respondent is a member				
None	314	(61.0)	206	(74.6)
One	152	(29.5)	58	(21.0)
Two	39	(7.6)	9	(3.3)
Three or four	10	(1.9)	3	(1.1)
Member of a political organization				
Yes	40	(7.8)	5	(1.8)
No	471	(92.2)	269	(98.2)
Member of a civic organization				
Yes	24	(4.7)	0	(0.0)
No	485	(94.9)	273	(100.00)
Member of a church group				
Yes	66	(13.0)	44	(16.4)
No	441	(86.9)	229	(83.6)
Takes into account group's views when forming opinions				
Yes	122	(24.0)	80	(29.2)
No	387	(76.0)	104	(70.8)

strongly suggests that political integration is an uneven and slow process for noncitizens, and both segments are more likely to be passive participants. Although links to the immigration experience serve as a shared experience for all three segments, the politicization and political learning processes that take place with all members, and their relation with their own community as well as the larger society, affect how they move through the stages of political integration. In this manner, concrete discussions of coalition formation can occur within the reality of a diverse Mexican-origin community.

COMMON GROUND FOR LATINO AND AFRICAN
AMERICAN COALITION FORMATION

Coalitions are action-oriented ventures among similarly situated groups. Thus, political activation and collective efforts depend on common experiences, values and priorities, and issues. At the same time, individuals inclined to act politically require some organization and leadership in order to realize goals.

This section explores bases for coalition formation between the Latino community or its subcommunities and the African American community. Obviously, approaches to the study of coalition formation center around the basis for any distinction among social interest groups.[2] Carmichael and Hamilton (1967) have identified some necessary requisites for coalition formation: recognition of each party's interests; the benefits to each party of allying; an independent base of support for each party; and the focus of the coalitional effort on specific and identifiable goals. In essence, the strategy of Jesse Jackson in the 1988 presidential campaign was to build rainbow coalitions based on reciprocity, leverage, and common interests (Henry and Munoz 1991).

Recent work by Uhlaner (1991) has examined a basis for coalitions between Latinos and African Americans that centers around not only common interests but also levels of perceived discrimination. Thus, the common condition of discrimination experienced by minority group members, although in varying degrees, may serve as a foundation for intergroup coalitions. Yet Uhlaner suggests that although sympathy may be generated across minority groups, the response may be more competitiveness or antagonism. That is, the recognition of differential treatment across groups could lead specific minority groups to feel more disadvantaged than others and be more inclined to protect their own. The level of one's perceived discrimination is related to the strength of an individual's racial or ethnic identity and to the impact of prejudice on one's interests and specific problems (Uhlaner 1991).

Discrimination can be experienced at various times in a person's life. Studies of minority elites (de la Garza and Baughn 1984; Marable 1985) have demonstrated that early socialization that included significant experiences with discrimination and prejudice influenced individuals toward activism and advocacy for their group. In addition, perceptions of differential treatment based on race, ethnicity, or gender can have a real effect on attitudes and behaviors even if a person has not directly experienced prejudicial treatment. Political behavior reflects linking the practice of discrimination with concerted actions to remove obstacles to policy adoption and implementation, actions that benefit African Americans or Latinos. The areas of interest for African Americans and Latinos may be very similar (economic mobility, jobs, the criminal justice system) or distinctive (immigration policies, cultural policies, English as the official language). The question of one's disadvantaged position can be tied to other groups in a manner to foster collaborative efforts, or one can see other groups as contributing to that disadvantaged status.

The key for coalitions, within this perspective, lies with the assessment of one's own disadvantaged status as tied to that of other groups so that each confronts similar problems and perhaps a common target. Although the emphasis of this perspective is at the individual level, the dynamics of coalition formation relies heavily on organizations and leaders to channel perceived common interests and discrimination toward focused activity.

Another perspective regarding coalitions centers around common status goals rather than welfare goals (Carmichael and Hamilton 1967; Sonenshein 1990). In this perspective, political ideology (liberalism, social change orientations such as economic individualism, and so on) serves as the glue for coalitions, and interests are secondary. In some manner, a coalition is built on a moral, sentimental, and friendly basis with direct appeals to one's conscience (Henry and Munoz 1991). This perspective is in contrast to the view that the basis for coalition formation lies with the recognition among minority groups that they share a common opponent. Thus, political coalitions are viable if both minority groups see themselves as combating the "white power structure" (McClain and Karnig 1990). A minimum level of trust between minority groups is essential for any degree of success. Work by Oliver and Johnson (1984) in Los Angeles indicates a low level of trust between Latinos and African Americans. The need for coalitions may be lessened if minority groups operate in independent arenas of decision-making. Thus, there are many factors affecting the formation of coalitions, ranging from the relative size of each minority group to similarity of perceived interests, levels of organizational development and leadership, and perceptions of discrimination and social distance (Dangelis 1977).

The strength of Latino and African American communities has become more evident in major U.S. urban areas. McClain and Karnig (1990) identified almost fifty cities with populations of 25,000 or more in which Latinos and African Americans each comprise more than 10 percent of the total population. Much of the previous urban research has focused on minority representation of African Americans and Latinos in local government (Eisinger 1982; Fraga, Meier, and England 1986; Robinson and Dye 1978; McManus and Cassel 1982). Works by Falcon (1988) and McClain and Karnig (1990) have focused on these groups' struggles for political power and economic mobility. More specific work on coalitions between these two groups has been focused on electoral issues (for example, Jackson's rainbow coalition) or specific local community efforts. With a focus on Latino–African American coalitional efforts, my purpose is to identify possible connectors that may facilitate specific cooperative efforts around particular issues.

Yet, ultimately, self-interest serves as a key factor for political motivation and for building linkages to intergroup activities. A cost-benefit ratio may be calculated by members of different groups to weigh the degree of overlapping interests and how each group's benefits would be enhanced (Henry and Munoz 1991). Interracial coalitions tend to be short-lived and sustained by very specific and identifiable goals.

Minorities' experiences in the United States are based on social stratification, differential treatment, and unequal access. Thus, there exists a common basis for members of minority communities to pool limited resources to empower their respective communities and resolve political inequities. Such cooperative efforts have occurred (the Civil Rights Act, the Voting Rights Act, class action litigation, and so on) during this century (Marable 1985). At the same time, minority communities have also displayed a competitive mode. Blalock (1967) identifies competition between minority groups when two or more groups strive for the same finite objectives so that success for one reduces the probability that the other will obtain its goals. These struggles can be described as power contests between minority groups for scarce system outputs and allocations (Oliver and Johnson 1984; Welch, Karnig, and Eribes 1983).

McClain and Karnig (1990) have introduced the idea of a covariation model. That is, both minority groups' goals lie in the same direction (education, income, employment, and social services) in the political arena so that system response is more at the expense of majority group members. Benefits derived do not reduce the probability of success for either minority group. Yet when one of the minority groups represents a dominant position in the political arena, there can be negative effects on the other minority community (McClain and Karnig

1990). Thus, the presence of competition and antagonism can influence the extent and nature of contact and interactions. For the purposes of this chapter, the crucial elements in the minority status model are actual experiences with discrimination, perceptions of discrimination for one's own group and other minority groups, and the extent of perceived social distance between different racial and ethnic groups.

Minority Status Model: The Latino Half

I am only able to present one-half of the intergroup equation in this inquiry. That is, the data from the Latino National Political Survey (LNPS) afford me the opportunity to examine dimensions of the minority experience for the Latino groups. There are other databases that can provide the African American half of these attitudinal aspects of minority status. Obviously, part of the research agenda entails more directly comparative analysis of African Americans and Latinos.

In this analysis, Latinos are not treated as a single group but are distinguished by national origin: Mexican, Puerto Rican, and Cuban. The basic minority status model incorporates the variables of the respondent's actual experience with discrimination; perceived levels of discrimination for his or her own group, other Latino groups, and African Americans; and the extent of social distance (empathy) between Latino subgroups and the other minority groups. I have expanded the basic model to include two other sets of potential explanatory variables: socioeconomic status and political integration. The analysis considers whether there is support for the minority status model. I use dimensions of passive participation to explore support for common interests (for example, level of support for policy funding) as the dependent variable.

Table 10.5 shows responses from the Latinos to the question "Because you are an [RG], have you ever been turned down as a renter or buyer of a home, or been treated rudely in a restaurant, or been denied a job, or experienced other important types of discrimination?"[3] Direct experiences with discrimination were more common among the Mexican and Puerto Rican respondents: 33 percent of Mexicans and 30 percent of Puerto Ricans said yes, in comparison with only 14 percent of Cubans. These results do not differ dramatically from other public opinion polls taken in the past decade.

Perceptions of discrimination may be derived from other experiences that are relayed to the respondent or through other indirect means. Table 10.6 shows the responses of African Americans and Latinos of Mexican, Cuban, and Puerto Rican origin to the question "Now I would like to ask you about how much discrimination or unfair treatment you think different groups face: do you think

Table 10.5
Latino Experience with Discrimination

Experienced Discrimination	Mexicans (N = 1,546)	Puerto Ricans (N = 589)	Cubans (N = 679)
Yes	516	176	95
No	1,024	413	584

Note: Data from the Latino National Political Survey; for the exact question, see text.

they face a lot, some, a little, or none at all?" The results indicate different levels of perceived discrimination among these groups. Blacks were seen as experiencing the greatest degree of discrimination by all three Latino groups. Yet there was some variation: more than one-half of the Puerto Ricans said blacks experienced "a lot" of discrimination, whereas only one-fourth of the Cubans said the same. Among the Latino subgroups, those of Mexican origin were seen as experiencing the greatest degree of discrimination by all three groups. Interestingly, a greater percentage of Puerto Ricans (35.8 percent) than Mexicans (31.6 percent) said that Mexicans experienced "a lot" of discrimination. Consistently, the Cubans perceived the lowest level of discrimination for all of the groups, especially themselves (6.6 percent said Cubans experienced "a lot"). Looking at both the extent of actual discrimination experienced and levels of perceived discrimination, I conclude that it is a significant part of these Latinos' lives (74.2 percent of Mexicans see a lot of bias against themselves, and 73.9 percent of Puerto Ricans see it directed against themselves).

Even though these responses are consistent with the concept of minority status, this does not automatically suggest a natural affinity across minority groups. Competition and possible antagonism may mark the nature of relations between minority groups. In order to further explore the minority status model for Latino subgroups and African Americans, I looked at statements of social distance in response to the question "Please rate each group using the feeling thermometer. Ratings between 50 and 100 degrees mean that you feel favorable toward the group. The ratings between 0 and 50 degrees means that you feel unfavorable toward the group." The groups differentiated for this question were Mexican Americans, Mexican immigrants, African Americans, U.S.-born Puerto Ricans, Puerto Ricans born on the island, and Cuban Americans. (The differentiations within the Mexican and Puerto Rican communities were made for the reasons discussed in the first section of this chapter.)

Table 10.6
Perceived Discrimination Against Latinos and African Americans by Latinos

Object of Discrimination	Mexicans		Puerto Ricans		Cubans	
	N	(Percentage)	N	(Percentage)	N	(Percentage)
African Americans		77.3		85.5		57
A lot	596	(38.6)	336	(57.0)	169	(24.9)
Some	599	(38.7)	168	(28.5)	218	(32.1)
Little	231	(14.9)	52	(8.8)	100	(14.7)
None	111	(7.2)	30	(5.1)	191	(28.1)
Mexicans		74		75		54
A lot	487	(31.6)	209	(35.8)	147	(2.1)
Some	657	(42.6)	229	(39.8)	212	(31.8)
Little	297	(19.2)	91	(15.6)	116	(17.4)
None	100	(6.5)	54	(9.3)	190	(28.5)
Cubans		59		58		40
A lot	254	(17.2)	127	(21.6)	45	(6.6)
Some	620	(41.9)	215	(36.6)	226	(33.4)
Little	398	(26.9)	56	(26.6)	297	(43.9)
Puerto Ricans		54		74		41
A lot	203	(13.7)	203	(34.7)	57	(8.3)
Some	608	(40.9)	230	(39.2)	231	(34.3)
Little	385	(25.9)	101	(17.3)	100	(14.9)
None	291	(19.6)	51	(8.7)	284	(42.2)
Total N:	1,546		589		679	

The overall pattern was that each respondent gave higher thermometer ratings for members of his or her own group than for the other groups. For example, the Mexican-origin respondents rated Mexican Americans and Mexican immigrants almost 20 points higher (between 75 and 85) than either Cubans or Puerto Ricans (between 55 and 60). Mexican immigrants were rated a little lower (75) than Mexican Americans (85) by the Mexicans. The second pattern is that no greater social distance is exhibited between Latino subgroups than between Latinos and African Americans. For example, the Cubans' average thermometer scores for Puerto Ricans and Mexican Americans were 66.5 and 58.0, respectively, whereas their rating of African Americans was 57.5.

With some basis for a common minority group status, the understanding of subordinate standing could also translate into a common set of concerns. In the

LNPS, the Latino respondents were asked: "Now we would like to ask you about your views on various types of government programs. [For each one] tell me if you would like to see it increased, even if it meant paying more taxes, if you would like to see it decreased, or would like to see it stay the same?" Table 10.7 shows the responses for public education, public assistance, medical care, child care services, crime prevention and drug control, and programs to help blacks. For the most part, levels of support for increased funding for these programs was consistently high across all three subgroups. Puerto Ricans showed high levels of support for funding for public assistance programs. The support for increases in funds for blacks ranged from 67.5 percent for Puerto Ricans to 58.7 percent for those of Mexican origin and 45.2 percent for Cuban Americans. Again the basis for an overlapping agenda has some support among the Latino groups in relation to support for black programs and social domestic programs.

There can be a basis for coalition between Latinos and African Americans due to common policy concerns and preferences. Yet similar policy preferences are not sufficient for coalition formation. I have introduced the idea of minority group status (as manifested in discrimination, perception of prejudice, and social distance) as an important attitudinal set. For this preliminary work, the dependent variable is the item that indicates Latino respondents' level of funding support for government programs to help blacks. The possible responses were "increase," "decrease," "maintain at the same level," or "no opinion." For analytical purposes, this variable was recoded to make it a dichotomous variable. The dichotomy was to favor increased spending or not (that is, a response of "maintain" was considered part of the "decrease" response), and "no opinion"

Table 10.7
Latino Support for Increased Spending for Programs, by Origin

	Mexicans		Puerto Ricans		Cubans	
Programs	N	(Percentage)	N	(Percentage)	N	(Percentage)
Education	1,286	(83.2)	516	(76.1)	513	(75.5)
Public assistance	596	(38.6)	295	(50.1)	246	(36.2)
Medical care	1,212	(78.4)	494	(83.9)	495	(72.9)
Child services	1,090	(70.5)	456	(74.4)	465	(68.5)
Drug and crime control	1,358	(87.8)	546	(92.7)	611	(90.0)
Programs to help blacks	908	(58.7)	398	(67.5)	307	(45.2)

Note: For question wording, see text.

responses were coded as missing data. The effect of removing the "no opinion" cases was the loss of 169 of 2,816 cases.

Logistic regression with a dichotomous dependent variable (support for black programs) and three models of explanation was used to test possible bases for coalition formation. Model 1 represents the minority status model. That is, subordinate status (experiencing discrimination and levels of perceived discrimination) and a perceived close social distance between different minority groups would serve as the basis for intergroup connections. I added to this model the presence of a pan-ethnic identity. This variable represents Latinos who chose to identify themselves in terms broader than just national origin (a pan-ethnic label). Model 2 uses the minority status variables as the base but also introduces sociodemographic factors (years of schooling, annual household income, language of the interview, and nativity). These are relevant factors mentioned in similarly focused research, as well as key components of the Latino experience. Using these factors also allows one to sort out the overlapping effects of the different variables.

Model 3 incorporates the dimension of passive participation (that is, political integration) that was developed in the first section of this chapter. I suggest that a sense of minority status and passive participation might serve as complementary forces for possible coalition formation. The sociodemographic variables serve to enhance political participation. In the analysis, variables that are categorical were entered in that manner, and the lower value served as the reference for the coefficients derived.

The results of the logistic regression are presented in table 10.8. The minority status variables in Model 1 showed some significant relationships. Specific Latino subgroup status has a positive association with support for black programs. Since Mexican Americans were the reference group, both Puerto Ricans and Cubans evidenced positive support for black programs relative to Mexican Americans. Overall, the Latino group variable was significant in the analysis. Interestingly, experiencing discrimination had the opposite effect: those who had experienced discrimination had lower support for black programs. One possible explanation for this result is that competition and disadvantaged status are not necessarily transferred to other minority groups. Finally, a positive group affinity between Latinos and African Americans had a direct effect.

The addition of socioeconomic variables, however, weakened the relations between social distance and experiencing discrimination and support for black programs. The direction of the relationships were the same, although the coefficients were smaller. Lower levels of years of schooling completed had a nega-

Table 10.8
Latinos' Support for Black Programs by Three Models of Coalition Formation

Variables	Model 1	Model 2	Model 3
Latino groups			
Puerto Ricans	.05 (.06)	.12 (.06)	.13 (.07)
Cubans	.43 (.07)	.43 (.08)	.41 (.08)
Experience discrimination	−.12 (.05)	−.09 (.05)	−.13 (.05)
Black social distance	.0004 (.002)	.0003 (.0002)	.0004
Black discrimination			
Little	−.33(.100)	−.47 (10)	−.46 (.11)
Some	.09 (.09)	−.03 (.09)	−.02 (.10)
A lot	−.11 (.07)	−.002 (.07)	.02 (.07)
Pan-ethnic identity	.0025 (.04)	−.05 (.04)	−.04 (.04)
Years of schooling	−.0225 (.01)	−.02 (.01)	−.02 (.01)
Household income	.0002 (.0002)	.0005 (.0019)	
Nativity	.10 (.06)	.05 (.06)	
Language of interview			
English and Spanish		−.25 (.10)	−.22 (.10)
Spanish only		−.01 (.15)	−.03 (.15)
Follows political events		.07 (.04)	
Pays attention to ethnic origin		.37 (.04)	
Works for ethnic identity		−.16 (.04)	
Constant	.30 (.06)	.37 (.15)	−.86 (.29)
−2 Log likelihood	3399.57*	3255.0*	3100.88*
Goodness of fit	2632.92	2575.76	2551.41

Note: The three models represent the following: Model 1 includes the minority status dimension with discrimination a critical component; Model 2 supplements the minority status variables with sociodemographic variables; and Model 3 supplements Model 2 with indicators of passive political participation.

tive effect on support for black programs; nativity and annual household income were statistically insignificant. The reference group for the language item was English-speaking respondents. Relative to this group, people who are bilingual are less supportive of black programs, and, to a lesser degree, so are Spanish speakers.

Model 3 includes the passive participation variables (political integration): how much a person follows political events; how much attention a person gives to matters affecting his or her Latino subgroup; and whether a person is willing to work with fellow ethnic group members to advance collective interests. The basic effects of the minority status variables remain essentially the same as in Model 2. The coefficient for Puerto Ricans was reduced. Experience with discrimination and social distance were statistically significant. Years of schooling and bilingualism also remained significant. The variable measuring how attentive the respondent was to the concerns of his or her group proved to be a salient factor in a positive way.

CONCLUSIONS

The results of this preliminary analysis provide some basis for the pertinence of minority status as a bridge to formation of coalitions between Latinos and African Americans. Support across all three Latino groups, as well as a positive social distance, enhances Latino support for programs for blacks. Lower educational attainment for Latinos, as well as bilingualism, reduces the level of support. If Latinos are aware of general political events, and particularly if they follow matters affecting their group, then these political integration variables complement the minority status model. In many ways, the keys to Latino coalition formation involve establishing participatory modes within their own communities and defining interests in minority status terms. This chapter only begins to explore a very complex dynamic. Some unexplored dimensions lie with power relations within specific Latino communities and their history of inter-minority relations, as well as the tendency of the Latino leadership to promote coalitions.

Coalitions, by definition, are designed to link group interests and common interests for specific purposes. The minority experience of differential treatment and disempowerment provides a basis for formation of coalitions between Latinos and African Americans. A critical element is greater degree of awareness among Latinos about the political system and its effects on their respective communities. In a sense, heightened political awareness can serve to politicize their own communities and enable them to become more aware of constructive alliances with other minority groups. At the same time, systemic factors can foster a more competitive situation between these two potential allies.

Concern about possible Latino–African American coalitions will remain a vital issue for the twenty-first century. The demographics of these two groups and their residential overlap compel both communities to seriously explore these potential links. The work by McClain and Karnig (1990) is insightful as to the overall conditions facilitating coalitions between these two groups. For Latinos and their various subcommunities, the development of more pervasive participatory patterns continues to be a major priority. It serves to define and enhance group interests. The staging of passive and active participation may be one way in which to move organizations and their leaders to increase participation in the political process. For the African American community, better understanding of what minority status has meant for Latino communities serves to forge a stronger bond between the two groups. In this way, shared interests can be better understood. Finally, the examination of coalition formation becomes one of multiple strategies to further empower both of these communities.

Notes

1. Throughout this book *black* and *African American* are used interchangeably, as are *Hispanic* and *Latino*.
2. *1992 Los Angeles County Social Survey,* Institute for Social Science Research Survey Research Center, UCLA, October 1992. The data for the analysis come from a survey of attitudes and beliefs of 1,869 residents of Los Angeles County—284 Asian (15 percent); 483 black (26 percent); 477 Latino (26 percent); and 625 white (33 percent). A grant from the Andrew W. Mellon Foundation enabled the 1992 survey to oversample Asian, black, and Latino Americans. A summary of the survey commissioned by the National Conference of Christians and Jews can be found in the *Washington Post,* 3 March 1994.
3. The list is long and getting longer. The following is merely a sample: Borjas 1987; Card 1990; Chiswick 1982; Greenwood and McDowell 1986; Grossman 1982; Johnson 1980; and Muller and Espenshade 1985. See also the chapters in Abowd and Freeman 1991 and Borjas and Freeman 1992.

CHAPTER 3: THE POLITICS OF BLACK-KOREAN CONFLICT

I am indebted to Adolph Reed, Jr., James C. Scott, Ira Katznelson, Rogers M. Smith, and Gerald Jaynes for their comments on an earlier draft. Support for this project was provided by the American Association of University Women, the Mellon Foundation, and the Institute for Intercultural Studies. For an expanded and updated analysis of the subject of this chapter, see Claire Jean Kim, Bitter Fruit: The Politics of Black-Korean Conflict (Yale University Press, forthcoming).

1. I use the term *blacks* to refer to both African Americans and immigrants from Haiti and other Caribbean nations.

2. Korean immigration to the United States grew dramatically after the implementation of the Immigration Reform Act of 1965, which dismantled the national-origin quota system that had effectively cut off Asian immigration since 1924. As of 1990, approximately 90 percent of New York City's two thousand or so greengroceries were Korean-owned and -operated (*Crain's New York Business,* 21 May 1990).

3. The demographic figures for New York City alone are striking. Between 1980 and 1990, 90 percent of the immigration into New York City came from the Caribbean, Asia, Africa, and Latin America (Armstrong 1989, 10). During this period, white non-Hispanics decreased by 15 percent to 43 percent of the city's total population of 7.3 million; black non-Hispanics increased by 9 percent to 25 percent of the total population; Hispanics increased by 27 percent to 24 percent of the total population; and Asians increased by 105 percent to 7 percent of the total population (Office of Community Board 14, n.d.). By the year 2000, 56 percent of the city's estimated population of 7.6 million will be foreign-born (Armstrong 1989, 28).

4. This chapter is based on research conducted for my dissertation, *Bitter Fruit* (see above). Types of data used include personal interviews, newspaper articles, television program transcripts, public documents such as hearing transcripts and official reports, and secondary literature. In all, I completed sixty-nine interviews with those involved in the Red Apple Boycott and the new black power movement.

5. Bonacich's more recent writings (1980, 1987) give the middleman minority theory a clearly Marxist cast. These writings attempt to dereify the structural arrangements surrounding middleman minorities and to highlight their class position; although they go further than her earlier work in denaturalizing and critiquing power relations, they remain focused on structural factors rather than purposive agency.

6. See Eugene Wong (1985) for a general critique of the middleman minority theory. Although a few recent works based on the middleman minority framework do address the ideational aspects of black-Korean conflict (Jo 1992; Cheng and Espiritu 1989), their treatment of collective beliefs as received, fixed, uniform, and passively experienced "opinions"—rather than as active instruments and products of collective action—does not advance our understanding of purposive agency.

7. I use the label "the new black power movement" to indicate that the movement was grounded in many of the ideas and practices of the black power movement of the late 1960s and early 1970s. Many of the new movement's leaders were veterans of the earlier movement.

8. The new black power movement's campaigns (including the Red Apple Boycott) have attracted little scholarly attention because many scholars bear unexplored assumptions about what collective action must look like before it can be deemed a bona fide movement. Fainstein and Fainstein (1991), for instance, argue that because the new black power movement campaigns were "not carried out under the auspices of established organizations" and

because they "failed to win much sympathy within the liberal white community," they did not "signa[l] the development of a coherent movement" (318–19).

9. Blacks were formally brought into the city's political system via political machines during the first few decades of the twentieth century, although this incorporation was—and arguably still is—nominal rather than meaningful. Until David Dinkins was elected mayor in 1989, all citywide elected officials in New York City had been white.

10. Between 1975 and the early 1990s, overall poverty rates and income inequality rose substantially in New York City and in the nation as a whole (Mollenkopf 1992; Mollenkopf and Castells 1991).

11. In the early 1980s, veteran activists Al Vann and Roger Green formed the Coalition for Community Empowerment (CCE) to promote radical black candidates for elective office. Known as "the Brooklyn insurgents," CCE members challenged both the Harlem black establishment and Brooklyn Democratic party regulars. Other campaigns crucial to the development of the new black power movement concerned the selection of the chancellor of the New York City school system in 1983, the mayoral election of 1985, and the presidential primary elections of 1984 and 1988. A note on terminology: I use *moderates* to refer to black leaders who are oriented toward elective office or willing to work with those who are and *radicals* to refer to black leaders who typically eschew working within the system in favor of a vision of more fundamental political, social, and economic change.

12. The December 12th Movement is a small, tight-knit group of the city's most radical African American and Caribbean activists. Each member espouses his or her own distinct set of radical beliefs ranging from cultural nationalism to Marxism-Leninism. Notable members include Sonny Carson, Coltrane Chimurenga, and Omowale Clay. In the early 1980s, these activists were all members of the New York Eight, a radical group subjected to COINTELPRO-style investigations by Mayor Edward Koch and New York police commissioner Benjamin Ward. The outer circles of the new black power movement's leadership included more "moderate" figures such as Reverend Herbert Daughtry of the House of the Lord Pentecostal Church in Brooklyn, Reverend Calvin O. Butts III of the Abyssinian Baptist Church, and Reverend Al Sharpton, as well as prominent community activists such as Jitu Weusi.

13. The following beliefs (or some variants thereof) are associated with the black power or the black nationalist perspective: that racial domination is an integral feature of American society; that blacks everywhere constitute an immanent nation or community; that blacks must unite, resist racial domination, and pursue self-determination rather than simply making moral appeals to the consciences of whites; and that civil rights are a superficial remedy for what is in fact a human rights problem in the United States.

14. Most relatively marginalized groups, who are compelled to work with strictly limited resources, exercise considerable tactical flexibility. Robert Allen (1969) wrote of black radicalism in the 1960s: "Anything workable goes—depending on specific conditions and the relation of forces—from legal struggle, to electoral politics, to direct action campaigns, to force. In short, what is required is a coordinated, multifaceted, multilevel struggle" (236). See also Woliver (1990).

15. The Caribbean population of New York City grew dramatically during the 1980s, due

largely to immigration. Philip Kasinitz (1992) argues that Caribbean blacks' ethnic assertions (i.e., their political assertions as Caribbeans rather than as blacks) during the 1980s suggest "the declining significance of race." In my view, ethnic and racial mobilizations are not mutually exclusive and can even happen in a complementary manner, as they did during the new black power movement.

16. Koch's vulnerability in 1989 was enhanced by earlier events such as the federal raid on the Bronx and Queens Democratic party organizations on corruption charges in 1986 and the Wall Street crash ("Black Monday") of October 1987.

17. Although blacks and Latinos together constituted a majority of the city's population in 1989, the majority of registered voters were white.

18. Dinkins won 50.7 percent of the total vote to Koch's 42 percent in the Democratic primary. Dinkins received 94 percent of the black vote, 56 percent of the Latino vote, and 33 percent of the white vote. Since New York City is overwhelmingly Democratic—registered Democrats outnumber Republicans by about five to one—the Democratic primary winner is usually the presumptive winner of the general election. Yet Dinkins barely won the election against a relatively unknown Republican opponent: he received 48.3 percent of the total vote to Giuliani's 45.8 percent. Did the politics of race affect this election outcome? Almost every white voter who said that he or she did not trust Dinkins to be fair to whites voted for Giuliani; 60 percent of those who thought he would be fair voted for Giuliani anyway. It was the smallest margin of victory for any New York City mayor in more than eighty years (Arian et al. 1991, 199).

19. This structural tension first became evident during the 1989 mayoral election when the Anti-Defamation League demanded that the Dinkins campaign fire black activists Sonny Carson and Jitu Weusi on the ground that both men were anti-Semitic. Although the Dinkins campaign let Carson and Weusi go, it lost ground among conservative Jewish supporters suspicious of Dinkins's ties to these activists.

20. December 12th Movement members claimed that the Haitian activists invited their participation, whereas the Haitian activists claimed that they welcomed but did not request the former's help. Whatever the behind-the-scenes tensions between the two groups, they neither erupted into open conflict nor prevented substantial cooperation during the course of the boycott.

21. December 12th activists adhered to a hard-line position because they were determined to avoid the outcome of the 1988 boycott in Bedford-Stuyvesant. In that conflict, Assemblyman Al Vann intervened to negotiate a settlement between the Nostrand Avenue Korean Merchants' Association and moderate black leaders over the objections of radical activists. The settlement effectively brought that boycott to a close.

22. Retail boycotts have been a staple of the black community's repertoire of collective actions since the late 1800s. Prior to the early 1970s, the merchants targeted by black-led boycotts were white, often Jewish. In fact, many Korean immigrants bought their stores from Jewish merchants who were leaving New York City for the suburbs.

23. Quotation is from an unpublished transcript. Korean merchants do literally take money out of black communities insofar as they rarely live in the neighborhoods where they operate businesses (Min 1996).

24. Every black person whom I interviewed recounted that he or she or a friend or family

member had been mistreated by a Korean merchant on at least one occasion. This finding is confirmed by countless newspaper stories, roundtables, and scholarly works.

25. Estimated at more than 200,000, the city's Korean American community is the second largest in the United States, after that of Los Angeles. Most of its members still belong to the first generation or the "1.5 generation" (born in Korea, raised and educated in the United States).

26. Since it was first introduced by the mainstream media in the mid-1960s, the model minority myth has functioned as racial ideology by valorizing the American political and economic system as open and fair by suggesting that blacks are responsible for their own plight (who are Asian Americans a model minority for?) and by glossing over the impact of racial domination on Asian Americans. It is the quintessential example of a construction that appears to be laudatory of a particular group when it in fact reinforces that group's marginalization. The most resolute critics of the model minority myth have been Asian American scholars and activists (Hurh and Kim 1989; Suzuki 1989).

27. Korean immigrants learn negative ideas about blacks from the Western media before they arrive in the United States. Most Korean Americans whom I interviewed acknowledged the prevalence of antiblack prejudice among Korean merchants.

28. Without these donations, both stores would have closed, since business dropped precipitously during the boycott: Jang had made $2,000 on a good day before the boycott; his daily income was at best $600 at the height of the picketing (*New York Times*, 1 February 1991).

29. New York City is the largest and most diverse media market in the world (Moss and Ludwig 1991). The argument proffered here applies only to mainstream media outlets. The black media in New York City treated the Red Apple Boycott as a legitimate political protest and were sharply critical of the mainstream media' coverage of the event.

30. Many offices and individuals within the Dinkins administration attempted to mediate the boycott, including the City Commission for Human Rights, the Office of African American and Caribbean Affairs, the Office of Asian American Affairs, the Community Assistance Unit, and Deputy Mayor Bill Lynch. Brooklyn borough president Howard Golden, Councilwoman Susan Alter, State Senator Marty Markowitz, State Assemblywoman Rhoda Jacobs, and Community Board 14 chairman Alvin Berk all attempted the same.

31. The City Council's criticism of the mayor over the boycott must be seen in historical context. The dismantling of the Board of Estimate (an important decisionmaking body) in 1989, pursuant to a U.S. Supreme Court decision, left the City Council vested with new powers and determined to challenge mayoral power. In this light, it is not surprising that a committee of the City Council held its own hearings on the boycott in the fall of 1990 and issued a report castigating the one issued by the mayor's committee on the boycott in April 1990 (see below).

32. The boycott generated only minor policy outcomes. The city's Office for Economic Development repackaged a microloan program for minority entrepreneurs that it had been planning and presented it as a policy response to the boycotters' concerns. Brooklyn borough president Howard Golden initiated a workshop on ethnic sensitivity for merchants and a second microloan program for minority entrepreneurs.

33. Aside from the efforts of the Committee Against Anti-Asian Violence, a progressive group that attempted to mediate between the black and Korean communities, there were no organized pan-Asian responses to the boycott (see Yen Le Espiritu 1992 for a discussion of the obstacles to pan-Asian solidarity).

34. Created by the city charter in the late 1970s as an experiment in decentralization and community control, the fifty-nine community boards are the lowest level of government in New York City. They deal with land use policy and service delivery in their respective areas. Fifty-nine percent of board members (all of whom are appointed) are nominated by City Council members, and borough presidents retain the final power of appointment over all members.

35. Since the late 1960s, whites have been leaving Flatbush, located in central Brooklyn, for the outermost reaches of Brooklyn and the suburbs, while immigrants of color (especially those from Haiti and other Caribbean nations) have been settling in Flatbush in unprecedented numbers. As a result, Flatbush became less white at a faster rate that did New York City as a whole during the 1980s (Office of Community Board 14, n.d.). Community Board 14 is often used as a statistical proxy for Flatbush.

36. The boycott spurred political development within the Korean American community not only by enhancing overall solidarity but also by clarifying existing ideological rifts—particularly those between generations. A few Korean American organizations and individuals called for a more conciliatory posture that acknowledged Korean racism against blacks, shouldered partial responsibility for urban social and economic conditions, and encouraged interminority cooperation against white racism. These groups consisted mostly of 1.5 or second-generation Korean Americans, who tended to be socially liberal and oriented toward politics in the United States. In contrast, the Korean Consulate, media, and business organizations were dominated by first-generation immigrants, who tended to be socially conservative and oriented toward politics in Korea.

37. During the campaign, Giuliani often linked the boycott with the Crown Heights uprising of 1991 (another movement episode). That event prompted the Hasidic community to accuse Dinkins of unlawful permissiveness toward black protesters. Like the boycott, the Crown Heights uprising highlighted the structural tension between moderate Dinkins and his radical movement allies.

CHAPTER 4: EDUCATING IMMIGRANT CHILDREN

1. The DCPS has begun giving newly entering Spanish-speaking students the SABE test, which assesses achievement in Spanish. (The program was originally Title I of the Elementary and Secondary Education Act. At the time this chapter was originally drafted, the program was called Chapter 1. In 1995 the program's name changed again, back to Title I.)

2. Figures are from the January 1993 "Chapter 1 Status Report 1," prepared by Boston Public Schools. Final selection of Chapter 1 students is based on teacher recommendations and multiple-criteria checklists aimed at determining whether a student is performing below the level of his or her peers. (The NAEP measures reading and mathematics proficiency by identifying five fundamental skill levels and then assigning each a numerical

value. The five levels and respective scores are rudimentary (150), basic (200), intermediate (250), adept (300), and advanced (350). In the area of reading, for example, these measures correspond to the following skills: rudimentary—the ability to carry out simple, discrete reading tasks; basic—the ability to understand specific or sequentially related information; intermediate—the ability to search for basic information, interrelate ideas, and make generalizations; adept—the ability to find, understand, summarize, and explain relatively complicated information; and advanced—the ability to synthesize and learn from specialized reading materials (see generally National Council of La Raza 1990).)

3. The Chapter 1 Policy Manual interpretation of the statute and regulations does not appear to prohibit paying such a supplement, however (U.S. Department of Education 1990).

4. See generally Citizens' Commission on Civil Rights (1998).

5. See August and Hakuta (1977). See also August, Piche, and Rice (1999).

CHAPTER 5: IMMIGRANTS, PUERTO RICANS, AND THE EARNINGS OF NATIVE BLACK MALES

Research for this chapter was supported by a grant from the Andrew W. Mellon Foundation. I thank Donna Sulak for programming assistance and Diane Villarreal and Sipra Roy for technical assistance in preparing the final manuscript.

1. The industry variables are indagr (agriculture), indmin (mining), indfoo (food, tobacco, textile, apparel, leather), indche (chemicals, petroleum products, rubber, and plastics), indpap (paper, lumber, stone, glass, or clay products), indmet (riary and fabricated metals), indmac (electrical and nonelectrical machines), indeqp (transportation equipment), indoth (other manufacturing), indtrn (transportation), indcom (printing and publishing, communications, utility), indwhl (wholesale trade), indret (retail trade), incifir (finance, insurance, real estate), indrep (business repair), indent (personal entertainment), and indadin (professional government administration). Workers in the construction industry ($N = 517$) constitute the omitted category, or the reference group.

2. The occupation variables are occpro (professional and technical workers), occmgr (managers and administrators), occsal (sales workers), ocock (clerical workers), occsrv (nonhouse services), occrep (craft and repair), occtrn (transport operatives), ocelab (laborers, handlers), and occoth (all others, including farm workers). Males who work as non-transportation operatives ($N = 1187$) are the omitted group for purposes of the regression analysis.

3. We also experimented with female and total unemployment rates in separate regressions, but the male unemployment rate was most closely associated with annual earnings. Similarly, the Puerto Rican male share of the labor market was more clearly related to the response variable than either the female or the total Puerto Rican share.

4. The point of inflection in the third-degree polynomial occurs at 12.7 years of education. Points of zero slope occur at 5.8 and 19.6 years. In our sample, "years of education" ranges from zero to twenty years, but only 3.4 percent of sampled black males have fewer than six years of schooling.

5. We fit a tobit model instead of a general linear model because the value of the response (annual weeks worked) is constrained to a maximum of fifty-two weeks.

CHAPTER 6: LABOR MARKET DYNAMICS AND THE EFFECTS OF IMMIGRATION
ON AFRICAN AMERICANS

1. In 1980 these correlations were r = -0.22 for African American and foreign-born and r = 0.42 for Hispanic Americans and foreign-born.

2. Employment data in the census are based on a one-in-six sample. Restricting the sample to metropolitan areas with at least five hundred black men in the labor force ensures that the unemployment rate for black men is computed with a sample of at least eighty. For an area with an unemployment rate of 10 percent, this implies a standard error for the estimated unemployment rate of about 3.3. The unemployment rate is measured by the percentage of unemployed for males aged sixteen and older in the civilian labor force. The 1990 data were calculated from the 5 percent PUMS files.

3. Honolulu and Miami were excluded because their percentages of foreign-born residents are much higher than those of other metropolitan areas. They are special cases deserving separate consideration. Janesville, Wisconsin, was deleted because it showed an unusual combination of high unemployment (the highest Anglo unemployment rate in our sample) and a low percentage of African Americans, which makes it a very influential case in some regressions. Our central findings, reported below, are strengthened when Janesville is included in the sample; we deleted Janesville as a conservative measure to ensure that the results do not depend on this influential case.

4. Additional variables were also considered but are not included in the final analyses because their effects proved unimportant or because the variables are redundant with other variables, including the percentage of the labor force in construction (closely correlated with population growth), white-collar employment (closely correlated with the mean socioeconomic status of jobs), a dummy variable for location in the South (correlated with the percentage black and receiving AFDC), and size of metropolitan area (no effect net of controls for the unemployment rate for Anglo men).

CHAPTER 9: POLITICAL ACTIVITY AND PREFERENCES OF AFRICAN AMERICANS,
LATINOS, AND ASIAN AMERICANS

1. Protest is another form of nonelectoral participation. It will not be discussed here, since our focus is on actions more directed toward conventional politics. This also reflects limitations in the available data.

2. Activity may be depressed because of ingrained habits. On the other hand, the effort to remove the barrier may mobilize and heighten activity.

3. There were virtually no foreign-born blacks in the California sample and very few noncitizen non-Hispanic whites. Recalculating rates for citizens only yields 80 percent turnout and 87 percent registration rates among non-Hispanic white citizens and 81 percent turnout and 88 percent registration rates among African Americans. The CPS reports rates for non-Hispanic citizens approximately two percentage points higher than the voting or registration rates reported for non-Hispanic whites. These differences are all minor, unlike the major distortions arising from ignoring citizenship status among Latinos and Asian Americans.

4. In the California data, the raw numbers show Filipinos the least likely to vote, followed by Chinese Americans and Japanese Americans, with the Korean Americans most likely to vote. The numbers of cases are so small, however, that these rankings should be taken as suggestive only.

5. For the first three estimations, the dependent variable takes on the value 1 for persons registered to vote in the indicated year and 0 for those not registered (using the validated registration data). The next three estimations are restricted to persons who were registered. Among them, the dependent variable takes on the value 1 if they were validated as voters and 0 otherwise. Family income is coded in thousands of dollars; education and age are coded in years. The five dummy variables (out of work, male, African American, Mexican American, and old [over 70]) take on the value 1 if the respondent has the characteristic and otherwise have the value 0. Thus nonblack, non-Hispanic females who are working are the implicit base case. For the second estimation, "Belongs to organization" has the value 1 if the respondent belonged to an organization allied with the group with which they most closely identify and 0 otherwise. Strength of partisanship was measured on a four-point scale (strong, weak, leaner, independent). Standard items were used for interest in politics, political efficacy, and sense of citizen duty.

6. Latinos of non-Mexican origin were excluded from this analysis for greater clarity. There are too few foreign-born African Americans and non-Hispanic whites in the sample for separate analysis.

CHAPTER 10: COALITION FORMATION

1. The results of the Latino National Political Survey, conducted in 1989–90, indicated still-low levels of organizational membership: among Mexican-origin, Puerto Rican-origin, and Cuban-origin respondents, 42.9 percent, 62.7 percent, and 47.1 percent, respectively, did not belong to any organization (de la Garza et al. 1993).

2. For the purposes of this chapter, racial and ethnic group status is being categorized as a definable social or interest group.

3. The RG designation refers to a respondent's own national origin reference. Thus, if the respondent was of Mexican origin, the RG denotes "Mexican."

References

Aberbach, Joel D., and Jack L. Walker. 1970. "The Meanings of Black Power: A Comparison of White and Black Interpretations of a Political Slogan." *American Political Science Review* 64, 2 (June): 367–88.

Abowd, John M., and Richard B. Freeman, eds. 1991. *Immigration, Trade, and the Labor Market.* Chicago: University of Chicago Press.

Abramson, Paul. 1976. "Generational Change and the Decline of Party Identification in America, 1952–74." *American Political Science Review* 70 (June): 469–78.

———. 1979. "Developing Party Identification: A Further Examination of Life-Cycle, Generational, and Period Effects." *American Journal of Political Science* 23 (February): 78–96.

Abramson, Paul, and William Claggett. 1991. "Racial Differences in Self-Reported and Validated Turnout in the 1988 Presidential Election." *Journal of Politics* 53 (February): 186–95.

Acuna, Rodolfo. 1981. *Occupied America.* New York: Harper and Row.

A. D. Jackson Consulting Services. 1990. *Women and Minority Contracting with the District of Columbia.* Silver Springs, Md.: A.D. Jackson.

———. 1993. *Discrimination Study on Minority Business Enterprises in the District of Columbia.* Silver Springs, Md.: A.D. Jackson.

Allen, Robert L. 1969. *Black Awakening in Capitalist America: An Analytic History.* Garden City, N.Y.: Doubleday.

Allport, Gordon W. 1958. *The Nature of Prejudice*. Garden City, N.Y.: Doubleday Anchor.

Almond, G., and S. Verba. 1965. *The Civic Culture*. Boston: Little, Brown and Co.

Altonji, Joseph, and Card, David. 1991. "The Effects of Immigration on the Labor Market Outcomes of Less-Skilled Natives." In Abowd and Freeman.

Altshuler, Alan A. 1970. *Community Control: The Black Demand for Participation in Large American Cities*. Indianapolis: Western.

Arian, Asher, et al., eds. 1991. *Changing New York City Politics*. New York: Routledge.

Armstrong, Regina. 1989. *New York and the Forces of Immigration in Future Shocks to New York*. New York: The Citizens Budget Commission, January 24.

August, Diane, and Kenji Hakuta, eds. 1997. *Improving Schooling for Language-Minority Children: A Research Agenda*. Washington, D.C.: National Academy Press.

August, Diane, Dianne Piche, and Roger Rice. 1999. "Inclusion of Limited English Proficient Students in Title I: An Assessment of Current Practice." In *The Test of Our Progress: The Clinton Record on Civil Rights*. Washington, D.C.: Citizens' Commission on Civil Rights.

Bach, Robert L., and Howard Brill. 1990. "Shifting the Burden: The Impact of the Immigration Reform and Control Act on Local Labor Markets." Report to the United States Department of Labor. Washington, D.C.: Government Printing Office.

Bach, Robert L., and Doris Meissner. 1990. *America's Labor Market in the 1990s: What Role Should Immigration Policy Play?* Washington, D.C.: Carnegie Endowment for International Peace.

Bailey, Thomas R. 1987. *Immigrant and Native Workers: Contrasts and Competition*. Boulder, Colo.: Westview.

Banton, Michael. 1983. *Racial and Ethnic Competition*. Cambridge: Cambridge University Press.

Barro, Stephen M. 1991. "The Distribution of Federal Elementary and Secondary Education Grants Among the States." Washington, D.C.: United States Department of Education.

Bean, Frank D., Jorge Chapa, Ruth Berg, and Kathy Sowards. 1991. "Educational and Sociodemographic Incorporation Among Hispanic Immigrants to the United States." Research paper, University of Texas, Austin.

Bean, Frank D., and Michael Fix. 1992. "The Significance of Recent Immigration Policy Reforms in the U.S." *Nations of Immigrants*, eds. G. Freeman and J. Jupp. Melbourne: Oxford U. Press.

Bean, Frank D., Lindsay Lowell, and Lowell Taylor. 1988. "Undocumented Mexican Immigrants and the Earnings of Other Groups in the United States." *Demography* 25: 35–52.

Bean, Frank D., Jeffrey Passel, and Barry Edmonston. 1990. *Undocumented Migration to the United States: IRCA and the Experience of the 1980s*. Washington, D.C: Urban Institute.

Bean, Frank D., Eduardo Telles, and Lindsay Lowell. 1987. "Undocumented Migration to the United States: Perceptions and Evidence." *Population and Development Review* 13: 671–90.

Bean, Frank D., and Marta Tienda. 1987. *The Hispanic Population of the United States*. New York: Russell Sage.

Bean, Frank D., George Vernez, and Charles B. Keely. 1989. *Opening and Closing the Doors: Evaluating Immigration Reform and Control*. Washington, D.C.: Urban Institute.

Bell, Derrick. 1987. *And We Are Not Saved: The Elusive Quest for Racial Justice*. New York: Basic.

————. 1992. *Faces at the Bottom of the Well: The Permanence of Racism.* New York: Basic.

Bellush, Jewel, and Dick Netzer, eds. 1990. *Urban Politics, New York Style.* Armonk, N.Y.: Sharpe.

Bendick, Marc, Jr., Charles W. Jackson, Victor A. Reinoso, and Laura E. Godges. 1991. *Discrimination Against Latino Job Applicants: A Controlled Experiment.* Washington, D.C.: Fair Employment Council of Greater Washington.

Bertram, Susan. 1988. *An Audit of the Real Estate Sales and Rental Markets of Selected Southern Suburbs.* Homewood, Ill.: South Suburban Housing Center.

Blalock, Hubert M., Jr. 1967. *Toward a Theory of Minority-Group Relations.* New York: John Wiley.

Bobo, Lawrence, and Franklin D. Gilliam, Jr. 1990. "Race, Sociopolitical Participation, and Black Empowerment." *American Political Science Review* 84 (June): 377–93.

Bobo, Lawrence, Howard Schuman, and Charlotte Steeh. 1986. "Changing Racial Attitudes Toward Residential Integration." In *Housing Desegregation and Federal Policy,* edited by John M. Goering. Chapel Hill: University of North Carolina Press.

Bonacich, Edna. 1973. "A Theory of Middleman Minorities." *American Sociological Review* 38, 5 (October): 583–94.

————. 1980. "Middleman Minorities and Advanced Capitalism." *Ethnic Groups* 2: 211–19.

————. 1987. "'Making It' in America: A Social Evaluation of the Ethics of Immigrant Entrepreneurship." *Sociological Perspectives* 30, 4 (October): 446–66.

Borjas, George. 1984. "The Impact of Immigrants on the Earnings of the Native-Born." In *Immigration: Issues and Policies,* edited by Vernon M. Briggs Jr. and Marta Tienda. Salt Lake City: Olympus.

————. 1985. "Assimilation, Changes in Cohort Quality, and the Earnings of Immigrants." *Journal of Labor Economics* 3: 463–89.

————. 1986. "The Sensitivity of Labor Demand Functions to Choice of Dependent Variable." *Review of Economic Statistics* 68: 58–66.

————. 1987. "Immigrants, Minorities, and Labor Market Competition." *Industrial and Labor Relations Review* 40, 3: 382–92.

————. 1989. "Economic Theory and International Migration." *International Migration Review* 23: 457–85.

————. 1990. *Friends or Strangers: The Impact of Immigrants on the U.S. Economy.* New York: Basic.

————. 1991. "Immigrants in the U.S. Labor Market: 1940–80." *American Economic Review* 81, 2: 287–91.

Borjas, George, and Richard B. Freeman, eds. 1992. *Immigration and the Work Force: Economic Consequences for the United States and Source Areas.* Chicago: University of Chicago Press.

Borjas, George, Richard B. Freeman, and Lawrence F. Katz. 1992. "On the Labor Market Effects of Immigration and Trade." In Borjas and Freeman.

Borjas, George, and James J. Heckman. 1979. "Labor Supply Estimates for Public Policy Evaluation." In *Proceedings of the Thirty-first Annual Meeting,* edited by Barbara D. Dennis. Madison, Wis.: Industrial Research Association Series.

Borjas, George, and Marta Tienda. 1987. "The Economic Consequences of Immigration." *Science* 235: 645–51.

Boston Public Schools. 1993. *Chapter 1 Status Report.* Boston: Boston Public Schools.

Bouvier, Leon, and Lindsay Graut. 1994. *How Many Americans?: Population, Immigration, and the Environment*. San Francisco: Sierra Club Books.

Boyd, Herb, and Don Rojas. 1992. "The Black Liberation Movement Lives: Village Voice Obits Notwithstanding." *The New York Amsterdam News.* 5, 38 (August 29): 38.

Brace, Kimball, Bernard Grofman, Lisa Handley, and Richard G. Niemi. 1988. "Minority Voting Equality: The 65 Percent Rule in Theory and Practice." *Law and Policy* 10: 43–62.

Brown, Christopher. 1990. "Import Workers or Train Americans." *Focus* 18, 9 (September).

Browning, Rufus P., Dale Rogers Marshall, and David H. Tabb. 1984. *Protest Is Not Enough: The Struggle of Blacks and Hispanics for Equality in Urban Politics*. Berkeley: University of California Press.

———. 1990. *Racial Politics in American Cities*. New York: Longman.

Bush, Rod, ed. 1984. *The New Black Vote*. San Francisco: Synthesis.

Butcher, Kristin F., and David Card. 1991. "Immigration and Wages: Evidence from the 1980s." *American Economic Review* 81: 292–96.

Butler, David, and Bruce Cain. 1992. *Congressional Redistricting*. New York: Macmillan.

Butler, John Sibley. 1991. *Entrepreneurship and Self-Help Among Black Americans: A Reconsideration of Race and Economics*. Albany: State University of New York Press.

Butler, Katharine I. 1985. "Reapportionment, the Courts, and the Voting Rights Act: A Resegregation of the Political Process?" *University of Colorado Law Review* 56: 1–97.

Cafferty, P., B. Chiswick, A. Greeley, and T. A. Sullivan. 1983. *The Dilemma of American Immigration*. New Brunswick, N.J.: Transaction.

Cain, Bruce E., and D. Roderick Kiewiet. 1984. "Minorities in California." Report to the Seaver Foundation.

Cain, Bruce E., D. Roderick Kiewiet, and Carole J. Uhlaner. 1991. "The Acquisition of Partisanship by Latinos and Asian Americans." *American Journal of Political Science* 35 (May): 390–422.

Campbell, Angus, Philip Converse, Warren Miller, and Donald Stokes. 1960. *The American Voter*. New York: Wiley.

Card, David. 1990. "The Impact of the Mariel Boatlift on the Miami Labor Market." *Industrial and Labor Relations Review* 43:245–257.

Carmichael and Hamilton. 1967. *Black Power: The Politics of Liberation in America*. New York: Vintage Books.

Carmines, Edward, and James Stimson. 1989. *Issue Evolution: Race and the Transformation of American Politics*. Princeton: Princeton University Press, 1989.

Castells, Manuel. 1983. *The City and the Grassroots*. Berkeley: University of California Press.

Cavanagh, Thomas E. 1985. *Inside Black America*. Washington, D.C.: Joint Center for Political Studies.

———. 1991. "When Turnout Matters: Mobilization and Conversion as Determinants of Election Outcomes." In *Political Participation and American Democracy*, edited by William J. Crotty. Westport, Conn.: Greenwood.

Cheng, Lucie, and Yen Espiritu. 1989. "Korean Businesses in Black and Hispanic Neighborhoods: A Study of Intergroup Relations." *Sociological Perspectives* 32, 4: 521–24.

Chiswick, Barry. 1978. "The Effect of Americanization on the Earnings of Foreign-Born Men." *Journal of Political Economy* 86: 897–921.

————. 1982. "The Impact of Immigration on the Level and Distribution of Economic Well-being." In *The Gateway: U.S. Immigration Issues and Policies*. Washington, D.C.: American Enterprise Institute.

Citizens' Commission on Civil Rights. 1998. "Title 1 in Midstream: The Fight to Improve Schools for Poor Kids." Washington, D.C.: Citizen's Commission on Civil Rights.

Clark, William A. V. 1991. "Residential Preferences and Neighborhood Racial Segregation: A Test of the Schelling Segregation Model." *Demography* 28: 1–19.

Cloward, Richard A., and Frances Fox Piven. 1972. *The Politics of Turmoil: Essays on Poverty, Race, and the Urban Crisis*. New York: Pantheon.

Cohen, Jean L. 1985. "Strategy or Identity: New Theoretical Paradigms and Contemporary Social Movements." *Social Research* 52, 4 (winter): 663–716.

Commission on Chapter 1. 1992. *Making Schools Work for Children in Poverty: A New Framework*. Washington, D.C.:

Converse, Philip. 1969. "Of Time and Partisan Stability." *Comparative Political Studies* 2: 139–71.

Conway, M. Margaret. 1991. *Political Participation in the United States,* 2d ed. Washington, D.C.: CQ.

Cornell, Stephen. 1988. *The Return of the Native*. New York: Oxford University Press.

Cottle, Simon. 1992. "'Race,' Racialization, and the Media: A Review and Update of Research." *Sage Relations Abstracts* 17 (May): 3–57.

Council of Chief State School Officers. 1991. *Summary of State Practices Concerning the Assessment of and the Data Collection About Limited English Proficient (LEP) Students*. Washington, D.C.:

Cross, Harry, Genevieve Kenney, Jane Mell, and Wendy Zimmermann. 1990. *Employer Hiring Practices: Differential Treatment of Hispanic and Anglo Job Seekers*. Washington, D.C.: Urban Institute.

Cross, Theodore. 1994. "Africans Now the Most Highly Educated Group in British Society." *The Journal of Blacks in Higher Education* 3, 1 (spring): 92–93.

Dangelis, Nicholas. 1977. "A Theory of Black Political Participation in the United States." *Social Forces,* 56, no. 1.

Davis, David Brion. 1975. *The Problem of Slavery in the Age of Revolution, 1770–1823*. Ithaca: Cornell University Press.

DeFreitas, Gregory. 1991. *Inequality at Work*. New York: Oxford University Press.

————. 1988. "Hispanic Immigration and Labor Market Segmentation." *Industrial Relations* 27, 2: 195–214.

de la Garza, Rodolfo. 1981. "Chicano Political Elite Perceptions of the Worker: An Empirical Analysis." Working Papers #31. U.S.–Mexican Studies. La Jolla Center for U.S.–Mexican Studies, UCSD.

de la Garza, Rodolfo, and D. Baughn. 1984. "The Political Socialization of Chicano Elites: A Generalitional Approach." *Social Science Quarterly,* 65 (2):290–307.

de la Garza, Rodolfo, A. Falcon, F. C. Garcia, and J. A. Garcia. 1991. "Will the Real Americans Stand Up: A Comparison of Political Values among Mexicans, Cubans, Puerto Ricans, and Anglos in the United States." Paper presented at the annual meeting of the American Political Science Association, Washington, D.C.

de la Garza, Rodolfo, A. Falcon, F. C. Garcia, and J. A. Garcia. 1993. "Mexican Immigrants, Mexican Americans and the American Political Culture"in Edmondson and Fix, eds., *Immigration and Public Policy*. Washington, D.C.: Urban Institute Press.

de la Garza, Rodolfo, Lorn DeSipio, F. Chris Garcia, John Garcia, and Angela Falcon. 1992. *Latino Voices: Mexican, Puerto Rican, and Cuban Perspectives on American Politics*. Boulder: Westview.

del Castillo, Richard Griswold. 1990. *The Treaty of Guadalupe Hidalgo*. Norman: University of Oklahoma Press.

Demerath, N. J., and H. W. Gilmore. 1954. "The Ecology of Southern Cities." In *The Urban South*, edited by Rupert B. Vance and N. J. Demerath. Chapel Hill: University of North Carolina Press.

Denton, Nancy A. 1992. "Are African Americans Still Hypersegregated in 1990?" In *Race and Housing in the United States: An Agenda for the 21st Century*, edited by Robert Bullard. Berkeley: University of California Press, 1992.

Denton, Nancy A., and Douglass S. Massey. 1988. "Residential Segregation of Blacks, Hispanics, and Asians by Socioeconomic Status and Generation." *Social Science Quarterly* 69: 797–817.

———. 1989. "Racial Identity Among Caribbean Hispanics: The Effect of Double Minority Status on Residential Segregation." *American Sociological Review* 54: 790–808.

———. 1991. "Patterns of Neighborhood Transition in a Multiethnic World." *Demography* 28: 41–64.

DeSipio, Louis. 1996. *Counting on the Latino Vote: Latinos as a New Electorate*. Charlottesville: University of Virginia Press.

de Tocqueville, Alexis. 1966. *Democracy in America*. 1835. Reprint, New York: Harper and Row.

Donato, K., J. Durand, and D. Massey. 1992. "Changing Conditions in the U.S. Labor Market: Effects of the Immigration Reform and Control Act of 1986." *Population Research and Policy Review*.

Dowdall, George W. 1974. "White Gains from Black Subordination in 1960 and 1970." *Social Problems* 22: 162–83.

Downs, Anthony. 1957. *An Economic Theory of Democracy*. New York: Harper and Row.

Drake, St. Clair. 1965. "The Social and Economic Status of the Negro in the United States." *Daedalus* 94, 4: 771–814.

Du Bois, W. E. B. 1948. "Race Relations in the United States, 1941–1947." *Phylon* 9 (September): 234–47.

———. 1989. *The Souls of Black Folk*. 1903. Reprint, New York: Penguin.

Duncan, Otis D., and Beverly Duncan. 1957. *The Negro Population of Chicago: A Study of Residential Succession*. Chicago: University of Chicago Press.

Easterlin, Richard. 1982. "Economic and Social Characteristics of the Immigrants." In *Dimensions of Ethnicity*, edited by S. Thernstrom. Cambridge: Harvard University Press, Belknap Press.

Edsall, Thomas Byrne, and Mary D. Edsall. 1991. *Chain Reaction*. New York: W. W. Norton.

Eisinger, Peter K. 1976. *Patterns of Interracial Politics: Conflict and Cooperation in the City*. New York: Academic.

————. 1982. "Black Employment in Municipal Jobs: The Impact of Black Political Power" *American Political Science Review.* 76:380–92.

Emshwiller, John R. 1992. "Tension Lurks in Los Angeles's Minority-Owned Firms." *Wall Street Journal,* 6 August.

Enchautegui, Maria E. 1993. "Immigration and the Wages and Employment of Black Males." Washington, D.C.: Urban Institute.

Equal Employment Opportunity Commission. 1989. *Annual Report on the Employment of Minorities, Women, and People with Disabilities in the Federal Government, 1989.* Washington, D.C.: Government Printing Office.

Erie, Steven P. 1988. *Rainbow's End.* Berkeley: University of California Press.

Espenshade, Thomas J. 1992. "Policy Influences on Undocumented Migration to the United States." *137th Proceedings of the American Philosophical Society.*

Espenshade, Thomas J., and Charles A. Calhoun. 1992. "Public Opinion Toward Illegal Immigration and Undocumented Migrants in Southern California." OPR Working Paper no. 92–2. Princeton: Office of Population Research, Princeton University.

Espiritu, Yen Le. 1992. *Asian American Panethnicity: Bridging Institutions and Identities.* Philadelphia: Temple University Press.

Estrada, L., F. C. Garcia, R. Macias, and L. Maldonado. 1981. "Chicanos in the United States: A History of Exploitation and Resistance." *Daedulus* 110:103–32.

Executive Office of the President of the United States. 1993. *A Vision of Change for America.* Washington, D.C.

Fainstein, Norman I., and Susan S. Fainstein. 1991. "The Changing Character of Community Politics in New York City: 1968–1988." In Mollenkopf and Castells.

Falcon, Angelo. 1988. "Black and Latino Politics in New York City" in *Latinos in the Political System,* F. C. Garcia, ed. Notre Dame: University of Notre Dame Press.

Farley, John E. 1987. "Disproportionate Black and Hispanic Unemployment in U.S. Metropolitan Areas: The Roles of Racial Inequality, Segregation, and Discrimination in Male Joblessness." *American Journal of Economics and Sociology* 46, 2: 129–50.

Farley, Reynolds. 1977. "Residential Segregation in Urbanized Areas of the United States in 1970: An Analysis of Social Class and Racial Differences." *Demography* 14: 497–518.

Farley, Reynolds, and Walter R. Allen. 1987. *The Color Line and the Quality of Life in America.* New York: Russell Sage.

Farley, Reynolds, Suzanne Bianchi, and Diane Colasanto. 1979. "Barriers to the Racial Integration of Neighborhoods: The Detroit Case." *Annals of the American Academy of Political and Social Science* 441: 97–113.

Farley, Reynolds, and Lisa J. Neidert. 1985. *Report to the Committee on the Status of Black Americans.* Washington, D.C.: National Research Council.

Farley, Reynolds, Howard Schuman, Suzanne Bianchi, Diane Colasanto, and Shirley Hatchett. 1978. "'Chocolate City, Vanilla Suburbs': Will the Trend Toward Racially Separate Communities Continue?" *Social Science Research* 7: 319–44.

Farley, Reynolds, Charlotte Steeh, Tara Jackson, Maria Krysan, and Keith Reeves. 1993. "The Causes of Continued Racial Residential Segregation: Chocolate City, Vanilla Suburbs Revisited." Population Research Center, University of Michigan.

Feins, Judith D., and Rachel D. Bratt. 1983. "Barred in Boston: Racial Discrimination in Housing." *Journal of the American Planning Association* 49: 344–55.

Ferree, Myra Marx. 1992. "The Political Context of Rationality: Rational Choice Theory and Resource Mobilization." In Morris and Mueller.

Fiorina, Morris. 1981. *Retrospective Voting in American National Elections.* New Haven: Yale University Press.

Fix, Michael, and Jeffrey S. Passel. 1991. *The Door Remains Open: Recent Immigration to the United States and a Preliminary Analysis of the Immigration Act of 1990.* Washington, D.C.: Urban Institute.

Fong, Timothy P. 1994. *The First Suburban Chinatown.* Philadelphia: Temple University Press.

Fraga, L., K. Meier, and P. England. 1986. "Hispanic Americans and Education Policy: Limits to Equal Access." *Journal of Politics* 48:850–76.

Francis, Samuel. 1992. "Bonfire of the Border Vanities." *The Social Contract* 2, 4: 219–20.

Freeman, Gary P., and James Jupp, eds. 1992. *Nations of Immigrants: Australia and the United States in a Changing World.* New York: Oxford University Press.

Freeman, Richard B. 1990. "Employment Earnings of Disadvantaged Men in a Labor Shortage Economy." In *The Urban Underclass,* edited by Christopher Jencks and Paul Peterson. Washington, D.C.: Brookings Institution.

Frey, William H. 1995. "Immigration and Internal Migration 'Flight' from U.S. Metro Areas: Toward a New Demographic Balkanization." *Urban Studies* 32: 733–757.

Frey, William H., and Reynolds Farley. 1993. "Latino, Asian, and Black Segregation in Multi-ethnic Metro Areas: Findings from the 1990 Census." Paper presented at the Annual Meeting of the Population Association of America, Cincinnati, April 1.

Frisbie, Parker, and Lisa Neidert. 1877. "Inequality and the Relative Size of Minority Populations: A Comparative Analysis." *American Journal of Sociology* 82, 5: 1007–30.

Fuchs, Lawrence D. 1961. *Hawaii Pono.* New York: Harcourt, Brace and World.

———. 1990. *The American Kaleidoscope.* Hanover, N.H.: University Press of New England.

Galster, George C. 1986. "More Than Skin Deep: The Effect of Housing Discrimination on the Extent and Pattern of Racial Residential Segregation in the United States." In *Housing Discrimination and Federal Policy,* edited by John M. Goering. Chapel Hill: University of North Carolina Press.

———. 1987. "The Ecology of Racial Discrimination in Housing: An Exploratory Model." *Urban Affairs Quarterly* 23: 84–107.

———. 1988. "HUD Could Forbid Affirmative Marketing Strategies." *Trends in Housing* 27: 3.

———. 1990a. "Neighborhood Racial Change, Segregationist Sentiments, and Affirmative Marketing Policies." *Journal of Urban Economics* 27: 344–61.

———. 1990b. "Racial Discrimination in Housing Markets During the 1980s: A Review of the Audit Evidence." *Journal of Planning Education and Research* 9: 165–75.

———. 1990c. "Racial Steering by Real Estate Agents: Mechanisms and Motives." *Review of Black Political Economy* 19: 39–63.

———. 1990d. "Racial Steering in Urban Housing Markets: A Review of the Audit Evidence." *The Review of Black Political Economy* 18: 105–29.

————. 1990e. "White Flight from Racially Integrated Neighbourhoods in the 1970s: The Cleveland Experience." *Urban Studies* 27: 385–99.

Galster, George C., Fred Freiberg, and Diane L. Houk. 1987. "Racial Differentials in Real Estate Advertising Practices: An Exploratory Case Study." *Journal of Urban Affairs* 9: 199–215.

Galster, George C., and W. Mark Keeney. 1988. "Race, Residence, Discrimination, and Economic Opportunity: Modeling the Nexus of Urban Racial Phenomena." *Urban Affairs Quarterly* 24: 87–117.

Garcia, Flaviano Chris. 1974. "Manitos and Chicanos in Nuevo Mexico Politics." *Aztlan* 5 (spring–fall): 177–88.

Garcia, Mario T. 1989. *Mexican Americans*. New Haven: Yale University Press, 1989.

Goldman, Sheldon, and Elliot Slotnick. 1997. "Clinton's First Judiciary: Many Bridges to Cross." *Judicature* 80 (May–June): 254–73.

Graham, Otis L., Jr., and Roy Beck. 1992. "Immigration's Impact on Inner City Blacks." *Social Contract* 2, 4: 215–16.

Green, Charles, and Basil Wilson. 1989. *The Struggle for Black Empowerment in New York City: Beyond the Politics of Pigmentation*. New York: Praeger.

Green, Shelley, and Paul Pryde. 1990. *Black Entrepreneurship in America*. New Brunswick, N.J.: Transaction.

Greenwood, Michael J., and John M. McDowell. 1986. "The Factor Market Consequences of U.S. Immigration." *Journal of Economic Literature* 24, 4: 1738–72.

Grimshaw, William J. 1992. *Bitter Fruit*. Chicago: University of Chicago Press.

Grofman, Bernard, and Chandler Davidson, eds. 1992. *Controversies in Minority Voting: A 25-Year Perspective on the Voting Rights Act of 1965*. Washington, D.C.: Brookings Institution.

Grofman, Bernard, Ura Handley, and Richard G. Niemi. 1992. *Minority Representation and the Quest for Voting Equality*. Cambridge: Cambridge University Press.

Grossman, Jean B. 1982. "The Substitutability of Natives and Immigrants in Production." *Review of Economics and Statistics* 64, 4: 596–603.

————. 1984. "Illegal Immigrants and Domestic Employment." *Industrial and Labor Relations Review* 37, 2: 240–51.

Guinier, Lani. 1992. "Voting Rights and Democratic Theory: Where Do We Go from Here?" In Grofman and Davidson.

————. 1994. *The Tyranny of the Majority*. New York: Free.

Gurin, Patricia, Shirley Hatchett, and James S. Jackson. 1989. *Hope and Independence: Blacks' Reponse to Electoral and Party Politics*. New York: Russell Sage.

Gurwitt, Rob. 1990. "Have Asian Americans Arrived Politically? Not Quite." *Governing* 4 (November): 32–38.

Guterbock, Thomas M., and Bruce London. 1983. "Race, Political Orientation, and Participation: An Empirical Test of Four Competing Theories." *American Sociological Review* 48: 439–53.

Haines, Herbert. 1988. *Black Radicals and the Civil Rights Mainstream, 1954–1970*. Knoxville: University of Tennessee Press.

Hakken, John. 1979. *Discrimination Against Chicanos in the Dallas Rental Housing Market:*

An Experimental Extension of the Housing Market Practices Survey. Washington, D.C.: Office of Policy Development and Research, U.S. Department of Housing and Urban Development.

Hamilton, Lawrence C. 1992. *Regression with Graphics.* Pacific Grove, Calif.: Brooks-Cole.

Hanushek, Eric A., and J. Jackson. 1977. *Statistical Methods for Social Scientists.* New York: Academic.

Harris, Joseph P. 1929. *Registration of Voters in the United States.* Washington, D.C.: Brookings Institution.

Harrison, Lawrence E. 1992. "Those Huddled, Unskilled Masses." *Social Contract* 2, 4: 222–24.

Harrison, Roderick J., and Daniel H. Weinberg. 1992. "Racial and Ethnic Residential Segregation in 1990." Paper presented at the Annual Meeting of the Population Association of America, Denver, Colorado, April 13.

Helper, Rose. 1969. *Racial Policies and Practices of Real Estate Brokers.* Minneapolis: University of Minnesota Press.

Henry, Charles, and C. Munoz. 1991. "Ideological and Interest Linkages to California's Rainbow Coalition" in *Racial and Ethnic Politics in California,* edited by B. Jackson and M. Preston. Berkeley: IGR.

Henry, M. L., Jr., Estajo Koslow, Joseph Soffer, and John Furey. 1985. *The Success of Women and Minorities in Achieving Judicial Office.* New York: Fund for Modern Courts.

Herman, Edward S., and Noam Chomsky. 1988. *Manufacturing Consent: The Political Economy of the Mass Media.* New York: Pantheon.

Heubert, Jay. 1991. "Low Achievers Can Catch Up: Chapter 1 Expects More of Schools." *Harvard Education Letter* (January–February).

Hill, Paul, and Lorraine McDonnell. 1922. "Schooling for Immigrant Youth." Typescript.

Hill, Peter J. 1975. *The Economic Impact of Immigration into the United States.* New York: Arno.

Hintzen, Hans. 1983. *Report of an Audit of Real Estate Sales Practices of 15 Northwest Chicago Real Estate Sales Offices.* Chicago: Leadership Council for Metropolitan Open Communities.

Hocking, Douglas. 1980. "Asian-Americans and the Law." In *Political Participation of Asian Americans,* edited by Yung-Hwan Jo. Chicago: Pacific-Asian American Mental Health Center.

Holzer, Harry, and Wayne Vroman. 1991. "Mismatches and the Urban Labor Market." Washington, D.C.: Urban Institute.

Huddle, Donald L. 1992a. "Immigration and Jobs: The Process of Displacement." Teaneck, N.J.: Negative Population Growth.

———. 1992b. "Immigration, Jobs, and Wages: The Misuses of Econometrics." Teaneck, N.J.: Negative Population Growth.

Hunt, Scott A., Robert D. Benford, and David A. Snow. 1994. "Identity Fields: Framing Processes and the Social Construction of Movement Identities." In Larana, Johnston, and Gusfield.

Hurh, Won Moo, and Kwang Chung Kim. 1989. "The 'Success' Image of Asian Americans: Its Validity and Its Practical and Theoretical Implications." *Ethnic and Racial Studies* 12, 4 (October): 512–38.

Hwang, Sean-Shong, and Steve H. Murdock. 1982. "Residential Segregation in Texas in 1980." *Social Science Quarterly* 63: 737–48.

Jackson, Byran O. 1991. "Racial and Ethnic Voting Cleavages in Los Angeles Politics." In *Racial and Ethnic Politics in California,* edited by Byran O. Jackson and Michael B. Preston. Berkeley: IGS.

Jackson, Peter. 1981. "Paradoxes of Puerto Rican Segregation in New York." In *Ethnic Segregation in Cities,* edited by Ceri Peach, Vaughn Robinson, and Susan Smith. London: Croom Helm.

James, David R., and Karl E. Taeuber. 1985. "Measures of Segregation." In *Sociological Methodology 1985,* edited by Nancy Tuma. San Francisco: Jossey Bass.

James, Franklin J., and Eileen A. Tynan. 1986. "Segregation and Discrimination Against Hispanic Americans." In *Housing Discrimination and Federal Policy,* edited by John M. Goering. Chapel Hill: University of North Carolina Press.

Jasso, Guillermina, and Mark R. Rosensweig, eds. 1990. *The New Chosen People: Immigrants in the United States.* New York: Russell Sage.

Jaynes, Gerald D., and Williams, Robin M., Jr., eds. 1989. *A Common Destiny: Blacks and American Society.* Washington, D.C.: National Academy.

Jaynes, Gerald D., and Franklin Wilson. 1996. "Labor Market Effects of Immigration on Native Americans." Typescript, University of Wisconsin.

Jennings, James. 1977. *Puerto Rican Politics in New York City.* Washington: University Press of America, 1977.

———. 1992. *The Politics of Black Empowerment: The Transformation of Black Activism in Urban America.* Detroit: Wayne State University Press.

Jo, Moon H. 1992. "Korean Merchants in the Black Community: Prejudice Among the Victims of Prejudice." *Ethnic and Racial Studies* 15, 3 (July): 395–411.

Johnson, Clifford M. 1991. *Child Poverty in America.* Washington, D.C.: Children's Defense Fund.

Johnson, George E. 1979. "The Labor Market Effects of Immigration into the United States: A Summary of the Conceptual Issues." In *Staff Report Companion Papers,* Interagency Task Force on Immigration Policy. Washington, D.C.: Departments of Justice, Labor, and State, 1979.

———. 1980. "The Labor Effects of Immigration." *Industrial and Labor Relations Review* 33, 3 (1980): 331–41.

Johnston, W. B., and A. E. Packer. 1987. *Workforce 2000: Work and Workers in the 21st Century.* Indianapolis: Hudson Institute.

Jones, Mack H. 1978. "Black Political Empowerment in Atlanta: Myth and Reality." *Annals of the American Academy of Political and Social Science* 439 (September): 90–117.

Kantrowitz, Nathan. 1973. *Ethnic and Racial Segregation in the New York Metropolis.* New York: Praeger.

Kasarda, John. 1985. "Urban Change and Minority Opportunities." In *The New Urban Reality,* edited by Paul Peterson. Washington, D.C.: Brookings Institution.

———. 1989. "Urban Industrial Transition and the Underclass." *Annals of the American Academy of Political and Social Science* 501: 26–47.

Kasinitz, Philip. 1992. *Caribbean New York: Black Immigrants and the Politics of Race.* Ithaca: Cornell University Press.

Keiser, Richard A. 1990. "The Rise of a Biracial Coalition in Philadelphia." In Browning, Marshall, and Tabb.

Kennedy, Mary. 1992. Personal communication, December 9: Washington, D.C.: U.S. Bureau of the Census.

Kim, Illsoo. 1981. *New Urban Immigrants: The Korean Community in New York.* Princeton: Princeton University Press.

Kinder, D., D. O. Sears. 1985. "Public Opinion and Political Action." *Handbook of Political Psychology.*

King, Alan, Lindsay Lowell, and Frank D. Bean. 1986. "The Effects of Hispanic Immigrants on the Earnings of Native Hispanic Americans." *Social Science Quarterly* 67: 673–89.

Kleppner, Paul. 1985. *Chicago Divided.* DeKalb: Northern Illinois University Press.

Kossoudji, Sherrie A. 1988. "English Language Ability and the Labor Market Opportunities of Hispanic and East Asian Immigrant Men." *Journal of Labor Economics* 6, 2: 205–28.

Kosters, Marvin H., ed. 1991. *Workers and Their Wages: Changing Patterns in the United States.* Washington, D.C.: American Enterprise Institute Press.

Kotkin, Joel. 1992. "California's Lesson: We're Looking at Our Future Again." *Washington Post,* 8–14 June, national edition.

Kousser, J. Morgan. 1974. *The Shaping of Southern Politics.* New Haven: Yale University Press.

———. 1984. "The Undermining of the First Reconstruction: Lessons for the Second." In *Minority Vote Dilution,* edited by Chandler Davidson. Washington, D.C.: Howard University Press.

———. 1992. "The Voting Rights Act and the Two Reconstructions." In Grofman and Davidson.

Kuznets, Simon. 1977. "Two Centuries of Economic Growth: Reflections on U.S. Experience." *American Economic Review* 67, 1: 1–14.

Kwong, Peter. 1987. *The New Chinatown.* New York: Noonday.

Lalonde, Robert J., and R. H. Topel. 1991a. "Immigrants in the American Labor Market: Quality, Assimilation, and Distributional Effects." *American Economic Review* 81: 297–302.

———. 1991b. "Labor Market Adjustments to Increased Immigration." In Abowd and Freeman.

Lamare, James. 1982. "The Political Integration of Mexican American Children: A Generational Analysis." *International Migration Review* 16(1): 169–88.

Landau, Ralph. 1988. "U.S. Economic Growth." *Scientific American* 258, 6: 44–52.

LaNoue, George R. 1993. "The Demographic Premises of Affirmative Action." *Population and Environment* 14, 5: 421–39.

Larana, Enrique, Hank Johnston, and Joseph R. Gusfield. 1994. *New Social Movements: From Ideology to Identity.* Philadelphia: Temple University Press.

Lau, Yvonne M. 1991. "Political Participation Among Chicago Asian Americans." In *Asian-Americans: Comparative and Global Perspectives,* edited by Shirley Hune, Hyung-chan Kim, Stephen S. Fugita, and Amy Ling. Pullman: Washington State University Press.

Lee, Hwasoo. 1980. "Toward Korean-American Participation and Representation in American Politics: The Case of Los Angeles." In *Political Participation of Asian Americans,* edited by Yung-Hwan Jo. Chicago: Pacific-Asian American Mental Health Research Center.

Lee, Sharon M., and Barry Edmonston. 1991. "Asian Immigrants and Patterns of Socioeconomic Achievement." Dept. Sociology, University of Richmond.

LeMann, Nicholas. 1986. "The Origins of the Underclass." *The Atlantic,* June: 35–36.

Levy, Frank. 1987. *Dollars and Dreams: The Changing American Income Distribution*. New York: Russell Sage, 1987.

———. 1998. *The New Dollars and Dreams*. New York: Russell Sage Foundation.

Levy, Frank, and Richard J. Murnane. 1992. "U.S. Earnings Levels and Earnings Inequality: A Review of Recent Trends and Proposed Explanations." *Journal of Economic Literature* 30, 3: 1333–81.

Lieberson, Stanley. 1980. *A Piece of the Pie: Blacks and White Immigrants Since 1880*. Berkeley: University of California Press.

———. 1981. "An Asymmetrical Approach to Segregation." In *Ethnic Segregation in Cities*, edited by Ceri Peach, Vaughn Robinson, and Susan Smith. London: Croom Helm.

Light, Ivan, and Edna Bonacich. 1988. *Immigrant Entrepreneurs: Koreans in Los Angeles, 1965– 82*. Berkeley: University of California Press.

Light, Ivan, and Angel A. Sanchez. 1987. "Immigrant Entrepreneurs in 272 SMSAs." *Sociological Perspectives* 30, 4 (October): 373–99.

Lipset, Seymour M., and Stein Rokkan. 1967. "Cleavage Structures, Party Systems, and Voter Alignments: An Introduction." In *Party Systems and Voter Alignments*, edited by Seymour M. Lipset and Stein Rokkan. New York: Free.

Lipsky, Michael. 1968. "Protest as a Political Resource." *American Political Science Review* 62 (December): 1144–58.

Lipsky, Michael, and David J. Olson. 1977. *Commission Politics: The Processing of Racial Crisis in America*. New Brunswick, N.J.: Transaction.

Logan, John R., and Harvey L. Molotch. 1987. *Urban Fortunes: The Political Economy of Place*. Berkeley: University of California Press.

Lopez, Manuel M. 1981. "Patterns of Interethnic Residential Segregation in the Urban Southwest, 1960 and 1970." *Social Science Quarterly* 62: 50–63.

Lupia, Arthur, and Kenneth McCue. 1990. "Why the 1980s Measures of Racially Polarized Voting Are Inadequate for the 1990s." *Law and Policy* 12: 353–87.

Luttwak, Edward N. 1992. "The Riots: Underclass vs. Immigrants." *Social Contract* 2, 4:221.

Macias, Reynaldo F. 1974. "Inheriting Sins While Seeking Absolution: English Language Literacy, Biliteracy, Language Diversity, and National Statistical Data Sets." In *Adult Biliteracy Education*, edited by David Spencer. Washington, D.C.: Delta Systems and the Center for Applied Linguistics.

Mandel, Michael J., and Christopher Farrell. 1992. "The Immigrants." *Business Week*, 13 July: 118–19.

Marable, Manning. 1985. *Black American Politics: From Washington Marches to Jackson*. London: Verso.

Massey, Douglas S. 1979. "Effects of Socioeconomic Factors on the Residential Segregation of Blacks and Spanish Americans in United States Urbanized Areas." *American Sociological Review* 44: 1015–22.

———. 1981a. "Dimensions of the New Immigration to the United States and the Prospects for Assimilation." *Annual Review of Sociology* 7: 57–85.

———. 1981b. "Hispanic Residential Segregation: A Comparison of Mexicans, Cubans, and Puerto Ricans." *Sociology and Social Research* 65: 311–22.

————. 1985. "Ethnic Residential Segregation: A Theoretical Synthesis and Empirical Review." *Sociology and Social Research* 69: 315–50.

————. 1987. "Do Undocumented Migrants Earn Lower Wages Than Illegal Immigrants? New Evidence from Mexico." *International Migration Review* 21: 236–75.

Massey, Douglas S., and Brooks Bitterman. 1985. "Explaining the Paradox of Puerto Rican Segregation." *Social Forces* 64: 306–31.

Massey, Douglas S., Gretchen A. Condran, and Nancy A. Denton. 1987. "The Effect of Residential Segregation on Black Social and Economic Well-Being." *Social Forces* 66: 29–57.

Massey, Douglas S., and Nancy A. Denton. 1987. "Trends in the Residential Segregation of Blacks, Hispanics, and Asians." *American Sociological Review* 52: 802–25.

————. 1988. "The Dimensions of Residential Segregation." *Social Forces* 67: 281–315.

————. 1989a. "Hypersegregation in U.S. Metropolitan Areas: Black and Hispanic Segregation Along Five Dimensions." *Demography* 26: 373–93.

————. 1989b. "Residential Segregation of Mexicans, Puerto Ricans, and Cubans in U.S. Metropolitan Areas." *Sociology and Social Research* 73: 73–83.

————. 1992. "Racial Identity and the Spatial Assimilation of Mexicans in the United States." *Social Science Research* 21: 235–60.

————. 1993. *American Apartheid: Segregation and the Making of the Underclass.* Cambridge: Harvard University Press.

Massey, Douglas S., and Eric Fong. 1990. "Segregation and Neighborhood Quality: Blacks, Hispanics, and Asians in the San Francisco Metropolitan Area." *Social Forces* 69: 15–32.

McAdam, Doug. 1982. *Political Process and the Development of Black Insurgency, 1930–1970.* Chicago: University of Chicago Press.

————. 1988. *Freedom Summer.* New York: Oxford University Press.

McCarthy, Kevin F., and R. Burciaga Valdez. 1986. *Current and Future Effects of Mexican Immigration in California.* RAND/R-3365-CR. Santa Monica, Calif. Rand Corporation.

McClain, P., and A. Karnig. 1990. "Black and Hispanic Socioeconomic and Political Competition." *American Political Science Review* 84(2): 535–45.

McDonnell, Lorraine M., and Paul Hill. 1993. "Schooling for Immigrant Youth." Santa Monica, Calif.: Rand Corporation.

McManus, S. and C. Cassel. 1982. "Mexican Americans in City Politics: Participation, Representation, and Policy Preferences." *Urban Interest* 4:57–69.

McNickle, Chris. 1993. *To Be Mayor of New York.* New York: Columbia University Press.

Miller, Arthur H., Patricia Gurin, Gerald Gurin, and Oksana Malanchuk. 1981. "Group Consciousness and Political Participation." *American Journal of Political Science* 25 (August): 494–511.

Min, Pyong Gap. 1996. *Caught in the Middle: Korean Communities in New York and Los Angeles.* Berkeley: University of California Press.

Miniclier, Kit. 1993. "Campbell Either 9th or 11th Indian in Congress." *Denver Post.*, 17 January.

Mishel, Lawrence, and R. A. Teixeira. 1990. *The Myth of the Coming Labor Shortage: Jobs, Skills, and Incomes of America's Workforce 2000.* Washington, D.C.: Economic Policy Institute.

Mladenka, Kenneth. 1989. "Blacks and Hispanics in Urban Politics." *American Political Science Review* 83(1):167–91.

Mollenkopf, John H. 1990. "New York: The Great Anomaly." In Browning, Marshall, and Tabb.

———. 1992. *A Phoenix in the Ashes: The Rise and Fall of the Koch Coalition in New York City Politics.* Princeton: Princeton University Press.

Mollenkopf, John H., and Manuel Castells, eds. 1991. Introduction. In *Dual City: Restructuring New York,* edited by John Mollenkopf and Manuel Castells. New York: Russell Sage.

Morgan, Edmund S. 1972. "Slavery and Freedom: The American Paradox." *Journal of American History* 59 (June).

Morris, Aldon D. 1984. *The Origins of the Civil Rights Movement.* New York: Free.

Morris, Aldon D., and Carol McClurg Mueller, eds. 1992. *Frontiers in Social Movement Theory.* New Haven: Yale University Press.

Morris, Milton D. 1985. *Immigration: The Beleaguered Bureaucracy.* Washington, D.C.: Brookings Institution.

Morton, Rebecca. 1991. "Groups in Rational Turnout Models." *American Journal of Political Science* 35 (August): 758–76.

Moss, Mitchell, and Sarah Ludwig. 1991. "The Structure of the Media." In Mollenkopf and Castells.

Moynihan, Daniel Patrick, and Nathan Glazer. 1963. *Beyond the Melting Pot: The Negroes, Puerto Ricans, Jews, Italians, and Irish of New York City.* Cambridge: MIT Press.

Mueller, Carol McClurg. 1992. "Building Social Movement Theory." In Morris and Mueller.

Muller, Thomas, and Thomas J. Espenshade. 1985. *The Fourth Wave: California's Newest Immigrants.* Washington, D.C.: Urban Institute.

Murphy, Kevin, and Finis Welch. 1988. "Wage Differentials in the 1980s: The Role of International Trade." Typescript.

Mydans, Seth. 1992. "Koreans Rethink Life in Los Angeles." *New York Times,* 21 June.

Myrdal, Gunner. 1944. *An American Dilemma: The Negro Problem and Modern Democracy.* New York: Harper and Brothers.

Nakanishi, Don T. 1989. "A Quota on Excellence? The Asian American Admissions Debate." *Change* (November–December): 39–47.

Nam, Charles B., and Walter E. Terrie. 1986. "Comparing the Nam-Powers and Duncan SEI Occupational Scores." Working Paper no. 86–27, Florida State University Center for the Study of Population.

National Council of La Raza. 1990. Agenda. Communications Center. Washington, D.C.

Nee, Victor G., and Nee, Brett de Bary. 1972. *Longtime Californ'.* New York: Pantheon; Norman: University of Oklahoma Press.

New Jersey State Data Center. 1992a. "Population: Citizenship and Residence in 1985, 1990 Census of Population and Housing." Profile 3 from Summary Tape File 3. Trenton: New Jersey Department of Labor, September.

———. 1992b. "Population: Race, Hispanic Origin, and Veteran Status, 1990 Census of Population and Housing." Profile 1 from Summary Tape File 3. Trenton: New Jersey Department of Labor, September.

Oberschall, Anthony. 1973. *Social Conflict and Social Movements.* Englewood Cliffs, N.J.: Prentice-Hall.

O'Brien, Sharon. 1989. *American Indian Tribal Governments.* Norman: University of Oklahoma Press.

Office of Community Board 14. n.d. *Statement of Community District Needs, Fiscal Year 1993.* New York: Office of Community Board 14.

Oliver, M., and J. Johnson. 1984. "Inter-Ethnic Conflict in an Urban Ghetto: The Case of Blacks and Latinos in Los Angeles." *Social Movements, Conflict and Change* 6:57–94.

Olson, James S., and Raymond Wilson. 1984. *Native Americans in the Twentieth Century.* Urbana: University of Illinois Press.

Olson, Mancur. 1965. *The Logic of Collective Action.* Cambridge: Harvard University Press.

Olzak, Susan. 1992. *The Dynamics of Ethnic Competition and Conflict.* Stanford: Stanford University Press.

Olzak, Susan, and Joane Nagel, eds. 1986. *Competitive Ethnic Relations.* San Diego: Academic.

Omi, Michael, and Howard Winant. 1986. *Racial Formation in the United States: From the 1960s to the 1980s.* New York: Routledge and Kegan Paul.

Ong, Paul, Kye Young Park, and Yasmin Tong. 1994. "The Korean-Black Conflict and the State." In *New Asian Immigration in Los Angeles and Global Restructuring,* edited by Paul Ong, Edna Bonacich, and Lucie Cheng. Philadelphia: Temple University Press.

Pachon, Harry P. 1985. "Political Mobilization in the Mexican-American Community." In *Mexican-Americans in Comparative Perspective,* edited by Walker Connor. Washington, D.C.: Urban Institute.

Pachon, H., L. Desipio, and R. Gold. 1990. "Future Research on Latino Immigrants and the Political Process." Paper presented at Latino Research Perspectives for the 1990s. Inter-University Program, Pomona, California.

Padilla, Fernando V., and Ramirez, Carlos B. 1974. "Patterns of Chicano Representation in California, Colorado, and Nuevo Mexico." *Aztlan* 5 (spring–fall).

Passel, Jeffrey, 1986. "Undocumented Immigration." *Annals of the American Academy of Political and Social Science* 487: 181–200.

Passel, Jeffrey S., and Barry Edmonston. 1992. "Immigration and Race in the United States: The 20th and 21st Centuries." Washington, D.C.: Urban Institute.

———. 1993. *Immigrant Children and the Children of Immigrant Children and the Children of Immigrants: The Next Fifty Years.* Washington, D.C.: Urban Institute.

Pearce, Diana M. 1979. "Gatekeepers and Homeseekers: Institutionalized Patterns in Racial Steering." *Social Problems* 26: 325–42.

Pedalino, Porter Rosalie. 1990. *Forked Tongue.* New York: Basic.

Persons, Georgia A., ed. 1993. *Dilemmas of Black Politics.* New York: HarperCollins.

Peterson, Helen L. 1957. "American Indian Political Participation." *Annals* 311 (May): 116–26.

Piore, Michael. 1979. *Birds of Passage: Migrant Labor in Industrial Societies.* Cambridge: Cambridge University Press.

Piven, Frances Fox, and Richard A. Cloward. 1979. *Poor People's Movements: Why They Succeed, How They Fail.* New York: Vintage.

———. 1988. *Why Americans Don't Vote.* New York: Pantheon.

Popkin, Samuel, John W. Gorman, Charles Phillips, and Jeffrey A. Smith. 1976. "Comment: What Have You Done for Me Lately? Toward an Investment Theory of Voting." *American Political Science Review* 70: 779–805.

Porter, Kirk H. 1918. *A History of Suffrage in the United States.* Chicago: University of Chicago Press.

Portes, Alejandro, and Rubin Rumbaut. 1990. *Immigrant America: A Portrait.* Berkeley: University of California Press.

Portes, Alejandro, and Mm Zhou. 1991. "Gaining the Upper Hand: Old and New Perspectives in the Study of Ethnic Minorities." Paper presented at the Urban Poverty Workshop, Northwestern University.

Presser, Stanley, Michael W. Traugott, and Santa Traugott. 1990. "Vote 'Over' Reporting in Surveys: The Records or the Respondents?" Paper prepared for the International Conference on Measurement Errors, Tucson, Arizona, Nov. 11–14.

Rae, Douglas. 1967. *The Political Consequences of Electoral Laws.* New Haven: Yale University Press.

Reder, Melvin W. 1963. "The Economic Consequences of Increased Immigration." *Review of Economics and Statistics* 45, 3: 221–30.

Reed, Adolph, Jr. 1988. "The Black Urban Regime: Structural Origins and Constraints." *Comparative Urban and Community Research.* 1: 138–88.

———, ed. 1999. *Without Justice for All: The New Liberalism and Our Retreat from Racial Equality.* Boulder: Westview.

Reimers, David M. 1983. "An Unintended Reform: The 1965 Immigration Act and Third World Migration to the United States." *Journal of American Ethnic History* (fall): 9–28.

———. 1985. *Still the Golden Door.* New York: Columbia University Press.

Reischauer, Robert. 1989. "Immigration and the Underclass." In *The Ghetto Underclass: Social Science Perspectives,* edited by William J. Wilson. Annals of the American Academy of Political and Social Science 501.

Richardson, Lynda. 1992. "Immigrants' Fear of Forms Imperils Aid to Schools." *New York Times,* 7 November.

Riker, William H., and Peter C. Ordeshook. 1968. "A Theory of the Calculus of Voting." *American Political Science Review* 62 (March): 25–42.

Rivlin, Gary. 1992. *Fire on the Prairie.* New York: Henry Holt.

Robinson, T. and T. R. Dye. 1978. "Reformism and Black Representation on City Councils." *Social Science Quarterly* 59:153–61.

Rosenstone, Steven J., and John Mark Hansen. 1993. *Mobilization, Participation, and Democracy in America.* New York: Macmillan.

Ruggles, Patricia. 1993. "Improving Poverty Estimates for States, Counties, and Other Jurisdictions." Testimony presented to a joint hearing of the Subcommittee on Elementary, Secondary, and Vocational Education, Committee on Education and Labor, and the Subcommittee on Census, Statistics, and Postal Personnel, Committee on Post Office and Civil Service. Washington, D.C.: Urban Institute.

Salisbury, Robert H. 1969. "An Exchange Theory of Interest Groups." *Midwestern Journal of Political Science.* 13: 1–32.

Saltman, Juliet. 1979. "Housing Discrimination: Policy Research, Methods, and Results." *Annals of the American Academy of Political and Social Science* 441: 186–96.

Sassen, Saskia. 1988. *The Mobility of Labor and Capital: A Study in International Investment and Labor Flow.* Cambridge: Cambridge University Press.

———. 1989. "New York City's Informal Economy." In *The Informal Sector: Theoretical and Methodological Issues,* edited by A. Portes, M. Castells, and L. Benton. Baltimore: Johns Hopkins University Press.

———. 1990. "Economic Restructuring and the American City." *Annual Review of Sociology* 16: 465–90.

Schelling, Thomas C. 1971. "Dynamic Models of Segregation." *Journal of Mathematical Sociology* 1: 143–86.

———. 1978. *Micromotives and Macrobehavior.* New York: Norton.

Schexnider, Alvin J. 1982. "Political Mobilization in the South: The Election of a Black Mayor in New Orleans." In *The New Black Politics,* edited by Michael B. Preston, Lenneal J. Henderson, Jr., and Paul Puryear. New York: Longman.

Schlesinger, Arthur M. 1991. *The Disuniting of America: Reflections on a Multicultural Society.* New York: Whittle.

Schmidley, Dianne, and Herman A. Alvarado. 1998. "The Foreign-Born Population in the United States: March 1997 (Update)," *Current Population Reports,* ser. P20–507. Washington, D.C.: U.S. Bureau of the Census.

Schneider, Mark, and John R. Logan. 1982. "Suburban Racial Segregation and Black Access to Local Public Resources." *Social Science Quarterly* 63: 762–70.

Schroeder, Ann. 1985. *Report on an Audit of Real Estate Sales Practices of Eight Northwest Suburban Offices.* Chicago: Leadership Council for Metropolitan Open Communities.

Schuck, Peter. 1991. "The Politics of Rapid Legal Change: Immigration Policy in the 1980s." Yale University Law School, November.

Schuman, Howard, and Lawrence Bobo. 1988. "Survey-Based Experiments on White Racial Attitudes Toward Residential Integration." *American Journal of Sociology* 2: 273–99.

Schuman, Howard, Charlotte Steeh, and Lawrence Bobo. 1985. *Racial Attitudes in America: Trends and Interpretations.* Cambridge: Harvard University Press.

Schwartz, Bernard. 1990. *The Ascent of Pragmatism: The Burger Court in Action.* New York: Addison-Wesley.

SCRIP (Select Commission on Immigration and Refugee Policy). 1981. *U.S. Immigration Policy and the National Interest.* Washington, D.C. U.S. Government Printing Office.

Shingles, Richard D. 1981. "Black Consciousness and Political Participation: The Missing Link." *American Political Science Review* 75 (March): 76–91.

Sierra, Christine. 1982. "The Organizational Development of the National Council of La Raza." Ph.D. diss., Department of Political Science, Stanford University.

———. 1987. "Latinos and the New Immigration: Responses from the Mexican American Community." In *Renato Rosaldo Lecture Series Monograph* 3. Tucson: MASRC (University of Arizona).

Simkus, Albert A. 1978. "Residential Segregation by Occupation and Race in Ten Urbanized Areas, 1950–1970." *American Sociological Review* 43: 81–93.

Simon, Julian. 1986. "Basic Data Concerning Immigration into the United States." *Annals of the American Academy of Political and Social Science* 487: 12–56.

———. 1989. *The Economic Consequences of Immigration.* Cambridge: Basil Blackwell.

Skerry, Peter. 1993. *Mexican Americans: The Ambivalent Minority.* New York: Free.

Slavin, Robert. 1991. "Chapter 1: A Vision for the Next Quarter Century." *Phi Delta Kappan.* (April).

Sleeper, Jim. 1990. *The Closest of Strangers: Liberalism and the Politics of Race in New York.* New York: Norton.

Smith, Barton, and Robert Newman. 1977. "Depressed Wages Along the U.S.-Mexican Border: An Empirical Analysis." *Economic Inquiry* 15, 1: 51–66.

Smith, James, and Barry Edmonston, eds. 1997. *The New Americans.* Washington, D.C.: National Academy Press.

Smith, James, and Finis R. Welch. 1989. "Black Economic Progress After Myrdal." *Journal of Economic Literature* 17, 2: 519–64.

Smith, Robert C. 1982. *Black Leadership: A Survey of Theory and Research.* The Institute for Urban Affairs and Research. Washington, D.C.: Howard University.

Sniderman, Paul M., and Thomas Piazza. 1993. *The Scar of Race.* Cambridge: Harvard University Press, Belknap Press.

Snow, David A., and Robert D. Benford. 1988. "Ideology, Frame Resonance, and Participant Mobilization." *International Social Movement Research.* 1: 197–217.

———. 1992. "Master Frames and Cycles of Protest." In Morris and Mueller.

Snow, David A., E. Burke Rochford, Jr., Steven K. Worden, and Robert D. Benford. 1986. "Frame Alignment Processes, Micromobilization, and Movement Participation." *American Sociological Review* 51: 464–81.

Sonenshein, Raphael J. 1990. "Biracial Coalition Politics in Los Angeles." In Browning, Marshall, and Tabb.

Sorenson, Elaine, Frank D. Bean, Leighton Ku, and Wendy Zimmermann. 1992. *Immigrant Categories and the U.S. Job Market: Do They Make a Difference?* Washington, D.C.: Urban Institute.

Sorenson, Elaine, and Maria Enchautegui. 1992. "Immigrant Male Earnings in the 1980s: Divergent Patterns by Race and Ethnicity." Washington, D.C.: Urban Institute.

Stanford Working Group. 1993. *Federal Education Programs for Limited English Proficient Students: Blueprint for the Second Generation.* Stanford: Stanford University Press.

Stewart, J., and T. Hyclak. 1986. "The Effects of Immigrants, Women, and Teenagers on the Relative Earnings of Black Males." *Review of Black Political Economy* 15: 93–101.

Stolzenberg, Ross M. 1979. "The Measurement and Decomposition of Causal Effects in Nonlinear and Nonadditive Models." In *Sociological Methodology 1980,* edited by Karl F. Schuessler. San Francisco: Jossey-Bass.

Strang, E. William, and Elaine Carlson. 1991. *Providing Chapter 1 Services to Limited-English-Proficient Students.* Washington, D.C.: Westat.

Strange, John Hadley. 1969. "The Negro and Philadelphia Politics." In *Urban Government,* edited by Edward Banfield. New York: Free.

Suzuki, Bob. 1989. "Asian Americans as the 'Model Minority': Outdoing Whites? Or Media Hype?" *Change* (November–December): 13–19.

Swain, Carol. 1993. *Black Faces, Black Interests.* Cambridge: Harvard University Press.

Takagi, Dana Y. 1992. *The Retreat from Race: Asian-American Admissions and Racial Politics.* New Brunswick: Rutgers University Press.

Takaki, Ronald. 1989. *Strangers from a Different Shore.* New York: Penguin.

Tam, Wendy. 1992. *Asians—A Monolithic Entity: A Study on the Heterogeneity of the Asian Subgroups.* Master's thesis, University of California, Berkeley.

Tarrow, Sidney. 1992. "Mentalities, Political Cultures, and Collective Action Frames: Constructing Meanings Through Action." In Morris and Mueller.

Tate, Katherine. 1991. "Black Political Participation in the 1984 and 1988 Presidential Elections." *American Political Science Review* 85 (December): 1159–76.

———. 1993. *From Protest to Politics: The New Black Voters in American Elections.* New York: Russell Sage.

Taylor, Lowell, Frank D. Bean, James B. Rebitzer, Susan Gonzalez Baker, and Lindsay Lowell. 1988. "Mexican Immigrants and the Wages and Unemployment Experience of Native Workers." Washington, D.C.: Urban Institute.

Thernstrom, Abigail M. 1987. *Whose Votes Count?* Cambridge: Harvard University Press.

Thomas, Brinley. 1973. *Migration and Economic Growth: A Study of Great Britain and the Atlantic Economy.* 2d ed. London: Cambridge University Press.

Tienda, Marta. 1989. "Looking to the 1990s: Mexican Immigration in Sociological Perspective." In *Mexican Migration to the United States: Origins, Consequences, and Policy Options: Dimensions of U.S.-Mexican Relations,* edited by W. Cornelius and J. A. Bustamante. San Diego: University of California Center for U.S.-Mexican Studies.

Tienda, Marta, and Zai Liang. 1992. "Horatio Alger Fails: Poverty and Immigration in Policy Perspective." Paper prepared for the Conference on Poverty and Public Policy, Madison, Wis., May 28–30.

Tienda, Marta, and Ding Tzann Lii. 1988. "Minority Concentration and Earnings Inequality: Blacks, Hispanics, and Asians Compared." *American Journal of Sociology* 93, 6: 141–65.

Tienda, Marta, and Haya Stier. 1990. "Joblessness and Shiftlessness: Labor Force Activity in Chicago's Inner City." In *The Urban Underclass,* edited by Christopher Jencks and Paul Peterson. Washington, D.C.: Brookings Institution.

Tilly, Charles. 1978. *From Mobilization to Revolution.* New York: Random House.

Turner, Eugene, and James P. Allen. 1991. *An Atlas of Population Patterns in Metropolitan Los Angeles and Orange Counties.* Occasional Publications in Geography 8. Northridge: Center for Geographical Studies, California State University.

Turner, Margery A., John G. Edwards, and Maris Mikelsons. 1991. *Housing Discrimination Study: Analyzing Racial and Ethnic Steering.* Washington, D.C.: U.S. Department of Housing and Urban Development, Office of Policy Development and Research.

Uhlaner, Carole Jean. 1989a. "Rational Turnout: The Neglected Role of Groups." *American Journal of Political Science* 33 (May): 390–422.

———. 1989b. "'Relational Goods' and Participation: Incorporating Sociability into a Theory of Rational Action." *Public Choice* 62: 253–85.

———. 1991a. "Electoral Participation: Summing up a Decade." *Society* 28 (July–August): 35–40.

———. 1991b. "Perceived Discrimination and Prejudice and the Coalition Prospects of

Blacks, Latinos, and Asian Americans." In *Racial and Ethnic Politics in California,* edited by Byran O. Jackson and Michael B. Preston. Berkeley: IGS.

———. 1991c. "Political Participation and Discrimination: A Comparative Analysis of Asians, Blacks, and Latinos." In *Political Participation and American Democracy,* edited by William Crotty. New York: Greenwood.

———. 1996. "Latinos and Ethnic Politics in California: Participation and Preference." In *Latino Politics in California,* edited by Aníbal Yáñez-Chávez. San Diego: UCSD Center for U.S.-Mexican Studies.

Uhlaner, Carole Jean, Bruce E. Cain, and Roderick D. Kiewiet. 1989. "Political Participation of Ethnic Minorities in the 1980s." *Political Behavior* 11 (3): 195–231.

Uhlaner, Carole Jean, and Chris Garcia. 1998. "Foundations of Latino Party Identification: Learning, Ethnicity, and Demographic Factors Among Mexicans, Puerto Ricans, Cubans, and Anglos in the United States." University of California, Irvine. Typescript.

United States Bureau of the Census. 1970. *Census of Population and Housing 1970.* Fourth Count Summary Tapes, File A. Washington, D.C.: U.S. Bureau of the Census.

———. 1980. *Census of Population and Housing 1980.* Summary Tape File 4A. Washington, D.C.: U.S. Bureau of the Census.

———. 1986. Current Population Reports, Series P-20, No. 405. *Voting and Registration in the Election of November 1984.* Washington, D.C.: U.S. Government Printing Office, March.

———. 1987. Current Population Reports, Series P-20, No. 414. *Voting and Registration in the Election of November 1986.* Washington, D.C.: U.S. Government Printing Office, September.

———. 1988. Current Population Reports, Series P-20, No. 434. *The Hispanic Population in the United States: March 1986 and 1987.* Washington, D.C.: U.S. Government Printing Office, December.

———. 1989a. Current Population Reports, Series P-20, No. 438. *The Hispanic Population in the United States: March 1988.* Washington, D.C.: U.S. Government Printing Office.

———. 1989b. Current Population Reports, Series P-20, No. 440. *Voting and Registration in the Election of November 1988.* Washington, D.C.: U.S. Government Printing Office, October.

———. 1989c. Current Population Reports, Series P-20, No. 442. *The Black Population in the United States: March 1988.* Washington, D.C.: U.S. Government Printing Office, November.

———. 1991a. Current Population Reports, Series P-20, No. 453. *Voting and Registration in the Election of November 1990.* Washington, D.C.: U.S. Government Printing Office, October.

———. 1991b. *Statistical Abstract of the United States: 1991.* 111th ed. Washington, D. C.: U.S. Government Printing Office.

———. 1991c. 1990 Census of Population and Housing. PL94–71. *Redistricting Data.* Washington, D.C.: U.S. Government Printing Office.

———. 1992a. 1990 Census of Population and Housing. 1990 CPH-1-1. *Summary Population and Housing Characteristics: United States.* Washington, D.C.: U.S. Government Printing Office, March.

———. 1992b. Current Population Reports, Series P-20, No. 459. *The Asian and Pacific Is-*

lander Population in the United States: March 1991 and 1990. Washington, D.C.: U.S. Government Printing Office, August.

———. 1992c. Current Population Reports, Series P-20, No. 464. *The Black Population in the United States: March 1991.* Washington, D.C.: U.S. Government Printing Office, September.

———. 1993. Current Population Reports, Series P-20, No. 466. *Voting and Registration in the Election of November 1992.* Washington, D.C.: U.S. Government Printing Office, April.

United States Commission on Civil Rights. 1992. *Civil Rights Issues Facing Asian Americans in the 1990s.* Washington, D.C.: Government Printing Office.

United States Congress, House Select Committee on Children, Youth, and Families. 1990. *Opportunities for Success: Cost Effective Programs for Children Update.* 101st Cong., 2nd Sess.

United States Department of Education. 1990. *Chapter 1 Policy Manual: Basic Programs Operated by Local Education Agencies.* Washington, D.C.: Government Printing Office.

———. 1992. *National Assessment of the Chapter 1 Program: The Interim Report.* Washington, D.C.: Government Printing Office, June.

———. 1993. *Reinventing Chapter 1: The Current Chapter 1 Program and New Directions.* Washington, D.C.: Government Printing Office.

United States Department of Labor. 1971. *Monthly Labor Review* 94, 3. Washington, D.C.: Government Printing Office.

———. 1981. *Monthly Labor Review* 114, 3. Washington, D.C.: Government Printing Office.

———. 1989. *The Effects of Immigration on the U.S. Economy and Labor Market.* Washington, D.C.: Bureau of International Labor Affairs, 1989.

———. 1991. *Monthly Labor Review* 124, 3. Washington, D.C.: Government Printing Office.

———. 1992. *1991 Statistical Yearbook of the Immigration and Naturalization Service.* Washington, D.C.: Government Printing Office.

Urban Institute. 1991. *Housing Discrimination Study: Methodology and Data Documentation.* Washington, D.C.: U.S. Department of Housing and Urban Development, Office of Policy Development and Research.

Valdieso, R., and C. Davis. 1988. "U.S. Hispanics: Challenging Issues for the 1990s." *Population Trends and Public Policy* No. 17 (December).

Verba, Sidney, and Norman H. Nie. 1972. *Participation in America: Political Democracy and Social Equality.* New York: Harper and Row.

Verba, Sidney, Norman H. Nie, and Jae-on Kim. 1978. *Participation and Political Equality: A Seven-Nation Comparison.* Cambridge: Cambridge University Press.

Vialet, Joyce. 1992. "Refugee Admissions and Resettlement Policy." Congressional Research Service Issue Brief. Washington, D.C.

Vigil, Maurilio E. 1987. *Hispanics in American Politics.* Lanham, Md.: University Press of America.

Waldinger, Roger. 1986. "Changing Ladders and Musical Chairs: Ethnicity and Opportunity in Post-Industrial New York." *Politics and Society* 15: 369–401.

———. 1989a. "Immigration and Urban Change." *Annual Review of Sociology* 15 (1989): 211–32.

———. 1989b. "Structural Opportunity or Ethnic Advantage? Immigrant Business Development in New York." *International Migration Review* 23: 48–72.

———. 1996. *Still the Promised City? African-Americans and New Immigrants in Postindustrial New York.* Cambridge: Harvard University Press.

Walter, John C. 1989. *The Harlem Fox.* Albany: State University of New York Press.

Walton, Hanes, Jr. 1972. *Black Politics.* Philadelphia: Lippincott.

Welch, S. A. Karnig, and R. Eribes. 1983. "Changes in Hispanic Local Employment in the Southwest." *Western Political Quarterly* 36: 660–75.

Westat, Inc. 1991. *A Summary of State Chapter 1 Participation and Achievement Information, 1988–89.* Washington, D.C.: U.S. Department of Education.

———. 1992. *A Summary of State Chapter 1 Participation and Achievement Information, 1989–90.* Washington, D.C.: U.S. Department of Education.

White, Michael J. 1986. "Segregation and Diversity: Measures in Population Distribution." *Population Index* 52: 198–221.

Wieck, Paul R. 1992. "The Problems Still Faced by Unskilled Workers." *The Social Contract* 2, 4: 217–18.

Wienk, Ronald, Cliff Reid, John Simonson, and Fred Eggers. 1979. *Measuring Racial Discrimination in American Housing Markets: The Housing Market Practices Survey.* Washington, D.C.: U.S. Department of Housing and Urban Development.

Wilkinson, Charles F. 1987. *American Indians, Time, and the Law.* New Haven: Yale University Press.

Williamson, Jeffrey G. 1982. "Immigrant-Inequality Trade-Offs in the Promised Land: Income Distribution and Absorptive Capacity Prior to the Quotas." In *The Gateway: U.S. Immigration Issues and Policies,* edited by Barry R. Chiswick. Washington, D.C.: American Enterprise Institute.

Wilson, James Q. 1960. *Negro Politics.* New York: Free.

———. 1961. "The Strategy of Protest: Problems of Negro Civic Action." *Journal of Conflict Resolution* 5, 3 (September): 291–303.

———. 1962. *The Amateur Democrat.* Chicago: University of Chicago Press.

Wilson, Paul. 1973. *Immigration and Politics.* Amistral: Australia National University Press.

Wilson, William Julius. 1987a. *The Declining Significance of Race: Blacks and Changing American Institutions.* 2d ed. Chicago: University of Chicago Press.

———. 1987b. *The Truly Disadvantaged.* Chicago: University of Chicago Press.

Woldemikael, Tekle Mariam. 1989. *Becoming Black American: Haitians and American Institutions in Evanston, Illinois.* New York: AMS.

Woliver, Laura. 1990. "A Measure of Justice: Police Conduct and Black Civil Rights." *Western Political Quarterly* 43, 2 (June): 415–36.

Wong, Bernard. 1977. "Elites and Ethnic Boundary Maintenance: A Study of the Roles of Elites in Chinatown, New York." *Urban Anthropology* 6: 1–22.

———. 1982. *Chinatown: Economic Adaptation and Ethnic Identity of the Chinese.* New York: Holt, Rinehart and Winston.

Wong, Eugene F. 1985. "Asian American Middleman Minority Theory: The Framework of an American Myth." *Journal of Ethnic Studies* 13, 1 (spring): 51–88.

Wunder, John R. 1994. *Retained by the People.* New York: Oxford University Press.

Yinger, John. 1986. "Measuring Racial Discrimination with Fair Housing Audits: Caught in the Act." *American Economic Review* 76: 991–93.

————. 1987a. *American Neighborhoods and Residential Differentiation.* New York: Russell Sage.

————. 1987b. "The Racial Dimension of Urban Housing Markets in the 1980s." In *Divided Neighborhoods: Changing Patterns of Racial Segregation,* edited by Gary A. Tobin. Newbury Park, Calif.: Sage.

————. 1989. "Measuring Discrimination in Housing Availability." Washington, D.C.: Urban Institute.

————. 1991a. *Housing Discrimination Study: Incidence and Severity of Unfavorable Treatment.* Washington, D.C.: U.S. Department of Housing and Urban Development, Office of Policy Development and Research.

————. 1991b. *Housing Discrimination Study: Incidence of Discrimination and Variations in Discriminatory Behavior.* Washington, D.C.: U.S. Department of Housing and Urban Development, Office of Policy Development and Research.

Contributors

Frank D. Bean is the Ashbel Smith Professor of sociology and public affairs and director of the Population Research Center at the University of Texas, Austin. A demographer with specializations in Mexican migration to the United States, international migration, family and fertility, the demography of racial and ethnic groups, and population policy, his most recent books include *At the Crossroads: Mexico and U.S. Immigration Policy* (edited with Rodolfo de la Garza, Bryan Roberts, and Sidney Weintraub) and *Help or Hindrance: Immigration and Its Economic Implications for Racial/Ethnic Minorities* (edited with Dan Hamermesh). His current research focuses on the labor market impacts of immigration; the relation of immigrants and their children to the U.S. system of public assistance; the public policy–related dimensions of U.S.-Mexico border control strategies; immigration and family and household behavior; and business activities and migration patterns among Mexican immigrants.

Bruce E. Cain is a professor in the Department of Political Science and IGS at the University of California, Berkeley. He formerly taught at the California Institute of Technology. A summa cum laude graduate of Bowdoin College (1970), he studied as a Rhodes Scholar (1970–1972) at Trinity College, Oxford. In 1976, he received his Ph.D. in political science from Harvard University. His writings include "The Reapportionment Puzzle" (1984); "The Personal Vote" with John Ferejohn and Morris Fiorina (1987); and "Congressional Redistricting" (1991), with David Butler.

Thomas E. Cavanagh is senior research associate at the Conference Board specializing in issues related to community economic development and global corporate citizenship. He has published numerous articles and monographs on the subjects of corporate development partnerships, racial politics, the party system, Congress, and voter turnout.

Thomas J. Espenshade is professor of sociology and a faculty associate at the Office of Population Research, Princeton University. He was formerly senior research associate and director of the Program in Population Studies at the Urban Institute. He is the author of *Investing in Children: New Estimates of Parental Expenditures* (1984), a co-author of *The Fourth Wave: California's Newest Immigrants* (1985), and editor of *Keys to Successful Immigration: Implications of the New Jersey Experience* (1997). His research interests include patterns of undocumented migration to the United States, the fiscal impacts of immigrants, and attitudes toward U.S. immigration. Currently Dr. Espenshade is directing a project on the contribution of foreign-born scientists and engineers to the U.S. workforce.

Michael Fix is a lawyer and principal research associate at the Urban Institute, where he directs the Immigrant Policy Program. He is a graduate of Princeton University and the University of Virginia Law School and a member of the Washington, D.C. bar. He has written or edited several books on immigration and civil rights policy including *Immigration and Immigrants: Setting the Record Straight* (1994), *The Paper Curtain: Employer Sanctions' Impacts, Implementation and Reform* (1991), *Enforcing Employer Sanctions: Challenges and Strategies* (1990), *Clear and Convincing Evidence: Testing for Discrimination in America* (1993), and *Opportunities Denied, Opportunities Diminished: Racial Discrimination in Hiring* (1991). Other areas of public policy in which Mr. Fix has worked include federalism and regulation. Books edited or authored in these fields include *Coping with Mandates: What Are the Options?* (1989); *Reagan's Regulatory Strategy* (1984), and *Relief or Reform? Reagan's Regulatory Dilemma* (1984).

Mark A. Fossett is associate professor of sociology and associate head of the Department of Rural Sociology at Texas A&M University. He has published articles in the *American Sociological Review, Demography, Social Science Quarterly,* and the *Journal of Marriage and the Family,* among others, focusing on topics dealing with race and ethnicity and social inequality. Most recently, he has authored *Long Time Coming: Racial Inequality in the Rural South, 1940– 1990.*

John A. Garcia is professor of political science at the University of Arizona. He received his Ph.D. from Florida State University. His major areas of research have been on the subjects of minority group politics, especially Latinos', and urban governments, survey research, and public policy. He was co-author of *Latino Voices: Perspectives of Cubans, Mexican Americans, and Puerto Ricans* (1992) and "Expanding Disciplinary Boundaries: Black, Latinos, and Racial Minority Group Politics in Political Science" in *The State of the Discipline II* (1993). He has co-edited three books. He serves as one of four co-principal investigators of the Latino National Political Survey (LNPS). Earlier he served on the research staff of the National Chicano Survey (1979) at ISR-University of Michigan. These projects represented the first national probability surveys of Latinos and Mexican-origin populations conducted.

Claire Jean Kim received her Ph.D. in political science from Yale University in 1996. She is currently an assistant professor at the University of California, Irvine, with a joint appointment in the Departments of Political Science and Asian American Studies, as well as a courtesy appointment in African American Studies. Her book *Bitter Fruit: The Politics of Black-Korean Conflict in New York City* is forthcoming from Yale University Press.

Douglas S. Massey is the Dorothy Swain Thomas Professor of sociology at the University of Pennsylvania and chair of its Sociology Department. He received his Ph.D. from Princeton University and did postdoctoral research there and at the University of California, Berkeley. He is co-author of *American Apartheid: Segregation and the Making of the Underclass* (1993), which won the Distinguished Publication Award of the American Sociological Association, the Otis Dudley Duncan Award of the Section on the Sociology of Population, and the Critics' Choice Award of the American Educational Studies Association. He has also published extensively on U.S.-Mexico migration, including the books *Return to Aztlan: The Social Process of International Migration from Western Mexico* (1987) and *Miracles on the Border: Retablos of Mexican Migrants to the United States* (1995). The latter, co-authored with Jorge Durand, won the 1996 Southwest Book Award. In collaboration with an international team of colleagues, he recently completed a new book, *Worlds in Motion: Understanding International Migration at Century's End* (1998).

Kyung Tae Park is assistant professor of sociology at Sung Kong Hoe University in Seoul, South Korea. He is a demographer with interests in statistical and demographic methodology, labor force, and immigration. In 1994, he received his Ph.D. from University of Texas, Austin. His dissertation, "Asian Immigration, Self Employment and Native Black Labor Market Outcomes," focused on the interconnections between Asian immigration and African American labor market outcomes, especially as these are affected by the structure of U.S. metropolitan labor markets.

Carole Jean Uhlaner is associate professor of political science at the University of California, Irvine. Her research on political behavior of ethnic minorities in the United States is part of a larger agenda examining the processes of political participation, political mobilization, and mass-elite linkages. Some of her work develops rational actor theories that can account for observed behavior. Her publications include "The Acquisition of Partisanship by Latinos and Asian-Americans: Immigrants and Native-Born Citizens" and "Rational Turnout: The Neglected Role of Groups," "Relational Goods and Participation: Incorporating Sociability into a Theory of Rational Action," in *Public Choice,* and "Political Participation of Ethnic Minorities in the 1980s," in *Political Behavior.*

Wendy Zimmermann is a research associate at the Urban Institute, where she conducts research on immigration and immigrant policy and civil rights issues. Her recent publications include "Welfare Reform: A New Immigrant Policy for the United States," written with Michael Fix and published in the Citizens' Commission on Civil Rights reports, *The Continuing Struggle: Civil Rights and the Clinton Administration,* and "Undocumented Immigrants in New Jersey: Numbers, Impacts and Policies," with Rebecca Clark, published in *Keys to Successful Immigration: Implications of the New Jersey Experience.* She is currently conducting research on state implementation of federal welfare reform's restrictions on immigrant eligibility and their impacts on immigrant communities.

Index

Immigration and race